The American Edge

THE AMERICAN EDGE

THE MILITARY TECH NEXUS AND THE SOURCES OF GREAT POWER DOMINANCE

SETH G. JONES

OXFORD
UNIVERSITY PRESS

Oxford University Press is a department of the University of Oxford.
It furthers the University's objective of excellence in research, scholarship,
and education by publishing worldwide. Oxford is a registered trade mark of
Oxford University Press in the UK and in certain other countries.

Published in the United States of America by Oxford University Press
198 Madison Avenue, New York, NY 10016, United States of America.

© Oxford University Press 2025

All rights reserved. No part of this publication may be reproduced, stored in a retrieval system, transmitted, used for text and data mining, or used for training artificial intelligence, in any form or by any means, without the prior permission in writing of Oxford University Press, or as expressly permitted by law, by license or under terms agreed with the appropriate reprographics rights organization. Inquiries concerning reproduction outside the scope of the above should be sent to the Rights Department, Oxford University Press, at the address above.

You must not circulate this work in any other form
and you must impose this same condition on any acquirer.

CIP data is on file at the Library of Congress

ISBN 9780197764602

DOI: 10.1093/oso/9780197764602.001.0001

Printed by Sheridan Books, Inc., United States of America

The manufacturer's authorised representative in the EU for product safety is
Oxford University Press España S.A., Parque Empresarial San Fernando de Henares,
Avenida de Castilla, 2 – 28830 Madrid (www.oup.es/en or product.safety@oup.com).
OUP España S.A. also acts as importer into Spain of products made by the manufacturer.

We must be the great arsenal of democracy.
—President Franklin D. Roosevelt

[In] a long-drawn-out Great Power (and usually coalition) war, victory has repeatedly gone to the side with the more flourishing productive base.
—Paul Kennedy, *The Rise and Fall of the Great Powers*

The U.S. struggle with China is the single greatest competition the United States has ever faced.
—U.S. Deputy Secretary of Defense Robert O. Work

CONTENTS

Introduction 1

1. The Arsenal of Democracy 17
2. The Cold War and Pax Americana 49
3. Desert Storm 89
4. The Last Supper 109
5. Drone Warfare and the Legacy of 9/11 127
6. Xi Jinping and the Third Offset 151
7. Private Capital and the Space Age 181
8. The New Cyber Wars 205
9. Slava Ukraini 223
10. China's Wartime Footing 239
11. Empty Bins in a Wartime Environment 261
12. Rebuilding the Arsenal of Democracy 285

Epilogue 299

Appendix 1: Kelly Johnson's 14 Rules   *305*
Appendix 2: Norman Augustine's 52 Laws   *307*
Appendix 3: Elon Musk's Algorithm and the Five Commandments   *311*
Notes   *313*
Acknowledgments   *397*
Index   *399*

INTRODUCTION

Time and again I would have to tackle that damnable peacetime mindset inside the Pentagon.
—U.S. Secretary of Defense and CIA Director ROBERT M. GATES

Continuous war will produce a predominance of rat-catchers, as classically demonstrated by the [British] Navy of the French Revolutionary and Napoleonic wars; continuous peace will produce a predominance of regulators.
—ADMIRAL SIR JOHN WOODWARD, British naval officer

THIS IS A BOOK ABOUT the defense industrial bases of the great powers over the 20th and early 21st centuries.[1] It seeks to explain how the industrial bases of the great powers—especially the United States—have risen, fallen, and evolved relative to each other, from the interwar period to Imperial Germany and Japan during World War II, the United States and Soviet Union during the Cold War, and the rise of China. Because of the constant U.S. position since World War II as a great power—indeed a global superpower—this book focuses in particular on the United States. The book pays specific attention to the interaction between the private sector and the government in the defense industrial base, which includes the ecosystem of government agencies and companies involved in the development and production of defense systems, emerging technology, and other matériel.

After all, it is the engineers, welders, technology specialists, electricians, production managers, and entrepreneurial men and women who design and produce what President Franklin Delano Roosevelt referred to as the "arsenal of democracy." As Roosevelt explained in his fireside chat to the United States on December 29, 1940, a year before Pearl Harbor, the "American industrial genius, unmatched throughout all the world in the solution of production problems, has been called upon to bring its resources and its talents into action."[2] This industrial prowess has provided an advantage—the American edge—in times of danger to the nation. Following World War I, U.S. leaders dismantled the country's defense industrial base. But President Roosevelt increased defense capacity in the late 1930s as war appeared imminent. By the end of World War II, the once mighty defense industries of Germany and Japan were decimated, and British and French industries were exhausted. For the next 45 years, the industrial might of the United States and the Soviet Union dominated international politics. But by 1990, the Soviet Union's defense industry was in shambles, thanks in part to the failure of Soviet-style communism and the collapse of the Soviet economy, leaving the United States alone atop the world. Without a global rival, the United States slashed its defense budget and its defense industry, epitomized by the "Last Supper" in 1993, in which Pentagon leaders urged defense companies to consolidate. Following the al-Qa'ida terrorist attacks on September 11, 2001, the United States and its industry shifted to counterterrorism and drone warfare to collect intelligence and conduct strikes against terrorists and their infrastructure.

But with Xi Jinping's emergence as leader, China began to slowly and methodically develop its defense industry as part of its effort to build military and economic power. A history of the defense industrial bases of the great powers—particularly the United States—is essential because the United States and China are locked in a competition that hinges to a great extent on their respective capabilities and industrial bases. As the historian Paul Kennedy wrote in *The Rise and Fall of the Great Powers*, it is "incontestable" that "in a long-drawn-out Great Power (and usually coalition) war, victory has repeatedly gone to the side with the more flourishing productive base—or, as the Spanish captains used to say, to him who has the last escudo."[3]

Yet the United States is in a precarious position. China is on a wartime footing, which means it is building a defense industrial base to deter the United States and—if deterrence fails—fight and win a war with the United States. But the U.S. defense industrial base is on a peacetime footing. It lacks the production capacity, responsiveness, flexibility, and surge capability to effectively deter China or defeat it in a great power war. The U.S. military has lost "overmatch"—the ability to overwhelm an adversary—in a war against China.[4] More broadly, the United States and other Western governments have been too prone to regulation and bureaucracy, too slow to integrate emerging technologies, and too risk-averse to change.

A failure to establish a robust industrial base could have disastrous consequences for the United States. After all, as former U.S. deputy secretary of defense Robert Work starkly noted, the struggle with China "is the single greatest competition the United States has ever faced."[5]

The main argument of this book is that countries in a wartime environment need to operate with urgency, spend money to maximize defense production, minimize excessive regulations, and streamline their defense acquisition and contracting systems. The primary goal of the defense industrial base should be to provide the military with what it needs to effectively deter adversaries and to fight and win wars. In the words of President Ronald Reagan, a country's defense industry needs to establish "peace through strength."[6] Building a defense industrial base for a wartime environment is neither cheap nor quick. To paraphrase British naval historian Andrew Gordon, policymakers and the private sector in wartime need to act more like *rat-catchers* (those who are committed to minimizing unnecessary regulations to effectively win wars) and less like *regulators* (those who are prone to bureaucracy and process).[7]

As the previous century of the U.S. defense industrial base suggests, periods of wartime require a different type of industrial base and a different approach than during peacetime. Wartime generally means a period when there is active combat (such as during the Korean War in the 1950s), conflict is likely imminent (such as during the late 1930s, when Germany was rapidly rearming), or there is a serious risk of war if deterrence fails (such as during the 1970s and 1980s, when the Soviet Union achieved nuclear parity with the United

States and had a significant conventional military advantage in Europe). In a wartime environment, there is much more at stake for a country—including survival—than in peacetime. In periods of peacetime, the U.S. defense industrial base has not needed to operate with the same sense of urgency, and there has been a strong and understandable impetus to consolidate defense companies, minimize risks, and develop rules, regulations, and policies to save money and protect sensitive technology.

The tragedy today is that the United States is in a wartime environment, but its defense industrial base is operating on a peacetime footing. The United States is at serious risk of losing deterrence to China and other adversaries because of a weak defense industrial base. Russia's invasion of Ukraine sparked the largest land war in Europe since World War II. China, Iran, and North Korea provided assistance to Russia, while the United States, other NATO countries, and even Indo-Pacific countries such as South Korea aided Ukraine. War persisted in the Middle East, with the United States providing aid to Israel and engaging in military operations in Yemen, the Red Sea, Iraq, Syria, and other countries. And tensions escalated in the Korean Peninsula, Taiwan Strait, South China Sea, and East China Sea. Yet regulators in the U.S. Congress and the executive branch predominate, not rat-catchers. A failure to alter this trajectory will weaken deterrence and warfighting in an era when the defense industrial bases of the main U.S. competitors—especially China—are on a wartime footing.

This intransigence to act in the face of serious danger is, in some ways, reminiscent of Britain in the 1930s. In the face of German rearmament, Winston Churchill's urgent calls to revitalize Britain's defense industrial base were ignored by significant portions of the Labour, Conservative, and Liberal parties. Standing before his colleagues in the House of Commons in May 1935, Churchill implored them to act: "During the last three years . . . Germany worked unceasingly upon a vast design of rearmament on a scale which would give that mighty, gifted, scientific, valiant race of 60,000,000 or 70,000,000 such a predominance in Europe as would enable it, if it chose—and why should it not choose?—to reverse the results of the Great War." Yet Churchill was repeatedly scorned by all political parties, including his own Conservative Party. "Want of foresight, unwillingness to act when action would be simple and effective, lack of clear thinking, confusion of counsel until the emergency comes, until self-preservation strikes its jarring gong—these are the features which constitute the endless repetition of history," Churchill lamented.[8] Britain's unpreparedness for war was nearly fatal.

Over the past century, U.S. policymakers have at times made poor decisions with their defense industrial bases. President Harry Truman's decision to dramatically cut the defense budget and scale back the defense industrial base after World War II was counterproductive and shortsighted. As Churchill remarked only a year after the end of World War II, Soviet leaders desired "the fruits of war and the indefinite expansion of their power and doctrines.... From what I have seen of our Russian friends and Allies during the war, I am convinced that there is nothing they admire so much as strength, and there is nothing for which they have less respect than for weakness, especially military weakness."[9] It made little strategic sense for the United States to switch so quickly to a peacetime industrial base. By 1950, Truman had to significantly increase the defense budget in response to Soviet expansionism and the Korean War.

In addition, the Johnson, Kennedy, and Nixon administrations underinvested in defense—including in defense capabilities—during the Cold War in ways that significantly weakened U.S. deterrence and jeopardized U.S. national security in the midst of Soviet expansion. In fact, U.S. Secretary of Defense Harold Brown sent a prescient memorandum to President Jimmy Carter lamenting that the United States had failed to invest sufficient resources in defense technology during the Vietnam War and in the immediate post-Vietnam War era. This failure put the United States in a perilous strategic position because the Soviets had conventional superiority.[10] Even during the height of the wars in Afghanistan and Iraq, U.S. defense officials failed to rapidly develop and produce defense material for U.S. military forces engaged in active combat. As Secretary of Defense Robert Gates bemoaned, "The hidebound and unresponsive bureaucratic structure that the Defense Department uses to acquire equipment performs poorly in peacetime. As I saw, it did so horribly in wartime. And then ... there was the department's inexplicable peacetime mind-set in wartime."[11]

As the history of the U.S. defense industrial base suggests, an effective industrial base in a wartime environment requires synergy between the government and the private sector to offset adversary advantages. The role of the private sector is a critical—and frequently overlooked—part of the process.[12] Without the private sector, little can be designed or produced. Since World War II, private sector engineers and other entrepreneurs have been instrumental in creating and shaping the design of aircraft, stealth technology, precision-guided weapons, drones, space and cyber capabilities, software, and advances in artificial intelligence and quantum computing. These breakthroughs were necessary for innovations in strategic bombing, strategic reconnaissance, precision strike, and drone warfare. As Margaret O'Mara argued in her book on industry and Silicon Valley, innovation is generally a tale "of entrepreneurship *and* government, new *and* old economies, far-thinking engineers *and* the many non-technical thousands who made their innovation possible."[13]

This book shines a specific light on *people* and their contribution to the arsenal of democracy. As President Roosevelt reminded Americans in his December 1940 fireside chat, "guns, planes, ships, and many other things have to be built in the factories and arsenals of America. They have to be produced by workers and managers and engineers with the aid of machines which in turn have to be built by hundreds of thousands of workers throughout the land."[14] Consequently, this book spends significant time examining some of the most important people who contributed to the U.S. defense industrial base.

For example, it is difficult to fully comprehend strategic bombing during World War II, including the use of B-29s against the Japanese mainland, without understanding the contributions of such Boeing engineers as George Schairer, Edward Wells, and Wellwood Beall, who were instrumental in designing the B-29. Still others, such as William Knudsen, president of General Motors and eventually a lieutenant general in the U.S. Army, played an outsized role in revitalizing the U.S. industrial base during World War II. The evolution of strategic reconnaissance during the Cold War occurred in part because of the pivotal contributions of Kelly Johnson and his team at Lockheed Skunk Works, who worked closely with Richard Bissell and others at CIA on the construction of the U-2 reconnaissance aircraft.

Some of the most important advances in precision-guided weapons, which were used to devastating effect in the lopsided U.S. victory in Iraq in 1991 during Operation Desert Storm, occurred because of the ingenuity of Weldon Word and his team at Texas Instruments, who built such laser-guided bombs as Paveway I, II, and III. Texas Instruments worked closely with Colonel Joseph Davis, vice commander of the Air Proving Ground at Eglin Air Force Base, who was searching for a weapon with the accuracy to routinely hit a target within 30 feet. The same was true of stealth and the development of such systems as the F-117 Nighthawk, which depended on the pathbreaking work of Ben Rich, Denys Overholser, and others at Lockheed Skunk Works.

In the post–Cold War era, the advances in drone technology and counterterrorism concepts of operations relied on pioneering work by engineers and executives such as Abraham "Abe" Karem, Linden and Neal Blue, and Tom Cassidy at General Atomics. These individuals worked closely with CIA officials like Director Jim Woolsey, the U.S. Air Force program Big Safari, and senior Pentagon officials like William Perry to develop and deploy drones into combat. Other U.S. government officials, such as General Stanley McChrystal, used drones and other systems to develop an innovative concept of operations characterized as "find, fix, finish, exploit, analyze."[15] By the 2000s, such companies as Palantir, which developed software that U.S. intelligence agencies and the military could use, emerged thanks to a partnership with the CIA and its nonprofit investment company, In-Q-Tel. Palantir was led by a visionary team of entrepreneurs and engineers, such as Alex Karp, Akash "Aki" Jain, and Stephen Cohen. Ruth David and others were crucial to the evolution of In-Q-Tel.

With the return of great power competition following the emergence of Xi Jinping and China, Elon Musk, Mark Juncosa, and Gwynne Shotwell at Space X and Starlink were instrumental in pathbreaking developments in space. The same was true in cyber, where such companies as Microsoft, led by chief executive officer Brad Smith and engineers like John Lambert, were crucial in the evolution of the cyber domain. Still other private sector entrepreneurs, such as Anduril's Palmer Luckey, Brian Schimpf, and Trae Stephens, were essential in developing advanced autonomous platforms, artificial intelligence, and sensor networks.

The defense sector in the West, including in the United States, also experienced a tectonic shift in the late 2010s with the rise of private capital led by venture capital and private equity investors, such as Peter Thiel and Marc Andreesen. During the Cold War, much of the defense-related funding for the private sector—including companies based in Silicon Valley and along Route 128 in Massachusetts—came from the Department of Defense, especially from such organizations as the Defense Advanced Research Projects Agency (DARPA). But funding changed dramatically in the late 2010s. Venture capital and private equity firms poured billions of dollars into start-ups and established defense companies that developed space and cyber capabilities, artificial intelligence, quantum computing, autonomous platforms, and a wide array of other hardware and software. Not to be outdone, a growing list of companies—such as Microsoft, Amazon Web Services, and Google—also entered the defense market and produced cutting-edge technologies and systems essential for military power. They joined such large defense "primes" as Lockheed Martin, Northrop Grumman, Raytheon (RTX), Boeing, and General Dynamics.

Calculations of power have long been at the heart of how states think about the world around them.[16] Some define power in terms of influencing others to get the outcomes they want.[17] Power, they argue, is largely about control or influence over others. In international politics, this definition of power translates into the ability of one state to force another to do something, even if it is against a state's own interests.[18] As Yale University professor Robert Dahl argued, "A has power over B to the extent that he can get B to do something that B would not otherwise do."[19] Others focus on economic power, including a country's natural resources, labor, capital, and entrepreneurship.[20] Still others emphasize "soft power," which includes the ability to co-opt rather than coerce.[21] Soft power rests on three components: culture, political values, and foreign policies. As Joseph Nye argues, "Soft power is not merely the same as influence.... It is also the ability to attract, and attraction often leads to acquiescence."[22]

While economic and soft power are important, military power remains primus inter pares in international politics.[23] Just ask Ukraine, which faced a brutal Russian invasion whose forces ravaged Ukrainian territory and committed gross human rights abuses against its population. Or Israel, which suffered a devastating attack by Hamas on October 7, 2023, and then two major Iranian missile and drone attacks in April and October 2024, respectively. Or Taiwan, which faced an alarming Chinese military buildup, aggressive military actions in the Taiwan Strait, and an unbridled determination by Beijing's leaders to unite the island with China. As Xi declared, Taiwan "must and will be" united with China by military force if necessary.[24] Military power is largely based on the size and strength of a state's army, air force, and navy—including their capabilities.[25]

This book focuses on military capabilities produced by the defense industrial base, which includes the hardware (such as ships, aircraft, tanks, and missiles) and software (such as technology and systems for command, control, communications, and intelligence) that military forces need. The defense industrial base comprises the set of companies and government agencies involved in the research, development, design, production, delivery, and maintenance of defense systems, material, and equipment for a country's armed forces.[26] In the United States, the defense ecosystem consists of well over 100,000 companies and their subcontractors across the globe, which conduct research, produce goods, and offer services.[27] Companies attempt to produce systems and technology that are increasingly more accurate and lethal, ensure greater mobility of forces over longer distances, and provide an ability to see, communicate, and process information in greater volumes over wider areas.[28]

Military forces use these capabilities to defend their countries, deter or coerce adversaries, fight wars, and provide other types of assistance.[29] But defense is not a free market system, especially in the West. It is a monopsony, a market arrangement in which there are several suppliers but only one buyer.[30] Defense is also a government-regulated industry. Government auditors carefully monitor the costs, purchases, and profits of defense contractors. In the United States, there are volumes of binding regulations that contractors must follow if they are to remain eligible to work on defense projects—some of which, as this book argues, need to be eliminated.[31]

Looking forward, military power will likely center on competition between the United States and China. The West's bottom-up approach to industrial production has inherent advantages over China's top-down model, especially if the United States can effectively leverage the private sector. But the U.S. and other Western governments need to be faster and less cumbersome against an adversary with substantial industrial might.

The Chinese defense industrial base is operating on a wartime footing and, in some ways, outpacing the U.S. and other Western defense industrial bases. China's colossal state-owned defense companies are producing a growing quantity and quality of military capabilities for the People's Liberation Army (PLA). As the U.S. commander of Indo-Pacific Command noted, "On a scale not since World War II, the PLA's buildup is occurring across land, sea, air, space, cyber, and information domains."[32] The PLA Navy is numerically the largest navy in the world, with an overall battle force of more than 370 ships—including major surface combatants and submarines.[33] Led by such companies as China State Shipbuilding, China is the world's largest shipbuilder by a significant margin. It has a military and commercial shipbuilding capacity that is roughly 230 times larger than that of the United States and enough capacity to build 23 million tons of vessels, compared to less than 100,000 tons in the United States.[34] One of China's shipyards also has more capacity than all U.S. shipyards combined.[35]

In addition, the PLA Air Force is growing more capable, with over 3,150 aircraft, including fifth-generation fighter aircraft and strategic bombers.[36] China's aviation industry is led by two major state-owned companies, the Aviation Industry Corporation of China and the Commercial Aircraft Corporation. China is also heavily investing in munitions and acquiring high-end weapons systems and equipment five to six times faster than the United States, according to some U.S. government estimates.[37] The PLA's nuclear force continues to expand, with plans for 1,000 warheads by 2030, along with new air- and sea-launched platforms.[38]

The PLA Army has nearly 1 million active-duty personnel with nearly 5,000 main battle tanks.[39] China's largest defense companies for ground systems—such as armored personnel carriers, main battle tanks, and artillery systems—include China North Industries Corporation and China South Industries Group Corporation. In space, the PLA continues to develop space and counterspace capabilities, including kinetic antisatellite weapons, high-power lasers, and microwaves.[40] "For the past three decades," concluded author Chris Brose in his book *The Kill Chain*, "the Chinese Communist Party has gone to school on the U.S. military and its entire way of war. . . . China has rapidly developed arsenals of advanced weapons intended to break apart U.S. battle networks, destroy the U.S. military's traditional platforms, and shatter its ability to close the kill chain."[41]

Yet as this book shows, there are also weaknesses in China's centralized model. A huge impediment is corruption, which is rampant in China's PLA and defense industrial base.[42] China's top-down, centralized model also inhibits innovation, which is partly why a major component of China's strategy is—and must be—to steal technology from the United States and other advanced Western countries. China uses espionage to acquire sensitive, dual-use, and military equipment. "China's strategy is the same: rob, replicate, and replace," said senior U.S. Department of Justice official John Demers. "Rob the American company of its intellectual property, replicate the technology, and replace the American company in the Chinese market and, one day, in the global market."[43] In addition, Chinese soldiers and civilians in the defense industry are expected to be both "red" (politically loyal and ideologically pure) and "expert" (professionally competent and capable of fighting). When the two conflict, loyalty normally is a safer route than taking the initiative.[44] It is also unclear how well the Chinese military can fight, including conducting combined arms and joint operations. The PLA has not fought a major war since the Sino-Vietnamese War in 1979, when it performed poorly.

The United States has significant advantages over China if the U.S. government can fundamentally shift to a system of rat-catchers, not regulators. The goals should be to increase production capacity, flexibility, innovation, and surge capability to meet the U.S. military's wartime needs. Accomplishing these goals will require rethinking core policies, rules, and regulations—from contracting and acquisitions to workforce, strategic stockpiles, and supply chain—in order to maintain technological and military superiority. The United States also needs to *offset* Chinese advantages in mass and scale by producing defense systems and developing concepts of operation that strengthen deterrence and warfighting. Examples include a mix of high-end systems (such as submarines, stealth bombers, and long-range precision missiles), cheap unmanned systems (such as unmanned underwater vehicles and drones), and cutting-edge technology (such as artificial intelligence and quantum computing).

But business as usual will not do. The U.S. government has slowly tried to change. The U.S. Department of Defense opened an office—the Defense Innovation Unit—in California's Silicon Valley and created such organizations as the Office of Strategic Capital to leverage emerging critical technologies. The CIA established In-Q-Tel as a nonprofit venture capital firm and created the Transnational and Technology Mission Center to focus on such emerging technologies as quantum computing, sensors, biotechnology, and blockchain-enabled technologies.[45] But public-private sector partnership is still far too ad hoc, and the government lacks a coherent strategy. As former U.S. Secretary of Defense Leon Panetta and Congressman Mike Gallagher argued, "The Defense Department must make the rapid adoption of new technologies a priority, particularly in the commercial sector. This will require Pentagon bureaucrats to overcome the aversion to risk that permeates their agency and to leverage the expertise of academia and the private sector. The goal will be to build a defense innovation ecosystem in which the brightest minds in technology, strategy and defense can collaborate without constraint."[46]

In exploring the history of the U.S. defense industrial base and the synergy between the government and the private sector, this book examines two types of innovation. The first is the invention of a new technology, system, or idea, such as the B-29 bomber, F-117 stealth aircraft, laser-guided weapons, and MQ-1 Predator drones. The second type of innovation involves a change in the conduct of warfare intended to improve the ability of a military to generate combat power.[47] This second type is more than just technology. A change in the conduct of warfare does not necessarily require a change in military doctrine, but it does involve change at the operational level of war. Change may occur throughout the entire military, or it may be in a narrower segment such as a military service.[48] Over the past century, major innovations have included the blitzkrieg, unrestricted submarine warfare, nuclear weapons, and strategic coordination of air, land, and naval forces (or joint operations).[49] This book also examines such innovations as strategic bombing, strategic reconnaissance, precision-guided warfare, and the evolving counterterrorism concept of "find, fix, finish, exploit, analyze" spearheaded by U.S. special operations forces.

Technology is an important part of military innovation, though it is generally not sufficient. Inventing technologies or being the first country to use a technology in warfare does not guarantee an advantage on the battlefield, since militaries still have to integrate the technology into combat.[50] For example, British engineers at William Foster & Company developed and produced the tank, including one dubbed "Little Willie," with the support of senior British officers such as Sir John French and Douglas Haig.[51] But it was German military officers such as Heinz Guderian that effectively *used* the tank to devastating effect during blitzkrieg operations in World War II. Consequently, military power is not just about the creation of critical technologies but also how the technology is adopted by a military.

Innovation can occur during peacetime when leaders—especially military leaders—respond to changes in the international landscape and create environments that facilitate and encourage junior officers to pursue innovations and new ways of war. Wartime also allows for testing innovations against a real adversary, as in Ukraine following Russia's 2022 full-scale invasion. But wartime comes with its own obstacles. Militaries must balance the incentive to innovate against the daily need of defeating an enemy who is trying to defeat them in battle. There is often insufficient time to assess wartime conditions, reformulate strategic conceptions, and build new forces before the outcome of a war is largely determined. Old and new methods can be tested in combat, but time constraints and limited intelligence make it difficult to take advantage of any apparent innovations in time to win the war.[52] In this book, several wars play an important part in innovation and the evolution of the defense industrial base, such as World War II, Korean War, Vietnam War, Desert Storm in Iraq, Afghanistan, the 2003 Iraq War, Ukraine, and wars between Israel and Hamas, Hezbollah, Iran, and other Iran-linked groups.

Despite amassing military capabilities and successfully innovating, militaries still have to employ their forces effectively.[53] Indeed, innovations are not always helpful; some may actually weaken a military's effectiveness.[54] While military capabilities and innovation are important, they do not guarantee successful military outcomes—despite Napoleon's comment that "God is on the side of the big battalions" and Thucydides's remark that "the weaker must give way to the strong."[55] There are a range of factors that impact outcomes in war beyond military capabilities, such as clever strategies, force employment, leadership, weather, and combat motivation.[56]

To better understand the changes afoot in military power, this book is organized into several eras that help track the rise and fall of the defense industries of the great powers, with a particular focus on the United States.

This book begins in Chapter 1 with the interwar period and World War II, which marked a fundamental change in the rise and fall of industrial powers with the collapse of Germany and Japan. President Roosevelt created the War Production Board and other bodies to provide general direction over U.S. procurement and production, cut through bureaucracy, ensure the defense industrial base had sufficient funds for production, and establish priorities regarding the distribution of materials and services. The book then shifts to the Cold War in Chapter 2 with the emergence of the Soviet Union and the United States as the two global superpowers. At various points during the Cold War, such as during the Korean War, the government prioritized defense production, reduced bureaucracy, and ramped up defense spending in the face of a growing Soviet threat.

Chapter 3 examines Operation Desert Storm, which benefited from stealth, precision-guided weapons, and other advances that emerged from the "second offset" in the late 1970s and 1980s. Following the collapse of the Soviet Union and its vast industrial base, Chapter 4 explores the Clinton administration's decision to consolidate the United States defense industrial base. Chapter 5 shifts to the era of counterterrorism after September 11, 2001, which led to advances in drones and new concepts of operation. Chapter 6 focuses on the emergence of China as a great power under Xi and the limited U.S. response in what some called the "third offset."

Chapter 7 tracks the surge in production capacity and innovation in space as a major domain of warfare and in other areas of the commercial sector, led by such companies as SpaceX. It also examines the growing role of venture capital and private equity investment in the defense sector. Venture capital investment in defense technology start-ups skyrocketed from $1.9 billion in 2013 to $31 billion in 2024.[57] In light of Russia's full-scale invasion of Ukraine in February 2022, Chapter 8 explores the role of Microsoft and other companies in the cyber domain. Chapter 9 highlights private sector support for Ukraine during its war with Russia, as well as the growing challenges faced by the U.S. defense industrial base.

Chapter 10 focuses on China's defense industrial buildup. Under Xi, China rapidly developed and produced weapons systems designed to deter the United States and, if deterrence failed, to win a great power war. Chapter 11 examines the central challenges facing the industrial bases of the United States. Chapter 12 provides an overview of how the United States can rebuild its arsenal of democracy. The book ends with an epilogue that harks back to Churchill's wilderness years before World War II and the failure of British policymakers to jumpstart the country's defense industrial base in the face of German rearmament.

Appropriately, our story begins with World War II, which was to a great extent a war of industrial might.

I

The Arsenal of Democracy

We won because we smothered the enemy in an avalanche of production, the likes of which he had never seen, nor dreamed possible.
—WILLIAM KNUDSEN, president of General Motors

No American will think it wrong of me if I proclaim that to have the United States at our side was to me the greatest joy.... So we had won after all!... I thought of a remark which Edward Grey had made to me more than thirty years before—that the United States is like "a gigantic boiler. Once the fire is lighted under it there is no limit to the power it can generate."
—Prime Minister WINSTON S. CHURCHILL

WILLIAM KNUDSEN, THE TOWERING PRESIDENT of General Motors, sat at his desk on May 28, 1940.[1] The world was at war. The front page of the *New York Times* ominously announced that the Belgian army had collapsed, and the German Wehrmacht was rapidly conquering Western Europe.[2] France would be next. Knudsen, wearing his black-ribbon eyeglasses, was intently studying a report on automobile production figures at his desk when the phone rang.

"This is Knudsen," he said, his heart pounding. Knudsen had been tipped off about the call by his friend Bernard Baruch, a self-made financier and former chairman of the War Industries Board, who described Knudsen as a production genius.[3]

"Mr. Knudsen," the voice responded, "the President of the United States wants to talk to you—here he is."

"Knudsen?" asked President Franklin D. Roosevelt.

"Yes, Mr. President."

"I want to see you in Washington." Roosevelt quickly explained. "I want you to work on some production matters. When can you come down here?"

There was a short pause. "I can be there the day after tomorrow, Mr. President," Knudsen replied. "First, I will have to go to New York to see the officials of my company."

"Good," said Roosevelt. "Let's see, the day after tomorrow? That will be Wednesday. Make it Thursday, instead. If you can, be here at ten o'clock. Come right to the White House."

"Yes, Mr. President," Knudsen responded.

"Thank you very much," said Roosevelt. "I'll be expecting you."[4]

Knudsen had heard the president speak on the radio earlier that week in one of his "fireside chats"—evening radio broadcasts in which Roosevelt presented some of his most important programs and ideas directly to the American public. Roosevelt announced that he intended to ask several U.S. business leaders to assist in carrying out a major effort to rebuild the defense industrial base in light of the Nazi advances. The success of this monumental program would hinge on the private sector: "We are calling upon the resources, the efficiency and the ingenuity of the American manufacturers of war material of all kinds—airplanes and tanks and guns and ships, and all the hundreds of products that go into this material. The Government of the United States itself manufactures few of the implements of war. Private industry will continue to be the source of most of this material, and private industry will have to be speeded up to produce it at the rate and efficiency called for by the needs of the times."[5]

After conferring in New York with General Motors chair Alfred Sloan about leaving the company, Knudsen headed to Washington.[6] A few minutes before 10:00 a.m. on May 30, Knudsen arrived at the White House and was greeted by Harry Hopkins, a tall, gaunt former commerce secretary who Roosevelt had tapped to help organize the defense effort. Hopkins had become such a critical advisor to Roosevelt that he had moved into the White House, where he kept a small bedroom on the second floor.

Hopkins graciously shook Knudsen's hand and then sheepishly remarked, "The president has asked me to tell you that we can't pay you anything, and he wants you to get a leave of absence from your company."

Knudsen was unmoved. "I don't expect any paycheck," he said matter-of-factly, "and the other matter has been taken care of."[7]

Hopkins accompanied Knudsen into the Oval Office, where Knudsen saw he was not the only one tapped to aid the war effort. Before him stood an assembly of industrial titans: Edward Stettinius Jr., president of U.S. Steel; Chester C. Davis of the Federal Reserve Board; Leon Henderson from the Securities and Exchange Commission; Sidney Hillman, president of the Amalgamated Clothing Workers of America; Ralph Budd, chairman of the board of the Chicago, Burlington, and Quincy Railroad; and Harriet Elliott, dean of women from the University of North Carolina.[8] These seven, including Knudsen, made up the National Defense Advisory Commission to help coordinate various segments of the U.S. industrial base as the country rapidly prepared for war.

Roosevelt explained in vague terms what Knudsen and the others would do. "We want to get some weapons for defense. We will begin that and superimpose the program on top of our ordinary production."

Roosevelt then ushered the group into the Cabinet Room, where members of the cabinet awaited them.

"These gentlemen, and Miss Elliott, are coming here to work on defense production," Roosevelt explained. "You gentlemen are to help them in every way you can."

Roosevelt noted that while there might be a thin legal basis to organize the commission, he believed he had sufficient authority under the Council of National Defense, a body formed during World War I to coordinate economic resources and industry in support of the country's war effort. Roosevelt also reassured his cabinet that the National Defense Advisory Commission would only be *advisory*.

Roosevelt paused, glanced around, and asked, "Are there any questions?"

"Yes, Mr. President," said Knudsen. "Who is boss?"

Roosevelt chuckled. "I guess I am."[9]

He suggested that the commission meet with him roughly once a week.[10] For Knudsen and his fellow commissioners, rapidly building the U.S. defense industrial base was a daunting task. The war in Europe was not going well. The day that Roosevelt welcomed Knudsen into the Oval Office, British Expeditionary Forces and other Allied troops were in the midst of Operation Dynamo, the evacuation from the French seaport of Dunkirk as the Wehrmacht completed its blitzkrieg of Western Europe.

Over the next five years, Knudsen and an army of U.S. policymakers and entrepreneurs—such as shipbuilder Henry Kaiser and former executive vice president of Sears Roebuck Donald Nelson—helped transform the U.S. defense industrial base from virtually nothing during the peacetime interwar years to the largest and most productive in the world. U.S. industry churned out a staggering 86,000 tanks, 2.5 million trucks, 286,000 warplanes, 8,800 navy ships, 2.6 million machine guns, and a whopping 41 billion rounds of ammunition.[11] Between 1940 and 1943, the U.S. Army Air Forces grew from a relatively small air force to the most capable in the world. In September 1939, the United States had barely 2,470 aircraft. By July 1944, it had nearly 80,000 aircraft thanks to a staggering production effort.[12]

Among the many achievements of the U.S. defense industrial base was the construction of the B-29 bomber, an extraordinary engineering feat that ushered in a new era of strategic bombing. A critical and generally overlooked part of strategic bombing was the role played by a group of Boeing engineers—including George Schairer, Edward Wells, and Wellwood Beall—in the design and production of the B-29. As the role of Knudsen, Wells, Beall, and others highlight, the private sector played a crucial role in innovation and military power.

The secret to this revitalization was Roosevelt's commitment to operating with speed in the defense industrial base, maximizing production capacity, minimizing excessive bureaucracy and red tape, and streamlining the acquisition and contracting systems. The Roosevelt administration created the War Production Board, with the full weight of the president, that cut through bureaucratic red tape, determined the policies and plans of federal departments regarding procurement and production, established priorities for materials and services, and created urgency to provide the U.S. military and its allies what they needed to fight and win the war.[13] U.S. and Allied air, ground, and naval forces used these weapons systems with lethal effectiveness to defeat Germany and Japan. As historian Richard Overy wrote in his book *Why the Allies Won*, one of the most important factors that led to the Allied victory in World War II was "the sheer speed and scale of American rearmament, which dwarfed anything that the Germans and Japanese, or even the British, had thought possible."[14]

But change didn't happen overnight for the United States.

By the time of Knudsen's meeting with Roosevelt, the U.S. defense industrial base was in shambles, wholly unprepared for the impending war and significantly smaller than that of most of the other great powers. Before World War II, the United States generally demobilized at the end of its wars. After World War I, civilian companies that had helped produce desperately needed arms and equipment returned to commercial production or went out of business as defense dollars dried up.[15] Some companies that had secured large contracts during World War I suffered serious dislocation and financial hardship when the military abruptly canceled their business at the end of hostilities. The nascent aircraft industry survived because of U.S. government airmail contracts, not U.S. military contracts.[16]

As a result of the collapse of the U.S. defense industrial base after World War I, the United States lacked a modern air force and a navy capable of operating in both the Atlantic and the Pacific. U.S. production plants had become obsolete and run down by the Great Depression. The United States also lacked domestic sources for some materials that were vital for a strong military. In 1940, for instance, the United States retained only 15 percent of the raw materials required for a two-year military emergency, a reality that terrified some senior U.S. officials.[17] There was *no stockpile* of such materials as mercury, industrial diamonds, mica, or wool—all of which were critical to the U.S. defense industry. Supplies were woefully low for manufacturing airplanes, including rubber, copper, ferroalloys, and aluminum.[18] Key segments of the U.S. economy were also underutilized. In 1938, the United States produced

26.4 million tons of steel—more than Germany at 20.7 million, the Soviet Union at 16.5 million, and Japan at 6.0 million. Yet a shocking two-thirds of U.S. steel plants were idle, while German, Soviet, and Japanese plants were working at full capacity.[19]

The U.S. government was more concerned about ensuring economic protectionism than supporting a robust defense industrial base, highlighted by congressional passage of the Smoot-Hawley Tariff Act, Roosevelt's support for labor unions, and the heavy taxation of businesses. Regulators dominated, and there was a serious—though illusory—hope that a peacetime environment would continue despite the military buildup happening in Europe and Asia. Starting in 1933, congressional legislation significantly restricted how much companies could make on their government contracts, even demanding advanced audits to guarantee that the company's profit would be no more than 8 percent before the contract was signed. Company investments in the construction of new plants took 16 years to be fully decided as a business expense, even with a contract.[20] Roosevelt and New Deal Democrats passed two Neutrality Acts, in 1935 and 1936, which prevented U.S. companies from selling defense material to any country involved in an armed conflict.[21] The Nye Commission, spearheaded by Senator Gerald Nye from North Dakota, condemned such companies as General Electric, General Motors, Colt Arms, Electric Boat, Curtiss, and Boeing as merchants of death, criticizing them for "lies, deceit, hypocrisy, greed, and graft."[22]

Isolationism reigned. Successive U.S. administrations under Presidents Herbert Hoover and Franklin D. Roosevelt, as well as significant segments of the U.S. population, had little interest in getting involved in foreign wars. As historian Paul Kennedy concluded in *The Rise and Fall of the Great Powers*, the United States "decidedly rejected a leading role in world politics, with all the diplomatic and military entanglements which such a posture would inevitably produce."[23] The Wall Street stock market crash on October 24, 1929, as well as the subsequent Great Depression, hurt the United States more than any other advanced economy. The U.S. gross national product plummeted from nearly $100 billion in 1929 to roughly half of that three years later, and at least 15 million workers lost their jobs.[24]

Before 1940, Roosevelt made a few efforts to revitalize the defense industrial base, but they were modest. In 1936, he supported a shipbuilding increase for the U.S. Navy after letting the Washington Naval Treaty lapse, which limited the navy's growth. Roosevelt also authorized an increase in aircraft construction for the U.S. Army Air Corps in 1938. But these were minimal steps. As Arthur Herman summarized, "After years of avoiding foreign affairs, Roosevelt began taking small, cautious steps, like a man feeling his way along in the dark."[25] As late as 1940, Roosevelt's treasury secretary, Henry Morgenthau Jr., wanted an additional $6 million cut out of the army's appropriations budget.[26]

The result was that the United States was far behind the great powers of the day in major weapons systems and defense production. In 1940, Germany's defense industry was the largest among the great powers at $6 billion, followed by the Soviet Union at $5 billion and the United Kingdom at $3.5 billion. In comparison, the United States spent a mere $1.5 billion.[27] That same year, the Soviet Union built 2,794 tanks, compared to 2,200 for Germany and 1,399 for the United Kingdom. The United States built only 400 tanks. The Soviet Union produced 15,300 artillery pieces, compared to 5,000 for Germany, 1,900 for the United Kingdom, and only 1,800 for the United States.[28]

The British defense industry lagged behind the German and the Soviet, thanks in part to several poor policy decisions. One was the Ten Year Rule, which was established in 1919 and supported by Winston Churchill. It decreed that the armed forces should draft their defense estimates on the assumption "that the British Empire will not be engaged in any great war during the next ten years and that no Expeditionary Force is required for this purpose."[29] The policy was eventually abandoned in 1932. But it caused grave damage because the British government made limited investments in the defense industrial base until 1940, despite German rearmament.[30] On the other hand, Japan began reorienting its economy toward war in the late 1920s. By 1940, total Japanese defense production had increased more than 75 percent, Japanese production of heavy industry rose by nearly 500 percent, and Japan directed roughly 17 percent of its total output to direct war material (compared to 2.6 percent for the United States).[31] Japanese defense production focused extensively on aircraft, naval, and merchant vessels, including such impressive systems as the Mitsubishi A6M "Zero" fighter.[32]

Country	1940	1941	1943
United Kingdom	$3.5	$6.5	$11.1
Soviet Union	$5.0	$8.5	$13.9
United States	$1.5	$4.5	$37.5
Germany	$6.0	$6.0	$13.8
Japan	$1.0	$2.0	$4.5
Italy	$0.75	$1.0	—

FIGURE 1.1 Arms production of the major powers, 1940–1943 (billions of 1944 dollars).[33]

In raw arms production, Germany and the Soviet Union led the way (Figure 1.1). Hitler had been rearming since 1933, and his instruction to Werner von Fritsch, commander-in-chief of the German Army, was clear: "to create an army of the greatest possible strength."[34] Albert Speer, Hitler's minister of armaments, oversaw German rearmament. By 1938, Hitler was spending more on weapons than the United Kingdom, France, and the United States combined as Germany mobilized for war and German industry furiously produced aircraft, tanks, ships, and other arms.[35] Kennedy summarized, "At sea, as well as on land and in the air, the German rearmament program was intent upon altering the balance of power as soon as possible."[36] In addition, Stalin focused on rapidly building the Soviet Union's defense industrial base, and he dramatically cut back funding to other sectors, such as agriculture, retail, and consumer goods.[37]

In comparison, the United States spent only 1.5 percent of its gross national product on defense in 1937—a paltry percentage compared to Japan (28.2), the Soviet Union (26.4), Germany (23.5), France (9.1), and the United Kingdom (5.7).[38] The United States also produced 2,195 aircraft in 1939, compared to 10,382 for the Soviet Union, 7,940 for Britain, and 8,295 for Germany.[39] In a shockingly short-sighted move, the head of U.S. Army Procurement, George Spalding, concluded that there was no mission requirement for the B-17 or any new four-engine long-range bomber. The Joint Army-Navy Board agreed with Spalding. In 1938, the U.S. military eliminated all funds for four-engine bomber procurement—including the B-17—from the fiscal years 1940 and 1941 military budgets.[40]

Despite the deficient U.S. defense industrial base, however, there was still a lot to build on. The United States had a remarkable juggernaut of an economy and led the world in manufacturing output, though its lead had shrunk over the 1930s (Figure 1.2). In addition, there were vast improvements across the globe in military technology—such as the torpedo, submarine, destroyer, machine gun, high explosives, calculating machines, main battle tank, and even fighter aircraft—that the United States could leverage.[41]

In short, the United States had significant *potential* to develop a strong defense industrial base to support its military. It just needed the organizational structure, money, and political leadership to do it, as well as a shift from a mentality of regulation to one of production. For William Knudsen and others involved in rebuilding the industrial base, the task was difficult—but entirely doable.

Knudsen developed a dogged work ethic at a young age and was a natural entrepreneur and innovator. As a teenager in Denmark, he became a junior clerk in the firm of Christian Achen in Copenhagen, which imported bicycle parts and tubing from Germany and England.[42] With

Country	1929	1932	1937	1938
United States	43.3%	31.8%	35.1%	28.7%
Soviet Union	5.0%	11.5%	14.1%	17.6%
Germany	11.1%	10.6%	11.4%	13.2%
United Kingdom	9.4%	10.9%	9.4%	9.2%
France	6.6%	6.9%	4.5%	4.5%
Japan	2.5%	3.5%	3.5%	3.8%
Italy	3.3%	3.1%	2.7%	2.9%

FIGURE 1.2 Share of world manufacturing output, 1929–1938 (percentage).[43]

one of Achen's salesmen, Knudsen built the first tandem bicycle in Denmark—his first manufacturing achievement.[44] But Knudsen had bigger dreams. In February 1900, the 20-year-old gangly Dane, who stood six feet three inches with a slope-shouldered frame, set off for New York on the *Norge*, a 6,000-ton ship, with his suitcase and $30. He quickly landed a job in the Seabury shipyards in the Bronx's Morris Heights reaming holes in steel plates for navy torpedo boats for just over 17.5 cents per hour. He was soon promoted to be a "bucker-up," holding the red-hot rivet in place with a combination of iron bars and brute strength so the riveters could hammer it in place. It was tedious activity. But Knudsen was proud of his work and inspired by the spirit of innovation in the United States.[45]

"When you go to Europe, they show you something that belonged to King Canute," Knudsen once remarked. "When you go to America they show you something they are going to build."[46]

Knudsen bounced around jobs in New York City, the suburbs of Buffalo, and ultimately Detroit, working his way up to production manager at Ford Motor Company's Highland Park Plant. But he increasingly butted heads with founder and president Henry Ford, and he resigned in 1921. Knudsen then caught the eye of Alfred P. Sloan, the new executive vice president at General Motors, who hired him the following year.[47] On May 3, 1937, Sloan became chairman of General Motors and made Knudsen his successor as president. Knudsen's time building cars at General Motors gave him a unique perspective in the art of mass production—the manufacturing of large quantities of standardized products using assembly lines to maximize efficiency—which would be invaluable to building the U.S. defense industrial base.

For Knudsen and other members of President Roosevelt's National Defense Advisory Commission, jump-starting U.S. industry meant helping the military rethink *what* it needed. Knudsen began by asking U.S. Army generals basic questions, such as "What do you want?"

The answers were always unsatisfactory. Many reverted to the army's mobilization plan with its goal of building a force of 400,000 soldiers within three months of mobilization, as well as another 800,000 soldiers after one year.

"That's not what I need," Knudsen had to explain, his patience waning. "I need to know what kind of equipment you need for these men—and how many pieces of each kind. Please tell me *how many pieces*."[48]

It rapidly became clear to Knudsen that none of the generals actually knew. This was a critical problem that needed to be resolved quickly. Knowing how many pieces the army needed was essential because the mass production of weapons systems and munitions could not be improvised at the last minute. It needed planning and time for development and production. After lunch with George C. Marshall in 1940, Knudsen grabbed a yellow legal pad and wrote furiously in his hotel room.

"The first thing to do," he scribbled down, "was to get started on the weapons that required a long cycle in manufacturing." Those would be ships, tanks, airplanes, guns, smokeless powder, and TNT. The second was to begin planning for the shorter-cycle items like trucks and other vehicles, clothing, food, and smaller arms like rifles and machine guns. The third was to assemble a team who understood the dynamic power of mass production and the technical problems facing a modern economy.[49]

At the first official meeting of the National Defense Advisory Commission on June 12, 1940, Knudsen described a way ahead based on his time in the automotive industry.

"Mass production has never depended on speed and never will," he said. "Speed, as such, is worthless. The only thing that produces good work is accuracy."

"I'm not a soldier, and I'm not a sailor," he acknowledged. "I am just a plain manufacturer. But I know if we get into war, the winning of it will be purely a question of material and production. If we know how to get out twice as much material as everyone else—know how to get it, how to get our hands on it, and use it—we are going to come out on top—and win."[50]

Knudsen's hunch was not entirely accurate. Winning wars is not—and never has been—just about material and production; it also requires the effective employment of forces, a sound strategy, and other factors.[51] Nevertheless, Knudsen was correct that material and production were critical to winning a protracted war. Over the next several months, he and the other commissioners worked tirelessly to jump-start industrial production and unwind the culture of regulation that had dominated the interwar period. For example, Knudsen helped streamline Army and Navy Department bureaucracy by establishing a "letter of intent," which indicated that the government planned to do business with a specific company before a formal contract was signed. He borrowed the concept from Britain's "letter of command," and it was enough to get a bank to advance the firm funds and to protect the firm's out-of-pocket expenses even if the contract never went through.[52]

The government negotiated contracts on a cost-plus basis, which meant that the government agreed to pay a company the cost of building an item—such as an aircraft, tank, munition, or uniform—plus a guaranteed percentage as profit. The more—and faster—a company produced, the more money it made. Roosevelt also issued an executive order in March 1942 suspending antitrust activities against companies that the government assessed were vital to defense production.[53] In a letter to President Roosevelt, senior U.S. government officials such as Attorney General Francis Biddle, Secretary of War Henry Stimson, and Secretary of the Navy Frank Knox argued that "in the present all-out effort to produce quickly and uninterruptedly a maximum amount of weapons of warfare, such court investigations, suits, and prosecutions unavoidably consume the time of executives and employees of those corporations which are engaged in war work."[54] Those who broke the law would still be aggressively punished, but the president of the United States could defer antitrust investigations for the duration of the war.

By October 1940, Knudsen had overseen some 920 contracts worth nearly $3 billion for the army and $6 billion for the navy. More than 500 companies were now involved in making everything from ships and tanks to aircraft engines and gunpower and ammonia plants.[55] Car companies were now heavily involved in defense production. Knudsen had enticed Henry Ford and the Ford Motor Company to manufacture 9,000 Pratt and Whitney engines for airplanes. In fact, Ford Motor Company produced more army equipment over the course of the war than the entire economy of Mussolini's Italy.[56] The General Motors Allison plant in Indianapolis produced engines for the Curtiss P-40 Warhawk. Chrysler built M3 Grant and Sherman tanks, as well as 40-mm anti-aircraft guns for the navy. Pontiac manufactured Oerlikon 20-mm anti-aircraft cannons.[57] Subcontractors were also critical. A company like General Motors employed at least 18,000 subcontractors.[58] Overall, automakers produced 50 percent of all aircraft engines, 35 percent of aircraft propellers, 47 percent of all machine guns, 87 percent of all aerial bombs, 80 percent of tanks and tank parts, 50 percent of the diesel engines for ships, submarines, and other naval craft, and 100 percent of U.S. Army trucks, half-tracks, and other vehicles.[59]

In December 1940, Roosevelt replaced the National Defense Advisory Commission with the Office of Production Management, which—unlike its predecessor—had the power to make decisions, issue directives, and cut through bureaucracy. Roosevelt wanted two heads: one to lead U.S. businesses, which was Knudsen; and one to lead labor, which was Sidney Hillman, who had served as president of the Amalgamated Clothing Workers of America.[60] "I told Knudsen that he was to be the chief figure," said Secretary of War Stimson, and that he "had won his position during the last six months by his outstanding work here in the Advisory Council."[61] Stimson wrote in his diary, "My impression of Mr. Knudsen's ability and his tact grows with each time I see him."[62]

On December 29, 1940, Roosevelt gave one of his most important speeches on defense production, arguing that the United States needed to be an "arsenal of democracy" for itself and its allies at war with Nazi Germany, including the United Kingdom and Russia. The speech, which has been referred to as "The Victory Program," is worth quoting at length:

> I want to make it clear that it is the purpose of the nation to build now with all possible speed every machine, every arsenal, every factory that we need to manufacture our defense material. We have the men, the skill, the wealth, and above all, the will. I am confident that if and when production of consumer or luxury goods in certain industries requires the use of machines and raw materials that are essential for defense purposes, then such production must yield, and will gladly yield, to our primary and compelling purpose.
>
> So I appeal to the owners of plants, to the managers, to the workers, to our own government employees to put every ounce of effort

into producing these munitions swiftly and without stint. With this appeal I give you the pledge that all of us who are officers of your government will devote ourselves to the same whole-hearted extent to the great task that lies ahead.

As planes and ships and guns and shells are produced, your government, with its defense experts, can then determine how best to use them to defend this hemisphere. The decision as to how much shall be sent abroad and how much shall remain at home must be made on the basis of our overall military necessities.

We must be the great arsenal of democracy.

For us this is an emergency as serious as war itself. We must apply ourselves to our task with the same resolution, the same sense of urgency, the same spirit of patriotism and sacrifice as we would show were we at war.[63]

Not everyone agreed with Roosevelt's approach and choice of industrial leaders. Secretary of the Interior Harold Ickes, a staunch liberal in the Roosevelt administration known as "the Old Curmudgeon," was responsible for implementing many of Roosevelt's New Deal policies. He criticized Knudsen and others involved in the war production effort for lining the pockets of rich industrialists and pushed to enforce a wide range of federal regulations. In his diary, Ickes fretted about "big business getting its nose under the Administration tent" and worried that Knudsen was a poor choice because he could never "dissociate himself from his past life, which has been in close cooperation with some of the biggest industrialists in the country."[64]

In addition, Thurman Arnold, whom Roosevelt appointed as head of the Justice Department's Antitrust Division in 1938, was apoplectic about the administration's support for big business. He had made his career breaking up companies and passing antitrust legislation, earning him the nickname "Trust Buster" in a *Saturday Evening Post* article.[65] Arnold protested, "[T]he vast government spending for war production . . . created a great opportunity for conspiratorial agreements between businessmen with respect to prices, bidding, consolidation, and mergers."[66] Likewise, Philip Murray, president of the Congress of Industrial Organizations, protested that industrial production was undermining the plight of workers. He charged that government agencies were "virtually infested" with corporate executives operating inside the government who were getting "fat, juicy, profitable contracts" for their own companies, calling them "dishonest, reprehensible, and vicious."[67] Not to be outdone, columnist Walter Lippmann blasted Knudsen for organizing the entire war effort to line his own pockets and those of corporate executives rather than serving "the public interest."[68]

But there were several problems with these arguments. First, Roosevelt had no serious option for jump-starting the defense industrial base but to work with major corporations such as General Motors and Ford since they already had the space, mass-production capabilities, and expertise to build defense systems. General Henry "Hap" Arnold, chief of the U.S. Air Corps and eventually commanding general of the U.S. Army Air Forces, remarked that Knudsen was simply indispensable: "[It] was no wonder that Army Air Corps officers were enthusiastic over the appointment of William S. Knudsen.... Bill Knudsen understood quantity production, machine tools and factory layouts, manufacturing technique and procedure, the skill and the spirit of both management and labor. With his arrival in Washington, the Air Corps production problems decreased as each day passed, and many of my headaches gradually disappeared."[69]

Second, there was little time to waste, making it important to rapidly shift from a peacetime environment of regulators to a wartime environment of rat-catchers. Hitler now controlled all of Europe, his Luftwaffe was pummeling cities like London during the Battle of Britain, and the Wehrmacht was preparing to invade the Soviet Union. Naysayers such as Ickes and Lippmann had no realistic alternative to quickly arm the United States in the face of German aggression.

Third, the efforts of Knudsen and others were already bearing fruit. By the end of 1940, the industrial base had built or secured under contract roughly 50,000 planes, 130,000 engines, 380 navy ships, 9,200 tanks, and 17,000 heavy guns for an army of 1.4 million soldiers.[70] As for raw materials, U.S. aluminum production had been only 25 million tons when Roosevelt brought Knudsen to Washington. But it was rising dramatically and would eventually hit 70 million by the end of 1941. Steel was moving in a similar direction.[71]

By December 7, 1941, these criticisms became moot when Japan attacked Pearl Harbor. The U.S. Congress responded the next day by declaring war on Japan, the House of Representatives voting 388–1 and the Senate voting 82–0.[72] The U.S. era of isolationism came to a sudden and decisive end. President Roosevelt gave a rousing speech to a joint session of Congress, warning that December 7 would be "a date which will live in infamy" in U.S. history.[73] In a gratuitous step, Hitler then declared war on the United States on December 11. The United States suddenly found itself in the most destructive war the world had ever witnessed.

Roosevelt moved with vigor and urgency to jump-start the defense industrial base. He signed the War Powers Act of 1941 on December 18, which gave him the authority to reorganize the executive branch and independent agencies, as well as censor mail and other forms of communication.[74] Three months later, he signed into law the Second War Powers Act, which allowed the government to acquire land for military or naval purposes. It also gave the federal government power to requisition supplies and property and force entire industries to produce wartime goods.[75]

In his January 1942 State of the Union address, Roosevelt echoed many of the themes from his "arsenal of democracy" speech. He argued that victory against the Japanese and Germans required not just defeating them on the battlefield but outpacing them in industrial production. And it wasn't enough to produce a "slightly superior supply of munitions"; the differences had to be significant. The superiority "in munitions and ships must be overwhelming—so overwhelming that the Axis Nations can never hope to catch up with it," Roosevelt thundered. "And so, in order to attain this overwhelming superiority the United States must build planes and tanks and guns and ships to the utmost limit of our national capacity."[76] He laid out an ambitious plan to build 60,000 airplanes in 1942 and another 125,000 in 1943, 45,000 main battle tanks in 1942 and 75,000 in 1943, 20,000 anti-aircraft guns in 1942 and 35,000 in 1943, and 6 million deadweight tons for merchant ships in 1942 and 10 million in 1943.[77] America's shipbuilding was led by such titans as Henry Kaiser, who established the Kaiser shipyards that built Liberty and Victory ships.

In his determination to rebuild the defense industrial base, Roosevelt grew impatient with Knudsen and the Office of Production Management for not moving fast enough. Knudsen likely knew his days were numbered when First Lady Eleanor Roosevelt blasted him and others in a speech to a national meeting of 4H directors. "The slowness of our officials in seeing ahead . . . is responsible for the whole [defense] mess."[78] With two heads, the Office of Production Management was in danger of becoming inefficient. Skeptics such as Ickes had long been circling like sharks around Knudsen, complaining that he was "handicapped by his own association with men like Ford and Sloan" and that "big business is having altogether too much to say about our preparedness program."[79]

On January 16, 1942, Roosevelt created the War Production Board. He fired Knudsen and appointed Donald Nelson, former executive vice president of Sears Roebuck, as the sole chair. Roosevelt explained that the board would exercise general direction over U.S. war procurement and production; determine the policies, plans, and procedures of federal departments regarding procurement and production; direct conversion of companies from peacetime to wartime work; establish priorities in the distribution of materials and services; and prohibit nonessential production.[80] It would also ration such commodities as gasoline, heating oil, metals, rubber, paper, and plastics.

Out of a job, Knudsen quickly turned to the army, who was thrilled to get him involved in production. Later in January, the army commissioned him as a lieutenant general, and he became the director of production in the Office of the Under Secretary of War.[81] Focused now on army production, Knudsen and other officials scrambled to increase the involvement of U.S. industry. As Knudsen remarked, "I placed most of the business with big companies for the reason that there was a lot of engineering to be done on practically every job. They were the only ones who had that kind of talent." Still, the subcontractors and "little businesses had an enormous part in the program."[82]

In addition to automobile companies, a growing number of other businesses began to develop and produce war materials. Examples ranged from Boeing to General Electric, Frigidaire, Rock-Ola, Underwood, National Postal Meter, Quality Hardware, IBM, Okonite, and Westinghouse. General Electric went on to make parts for destroyer engines, turbosuperchargers for high-altitude bombers, radar sets, and electrical systems that went inside the Landing Ship, Tanks (LST) and Landing Craft Infantry (LCI).[83] Boeing had more than 1,400 subcontractors for its B-29 project alone.[84]

To implement these changes, the United States also needed the raw materials. Aluminum was, in many ways, the era's defining war material. It was lightweight, high strength, and noncorrosive. Nearly as strong as iron and steel but much lighter, aluminum enabled planes to carry more weight, fly faster, and travel farther than ever before. Aluminum made up 60 percent of a modern heavy bomber's engines, 90 percent of its wings and fuselage, and all of its propellers.[85] It was also critical for the rudder, cockpit instrumentation, seats, doors, and other areas. "Aluminum," one observer noted, "has become the most important single bulk material of modern warfare. No fighting is possible, and no war can be carried to a successful conclusion today, without using and destroying vast quantities of aluminum."[86] Between 1939 and 1943, U.S. aluminum production grew sixfold, surpassing all other essential metals.[87] By the end of the war, roughly 70 percent of U.S., German, Japanese, and British aluminum production went into building aircraft.[88]

But the United States faced a serious supply-chain problem in manufacturing aluminum. Initially, the United States obtained most of its bauxite, the main source of aluminum, from mines in Suriname on the northeast coast of South America. However, German submarines disrupted this supply. During a three-week period in the early fall of 1942, German submarines torpedoed 15 bauxite carriers and reduced availability by more than 75,000 tons of bauxite.[89] Launching an "all-out" program to develop domestic sources, the War Production Board turned to bauxite from Arkansas, newly usable because of a technological breakthrough called the lime-soda sintering process.[90] In 1941, foreign suppliers provided 54 percent of America's bauxite, but this dropped to less than 20 percent in 1943—despite the massive increase in aluminum production.[91] "Had the United States not possessed a deposit of bauxite in Arkansas," a U.S. government study explained, "it might have been forced to cut back on airplane production."[92]

Thanks to these efforts, Knudsen, Kaiser, Nelson, and others revitalized the U.S. defense industrial base. In 1943, the United States produced a total of 18,434 battleships, cruisers, destroyers, carriers, and submarines; 16,000 landing craft; 9,616 bombers; 29,495 tanks; 7 million small arms; 800,000 tons of artillery shells; and 830,000 machine guns.[93] The balance of power was shifting dramatically. By 1943, the United States, the Soviet Union, and Britain had twice the manufacturing strength, three times the war potential, and three times the national income of Germany, Japan, and Italy.[94] The United States alone had more than double the arms production of Germany and Japan combined. In an incredible feat, U.S. arms production increased more than eight times between 1941 and 1943.

While arms production did not translate directly into fighting effectiveness, these weapons were *essential* in the European and Pacific theaters. They helped U.S. forces in the European theater push through North Africa and Italy, conduct a blistering air offensive against German forces in Europe, and prepare for D-day. In the Pacific theater these weapons enabled the U.S. military to blunt the Japanese push into the Coral Sea in May 1942 and Midway Island in June 1942.

In addition to these raw numbers, there are numerous examples of military innovation during World War II which contributed to the U.S. and Allied victory. Among the most significant was the transformation of U.S. submarine fleets from targeting Japanese battleships to waging unrestricted warfare against Japanese merchant ships, or *maru*, that carried oil, food, munitions, and other matériel. The goal was to decimate Japan's logistics pipeline, which supported its military.[95] The combination of submarine attacks and strategic bombing reduced Japan's stockpiles of oil from 43 million barrels at the end of 1944 to less than 4 million barrels in March 1945.[96] It was a difficult transition. In 1943, 30 percent of U.S. submarine commanders in the Pacific were relieved for cause because they were unable to shift their missions. This innovation involved a change in the character of the submarine fleet's officer corps and evolution into an organization with a radically decentralized command structure and good intelligence about the enemy.[97] Harvard professor Stephen Rosen concluded, "During the course of World War II, the American submarine fleet in the Pacific was transformed from a force targeted on the Japanese battlefleet into a force concerned with raiding merchant shipping."[98]

Another example of U.S. innovation was strategic bombing and the development of the four-engine B-29 Superfortress bomber. One of the most significant problems for the United States in the Pacific was the tyranny of distance, especially when it came to targeting the Japanese mainland. The U.S. military needed a bomber that could fly between 3,000 and 4,000 miles from U.S. air bases in China or the Pacific islands, climb to 30,000 feet to avoid Japanese anti-aircraft fire, reach a top speed of over 350 miles per hour, and carry a heavy payload—potentially including nuclear weapons. The B-17 Flying Fortress, built by Boeing and introduced in 1938, wasn't adequate. It had the range and ceiling but lacked the speed and especially the payload capacity.

Building such a bomber—which became the B-29—was an engineering feat. It would have to carry a massive bomb load several thousand miles and fly at a higher altitude than Mt. Everest to avoid enemy fighters and anti-aircraft fire.[99] It would also have to be built in large numbers "off the drawing board," which meant that multiple companies would have to produce components before the first plane was even built. It was virtually unprecedented—and extremely risky—for engineers to begin production *without* flight-testing a prototype.[100]

Shortly after the German invasion of Poland, the U.S. Army Air Corps turned to industry to build a bomber with higher speed, longer range, and greater overall performance than previous bombers. General Arnold, the commander, helped spearhead the initiative.[101] Boeing won a competitive bid with a prototype that met the main army air corps engineering requirements: a pressurized cabin to improve comfort for the crew, tricycle landing gear to enhance landings and handling on the ground, greater speed than the B-17 bomber, greater range, greater bomb capacity, and greater interchangeability between fuel and bombs (which meant a larger fuselage).[102]

The engineering feat to build the B-29 was staggering. The aircraft had to be constructed around aeronautical principles that had never before been applied. It needed to be almost twice the size of the B-17, close to 60,000 pounds when empty compared to 30,000 pounds for the B-17. It would need four engines and a wing area of at least 1,700 square feet to get a 70-ton plane with a full payload into the air and above 30,000 feet. It also needed a pressurized cabin so that the crew wouldn't pass out climbing to such high altitudes or suffer decompression sickness coming back down.[103] The B-29 was the largest project in the history of aeronautics up to that point. A U.S. company had never been asked to undertake an industrial project of this size, cost, and complexity this quickly.

In the end, five main companies—Boeing, North American Aviation, Bell Aircraft Corporation, Wright Aeronautics, and General Motor's Fisher Body Division—joined forces with the U.S. Army Air Force to work out a comprehensive production plan, with Boeing in the lead. It had a development and production cost of between $3 billion and $3.7 billion, even larger than the $2 billion for the Manhattan Project.[104] Boeing provided all the engineering data to the primary contractors, oversaw all design changes, and supplied the master gauges to maintain interchangeability of parts. Because of the enormous complexity of designing and producing an aircraft in the middle of a world war, Boeing put its best engineers on the project—including Wellwood Beall, Edward "Ed" Wells, and George Schairer. Claire Egtvedt, Boeing's president, was heavily involved, as was Boeing's best test pilot, Edmund "Eddie" Allen.

Beall was vice president in charging of engineering and a native of Canon City, Colorado, who had attended the University of Colorado and New York University.[105] Wells was the chief engineer and a cum laude graduate of Stanford University's Engineering School; he grew up in Portland, Oregon, and had designed major portions of the B-17 Flying Fortress. At the age of 10, Wells built his first airplane, a scale model of the Curtiss Jenny training plane.[106] But the B-29 would be his most daunting challenge. Schairer was Boeing's chief aerodynamicist; he had an undergraduate degree from Swarthmore College and a master's degree from MIT. "George was hard to get along with," according to one of his colleagues, but he "was to Boeing what Bill Gates has been to Microsoft."[107] Allen was the chief of Boeing Flight Test, a thin, balding native of Chicago who had achieved legendary status as one of the best test pilots in the world. He died on February 18, 1943, during a flight test of the B-29's second prototype, the XB-29, when the aircraft experienced an engine fire, narrowly missed downtown Seattle skyscrapers, and crashed into the Frye Packing Plant just short of the runway at Boeing Field. The death of Allen was a result, in part, of the War Department's urgent need to produce the B-29 in the middle of a world war before the prototype had been completed.[108]

With these individuals in the lead, Boeing designed the B-29 in multiple sections: the body and nacelles (the streamlined enclosure that housed the engine and its components), wing and control surfaces, power plant installations, electrical and hydraulic systems, landing gear and controls, and all internal equipment. Boeing's engineers faced numerous challenges along the way. One was designing and producing a massive aircraft that was twice the weight of the B-17, able to fly with 30 percent more speed but with only 83 percent more horsepower. It defied the general principles of aeronautical engineering at the time, which assumed that, "all other things being equal, to double the speed you must have eight times as much power; for in doubling the speed this ordinarily produced four times the drag."[109] The answer, it turned out, was an extraordinary innovation: the Model 117 wing, which offered greater range performance because of refinements in drag characteristics. Boeing engineers, led by Schairer, designed an extendable wing flap that allowed the wings to carry a greater load of fuel and bombs per square foot than any other plane built up to that point.[110] The wing also had a web-type construction rather than the tubular spar construction of the B-17, with a heavy extruded duralumin chord.[111]

In addition, the U.S. chemical company DuPont had developed special Plexiglas-like observation blisters to fit into the fuselage. But they had a tendency of blowing out when the pressure outside the plane changed too quickly. Boeing had designed an automatic cabin pressure regulator for the cabin for high altitudes. On one test at 30,000 feet, all the crew were at their stations wearing their parachutes when the blister popped.

"It was like an elephant kicking me in the pants, sir," one of the crew members said to Knudsen, who helped coordinate the B-29 program.

"So, what did you do?" asked Knudsen.

"Well, sir, I found myself up there without any airplane and just pulled my cord," the crew member shrugged.[112]

Another engineering puzzle was how to build a workable central fire control system directed by an analog computer that corrected for wind, gravity, airspeed, and other factors. Working with Sperry Gyroscope, Boeing and General Electric created a remote fire-control system for the B-29—the first "smart" automated weapons system.[113] There were numerous other innovations. One was the so-called wet wing fuel tank. At the time, self-sealing fuel tanks were still clumsy. Consequently, the engineers spread the interior of the wing fuel tank with Duprene sealer from DuPont, which prevented wing punctures from leaking or igniting a fire—or even exploding.[114]

In May 1941, the War Department alerted Boeing in a letter that it would place an order of 250 B-29 bombers. The letter specified that "procurement is conditioned upon expansion of facilities at Boeing-Wichita to permit" increased productive capacity and emphasized, "[T]he Secretary of War advises that in the interest of national defense it is necessary that production be not delayed."[115]

The production task fell to Wellwood Beall and his team. They agreed that Boeing would build many of the B-29s at a plant in Wichita, which had to be expanded.[116] The project would become known as the "Battle of Kansas," or more formally the PQ Project, because of the immense challenges that Boeing personnel endured in the winter of 1944 to build and modify aircraft through extreme cold, bitter wind, and blowing snow.[117] No one, not even the Ford Motor Company at its massive Willow Run factory in Michigan, where it built B-24 Liberator bombers, had come up with an assembly line layout that could handle the size and complexity of the B-29. The plant in Wichita had 40,540 different parts and a million rivets. The multi-staffed assembly-line method marked a revolution in U.S. manufacturing. Compared to Willow Run, with its long-winding L-shaped construction, a B-29 plant could be built as a square or rectangle, which saved money.[118] But Boeing-Wichita wasn't large enough to build all the airplanes the War Department requested. Boeing also produced B-29s in Renton, Washington; Bell Aircraft produced B-29s in Marietta, Georgia; and the Glenn L. Martin Company produced some at its plant in Omaha, Nebraska.[119] In all, 3,300 engineers helped design the aircraft, and 80,000 men and women built it.[120]

There were significant challenges along the way, including with the Wright R-3350 engines. All the early ones were inadequate and unreliable. The engine cowling for the B-29 was wrong, the flaps were problematic, and the engines would overheat and catch fire.[121] The second prototype caught fire during testing, leading to Allen's death. There were serious discussions about canceling the program.[122] Knudsen was so worried about the engines that he insisted the results be phoned directly to him every day in his office in the Pentagon. "It gave me the jitters," he recalled.[123] The list of problems seemed endless: overheating engines, overheating and blown cylinders, defective valve push rods, busted valve springs, defective fuel pumps, and faulty fuel transfer systems.[124] But these were risks the U.S. military was willing to take to quickly produce an aircraft that could be used for strategic bombing against Japan.

The result was an engineering feat. The final B-29 was a midwing, four-engine, all-metal monoplane with pressurized cabin and tricycle-type landing gear. It was the heaviest high-speed airplane in the world. It was half the size of the B-17 Flying Fortress but double its weight and considerably faster. It absorbed multiple engineering developments, including the design of nacelles to house and cool the massive power plants and still be aerodynamic. To cool the engines, it was necessary to design the largest cowl flaps ever installed on an airplane. The nose wheel figure of the tricycle landing gear was the first double-wheel arrangement ever placed on an airplane produced in quantity. The 16.5-foot four-bladed Hamilton-Standard propellers were the largest metal propellers ever installed on a production airplane.[125] In addition, the B-29 was the first altitude-conditioned, four-engine heavy bomber, as well as the first with complete remote-control gun firing systems. Boeing built 1,644 B-29s, the last one delivered on October 2, 1945.[126] The bomber could reach a maximum speed of 350 miles per hour, fly over 3,500 miles without refueling, reach a ceiling over 35,000 feet, and carry a 10-ton bomb load—including nuclear weapons.[127]

With the B-29s in hand—or, perhaps more appropriately, in flight—U.S. Air Force General Curtis LeMay oversaw their use from his perch at XX Bomber Command in China and then XXI Bomber Command in the Pacific. LeMay was eventually placed in charge of all strategic air operations against the Japanese home islands and commanded multiple B-29 operations against Japan, including massive incendiary attacks on 67 Japanese cities and the atomic bombs dropped on Hiroshima

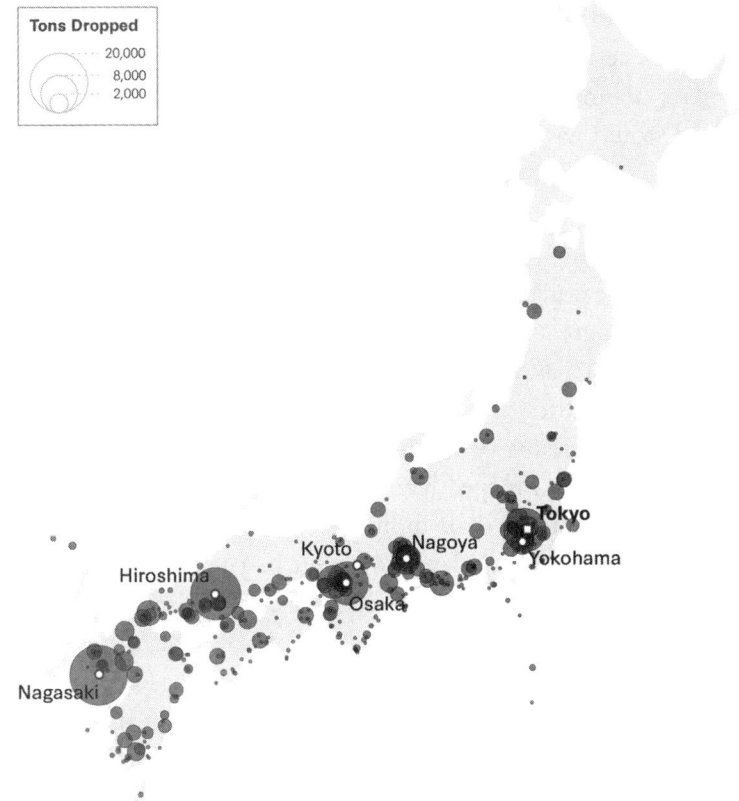

FIGURE 1.3 Map of B-29 bombing of Japan during World War II (by tonnage). Includes the atomic bombings of Hiroshima and Nagasaki.[128]

and Nagasaki (Figure 1.3). The B-29 firebombing of Tokyo—known as "Operation Meetinghouse" and conducted on the night of March 9–10, 1945—was the single most destructive bombing raid of the war. Initially, B-29s had to operate at night or at relatively high altitudes, 17,000 feet or more, to minimize losses from Japanese guns. Over the course of 1945, however, they bombed Japan at will and flew missions as low as 8,000 and 5,000 feet with virtually no losses.[129] B-29s destroyed most of Japan's industries, and some Japanese leaders assessed that B-29 attacks had reduced their nation's military production by roughly 50 percent.[130] The use of B-29s for strategic bombing helped end the war in the Pacific, along with strategic interdiction and the naval blockade of Japan.[131] As historian Paul Kennedy argued, the B-29 offered "an enormous shortcut to a war that many planners originally thought might go on until 1946 or 1947 and would have to include a giant Allied invasion of mainland Japan."[132]

By the end of the war, there was a major reordering of the defense industrial bases of the great powers. Allied strategic bombing had devastated Germany's industrial base, including in the Ruhr industrial region. After the war, the Allies divided Germany into four occupation zones, and the "level of industry" plans, spearheaded by U.S. Secretary of the Treasury Henry Morgenthau, led to the destruction of German defense factories and civilian industries that could support defense. Morgenthau wrote to President Roosevelt in 1944, "It should be the aim of the Allied Forces to accomplish the complete demilitarization of Germany in the shortest possible period of time after surrender." He explained that this meant "completely disarming the German Army and people (including the removal or destruction of all war material), the total destruction of the whole German armament industry, and the removal or destruction of other key industries which are basic to military strength."[133] After the war, German national income and output in 1946 were less than one-third that of 1938—a stark decline.[134]

Japan's defense industry was also in tatters, thanks in part to the U.S. strategic bombing campaign. In addition to factories, U.S. bombing targeted Japan's raw materials such as iron ore and bauxite, the latter of which was critical for aircraft production; oil and fuel production; and other industrial and civilian targets. According to Teijiro Toyoda, an admiral in the Imperial Japanese Navy during the war, the impact was significant: "The destruction of the two Mitsubishi plants in Nagoya was remarkably complete and the loss of those plants was very important to us. You know that the growth of the Japanese aircraft industry had been remarkably rapid and as a result relies heavily on small and home industries. Besides the precision attacks, your destruction of the little plants in the smaller cities hit by bombing reduced our productive power greatly."[135]

Even though Italy switched sides in 1943, the fate of its defense industrial base—and economy more broadly—was nearly as grim. France's industrial base was also decimated. After several years of plundering by the Nazis, war itself destroyed much of what was left of French industry in 1944. British production of air, sea, and land systems was impressive over the course of the war, including such platforms as the heavy four-engine bomber, the Lancaster.[136] Nevertheless, the British industrial base was in seriously bad shape by the end of the war. The economist John Maynard Keynes likened the situation to a "financial Dunkirk," since the United Kingdom faced a massive trade gap, weakened industrial base, and heavy reliance on U.S. military and economic assistance.[137]

It was the Soviet and U.S. defense industrial bases that emerged ahead of the pack. On the Eastern Front, the Soviet industrial base outproduced Germany and was able to accelerate faster than Germany's over the course of the war.[138] During implementation of the First Five-Year Plan, 1928 to 1932, Soviet leaders had lavished resources on their defense industrial base, even as millions starved in the early 1930s because of forced collectivization and a crash industrialization policy. Following Hitler's invasion of the Soviet Union in 1941, Soviet industrial efforts dramatically increased. Between 1941 and 1945, the Soviets churned out 112,100 aircraft (compared to 80,600 for Germany), 1,515,900 machine guns (compared to 1,096,400 for Germany), over 12 million rifles (compared to 8.5 million for Germany), and 102,800 tanks and self-propelled artillery (compared to 43,400 for Germany) (Figure 1.4).[139] As University of Chicago professor John Mearsheimer wrote in *The Tragedy of Great Power Politics*,

Weapons System	Soviet Union	Nazi Germany
Aircraft	112,100	80,600
Machine Guns	1,515,900	1,096,400
Rifles	12,139,300	8,525,200
Tanks and Self-propelled Artillery	102,800	43,400
Artillery	482,200	311,500

FIGURE 1.4 Soviet and German war production, 1941–1945.[140]

"[T]he Soviet war economy was able to compete effectively with the German war economy in World War II. Indeed, the Soviets outproduced the Germans in virtually every category of military weaponry for the years from 1941 through 1945.... No wonder the Red Army defeated the Wehrmacht on the eastern front."[141] The Soviet Union was the dominant land power—even compared to the United States—producing 15,400 tanks in 1945 (compared to 11,968 for the United States) and 31,000 artillery pieces (compared to 19,699 for the United States).[142]

Over the last several years of the war, the United States produced an extraordinary number of weapons systems, particularly aircraft.[143] U.S. industry achieved a stunning 1,545 percent increase in aircraft production between 1939 and 1944. By 1944, U.S. industry produced more aircraft than Germany and Japan combined, more than twice the amount of the Soviet Union, and nearly four times the amount of the United Kingdom.[144] The United States also produced far more vessels (1,513) than the United Kingdom (64), Japan (51), or Soviet Union (11) (Figure 1.5).

Churchill had been prescient in December 1941 after Pearl Harbor, believing that U.S. entry into the war would turn the tide. "Hitler's fate was sealed. Mussolini's fate was sealed," he wrote. "As for the Japanese, they would be ground to powder. All the rest was merely the proper application of overwhelming force. The British Empire, the Soviet Union, and now the United States, bound together with every scrap of their life and strength, were, according to my lights, twice or even thrice the force of their antagonists."[145]

News of the atomic bombs on Hiroshima and Nagasaki, which were dropped from B-29s, reached Knudsen in his office in Dayton, Ohio, at the air force's Wright-Patterson Field. Emperor Hirohito announced Japan's surrender on August 15, 1945, and the formal surrender took place in September on the deck of the USS *Missouri*. Knudsen formally resigned from the army after half a decade dedicated to building the U.S. defense industrial base. He eventually returned to Detroit and was honored at a parade attended by Washington dignitaries, including Chief of Staff of the U.S. Army George C. Marshall. When it was

Aircraft							
	1939	1940	1941	1942	1943	1944	1945[1]
United Kingdom	7,940	15,049	20,094	23,672	26,263	26,461	12,070
United States	5,856	12,804	26,277	47,826	85,998	96,318	49,761
Soviet Union	10,382	10,565	15,735	25,436	34,900	40,300	20,900
Germany	8,295	10,247	11,776	15,409	24,807	39,807	7,540
Japan	4,467	4,768	5,088	8,861	16,693	28,180	11,066
Major Vessels[2]							
	1939	1940	1941	1942	1943	1944	1945
United Kingdom	57	148	236	239	224	188	64
United States	–	–	544	1,854	2,654	2,247	1,513
Soviet Union	–	33	62	19	13	23	11
Germany (U-boats Only)	15	40	196	244	270	189	0
Japan	21	30	49	68	122	248	51
Tanks[3]							
	1939	1940	1941	1942	1943	1944	1945
United Kingdom	969	1,399	4,841	8,611	7,476	5,000	2,100
United States	–	400	4,052	24,997	29,497	17,565	11,968
Soviet Union	2,950	2,794	6,590	24,446	24,089	28,963	15,400
Germany	1,300	2,200	5,200	9,200	17,300	22,100	4,400
Japan	200	1,023	1,024	1,191	790	401	142
Artillery Pieces[4]							
	1939	1940	1941	1942	1943	1944	1945
United Kingdom	1,400	1,900	5,300	6,600	12,200	12,400	–
United States	–	1,800	29,615	72,658	67,544	33,558	19,699
Soviet Union	17,348	15,300	42,300	127,000	130,300	122,400	31,000
Germany	2,000	5,000	7,000	12,000	27,000	41,000	–

FIGURE 1.5 Weapons production of the major powers, 1939–1945.[146]

Notes: [1] 1945 figures for the United Kingdom, United States, and Japan for January–August; for the Soviet Union, all year for aircraft, January–March for artillery; for Germany, January–April.
[2] Excludes landing-craft and smaller auxiliary vessels.
[3] Includes self-propelled guns for the Soviet Union and Germany.
[4] Medium and heavy caliber only for Germany, the United States, and the United Kingdom; all artillery pieces for the Soviet Union. Soviet heavy artillery production in 1942 was 49,100; in 1943, 48,400; and in 1944, 56,100.

Knudsen's turn to speak, he was concise: "Good night, my friends, and God bless you all."[147]

Many others were not willing to let Knudsen off the hook so fast. General Arnold was effusive in praising Knudsen as a quintessential example of U.S. innovation and productivity. "Lieutenant General

William Knudsen's genius continued to dominate the production picture," he concluded. "There are few countries (Britain was one of them) that could, as we did here in America, change a piano company into an outfit that would turn out airplane wings within a few months, or change a railroad car factory over to an airplane factory, a toy factory into an agency from which we were able to get all kinds of gadgets and accessories for our airplanes."[148] But Knudsen was such an industrial leader.

Led by Knudsen, Nelson at the War Production Board, and Kaiser with shipbuilding, the Roosevelt administration fundamentally transformed the defense industrial base from obsolescence in the peacetime interwar years to a juggernaut during World War II. To maximize production capacity, the administration operated with urgency, limited unnecessary regulations, and provided incentives to the private sector for innovation (including to Boeing for its B-29 production). "We are going to have to rely on our great mass production industries for the bulk of our increase under this war production," said Nelson while he was chair of the War Production Board. "The only gauge we can apply to this process is: 'What method will most quickly give us the greatest volume of war production in this particular industry?'"[149] But it wasn't easy. There was strong resistance from the likes of Secretary Ickes, Assistant Attorney General Thurman Arnold, Congress of Industrial Organizations president Philip Murray, columnist Walter Lippman, and others. Many wanted industry to be regulated, not empowered. But they lost in the end.

From the moment Knudsen and others helped kick off the armaments program in 1940 until August 1945, the United States produced a staggering $183 billion in arms to defeat Nazi Germany and Imperial Japan. During that time, an assortment of large and small companies churned out 141 aircraft carriers; 8 battleships; 807 cruisers, destroyers, and destroyer escorts; 32 tons of merchant shipping; 88,410 tanks and self-propelled guns; 257,000 artillery pieces; 2.4 million trucks; 2.6 million machine guns; 41 billion rounds of ammunition; and 24,750 aircraft. Not only had U.S. industry equipped its own military, but it had provided roughly $50 billion in aid through Lend-Lease to its allies.[150] By 1944, the U.S. industry had produced more than

Company	Total Amount of War Supply Contracts (Millions of Dollars)	Percentage of Total
General Motors Corporation	$13,812.7	7.9%
Curtiss-Wright Corporation	$7,091.0	4.1%
Ford Motor Company	$5,269.6	3.0%
Consolidated Vultee Aircraft Corporation	$4,875.4	2.8%
Douglas Aircraft Company	$4,431.3	2.5%
United Aircraft Corporation	$3,923.0	2.2%
Bethlehem Steel Company	$3,789.3	2.2%
Chrysler Corporation	3,394.8	1.9%
General Electric Company	3,300.1	1.9%
Lockheed Aircraft Corporation	3,246.2	1.9%

FIGURE 1.6 Top 10 U.S. companies involved in defense production, 1940–1944.[151]

two-fifths of the globe's munitions and roughly 50 percent more than all its enemies combined.[152] Key companies were General Motors, Ford, Chrysler, Curtiss-Wright Corporation, Douglas Aircraft Company, General Electric Company, and Lockheed Aircraft Company (Figure 1.6). And within those companies, engineers and workers like Schairer, Wells, and Beall turned ideas into hardware.

There were, of course, other factors that contributed to the U.S. and Allied victories in the European and Pacific theaters. One was the successful employment of force by U.S. and Allied air, sea, and land power. In addition, the United States and its allies effectively targeted German and Japanese war production through the successful application of air and maritime bombing.[153] But the U.S. defense industrial base, which was able to develop and produce a staggering amount of equipment and achieve impressive innovations like the B-29 and strategic bombing, was essential to victory. Roosevelt said it best in January 1942, less than a month after Pearl Harbor: "Powerful enemies must be outfought *and outproduced*."[154]

Hope that the surrender of Japan would usher in an era of peace and tranquility was fleeting. The next task of the industrial base was to prepare the United States for the coming Cold War with the Soviet Union.

2

The Cold War and Pax Americana

Our aim is to get results cheaper, sooner, and better through application of common sense to tough problems. If it works, don't fix it.

Be quick, be quiet, be on time.
—CLARENCE "KELLY" JOHNSON, Lockheed Skunk Works

THE DEFENSE COMPANY LOCKHEED HAD pestered the U.S. Army Air Corps for years about building a jet-powered aircraft.[1] Based in the bustling city of Burbank, 10 miles northwest of Los Angeles in the San Fernando Valley, Lockheed had boomed during World War II and employed 90,000 workers.[2] A few prescient aeronautical engineers, such as Lockheed's Clarence "Kelly" Johnson, believed they could build fighter aircraft with speeds that would far exceed those of current engines and propellers. The air corps dragged its feet, worried that jet airplanes would be inefficient gas guzzlers that couldn't fly the long distances needed in the Pacific.

But not the British. In 1941, the Royal Air Force installed a jet engine designed by Frank Whittle into one of its small fighters, the Gloster E.28/39 Meteor. The innovation was to use centrifugal flow, in which air is directed outward through centrifugal action to power the engine. At the same time, the Germans were working on a separate jet engine design, led by Herbert Wagner, chief structural engineer for the German company Junkers. Instead of a centrifugal flow jet engine, Wagner's Junkers Jumo 004 was an axial flow turbojet engine, in which air flows parallel to the axis of rotation.[3]

The innovation sent shock waves through Allied and Axis countries: they could now manufacture fighter aircraft that could achieve unprecedented speeds. The race was on to mass-produce jet-powered fighter aircraft. At the front of the pack was Lockheed's Kelly Johnson. Born in 1910 in the town of Ishpeming in northern Michigan to Swedish immigrants, Johnson was a tough, bare-knuckles kid. In elementary school, he snapped during an argument on the playground with the class bully, Cecil. Johnson kicked him in the back of the knee and pounced on him, making him a legend among his classmates.[4] They christened him "Kelly" from a popular music hall song of the day:

> Has anybody here seen Kelly?
> K-E-double-L-Y
> Has anybody here seen Kelly?
> Have you seen him smile?
> Oh, his hair is red and his eyes are blue
> And he's Irish through and through.
> Has anybody here seen Kelly?
> Kelly from the Emerald Isle.[5]

The name stuck. As a youth, Kelly Johnson carried bricks and other supplies to bricklayers and stonemasons, and he developed arms as thick as tree trunks that were useful for arm wrestling. He also developed an early passion for airplanes. He was a voracious reader of books like *Tom Swift and His Air Scout*, a novel from the dashing adventure series created by Edward Stratemeyer. "I read other books on aircraft—the Rover Boys, Collins' book on model airplanes—and decided by the time I was 12 years old that I would be an aircraft designer," Johnson recalled. "My whole life from that time was aimed at preparing for that goal."[6] Johnson briefly went to Flint Junior College before transferring to the University of Michigan, where he received a bachelor's and a master's degree in aeronautical engineering.[7]

In 1933, Lockheed took a chance on Johnson, starting him off in tool design and paying him $83 per month.[8] After the British installed Whittle's engine in its Meteor fighter aircraft, the U.S. Army Air Corps finally agreed to listen to a pitch from Johnson and Lockheed. On June 8, 1943, the Lockheed team traveled to Wright Field in Dayton, Ohio, to meet with Major General Frank Carrol, chief of the experimental engineer section.

"We'll give you a contract for the airplane, Kelly," Carrol announced after the briefing. "But you'll have to use the British engine in the first airplane because we need it—and all the jet fighters you can build—as soon as possible to use against the Me-262." This was the Luftwaffe's vaunted fighter-bomber that used the Junkers' jet engine. "Your new engine couldn't possibly be ready for service in time."

Johnson was ecstatic. "When will we get a contract? When will the time start?" he inquired.

"You will have a Letter of Intent this afternoon by 1:30 p.m.," Carrol said, highlighting the speed and agility with which the U.S. military contract process was able to move. "There is a plane leaving Dayton for Burbank at two o'clock. Your time starts then."9

Johnson had pestered Lockheed leadership to set up an experimental department where the engineers, mechanics, and designers could work together in a confined location without having to worry about the excessive regulations and delays of working in much of the traditional defense industry. But Lockheed's corporate leadership was not convinced it was worthwhile—until now. Back in Burbank, Johnson cobbled together 22 of Lockheed's best engineers, among them W. P. Ralston, Don Palmer, and Art Viereck. They created their own purchasing department to operate independently of the rest of Lockheed, and they worked out of a two-story, windowless building that looked like an uninhabited concrete blockhouse. Lockheed's Advanced Development Projects, known as Skunk Works, was the epitome of an agile organization that was committed to innovation with a streamlined system and limited bureaucracy. Led by Johnson, Skunk Works created some of the most important and innovative defense systems of the Cold War, including the P-80 Shooting Star, U-2 reconnaissance aircraft, SR-71 Blackbird reconnaissance aircraft, F-117 Nighthawk stealth attack aircraft, and F-22 Raptor stealth aircraft. Skunk Works was symbolic of a defense industry that could produce critical material for the military and intelligence community given the money, urgency, and streamlined contracting process.

Over the course of the Cold War, the U.S. defense industrial base ebbed and flowed during six major periods that make up the core of this chapter: (1) the demobilization of the defense industry after World War II as the United States shifted to a peacetime environment; (2) the rapid shift to a wartime environment with the outbreak of the Korean War; (3) the transition back to a peacetime industrial base with the end of the Korean War and the first offset; (4) the Soviet launch of Sputnik and the return to a wartime environment; (5) the move to a peacetime industrial base in the 1960s and 1970s; and (6) the second offset and Reagan buildup in the final stages of the Cold War.

As this chapter argues, during periods of wartime the U.S. government generally increased funding for defense, focused on the rapid production of essential systems and platforms for the military, streamlined acquisitions and contracting, and operated with an overall sense of urgency. This occurred during the Korean War and in the late 1970s when the Soviets achieved nuclear parity and possessed significant conventional capabilities in Eastern and Central Europe. But the immediate aftermath of World War II, the years after the end of the Korean War, and the 1960s were all periods in which U.S. policymakers mistakenly assessed they were living in a peacetime environment. Cuts in defense and industry during several of these periods—such as in the late 1940s and 1960s—weakened deterrence and undermined U.S. national security. While the Truman, Kennedy, and Johnson administrations hoped for a peacetime environment, the Soviet Union had a vote.

The first major debate about the international security environment was after World War II, when Truman administration officials and many Americans hoped they could put war and security competition behind them. In many ways, these views were understandable after such a destructive war. But it was ultimately a mistake to gut the U.S. defense industry while Soviet leader Joseph Stalin was attempting to expand Soviet power and strengthen military capabilities.

With the defeat of Germany and Japan, the United States was exhausted by war. President Truman slashed the defense budget, which declined sevenfold between 1946 and 1948.[10] He also abolished the

War Production Board in October 1945, which had streamlined contracting and production, eliminated unnecessary regulations, and allocated scarce materials.[11] William Knudsen retired to his manor at 1501 Balmoral Drive in an upscale neighborhood of Detroit. Henry Kaiser struggled to keep his shipyards open in Richmond, California, and Portland, Oregon. But Kaiser pushed into other areas, such as healthcare, aluminum, housing, and a wide array of construction projects.

While the U.S. government made large capital investments in plants and equipment during World War II, it sold off those holdings after the war to those companies that had produced matériel at the plants. The result was that approximately 250 of the largest U.S. companies secured more than 70 percent of the plants that were sold.[12] In other instances, the government continued to own the facility, but the companies located there took over management.[13] Companies that had produced weapons systems and platforms during the war—such as Ford and Chrysler—transitioned back to commercial production. In addition, nearly 10 million American soldiers returned to the United States, hoping for a normal life, a paycheck, and a home.[14] The labor unions, which had been partially neutered during World War II, returned with a vengeance and demanded postwar pay raises as high as 30 percent from such companies as Ford and General Motors.[15]

The United States rapidly reduced its number of forces in Europe as domestic pressure intensified in late 1945 and 1946 to speed up withdrawal. The U.S. military had planned for a nine-division force in Germany but reduced it to five divisions.[16] U.S. end strength fell from over 12 million personnel in Europe in 1945 to just 1.4 million by 1948.[17] By 1950, the army's European Command controlled only one infantry division in Germany, while four were stationed in Japan.[18] By the time of the creation of NATO in 1949, the United States, the United Kingdom, and France could barely account for 12 total divisions, which were dedicated primarily to the occupation of Germany.[19]

While the United States cut back its defense spending and industry, the country emerged from World War II as a global economic power. The gross national product skyrocketed from $88.6 billion in 1939 to $135 billion in 1944, a period that witnessed the greatest expansion of industrial production in the country's history.[20] The United States had $20 billion in gold reserves, which was nearly two-thirds of the globe's total of $33 billion.[21] By 1950, total U.S. gross national product was significantly larger than that of the United Kingdom, France, West Germany, Japan, and Italy *combined*—and over three times larger than the Soviet Union's (Figure 2.1).[22] Europe's traditional powers struggled with wartime debt, signaling the end of the Age of Europe, and Japan collapsed as a major power. Though free of Japanese imperialism, China was economically backward and had a tiny defense budget compared to the United States and Soviet Union. In 1953, China was responsible for only 2.3 percent of world manufacturing production and had a total industrial potential equal to only 71 percent of the United Kingdom's in 1900.[23]

But was the international landscape truly a peacetime environment? No—and certainly not for Stalin. After the war, the Soviets possessed the largest military in the world, with 4 million soldiers in the armed forces in 1948, including 2.6 million in the army.[24] Stalin expanded his country's territory by annexing parts of Finland, Poland, Romania, East Prussia, and Czechoslovakia, and he swallowed up Estonia, Latvia, Lithuania, and Moldova. The Soviet Union also established a sphere of influence in Eastern Europe, which was formalized by the creation of the Warsaw Pact.

Country	Total GNP (Billions of Dollars, 1964 Prices)	Per Capita GNP
United States	$381	$2,536
Soviet Union	$126	$699
United Kingdom	$71	$1,393 (USD 1951)
France	$50	$1,172
West Germany	$48	$1,001
Japan	$32	$382
Italy	$29	$626 (USD 1951)

FIGURE 2.1 Total GNP and per capita GNP of the major powers, 1950.[25]

In addition, the Soviet Union possessed a robust defense industrial base. Beginning in the 1930s, Stalin had designed an ambitious plan to establish a capital base oriented to heavy industry—including the defense industry—and to abandon the country's traditional reliance on agriculture. Unlike the United States and most Western countries, the Soviet Union had a command economy and centrally administered industrial base. The Military-Industrial Commission of the USSR oversaw the defense industrial ministries and developed laboratories, design bureaus, and production plants—including for raw material production.[26] Because of centralized planning, Soviet leaders could direct massive amounts of investment, labor, and high-quality material to the industrial base, generally at the expense of nondefense sectors.[27] In establishing the world's largest weapons industry, Soviet leaders also relied on Western technological advances, including through an aggressive KGB espionage campaign.[28]

Soviet leaders focused on several priorities: developing selective technologies with the greatest likelihood of advancing future military capabilities; producing weapons with the highest technical characteristics but the lowest possible cost; monitoring Western technological advances, in part to target for espionage; and establishing weapons and equipment that were easy to operate or could allow for reductions in military labor through automation.[29] These priorities were often in direct conflict with each other, such as the desire for high technical capabilities and low cost.

One of the biggest challenges of the Soviet system—which Chinese leader Xi Jinping grappled with several decades later—was that it consistently lagged behind the United States and some other Western states in technological development. It was frequently difficult for a command economy and a communist system to compete with a democratic and capitalist system in innovation. Nevertheless, one benefit of the Soviet's command economy was that Moscow could direct—or redirect—substantial resources to its defense industrial base and achieve mass and scale in selected areas. The result was that the Soviets produced massive amounts of some weapons systems after World War II, such as the MiG-15 fighter aircraft, guided missiles, submarines, and heavy cruisers. Soviet leaders gave high priority and privileged access to the defense sector, and the defense industrial base became the most capable sector of the economy.[30]

English geographer Sir Halford John Mackinder had predicted the rise of the Soviet Union as a superpower, presciently noting during World War II, "[T]he conclusion is unavoidable that if the Soviet Union emerges from this war as conqueror of Germany, she must rank as the greatest land Power on the globe. . . . The Heartland is the greatest natural fortress on earth. For the first time in history it is manned by a garrison sufficient both in number and quality."[31] For Mackinder, the significance of the Soviet Union's ascension was central to his argument that balance-of-power competition would eventually be global and span large landmasses of Euro-Asia (which he called "the Heartland") and littoral areas (which he labeled "world-islands"). The resource-rich areas of Eastern Europe and Central Asia were particularly valuable for major powers in the industrial age.[32] And the Soviet Union now dominated these regions.

In spite of this reality, some U.S. leaders, including Truman himself, miscalculated. The decision to cut defense budgets and the defense industry was ultimately mistaken and counterproductive. Truman acknowledged he was a Russophile at the time, along with some other influential figures, such as former U.S. ambassador to the Soviet Union Joe Davies. The president supported an "amicable divorce" from the Soviet Union and believed he could ultimately live with Stalin. "I liked the little son of a bitch," he acknowledged.[33] But other U.S. leaders, such as Secretary of State James Francis Byrnes and diplomat George Kennan, did not trust Stalin or his intentions, as suggested by early disagreements between the United States and Soviet Union over Iran and Turkey.[34] A year before the end of World War II, a Joint Staff assessment had accurately predicted that the balance of power would shift dramatically after the war, with the United States and Soviet Union possessing vast military capabilities:

> The successful termination of the war against our present enemies will find a world profoundly changed in respect of relative national military strengths, a change more comparable indeed with that occasioned by the fall of Rome than with any other change occurring during the succeeding fifteen hundred years. This is a fact of fundamental

importance in its bearing upon future international political settlements and all discussions leading thereto.... After the defeat of Japan, the United States and the Soviet Union will be the only military powers of the first magnitude. This is due in each case to a combination of geographical position and extent, and vast munitioning potential.[35]

The international security environment that emerged in the mid- and late-1950s was highly competitive. Contrary to Truman administration hopes, war was imminent and peace was not.

The outbreak of the Korean War in June 1950 ended all pretense of a peacetime environment, and the U.S. defense industrial base rapidly shifted to a wartime footing. That year the Truman administration concluded in its 66-page top-secret report "United States Objectives and Programs for National Security" that the nation needed a muscular defense industrial base. Better known as NSC-68, the report determined that the fundamental goal of the Kremlin was to solidify absolute power and to establish governments around the world that were "subservient to and controlled from the Kremlin."[36] This reality created an urgency to strengthen U.S. military capabilities and, just as important, the country's defense industrial base. It was imperative, NSC-68 concluded, "to increase as rapidly as possible our general air, ground, and sea strength and that of our allies to a point where we are militarily not so heavily dependent on atomic weapons."[37]

The U.S. defense industrial base already showed promise. At Lockheed Skunk Works, Johnson and his team produced the P-80 Shooting Star (eventually renamed the F-80), which originated from Johnson's 1943 meeting with General Carrol in Dayton. Johnson and Lockheed engineers worked in strict secrecy at the company's facility in Burbank, California, and designed the P-80 as the first U.S. jet-powered combat aircraft.[38]

Following North Korea's invasion of South Korea, the United Nations, led by the United States, joined the war on the side of South Korea. Between 1950 and 1953, total U.S. ground forces tripled in size. The Korean War catapulted the United States back into a wartime environment. Harvard professor Samuel Huntington wrote, "[A]fter the outbreak of the Korean War, it became obvious that the Cold War military demand was going to be substantial and relatively stable. The dollar volume of military orders and the complex technological requirements of the modern armed forces brought a significant permanent defense industry into existence for the first time in the United States."[39] Johnson and his team at Skunk Works interviewed Korean War fighter pilots and designed an innovative aircraft—the F-104 Starfighter—a supersonic attack fighter that was lightweight, capable of reaching altitudes of over 90,000 feet and of exceeding Mach 2 in level flight, and adaptable for ground attack, intercept, or tactical support.[40] It was nicknamed "the Sipper," but some in the press referred to it as "the missile with the man in it."[41]

The Truman White House authorized a spike in military spending and pushed for greater production and less regulation. Though Truman had abolished the War Production Board, he quickly switched gears following the outbreak of war and established the cabinet-level Office of Defense Mobilization to plan, coordinate, direct, and control all wartime mobilization.[42] He also created the National Security Resources Board to mobilize industrial resources and the scientific community to meet the growing military demands.[43]

Perhaps Truman's most significant step for strengthening the defense industry was signing the Defense Production Act on September 8, 1950, which sailed through the Senate by a vote of 85–3 and the House by 383–12. The law authorized the president to force companies to prioritize defense production, set aside price ceilings, and expand private and public production capacity.[44] It also permitted the federal government to mobilize the economy for war through regulation of the private market and takeover of industrial production. Under the act, the government could control prices, build defense plants, regulate credit, and streamline resources and products for manufacturing. Congress would go on to reauthorize the Defense Production Act at least 53 times over the next seven decades.[45] The Defense Production Act also created the Defense Priorities and Allocation System, which allowed the U.S. government to prioritize national defense-related contracts and orders.

There was some grumbling by fiscal conservatives that the act would lead to greater government intrusion in the private sector and distort a free market. Others worried that the Defense Production Act would direct money into the pockets of greedy corporate executives.[46] But as Truman explained to the nation in an address from the Oval Office, the act was essential to build the U.S. arsenal of democracy:

> To do our part in building up our military strength and the military strength of the free nations throughout the world, the United States must more than double its defense efforts. We have been spending about $15 billion a year for defense. We are stepping up this rate rapidly. By next June, under our present plans, we expect to be spending at the rate of at least $30 billion a year. In the year after that we shall probably have to spend more than $30 billion. And we must be prepared to maintain a very strong defense program for many years to come.[47]

With a major increase in defense spending and a newly passed Defense Production Act to jump-start manufacturing, the U.S. defense industry provided critical equipment to U.S. forces fighting in Korea. Examples included Douglas B-26C Invader light bombers, North American Aviation F-86A Sabre fighter aircraft, Boeing B-29 bombers, Rock Island Arsenal M114 155-mm howitzers, and Chrysler M4A3E8 Sherman tanks. By the end of 1951, the United States had put more than $45 billion into military procurement.[48] Defense contracts transformed budding areas like Silicon Valley from fruit orchards into a hub of electronics production and innovation. The U.S. Army and Navy outsourced the tasks of designing and building high-tech weapons to private electronics and aerospace companies, reanimating industries that had boomed during World War II and slumped after the end of the war. Pentagon leaders worked with Congress to authorize bigger tax breaks for companies to build electronics plants.[49]

One example was naval power. The United States possessed eight naval shipyards—among them Groton (Connecticut), Bethlehem Sparrows Point (Maryland), Bethlehem Quincy (Massachusetts), Ingalls (Mississippi), and Newport News (Virginia)—and several dozen private-sector shipyards that built naval and merchant ships, including submarines.[50] The United States had, by far, the strongest navy in the world. It boasted 1,633 ships of 1,000 tons or larger, including 99 aircraft and 8 fast battleships, compared to only 189 ships in the Soviet

Country		1936	1941	1944	1946	1956
France	Tons (Thousands)	500	425	281	292	378
	Number of Ships	158	145	68	60	95
Japan		845	963	916	–	38
		211	250	244	–	27
Soviet Union		156	360	432	657	1,058
		51	253	285	189	413
United Kingdom		1,100	1,360	1,875	1,468	1,235
		265	334	391	345	355
United States		1,021	1,387	3,847	5,741	5,806
		294	326	1,684	1,633	1,518
Total		3,622	4,495	7,351	8,158	8,515
		979	1,308	2,672	2,227	2,408

FIGURE 2.2 Major fleet sizes, 1936–1956.[51]

navy. This total constituted 70 percent of combat vessels of the major powers in 1946 (Figure 2.2).[52]

Another example was the aircraft industry. The U.S. Air Force, established in 1947, had a fleet of more than 2,000 bombers, such as Boeing B-29s, and atomic bombs that could be loaded onto the aircraft.[53] Lockheed, Douglas, McDonnell, Grumman, Convair, and other companies churned out a steady line of bombers, fighters, and other aircraft to support the war effort in Korea.

However, this environment would not last forever.

On July 27, 1953, the United States, China, North Korea, and South Korea signed an armistice that established a demilitarized zone dividing North and South Korea. With the end of the war, the Eisenhower administration shifted away from a wartime environment. Eisenhower demoted the Office of Defense Mobilization from cabinet rank.[54] He also worried that a large defense budget would cripple the vibrant U.S. economy of the mid-1950s, bankrupt the United States, and trigger a $44 billion deficit over five years.[55] In 1953, Eisenhower declared that the defense industrial base was no longer a priority:

> Every gun that is made, every warship launched, every rocket fired signifies, in the final sense, a theft from those who hunger and are not fed, those who are cold and are not clothed....

The cost of one modern heavy bomber is this: a modern brick school in more than 30 cities.

It is two electric power plants, each serving a town of 60,000 population.

It is two fine, fully equipped hospitals.

It is some 60 miles of concrete highway.

We pay for a single fighter plane with a half million bushels of wheat.

We pay for a single destroyer with new homes that could have housed more than 8,000 people.[56]

Though defense dollars began to dry up, Eisenhower supported research, development, and production in nuclear weapons and bombers to counter—or "offset"—Soviet conventional superiority in Europe, leading some U.S. defense officials decades later to refer to this effort as the "first offset."[57] The Soviets had nearly three times the number of ground forces in Europe as the United States and its allies.[58] But Eisenhower assessed that sustaining a large standing army would likely cripple the U.S. economy.

Instead, his administration developed a strategy called "New Look," which was designed to counter Soviet advantages in conventional forces. New Look involved building an overwhelming nuclear advantage and, if necessary, using tactical nuclear weapons against Red Army troops—including inside West Germany.[59] As described in the administration's top-secret policy paper NSC 162/2, the United States need to develop the capability to inflict "massive retaliatory damage by offensive striking power," including with tactical and strategic nuclear weapons.[60] For Secretary of State John Foster Dulles and other officials, this doctrine of massive retaliation meant that the United States would respond disproportionately to an attack.[61] The goal was to use nuclear weapons to strengthen deterrence and to persuade the Soviet Union *not* to start a war.

NSC 162/2 argued that the "risk of Soviet aggression will be minimized by maintaining a strong security posture, with emphasis on adequate offensive retaliatory strength and defensive strength. This must be based on massive atomic capability including necessary bases."[62] Half a century later, Pentagon officials, such as Secretary of Defense Ashton Carter and Deputy Secretary of Defense Robert Work, referred to New Look as the first offset.[63] It was later followed by a second offset in the late 1970s and 1980s to counter growing Soviet capabilities. As Work summarized about the first offset: "The United States enjoyed nuclear superiority, and what we did is we used tactical nuclear weapons, battlefield nuclear weapons, for conventional deterrence. We told the Soviet Union that if they attacked, we would respond with tactical nuclear weapons."[64] U.S. nuclear capabilities were designed to offset Soviet conventional advantages.

Consequently, New Look led to a major investment in two main areas of the defense industrial base: nuclear weapons and long-range bombers. The first involved a rapid increase in the development and production of nuclear weapons and delivery vehicles, especially ICBMs. The U.S. Air Force ramped up development of the liquid-fueled Atlas ICBM, built by the Convair Division of General Dynamics. Testifying before Congress in 1956, Chairman of the Joint Chiefs of Staff General Nathan Twining explained that the Pentagon gave "the very highest priority" to Atlas production to offset Soviet military capabilities.[65] The U.S. military also increased development of Titan I, the U.S.'s first multi-stage ICBM developed by Martin Marietta, as well as two types of guided missiles: the subsonic Snark, a ground-launched cruise missile developed by Northrop; and the supersonic Navaho, a cruise missile developed by North American Aviation.[66] The Eisenhower administration also supported development of several other missiles capable of carrying nuclear warheads: the Polaris submarine-launched ballistic missile by Lockheed, Thor intermediate-range ballistic missile by Douglas Aircraft Company, and Jupiter medium-range ballistic missile by Chrysler.

A second priority was long-range bombers that could carry nuclear weapons. The United States military had several bombers, including the B-52 Stratofortress (Boeing), B-47 Stratojet (Boeing), B-58 Hustler (General Dynamics), and B-36 Peacemaker (General Dynamics).[67] But the mainstay was the B-52, a long-range bomber capable of flying at subsonic speeds that could carry nuclear and conventional ordnance and perform a range of missions, including strategic attack, close air support, air interdiction, and offensive counter-air operations. In 1956, President Eisenhower and Secretary of Defense Charles E.

Wilson asked Congress for an additional $248.5 million to increase B-52 production from 17 aircraft per month to 20 per month. They also requested another $128 million to expand air base infrastructure necessary for the B-52 force.[68] In addition, there was a major effort to support the electronics and technology used to support nuclear weapons and bombers.[69]

Yet Eisenhower's New Look was in many ways irresponsible in its focus on fighting a nuclear war on NATO soil. Secretary of Defense William Perry later lamented, "As I look back at this strategy and the weaponry, I think that we showed an almost primordial behavior that in our perilous new times was extraordinarily reckless."[70] Unlike Truman, who realized that nuclear weapons were not really usable on the battlefield despite General Douglas MacArthur's desire to use them in Korea, Eisenhower developed a strategy to employ nuclear weapons in Europe. In addition, Eisenhower's decision to cut back on the defense industry was premature in the midst of the Cold War, as he would soon find out with major advances in Soviet military and technological capabilities. It was a difficult time for defense companies, which needed to be particularly creative and innovative.

One of the gems was Kelly Johnson's Skunk Works and its contribution to strategic reconnaissance.

The name "Skunk Works" came from the mystery at Lockheed about what went on at Johnson's compound, which was walled off from the rest of the company.

"What the heck is Kelly doing in there?" was the question.

"Oh, he's stirring up some kind of brew," was the typical answer.[71]

The image of a shadowy group tiptoeing around the Lockheed campus in Burbank elicited images of Al Capp's *Li'l Abner*, a satirical comic strip that graced newspapers in the United States, Canada, and Europe. One of the local attractions in the comic strip was "Skonk Works," a deteriorated factory situated on the fringes of Dogpatch, USA, the comic strip's fictitious hillbilly town. Locals brewed all day in the dilapidated factory by grinding dead skunks, worn shoes, and sundry other items into a mysterious concoction. And so was born Lockheed's legendary

Skunk Works, officially the Advanced Development Projects, or ADP, in 1943 with only 120 people.[72]

A good example of the production capacity and innovation at Skunk Works was in strategic reconnaissance—the effort to spy on the Soviet Union from the air. And it was the forward-leaning CIA, not the Pentagon, that became Johnson's partner. In particular, Johnson and his team produced the U-2 reconnaissance aircraft, nicknamed "Dragon Lady." It was a marvel in innovation and provided unprecedented day and night, high-altitude, all-weather intelligence gathering of the Soviet Union. And it typified the U.S. model of innovation, which consisted of a vibrant culture that valued private-sector creativity, intense competition, and a thirst for new ideas.

Lockheed benefited from growing U.S. concern about the Soviet Union's expanded nuclear weapons effort, including bomber forces, ballistic missiles, submarine forces, and nuclear weapons infrastructure. U.S. and allied spies largely failed to penetrate the Soviet Union's nuclear program, and Moscow improved the security of its telephone, telegraph, and radio-telephone communication. In addition, the Soviet Union's air defense systems had become more aggressive in defending their air space, and the Soviet military had improved its radar technology.[73] Consequently, President Eisenhower approved a program in which the CIA, working with the U.S. Air Force, would develop and produce a reconnaissance airplane that could fly higher than any aircraft had *ever* flown and take photographs of Soviet military capabilities.[74] As a classified CIA assessment concluded, the objectives included "appraising Soviet guided missile development," "improving estimates of Soviet ability to deliver nuclear weapons and of their capacity to produce them," and "appraising Soviet industrial and economic progress."[75]

The engineering requirements were excruciatingly difficult. The airplane would need to soar at an altitude above 70,000 feet to ensure that its condensation trails would not be visible by Soviet tracking systems, fly between 3,000 and 4,000 miles, and provide a stable platform for highly accurate photographs from high altitudes.[76] Led by Johnson, Lockheed had already been working on a prototype for the air force in 1954, which was originally known as the CL-282. Johnson adapted many of the features of the aircraft from gliders. However, senior air force officers were not impressed. General Curtis LeMay became agitated during one of Johnson's briefings and protested that it was a waste of time and money to build an aircraft that lacked guns to protect itself. LeMay said the solution was simple: put cameras on his B-36 bombers. He then stormed out of the room.[77]

But President Eisenhower was interested in developing an *intelligence* program. "I want this whole thing to be a civilian operation," he asserted. "If uniformed personnel of the armed services of the United States fly over Russia, it is an act of war—legally—and I don't want any part of it."[78] On November 19, 1954, Johnson met with Director of Central Intelligence Allen Dulles, who approved what became "Project AQUATONE" as a joint U.S. Air Force–CIA effort.[79] Between November 29 and December 3, 1954, Johnson pulled together a team of 25 engineers by raiding them from other Lockheed projects. They immediately began developing the U-2, which they nicknamed the "Angel" because it was designed to fly so high.[80]

Virtually everything about the project was cloak and dagger. Skunk Works used a mail drop in nearby Sunland, California, situated between the Verdugo and San Gabriel mountains north of Burbank, where suppliers could send parts. Johnson also set up a phony company called C&J Engineering to bank CIA funds. He worked closely with Richard Bissell, a former Yale economics professor and special assistant to Director Dulles, who oversaw the U-2 program for CIA. In early 1955, after Lockheed submitted its first vouchers for progress on the contract, Bissell wrote two checks for a total of $1.25 million and mailed them directly to Johnson's home in Encino, California.[81]

Johnson was not always easy to work with. He could be a bully—even to senior air force officers—and his temper was renowned. He shuffled around Skunk Works with an untucked shirt, slicked-back white hair, and an oversized attitude.[82] One of his colleagues described him as developing "the reputation of an ogre who ate young, tender engineers for between-meal snacks."[83] But he was a legendary engineer. And he and his Lockheed team faced perhaps their biggest test designing the U-2.

The aircraft had to carry a sufficient supply of fuel to fly thousands of miles. But it also had to be light enough to reach ultra-high altitudes out of range of Soviet air defense systems and fighter jets. To save weight, Johnson and his team attached the tail to the main body with just three tension bolts, an adaptation from sailplane designs. Unlike most traditional aircraft, whose main wing spar passed through the fuselage to provide continuity and strength to the wings, the U-2 had two separate wing panels. Engineers attached these panels to the fuselage sides with tension bolts, again much like in sailplanes. Since the wing spar did not pass through the fuselage, Johnson and his team placed a camera behind the pilot and in front of the engine, reducing the aircraft's weight.[84]

The wings were perhaps the most challenging part of the design. Johnson came up with an innovative concept that incorporated the fuselage of the F-104 jet fighter but included a higher-aspect-ratio wing, which had a lower drag and a higher lift than a lower-aspect-ratio wing. The wings carried virtually all the U-2's supply of fuel. Johnson also devised a "gust control" mechanism that set the ailerons (the flight control surfaces on the wing) and horizontal stabilizers (the fixed wing sections on the tail) into a position that kept the nose up, which would protect the aircraft from huge gusts of wind at altitudes below 35,000 feet.[85] Johnson and his team used the J-57 Pratt & Whitney engine, which was built outside Hartford, Connecticut.[86] The aircraft also had to carry lightweight, high-tech cameras able to take clear pictures at high altitudes. They used modified K-38 cameras, which became known as A-1 cameras, and included two 24-inch framing cameras. A CIA assessment of the U-2 program lauded Johnson's innovative organizational strategy: "Kelly Johnson's approach to prototype development was to have his engineers and draftsmen located not more than 50 feet from the aircraft assembly line. Difficulties in construction were immediately brought to the attention of the engineers, who gathered the mechanics around the drafting tables to discuss ways to overcome the difficulties. As a result, engineers were generally able to fix problems in the design in a matter of hours, not days or weeks."[87]

Johnson and his team delivered the U-2 on time (an incredible nine months for a test flight after signing the first contract) and under budget to Bissell and his CIA colleagues. The U-2 was an extraordinary engineering feat that revolutionized strategic reconnaissance. The CIA conducted roughly two dozen U-2 flights over Soviet territory and developed more than 1,285,000 feet of film—nearly 250 miles. The U-2s took pictures of more than 1,300,000 square miles of the Soviet Union, roughly 15 percent of its total area. Information from U-2 photographs was used to prepare separate photo analytical reports.[88] The reconnaissance flights were pivotal in understanding the Soviet Union's bomber forces, missile force, nuclear weapons program, and air defense systems. They also provided substantial evidence that the Soviet Union's intercontinental ballistic missile (ICBM) program was not as large as some had feared, leading President Eisenhower to resist political pressure to develop a large-scale U.S. program.[89] In a memorandum, Dulles summarized the U-2's successes: "Five years ago, before the beginning of the U-2 program . . . half knowledge of the Soviet Union and uncertainty of its true power position posed tremendous problems for the United States. We were faced with the constant risk of exposing ourselves to enemy attack or of needlessly expending a great deal of money and effort on misdirected military preparations of our own."[90]

The U-2 program entailed serious risks. In 1960, the Soviet Union shot down CIA pilot Francis Gary Powers while photographing missile sites at Sverdlovsk and Plesetsk, though Soviet leaders later released him in exchange for a Soviet intelligence agent.[91] But these risks were worth it. Johnson and his team's contributions put the United States in a much better position to understand Soviet defense production. In direct contrast to U.S. Air Force estimates, the Soviet Union was *not* building a huge force of long-range bombers; the "bomber gap" between the two countries was largely a myth. The U.S. private sector had done it again, this time led by Johnson. The U-2 helped usher in a new era of innovation in strategic reconnaissance in which the United States could collect intelligence on Soviet conventional and nuclear capabilities operating *directly over* Soviet and other hostile territory. Strategic reconnaissance was important not just for war planning during the Cold War but also to prevent strategic surprise.[92]

But while the U-2 helped avert surprise in Soviet nuclear capabilities, the United States was about to face one of the most significant surprises of the Cold War.

On October 4, 1957, the Soviets launched Sputnik 1, a 184-pound satellite that remained in orbit until January 4, 1958. Sputnik 1 stunned the U.S. population and government, which had assumed the United States was technologically ahead of the Soviet Union. Eisenhower responded, "There was no point in trying to minimize the accomplishment or the warning it gave."[93] Soviet leader Nikita Khrushchev then doubled down by ramping up the Soviet Union's program to develop long-range missiles, including ICBMs. The Soviets were also catching up to the United States in other areas. A CIA report in 1959 assessed that the Soviet Union was only two to four years behind the United States in the quality and quantity of transistors produced.[94]

Several months after the Sputnik 1 launch, a study financed by the Rockefeller Brothers Fund and directed by Henry Kissinger released its findings: the United States needed an immediate $3 billion boost in the defense budget and similar increases each year for the next several years; otherwise, Kissinger and the other participants warned, the Soviet Union would gain military superiority within two years.[95]

The industrial base was back on a wartime footing and once again focused "on time, rapid experimentation, multiple technological pathways, and rapid operational prototyping."[96] U.S. policymakers feared the emergence of a "missile gap," which was a major focus of the Gaither Committee, a civilian group tasked by President Eisenhower with making recommendations to strengthen military defensive systems and better prepare the country for a nuclear attack. The committee issued its report in November 1957. The Gaither Report, as it became known, concluded that the Soviet Union had fundamentally reinvigorated its defense industrial base: "The singleness of purpose with which they have pressed their military-centered industrial development has led to spectacular progress."[97]

Soviet advances were widespread and included the development of nuclear weapons, long-range bombers, jet aircraft, ICBMs, and air defense systems. In addition, Soviet leadership directed the defense industrial base to conduct a major expansion of the navy, including cruisers, destroyers, and aircraft carriers.[98] More broadly, the Soviets engaged in a rapid industrial effort to develop solid-rocket production technology, composite materials, advance metallurgy, and semiconductors, though most Soviet weapons were produced by a defense industrial base that was relatively obsolete by Western standards.[99]

The Gaither Report assessed that the United States was vulnerable to a Soviet nuclear attack and that deterrence had severely eroded. It recommended significantly increasing defense research and development in such areas as air defense: "An effective air defense system is so important to ensure continuity of government, and to protect our civil population, our enormously valuable civil property and military installations, that these development programs we suggest should be pushed with all possible speed."[100]

While Eisenhower rejected some of the Gaither Report recommendations as unnecessary and exorbitant, the Sputnik 1 launch nevertheless had a notable impact on the U.S. defense industrial base by dramatically increasing research and development investments.[101] The defense contracting spigot opened into a firehose.[102] There was a major acceleration of ICBM production as a result of prodding and promotion from the air force research and defense community, the Joint Chiefs of Staff, and some members of Congress.[103] General Bernard Schriever took over the air force's ICBM efforts and oversaw production of the Atlas ICBM and the land-based intermediate-range ballistic missile, Thor.[104] Under Schriever, the military completed several programs within a five-year window from development to operational use. The government awarded the Titan II initial contract in 1960, and the missile was operational by 1963. Development of the Minuteman I ICBM began in 1957, and it was operational by 1962. Not to be outdone, the timelines for Minuteman II and III were five and four years, respectively.[105]

In addition, the government was increasingly involved in the electronics business and became, in a sense, Silicon Valley's first and greatest venture capitalist. In 1958, the Eisenhower administration created the Advanced Research Projects Agency, which later became the Defense Advanced Research Projects Agency (DARPA). Its goal was to spur collaboration between academia, industry, and the government by formulating and funding research and development projects to expand the frontiers of technology and science, often beyond immediate military requirements. DARPA poured money into the electronics and microchips used in satellites, computers, and nuclear missile guidance systems.

DARPA was a direct reaction to Sputnik 1 and, at its core, focused on developing technologies to avoid strategic surprises. "What made

DARPA successful," wrote Sharon Weinberger in her book *The Imagineers of War*, "was its ability to tackle some of the most critical national security problems facing the United States, unencumbered by the typical bureaucratic oversight and uninhibited by the restraints of scientific peer review."[106] DARPA was designed to be the champion—not the victim—of technological surprises. It created the Advanced Research Projects Agency Network, or ARPANET, which laid the foundation for the modern internet.

On the East Coast, companies like Raytheon, founded by MIT's Vannevar Bush, flourished along Route 128 in Massachusetts, which was competing with Silicon Valley as "America's Technology Highway."[107] During World War II, President Franklin D. Roosevelt had tapped Bush to run the wartime Office of Scientific Research and Development, an operation that mobilized thousands of PhDs and spent half a billion government dollars by the end of the war.[108] A 1944 *Time* magazine cover story dubbed Bush the "General of Physics."[109]

Bush and Raytheon were not alone. In response to Sputnik 1, the U.S. Air Force began looking for a new computer to guide its Minuteman II missile. Pat Haggerty, president of Texas Instruments, which dominated integrated circuits, promised the air force that computers using integrated circuits invented by Jack Kilby, the company's legendary engineer and eventual Nobel prize winner in physics, could perform twice the computational power with half the weight. Texas Instruments won the Minuteman II contract and fundamentally transformed its business to supply thousands of circuits to the air force to help close the missile gap. By the end of 1964, Texas Instruments had sold a stunning 100,000 integrated circuits to the Minuteman program. By this time, the U.S. military was using chips on all types of weapons systems, such as telemetry systems, satellites, missiles, and sonar.[110]

On the West Coast, Lockheed was a good example of defense technology. It had moved from southern California and opened shop in Silicon Valley, next to Moffett Field. Lockheed executives were drawn by a desire to be close to Stanford's electronics experts and the high-speed aerodynamics research going on at the National Advisory Committee for Aeronautics' Ames Aeronautical Laboratory. Within a matter of months after Sputnik 1 launched, Lockheed became Silicon Valley's largest and richest employer, with its 300-acre campus along Highway

101 employing 19,000 people and raking in close to $400 million in sales in 1959 alone.[111]

By the early 1960s, however, the defense boom was on its last legs. President John F. Kennedy and his successor, Lyndon Johnson, were not sold on defense. They had bold ambitions to wage war on poverty, deliver new social programs, send U.S. astronauts to the moon, and cut taxes.[112] Their decision to slash defense—despite the continuation of the Cold War—ultimately weakened deterrence. In December 1963, Secretary of Defense Robert McNamara announced significant cuts in U.S. defense spending, a decision that led to the closing of military bases, elimination of defense programs, shuttering of defense production facilities, and a rise in the number of unemployed defense workers.[113] The Department of Defense closed a number of major production lines, such as Martin's P5M-2 patrol aircraft line in Baltimore, Convair's F-106 aircraft line in San Diego (owned by General Dynamics), Chance-Vought's F8U-2N fighter line in Dallas, and Republic's F-105 line in Farmingdale, New York.

These actions came on top of several additional closures, such as Curtiss Aircraft's F-87 line in Columbus, Ohio; Westinghouse's J-40 engine line in Kansas City, Missouri; and Wright Aeronautical's J-65 line in Woodbridge, New Jersey (Figure 2.3). Curtiss-Wright Corporation, which was once the second largest manufacturer in the United States,

Company	Plant	Last Project	Year
Curtiss Aircraft	Columbus, OH	F-87, SB2C	1951
Westinghouse	Kansas City, MO	J-40 engine	1955
Wright Aeronautical	Woodridge, NJ	J-65 engine	1957
Martin	Baltimore, MD	P5M-2	1960
General Dynamics (Convair Division)	San Diego, CA	F-106	1960
Chance-Vought	Dallas, TX	F8U-2N	1961
Republic	Farmingdale, NY	F-105	1965
New York Ship	Camden, NJ	Nuclear-powered ships	1967

FIGURE 2.3 Partial list of closed prime contractor production lines, 1951–1967.[114]

collapsed after refusing to conduct research and development for the air force and navy until they had funded projects.[115] On top of these closures, the Pentagon constructed an increasingly sprawling regulatory environment to oversee the acquisition process.

McNamara, who had been president of Ford Motor Company, created new layers of oversight in the acquisition process, including through the establishment of the Planning, Programming, Budgeting System (which later became the Planning, Programming, Budgeting, and Execution System). The government also established the Truth in Negotiations Act, which compelled contracts to provide full and complete price and cost information when submitting bids. The impetus for the act was straightforward and understandable: to reduce fraud and improve the accuracy of information. Over time, however, the Truth in Negotiations Act contributed to a significant bureaucracy that slowed down contracting.

Commercial companies shied away from defense contracts because the contracting process became far too cumbersome and defense dollars dried up. As one assessment concluded, "The result was that the process of developing military technology became harder, slower, and less creative."[116] Overall, the Pentagon during this era established growing barriers to commercial firms that wanted to participate in the defense industrial base: suffocating procurement and oversight requirements, increased Pentagon control of intellectual property, mounting security requirements, and greater controls on arms exports.[117] Virtually the only way to innovate quickly was to take big defense programs *outside* of the traditional acquisitions and contracting system, as Johnson had done with the U-2 reconnaissance aircraft at Skunk Works.

General Schriever, who headed Air Force Systems Command and oversaw all air force research and development, was frustrated at the growing regulatory environment and lack of foresight by McNamara. Schriever oversaw Project Forecast, which anticipated technological breakthroughs in such areas as hypersonics. But McNamara cut funding for many of these efforts to maximize cost-effectiveness. He also put in place a range of procedures, which were formalized in July 1965 in Department of Defense Directive 3200.9, that stifled experimental research and development. Schriever complained that McNamara's staff "started getting into every . . . nit-picking detail that you can possibly imagine."[118] A disillusioned Schriever retired in 1966, several years before his mandatory retirement date.

During this time, a growing number of engineers and entrepreneurs in Silicon Valley had become uncomfortable working for the U.S. government as the Vietnam War became more politically divisive. There were also mounting criticisms of the defense industrial base as hopelessly expensive, if not fraudulent. William Proxmire, a Democratic senator from Wisconsin, grew increasingly concerned about alleged Pentagon waste and abuse: "It is discouraging for me, as a citizen and senator, to know that weapons cost far too much, are delivered far too late, and function far below their specifications."[119] The litany of examples was long. Industry supposedly charged the government $640 for a toilet seat, $91 for a screw, and $7,000 for a coffee pot.[120] These alleged outrageous instances of contractor fraud attracted media and congressional attention.

The problem was that many of these examples were either patently false, exaggerated, or—in a few cases—the result of outdated or absurd Department of Defense acquisition requirements. For example, the U.S. Navy wanted an entire toilet assembly kit for its P-3 Orion antisubmarine and maritime surveillance aircraft. Lockheed, which built the P-3, offered to give the task to anyone who claimed they could pick up the part at Walmart or Sears for $15. But Lockheed found no takers who could meet the navy's requirements. The screw was composed of titanium and purchased as a special order. The coffee pot was an entire assembly kit for the C-5 Galaxy military transport aircraft and the result of excessive and perhaps unnecessary air force crash survivability standards.[121]

In April 1971, two cheeky real estate agents, Bob McDonald and Jim Youngren, put up an iconic billboard in Seattle following crushing job cuts. Its lines were simple but powerful: "Will the last person leaving SEATTLE—Turn out the lights."[122] The phrase took off. Workers across the country embraced the dark humor, replacing "Seattle" with "Detroit," "St. Louis," "Kansas City," and other cities. Defense cuts contributed to the loss of 10,000 manufacturing jobs in the San Jose metropolitan area between 1969 and 1971.[123] In Boston's high-tech defense corridor, more than 100,000 manufacturing jobs evaporated between 1967 and 1972, and the defense contracts awarded to the New England region shrank by 40 percent. Just as in San Jose, the Vietnam-era cutbacks left scores of scientists and engineers out of work. Massachusetts took a larger hit to its defense sector than anywhere else in the country.[124] The government also relegated its shipyards to repair work and outsourced most ammunition manufacturing, leaving almost no government production at all.[125]

As would soon become clear, the United States underinvested in defense technology, created an oppressive regulatory environment for the defense industry, and ultimately jeopardized deterrence. The Soviets had spent $240 billion more than the United States in equipment and technology during the Vietnam War and in the immediate postwar period.[126] By the 1970s, there were multiple signs that the United States was in trouble.

Of particular concern for U.S. policymakers was that the Soviet Union had increased its nuclear capabilities and achieved nuclear parity with the United States. "[An] inescapable reality of the 1970s," concluded President Richard Nixon in his February 1970 report to Congress, "is the Soviet Union's possession of powerful and sophisticated strategic forces approaching our own."[127] By the late 1970s, the Soviets also possessed a large and imposing air defense system—complete with long-range early-warning radar systems, advanced interceptor aircraft, and radar-guided surface-to-air missile systems—and a 3:1 lead in conventional weapons, such as main battle tanks and artillery.[128] U.S. analysis of Israel's Yom Kippur War with Egypt and Syria suggested that U.S. tactical air would be destroyed in roughly two weeks of a European conflict with the Soviet Union. Egypt and Syria possessed Soviet radar-guided surface-to-air missiles and anti-aircraft guns, which inflicted 109 losses in 18 days on skilled Israeli pilots flying in U.S. aircraft and using the same tactics utilized by U.S. pilots.[129]

The U.S. defense industry was still capable of producing innovative systems. For example, Johnson's Skunk Works designed and produced the SR-71 Blackbird. Much like its predecessor, the U-2, the SR-71 continued innovation in strategic reconnaissance. More than 100 feet in length, the SR-71 achieved a sustained speed above Mach 3 at an incredible altitude of over 80,000 feet—more than 15 miles above the Earth. It carried a wide variety of observation equipment for pre-attack and post-attack reconnaissance. The air force used the SR-71 extensively in Asia and Europe.[130] As Johnson explained, "[A]ircraft operating at those speeds and altitudes would require development of special fuels, structural materials, manufacturing tools and techniques, hydraulic fluid, fuel-tank sealants, paints. . . . Everything about the aircraft had to be invented. Everything."[131]

But cuts in the defense budget and a regulatory framework during the 1960s and early 1970s widened Soviet advantages. In 1977, the Defense Science Board released a study concluding that while industry was still capable of executing a program rapidly, the government's timeline to make a decision had increased from two years in the 1950s to over five years by the early 1970s. The board blamed the problem on the accumulation of layers of bureaucracy involved in the decision-making process.[132] Perhaps most alarming, the United States was losing deterrence capability. Deterrence of a Red Army invasion of Western Europe hinged on U.S. superiority in strategic nuclear weapons. According to U.S. government estimates, however, the Soviets had reached strategic parity with the United States by 1977; some U.S. assessments even claimed that the Soviets had pulled ahead.[133] By some accounts, the Soviets also had a 3:1 advantage in conventional capabilities in Central Europe.[134] Experts like Johnson praised Soviet military production: "If we're six feet, their about six feet two, in my book. . . . Their planes are getting pretty darned good. They are ahead of us in numbers and in certain aircraft for which we don't have competitive types."[135]

Pentagon officials during the Carter administration—led by Secretary of Defense Harold Brown and Undersecretary of Defense for Research and Engineering William Perry—sparked a fundamental shift in U.S. defense policy in what became known as the "second offset."[136] As Perry explained, there was a mad rush to design projects to "compensate for the Soviet size advantage in conventional forces and thus re-establish general military parity and shore up deterrence."[137] In 1977, Brown, Perry, and others spearheaded an effort to develop military technologies—such as digital sensors, microprocessors, high-speed digital programs, technology for precision strikes, synthetic aperture radar, and stealth technology—into a system for deep attack to counter, or "offset," Soviet capabilities. They called the program "Assault Breaker."

Even if the Soviets could successfully break through U.S. and other NATO military lines in Central Europe, the main objective of Assault Breaker was to destroy successive waves of Soviet forces using those sensors, precision strike, stealth, and other capabilities. According to Perry, the technical goals of Assault Breaker were "to be able to see all high value targets on the battlefield at any time; to be able to make a direct hit on any target we can see; and to be able to destroy any target we can hit."[138] To achieve these goals, Assault Breaker required the research, development, production, and ultimately the deployment of sensors, computer programs, stealth, high-speed digital communications, and precision weapons to strike hardened mobile targets—such as tanks—that operated in all weather conditions, day or night.[139] As Perry noted in a memo to Brown in August 1978, "In order to stop the second and third echelons [of a Soviet and broader Warsaw Pact attack against Western Europe] with conventional weapons, we need to 'see deep' and 'shoot deep'; that is, detect and place precision weapons on targets 30 to 50 KM behind the FEBA [forward edge of the battle area]."[140]

The efforts of Brown, Perry, and other Pentagon officials led to the production of an array of smart weapons, including artillery shells such as the Copperhead 155mm caliber cannon-launched guided projectile, short-range missiles such as the Maverick and Hellfire, and long-range cruise missiles such as the air-launched cruise missile and Tomahawk Land Attack Missile.[141] They also developed a series of satellite-based systems, such as the Global Positioning System (GPS), and smart sensors, such as Joint Surveillance Target Attack Radar System. The latter was a modified Boeing 707 aircraft used for airborne ground surveillance, battle management, and command-and-control tasks, including tracking friendly and hostile forces. The Pentagon under Brown also modernized the nuclear triad, including airborne bombers, seaborne missiles, and land-based ICBMs. In September 1978, Brown briefed President Carter on Assault Breaker: "This program is a new initiative intended to break up an assault of massed armor without using nuclear warheads. It applies the MIRV [multiple independently targetable reentry vehicle] concept to tactical forces: a tactical missile is launched at a column of tanks; as it approaches the column, its warhead separates into 20 or 30 bomblets, each of which has a heat seeker which guides that bomblet to an individual tank."[142]

One of the most important developments of the second offset—stealth technology, which is discussed in more detail in the next chapter—was possible in part because Brown and Perry shed many of the regulations for its research, development, and production. They significantly shortened the development time of the prototypes for what became the F-117 Nighthawk, allowing the aircraft to move from contract to first flight of the production model in just under four years.[143]

Moscow viewed Assault Breaker and the U.S. development of sensors, stealth, and precision weapons with alarm. Led by General Nikolai Ogarkov, Soviet leaders conducted a massive exercise to respond to Assault Breaker advances.[144] He and other Soviet leaders became increasingly concerned that their country was falling behind. Minister of Defense Dmitri Ustinov told a meeting of the Warsaw Pact Committee of Defense Ministers that the military balance between NATO and the Warsaw Pact was "at the moment not in our favor."[145] The second offset strategy provided the U.S. military and its allies with an operational advantage.[146]

Contrary to some historical accounts, it was Brown, Perry, and other Pentagon officials during the Carter administration—not the Reagan administration—who *first* initiated the shift from a peacetime to a wartime industrial base in response to growing Soviet capabilities. Yet the Carter administration was too slow and too late in implementing a broader revitalization of the defense industrial base. A House Armed Services Committee study concluded in December 1980, "[T]he general condition of the defense industrial base has deteriorated and is in danger of further deterioration in the coming years." It also criticized the Department of Defense for policies and procedures that were "excessively inflexible and discourage the use of contract types [that] would promote the best interests of the United States," including tax policies that "discourage capital investment in new technology, facilities and equipment that would increase productivity and improve the condition of the defense industrial base."[147]

President Reagan jumped at the opportunity to further strengthen defense in a wartime environment.

During his campaign for president, Reagan had scored political points by lambasting incumbent president Carter for a lackluster foreign policy, which many saw as being weak on Moscow. "Militarily, our nation was in danger of falling behind the Soviet Union," Reagan warned. "Abroad the Soviet Union was engaged in a brutal war in Afghanistan and Communism was extending its tentacles deep into Central America and Africa."[148] He did not want reconciliation with Moscow but rather the *end* of communism.[149]

One of the biggest drivers of the Reagan buildup was the growth of Soviet military spending and weapons procurement, which jeopardized deterrence and threatened to put the United States dangerously behind the Soviet Union. Over the previous decade, the Soviet Union had spearheaded a major modernization effort, led by Minister Ustinov. The campaign involved capital improvements for the construction of aircraft, such as the MiG-29 and Su-27; main battle tanks, such as the T-80; missiles, such as the SA-12 surface-to-air missile; and ships, such as the Sierra-, Oscar-, and Akula-class attack submarines. One CIA assessment concluded, "Our analysis of the Soviet machinery sector—responsible for the production of consumer durables, investment goods, and military hardware—suggests that between the early and late 1970s the share of investments in the defense-industrial ministries increased substantially."[150] There were nine ministries, such as for the aviation industry, the shipbuilding industry, and the electronics industry, devoted to defense industrial production.[151] Since Soviet industry was generally not as technologically advanced as Western industry, the Soviet government organized an aggressive effort to acquire Western technology through legal and illegal means—including espionage led by the KGB.[152]

The overall result was that Soviet defense production of major weapons systems—such as missiles, bombers, fighters, helicopters, tanks, and artillery—exceeded U.S. production. According to U.S. intelligence estimates, the Soviet Union produced 3,400 ICBMs and submarine-launched ballistic missiles between 1974 and 1984, compared to 980 for the United States; 130,000 surface-to-air missiles, compared to 24,000 for the United States; 11,700 fighters, compared to 5,600 for the United States; 31,500 tanks, compared to 8,795 for the United States; and 30,000 pieces of artillery, compared to 5,250 for the United States.[153] In addition, the Soviet Union significantly increased its strategic offensive and defensive capabilities, including SS-25 ICBMs, Typhoon-class and Delta-class strategic ballistic missile submarines, BLACKACK and BEAR H bombers, the world's only antiballistic missile system around Moscow, and an impressive antisatellite capability (Figure 2.4).[154]

The Reagan buildup accelerated defense spending and continued the second offset, including stealth and precision-guided weapons. Under the leadership of Secretary of Defense Casper "Cap" Weinberger, the defense budget rose by almost $100 billion between 1981 and January 1985, defense sales increased by 60 percent in real terms in the early 1980s, and the aerospace workforce grew by 15 percent from 1983 to

Weapons System	United States	Soviet Union
Intercontinental Ballistic Missiles and Submarine-launched Ballistic Missiles	980	3,400
Intermediate-and Medium-range Ballistic Missiles	116	735
Surface-to-Air Missiles	24,000	130,000
Long- and Intermediate-range Bombers	6	340
Fighters	5,600	11,700
Helicopters	3,000	10,000
Submarines	40	121
Major Surface Combatants	90	110
Tanks	8,795	31,500
Artillery	5,250	30,000

FIGURE 2.4 U.S. and Soviet production of major weapons systems, 1974–1984.[155]

1986.[156] Reagan's defense buildup led to new systems, such as the M-1 Abrams tank, M-2 Bradley infantry fighting vehicle, and a wide range of missiles capable of precision strike.[157] In 1985, the Department of Defense requested—and Congress authorized—more than 900 aircraft, 50 ICBMs, 23 naval ships, 2,000 tanks and armored personnel carriers, more than 5,000 guided missiles, and 72,000 unguided rockets.[158] The air force funded the B-1B heavy bomber, B-2 stealth bomber, F-15 tactical fighter, F-16 multi-role fighter, and investments in electronic warfare and night operations. Reagan and Weinberger also supported strategic modernization, including the land-based Minuteman ICBM force, missile experimental ICBMs, and Ohio-class submarines with Trident missiles. They stationed Pershing II missiles and ground-launched cruise missiles in Western Europe to counter the threat of Soviet SS-20 road-mobile, intermediate-range ballistic missiles. The U.S. defense budget rose to roughly $550 billion in 1985, second only to $650 billion in 1952 during the Korean War.[159] As a percentage of gross domestic product, however, U.S. defense spending was still only 6 percent in 1985, notably smaller than the peak of 14 percent during the 1950s and 9 percent during the 1960s.[160]

Another component of the defense buildup was the administration's missile defense system, termed the Strategic Defense Initiative (SDI) and nicknamed "Star Wars."[161] It was designed to protect the U.S. homeland from attack by shooting down Soviet ballistic missiles.[162] The SDI had been championed by Berkeley's Edward Teller, director of the Lawrence Livermore Laboratories and one of the fathers of the hydrogen bomb.[163] While governor of California, Reagan had several meetings with Teller about the possibility of destroying ICBMs or their warheads with X-ray lasers and other systems.[164] In the end, the technologies needed for a national missile defense system were decades away from readiness, and Congress cut SDI's budget beginning in the late 1980s.

The United States also strengthened its already formidable navy, which Weinberger expanded from 479 to 525 deployable battle-force ships.[165] While the Soviet Union had an impressive navy with new and increasingly powerful nuclear and diesel submarines, surface warships, and naval aircraft, it did not have the power projection capabilities of the United States with its 15 carrier task forces. Neither the Soviet Union nor any other Warsaw Pact country had a single aircraft carrier (Figure 2.5).[166]

Country	Warsaw Pact			NATO		
	Soviet Union	Non-Soviet	Total	U.S.	Non-U.S. NATO	Total
Nuclear-powered Submarines	130	0	**130**	97	18	**115**
Diesel-powered Submarines	143	8	**151**	4	124	**128**
Principal Surface Warships[1]	270	11	**281**	222	240	**462**
Naval Combat Aircraft	984	67	**1,051**	1,701	295	**1,996**
Naval Armed Helicopters	335	40	**375**	313	355	**668**
Aircraft Carriers	6	0	**6**	15	8	**23**

FIGURE 2.5 NATO and Warsaw Pact naval strength, 1986.[167]

Note: [1] Includes frigates, cruisers, destroyers. Excludes aircraft carriers.

There were no other major powers on the horizon. European militaries remained relatively weak. So did China's. In February 1979, China invaded Vietnam, captured several cities near the border, and then began withdrawing in March. China had mobilized as many as 400,000 People's Liberation Army soldiers against a much smaller Vietnamese force.[168] But the PLA performed poorly and suffered from weak leadership, lackluster coordination between units at the tactical level, antiquated weapons and logistics equipment, and inadequate training and readiness.[169] Casualties were high. The war lasted less than four weeks, but the costs were staggering. Battle-hardened Vietnamese troops killed 26,000 Chinese and wounded 37,000 others.[170]

Defense was not the top priority for China; it was the fourth of Chinese leader Deng Xiaoping's "four modernizations," behind science, agriculture, and industry. As historian Paul Kennedy summarized, China was in a woeful position by the end of the Cold War: "The competing claims of weapons modernization, the people's social requirements, and the need to channel all available resources into 'productive' nonmilitary enterprises is nowhere more pressing than in the People's Republic of China (PRC), which is simultaneously the poorest of the major powers and probably the least well placed strategically."[171] To make matters worse, the United States and Europe imposed an arms embargo on China and broader sanctions after the June 1989 Tiananmen Square crackdown.

Back in the United States, the defense industry focused on the production and innovation of systems and platforms to strengthen deterrence.

One important part of the Reagan buildup was to loosen up the defense regulatory environment and focus on speed, production capacity, and innovation. The Reagan administration orchestrated a series of acquisition reforms led by Secretary Weinberger, Deputy Secretary of Defense Frank Carlucci, and Comptroller Vincent Puritano. They increased multiyear procurements for several weapons systems, which involved the congressional appropriation of funding for more than a single year to reduce per-unit production costs and improve quality. Pentagon leaders focused on 32 management initiatives to address long-standing problems with major weapons systems acquisition.[172] The General Accounting Office reported, "We found that although the initiatives have not fully achieved their intended results, there have been improvements in the acquisition process."[173]

In response to concerns about waste, fraud, and abuse, President Reagan established the Packard Commission, chaired by Hewlett-Packard cofounder David Packard, who had served as deputy secretary of defense under President Nixon.[174] The goal of the commission was to examine procurement problems within the Department of Defense.[175] Yet one of the commission's most important contributions was to recommend improvements in the Pentagon's acquisition process, including changes to federal procurement law:

> [A] much more serious result of this management environment is an unreasonably long acquisition cycle—ten to fifteen years for our major weapon systems. This is a central problem from which most other acquisition problems stem:
>
> - It leads to unnecessarily high costs of development. Time is money, and experience argues that a ten-year acquisition cycle is clearly more expensive than a five-year cycle.

- It leads to obsolete technology in our fielded equipment. We forfeit our five-year technological lead by the time it takes us to get our technology from the laboratory into the field.
- And it aggravates the very gold-plating that is one of its causes. Users, knowing that the equipment to meet their requirements is fifteen years away, make extremely conservative threat estimates. Because long-term forecasts are uncertain at best, users tend to err on the side of overstating the threat.[176]

The result was devastating: "[F]ederal law governing acquisition has become steadily more complex, the acquisition system more bureaucratic, and acquisition management more encumbered and unproductive."[177] The regulators were winning. In response, the Packard Commission made numerous recommendations to expand the use of commercial products and streamline acquisition procedures. For example, the commission recommended the adoption of commercial processes and practices to allow the Department of Defense to broaden its access to cutting-edge commercial products, services, and solutions.[178] Several of the recommendations were implemented in the Goldwater-Nichols Department of Defense Reorganization Act of 1986, such as the creation of an undersecretary of defense for acquisition.[179]

In this environment, engineers and other workers at Lockheed's Skunk Works, where Kelly Johnson's longtime deputy Ben Rich had replaced him as director, were so excited that they adopted as their theme song "Happy Days Are Here Again." Written and composed in 1929 by Milton Ager and Jack Yellen, Barbra Streisand rerecorded it in 1962.[180] The song's lyrics were, quite literally, music to the ears of those at Skunk Works and other locations:

> Cloudy gray times,
> You are now a thing of the past.
> 'Cause happy days are here again!
> The skies above are clear again.
> Let us sing a song of cheer again.
> Happy days are here again![181]

In fact, the defense business was so good that Skunk Works ran into deficiencies in supplies and labor. "I suddenly found myself on the short end of materials, subcontracting work, machine shop help, and skilled labor," recalled Rich. "Without warning there was a dire shortage of everything used in an airplane. Lead times for basic materials stretched from weeks to literally years."[182]

Much like after Sputnik 1, the defense surge involved a financial boost for university research. But this time it wasn't primarily for missiles and rockets; it was for supercomputers, artificial intelligence, and other advanced technology. In September 1982, DARPA released a report titled "A Defense Program in Supercomputation from Microelectronics to Artificial Intelligence for the 1990s," which led to the so-called Strategic Computing Initiative. DARPA-funded work put the United States back in the lead of a global high-tech race and made such areas as Silicon Valley more influential than ever. Military spending at universities soared from less than $500 million in 1980 to $930 million in 1985. The surge was particularly noteworthy in computer science. Two years into the Reagan era, nearly 60 percent of federal funds for basic research in computer science came from the Pentagon.[183]

The Pentagon recruited several technology luminaries, such as Jack Kilby from Texas Instruments and Bob Noyce from Fairchild Semiconductor, to prepare a report on revitalizing the U.S. semiconductor business. Their report concluded that roughly 17 percent of military spending went to electronics in the 1980s, compared to only 6 percent at the end of World War II. Satellites, early-warning radar, missiles, and a wide range of other weapons systems relied on advanced chips. The report came to several major conclusions: U.S. military forces relied primarily on technological superiority to win wars; electronics was the technology that could be most productively leveraged; semiconductors were critical to electronics; and U.S. defense would soon depend on foreign sources for advanced technology in semiconductors.[184]

The number of employees at defense contractors doubled between 1976 and 1986, rising to more than 3.3 million from about 1.7 million. The Reagan buildup was intended to recapitalize U.S. forces, providing them with the most modern weapons systems in preparation for a major European war. That war, though, was never fought.[185] The "Massachusetts Miracle" of the 1980s resulted in part from an influx of defense spending, which by the middle of the decade reached $12 billion—greater than 8 percent of the net state product.[186] The story was similar on the West Coast. By the early 1980s, Santa Clara County, California, enjoyed more defense spending per capita than any other county in the United States. Approximately one-fifth of Silicon Valley's output came from the defense sector. The heartbeat remained Lockheed, whose workforce of 24,000 was nearly double the size of Intel's and roughly five times larger than Apple's.[187]

As usual, there were fierce opponents of the defense buildup. Lockheed was a major target of protesters, who regularly gathered at the facility's gates with banners and chants to register their objections. In October 1986, police arrested 150 people for hurling pumpkins at cars and assaulting an officer to protest Lockheed's involvement in the SDI.[188] In April 1986, the police arrested 138 protesters outside the headquarters of Honeywell during a demonstration against the company's production of nuclear weapon components.[189]

But such opposition was limited, and the defense boom was critical to technological advances on the commercial side. As Margaret O'Mara concluded, "The big money that flowed in via [Strategic Computing Initiative] and SDI contracts in the 1980s was a reminder that defense remained the big-government engine hidden under the hood of the [Silicon] Valley's shiny new entrepreneurial sports car, flying largely under the radar screen of the saturation media coverage of hackers and capitalists."[190] These federal contracts subsidized the development of cutting-edge technologies that otherwise wouldn't have seen the light of day.

Reagan's defense strategy of peace through strength outlasted the Soviet Union and its defense industrial base, which was on its last legs. On November 9, 1989, exuberant East Germans poured through checkpoints at the Berlin Wall, which divided East and West Germany, and used *Mauerspechte*, or "wallpeckers," to chip off parts of the wall. One large slab eventually made its way to Reagan's presidential library in Simi Valley, California.

Over four and a half decades of the Cold War, the U.S. defense industrial base had ebbed and flowed during six major periods: the demobilization of the defense industry after World War II; the shift to a wartime environment with the outbreak of the Korean War; the transition back to a peacetime industrial base with the end of the Korean War; the Soviet launch of Sputnik and the return to a wartime environment as the United States attempted to deter Soviet aggression; the move to a peacetime industrial base in the 1960s and 1970s; and the Reagan buildup in the final stages of the Cold War following incremental changes during the Carter administration.

In wartime—such as during the Korean War, the second offset, and the Reagan buildup—the U.S. defense industry received a surge of additional funding and U.S. officials streamlined acquisition processes and focused on the manufacturing of defense products for deterrence and warfighting. In peacetime, regulators reigned. But policymakers sometimes miscalculated. Truman's decision to slash defense budgets and industry after World War II was shortsighted because of Stalin's defense buildup and expansionist policies—as some U.S. officials at the time predicted.

The Johnson and Kennedy administrations underinvested in defense—including in defense technology—in ways that weakened U.S. deterrence and jeopardized U.S. national security against growing Soviet capabilities. Secretary of Defense Brown told President Carter in December 1980 that the United States had seriously underinvested in defense technology during the Vietnam War era, while the Soviets had spent more than $240 billion in defense equipment and technology.[191] As a percentage of gross domestic product, the U.S. defense budget peaked at 14 percent during the Korean War, varied between 9 and 11 percent during New Look, and remained over 6 percent during President Reagan's defense buildup in the 1980s (Figure 2.6).[192]

The Cold War brought with it a flood of defense dollars that—for the first time in U.S. history—created an enduring defense industrial base. The U.S. military relied on private companies for most military-technical skills.[193] Engineers and entrepreneurs like Kelly Johnson at Lockheed's Skunk Works served as the engines of private-sector innovation through production of such aircraft as the U-2, which fundamentally reshaped U.S. strategic reconnaissance. Johnson's contribution

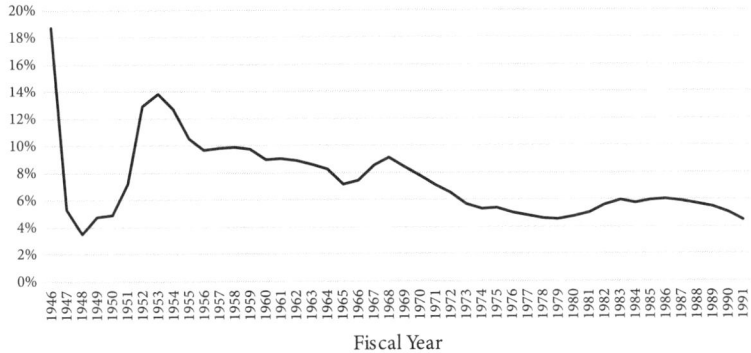

FIGURE 2.6 U.S. defense spending as a percentage of GDP, 1946–1991.[194]

was particularly significant, and he was ruthless about limiting unnecessary regulations, cutting bureaucracy, and simplifying processes.[195] In a Christmas speech to his staff, he defined Skunk Works as "a concentration of a few good people solving problems far in advance at a fraction of the cost of other groups in the aircraft industry by applying the simplest, most straightforward methods possible to develop and produce new projects."[196] Senator Barry Goldwater praised Johnson as an innovative "genius."[197] But perhaps President Lyndon Johnson said it best when presenting him with the National Media of Science: "Kelly Johnson and the products of his famous Skunk Works epitomize the highest and finest goal of our society—the goal of excellence. His record of design achievement in aviation is both incomparable and virtually incredible. Any one of his many airplane designs would have honored any individual's career."[198]

Johnson died on December 21, 1990, just weeks before Operation Desert Storm in Iraq. The U.S.-led war was one of the most awesome displays of U.S. military power since World War II, and Skunk Works yet again played a crucial role.

3

Desert Storm

There are two major ideas about how warfare may change that seem very plausible. The first is that of long-range precision strike becoming the dominant operational approach.... The second idea is the emergence of what might be called information warfare.
—Andrew Marshall, U.S. Department of Defense

Well, how about laser-guided stuff? We never built any, but we're sure talking the hell out of it.
—Weldon Word, Texas Instruments

AT 2:40 A.M. ON January 17, 1991, the United States fired the first shots of Operation Desert Storm, the U.S.-led campaign to oust Iraqi forces from Kuwait. Task Force NORMANDY, which included nine AH-64 Apache helicopters and four Air Force MH-53 Pave Low special operations helicopters, flew silently into Iraq in near total darkness.[1] The helicopters hugged the cold desert floor to evade detection from Iraqi radars. Task Force NORMANDY was on a mission to destroy two critical early-warning radar installations in western Iraq not far from the country's borders with Saudi Arabia and Jordan, clearing the way for a mass of U.S. and allied airpower. More than five months earlier, Saddam Hussein's army had invaded Kuwait, occupied it, and then formally annexed the country. After several minutes of tense silence, Colonel Jesse Johnson, head of U.S. Special Operations Command Central and a former deputy commander of the elite Delta Force, reported back to General Norman Schwarzkopf, head of U.S. Central Command, and other leaders: "0247: SOF TARGETS DESTROYED."[2]

The mission was successful. Approximately 27 Hellfire missiles and 100 Hydra-70 rockets demolished the radar sites and anti-aircraft guns. F-15E fighter aircraft then screamed into Iraqi airspace and destroyed an Iraqi air defense command center, supported by two EF-111s that jammed Iraqi radars. These strikes paved the way for hundreds of U.S. aircraft—including F-117 stealth fighters—to begin striking targets throughout Iraq. The F-117s carried a wide range of precision-guided munitions, such as Paveway II and III laser-guided bombs and Maverick air-to-ground missiles.[3] Brigadier General Jack Leide, U.S. Central Command's intelligence chief, sent an update to headquarters: "0310: PHONES OUT BAG."[4]

Telephone communications were now out in Baghdad. An hour later, the city went dark after U.S. Navy Tomahawk missiles destroyed multiple Iraqi power plants. Over the next several hours, U.S., U.K., French, and Italian fighters pounded Iraqi airfields, missile sites, and other targets. Lieutenant General Chuck Horner, head of U.S. Central Command Air Forces, reported from his command post in the basement of Saudi Air Force headquarters in Riyadh: "0415: NO FEEDBACK ON AIR TO AIR/NO BEEPERS ON SHOOTDOWN."[5]

There were no intelligence reports of Iraqi Air Force opposition and no radio beacons that indicated the survival of Iraqi pilots. All were dead. Over the next month, U.S. aircraft carrying precision-guided munitions conducted an aggressive air campaign against Iraqi airfields, oil facilities, command-and-control facilities, main battle tanks, strategic air defenses, missile sites, and scores of other targets. The U.S. objectives were straightforward: to cripple Iraqi air defenses, undermine Iraqi military morale, and severely weaken Iraqi military capabilities—including ground forces—to facilitate a U.S.-led ground assault.[6]

At 1:00 a.m. on February 24, 1991, U.S. and other coalition forces began their ground invasion against Iraqi forces in Kuwait. They moved with lightning speed against depleted Iraqi forces. On February 26, Iraqi troops began retreating from Kuwait after setting fire to over 700 oil wells. A long convoy of retreating Iraqi troops gathered along the main Iraq-Kuwait highway, creating an easy target for coalition aircraft and army and marine corps units. U.S. and coalition strikes killed hundreds of Iraqi troops and decimated their vehicles on what became known as the "Highway of Death."[7] U.S., British, and French forces continued to pursue retreating Iraqi forces back into Iraq, eventually moving to within 150 miles of Baghdad, before withdrawing back to Iraq's border with Kuwait and Saudi Arabia.

On February 28, 100 hours after the ground campaign started, President George H. W. Bush declared a ceasefire and announced that Kuwait had been liberated. It was a remarkable success. Operation Desert Storm benefited from the offset initiated by Secretary of Defense Harold Brown and Undersecretary of Defense William Perry in response to Soviet military capabilities and concerns about the erosion of U.S. deterrence. The Reagan and Bush administrations continued many of these programs. Operation Desert Storm also highlighted synergy between the private sector and government. Weldon Word and his colleagues from Texas Instruments and Ben Rich, Denys Overholser, and their team from Lockheed Skunk Works were instrumental in working with the Defense Department to develop precision-guided weapons and stealth technology, respectively. They benefited from a wartime environment and a defense industrial base that was given adequate resources and could focus on production and innovation.

But U.S. military advances did not happen overnight.

U.S. research and development efforts on guided weapons had progressed in fits and starts since World War II, with the radio-guided, azimuth-only bomb (Azon); range and azimuth-only bomb (Razon); and much larger Tarzon "tall boy" guided bomb. But the results were disappointing. The bombs suffered from serious weather restrictions, a low success rate of hitting targets, high maintenance costs, and reliability problems—including bomb malfunctions.[8]

Research and development advances continued to progress through the Vietnam War. Companies like Texas Instruments and Hughes Aircraft—whose defense businesses were eventually bought by Raytheon—were happy to oblige. Texas Instruments, based in Dallas, had developed a series of infrared and radar technologies, and its executives and engineers were increasingly interested in the lucrative missile business. One was Weldon Word, who had a Master of Science in Electrical Engineering from Southern Methodist University and joined Texas Instruments after retiring from the U.S. Army. Word worked on a wide range of projects, from developing anti-submarine sonars to the Shrike antiradar missile.[9]

He was increasingly frustrated with the poor accuracy of U.S. bombs for most of the Vietnam War and, as a result, was intrigued about the prospect of laser-guided weapons. The problem was that no one in the Department of Defense would listen to him or his engineering team. "They took great offense at our 'Buck Rogers' idea," Word said of general officers he briefed, referring to the science fiction adventure television series. But Word insisted that the U.S. Air Force could not accurately hit their targets and instead left behind a string—or "train"—of pockmarks in the Vietnam landscape during bombing raids. "You have bomb-damage assessment photos," he said mockingly, "with 800 craters and you ain't hit the target yet."[10]

Word and his team—which included subsonic aerodynamicist Dick Johnson, retired Navy pilot Jack Sickle, and engineers Robert Wagner and Ken Goldstein—found a supporter in Colonel Joseph Davis, vice commander of the Air Proving Ground at Eglin Air Force Base.[11] Davis was searching for a weapon with the accuracy to routinely hit a target within 30 feet.[12] One early hurdle was how to work around stifling regulations. At the time, a service secretary generally had to sign a defense contract above $100,000, which, as Word lamented, meant "a long cycle" and "lots of paperwork."[13] So they pushed for a contract just under $100,000—$99,000 to be exact—to minimize the bureaucracy.[14]

After multiple discussions with Colonel Davis, who was also frustrated with the bombing inaccuracy in Vietnam, Word and his team proposed—and delivered—a laser kit that could be bolted onto 500- and 2,000-pound "dumb bombs." A dumb bomb is a bomb that does not have a guidance system, follows a ballistic trajectory instead, and generally cannot hit a target with the same accuracy as a precision-guided—or "smart"—bomb. Word and his team's kit consisted of four main components: a seeker head that was aerodynamically stabilized, a control assembly, wings, and a guidance electronic system. The weapons system's seeker head and four-quadrant silicon detector were particularly innovative and represented major engineering breakthroughs.[15] As Word recalled, the seeker head "resembled a badminton birdie, and so from then on it was dubbed the 'birdie head.'"[16]

Two airplanes were necessary to use the laser-guided bomb: one, which was called the designator aircraft, "painted" the laser beam on the target; the other dropped the bomb. Once the bomb's seeker detected the reflected energy on a compatible frequency, the bomb could ride the laser beam all the way to the target. The bomb generally took a zigzag route to the target since the fins had to make corrective switches to bring the laser reflection to the center of the seeker's field of view.[17] As highlighted in the patent description, the design was both simple and remarkably innovative: "The guided bomb can be delivered from an unmodified aircraft in the same manner as a conventional bomb. There is no requirement for target lock-on or bomb guidance tracking before launch. Electronic circuits are activated by a simple bomb fuse-type arming wire that is withdrawn from a spring-loaded switch when the bomb is released from the airplane. This activates the battery which is housed in the control section and provides sufficient electrical power for the system to operate."[18]

U.S. aircraft deploying what became known as the Paveway I bomb could drop it from well before the enemy's main air defense systems, which significantly reduced the threat to the aircraft. Air force acquisition managers were giddy, noting that "the capability . . . to vastly improve bombing impact accuracy was emphatically demonstrated."[19] Paveway I was enormously successful. It had a 25-foot circular error of probability, which is a measure of a weapons system's precision. The circular error of probability refers to the radius of a circle centered at the intended target, within which 50 percent of the missiles would be expected to hit. During Operation Rolling Thunder in Vietnam, for example, U.S. bombs typically had a circular error of probability of 450 feet and hit their target 4.4 percent of the time.[20] Consequently, the shift from a circular error of probability of 450 feet during Vietnam to 25 feet with Paveway I was dramatic.

A second laser-guided bomb, Paveway II, was even more precise. It had several variants, such as Guided Bomb Unit (GBU)-12 and GBU-10. Word and his team made several improvements, such as folding tailfins that opened (or "popped") when released to improve aircraft payload; improved electronics, such as integrated circuitry, that increased reliability and decreased production time; enhanced bomb guidance and maneuverability; and plastic lenses and ringtails that reduced the price tag.[21] Word explained, "Paveway I was just riddled with problems. Paveway II was really the cleanup."[22] Texas Instruments engineers designed Paveway II to strike stationary armored targets, such as main battle tanks, in what became known as "tank plinking."[23] As early tests showed, the missile could strike within inches of a designated target from such aircraft as the F-111F all-weather attack aircraft.[24] The Soviet Union took notice. One Soviet military analyst reported, "[A] new line in non-nuclear means of armed struggle had been developed."[25]

Paveway III (which also had several variants, such as GBU-24 and GBU-27) involved even more improvements. With the enhancement of enemy air defense systems, fighter aircraft had to fly low to defeat ground-based radar and avoid sophisticated surface-to-air missiles and anti-aircraft artillery. But the technology on Paveway I and Paveway II wouldn't allow the bomb to hit targets with precision when pilots dropped them at a low altitude. Paveway III had a microprocessor-based autopilot that allowed for proportional control, a scanning laser with a larger field of view, and enlarged tailfins for greater maneuverability. These modifications significantly improved the accuracy of the bomb at low altitude.[26] With laser-guided bombs, the United States could now hit a target with a *single* bomb—an extraordinary evolution from the dumb bombs and pockmarked landscapes of the Vietnam War.

Another example of the evolution in precision-guided munitions was the Maverick missile, or AGM-65, produced by Hughes Aircraft Company and later by Raytheon. Maverick was a tactical, air-to-surface guided missile designed for such missions as close air support and interdiction. It provided stand-off capability and precision strike against a wide range of targets, including main battle tanks, air defense systems, ships, and fuel storage facilities. Hughes engineers began development of Maverick in the 1960s, when the air force initiated a program to replace the AGM-12 Bullpup short-range air-to-ground missile. Over the course of the 1970s and 1980s, Hughes engineers made numerous advancements to the missile. It was a modular design weapon, which meant that different combinations of guidance packages and warheads could be attached to the rocket motor section to produce a different weapons system. For example, the Maverick had three different seeker options: electro-optical imaging, imaging infrared, and a laser guidance package.[27]

The Paveway I, II, III, Maverick, and other precision-guided bombers and missiles were still fallible; they could be thrown off course by pilot error and clouds, and the bombs could slip out of the "basket" of the radar beam if the pilot swerved too sharply to avoid ground fire and missiles. Nevertheless, these precision-guided weapons gave the U.S. military a significant advantage over other countries—including the Soviet Union—in conducting precision strikes against enemy targets.

And they were a boon for military theorists.

Andrew Marshall, director of the Pentagon's Office of Net Assessment, was a luminary in the annals of U.S. defense strategy. Marshall's burgeoning career as a strategic thinker began in 1949 at the RAND Corporation, based in Santa Monica, California. Henry Kissinger, President Richard M. Nixon's national security advisor, brought Marshall onto the National Security Council staff in 1972. A year later, Marshall established the Office of Net Assessment in the Pentagon and began studying Soviet military strengths, weaknesses, and long-range trends. He had an extraordinary knack for asking difficult questions that the U.S. intelligence community could not—or would not—ask and for conducting "net assessments." Instead of examining countries like the Soviet Union in isolation, Marshall advocated a more systematic approach that included examining the military balance between two or more countries. During the Cold War, this approach involved analyzing the United States and Soviet Union *together*—both strengths and weaknesses—by examining their respective doctrines, logistics systems, weapons systems, training regimens, and other factors.[28]

Marshall had been thinking for years about what he called a "military revolution."[29] In looking back at major military breakthroughs, he was particularly interested in periods when there were significant technological developments *and* major changes in how militaries used the technology or weapons system. "The most important thing that we can focus on in the next several years," Marshall wrote, "is the investigation of, and experimentation with, novel concepts of operation and new organizations to exploit the technologies available now and likely to be available in the next 20 years."[30] One potentially new concept of operation centered on how the U.S. military could use precision-guided weapons for military operations.

In the 1970s, DARPA supported an effort called the Long Range Research and Development Planning Program, which prioritized the development of precision weapons and other technologies and capabilities that could offset the Soviet Union's military power.[31] The program assumed that accurate conventional munitions could cause massive damage and, in most cases, avoid the need for using nuclear weapons.[32] William Perry, who was serving as under secretary of defense for research and engineering under Harold Brown, explained that the United States could offset the Soviet Union's advantage in conventional capabilities by shifting the arms race to a technological arena, where the United States had an advantage. Perry told members of Congress in 1978, "Precision-guided weapons, I believe, have the potential of revolutionizing warfare. More importantly, if we effectively exploit the lead we have in this field, we can greatly enhance our ability to deter war without having to compete tank for tank, missile for missile with the Soviets. We will effectively shift the competition to a technological area where we have a fundamental long-term advantage."[33]

While the U.S. military was at the forefront of developing new technologies, including precision strike, Marshall assessed that Soviet military leaders were at the forefront of *theorizing* about the changing character of war.[34] He believed "it was the Soviet military theorists, rather than our own, that were intellectualizing about it, and speculating on the longer-term consequences of the technical and other changes that the American military had initiated."[35] In an article in *Red Star*, the official newspaper of the Soviet Ministry of Defense, General Nikolai Ogarkov, chief of the General Staff, concluded that there were significant changes afoot in warfare because of "precision weapons, reconnaissance-strike complexes, and weapons based on new physical principles."[36] In an interview with *Red Star*, he noted that "the development of conventional means of destruction . . . is making many kinds of weapons global" and triggering a rise "in the destructive potential of conventional weapons, making them almost as effective as weapons of mass destruction."[37]

Integrating precision strike and other technologies into warfare would require an evolution in concepts. One of the most important was an evolution in what the Soviets called the "reconnaissance strike complex," which involved the collection of real-time intelligence and rapid movement of information to air, ground, and maritime units for strike.[38] A major goal of the reconnaissance strike complex was to improve command, control, communications, computers, intelligence, surveillance, and reconnaissance on the battlefield to facilitate the coordinated use of high-precision, long-range weapons linked to real-time intelligence data.

While the Soviets may have been a step ahead of the United States in fully comprehending the changing character of warfare, some U.S. companies were innovating at a scorching pace. They benefited from an era in which U.S. policymakers recognized that the country was in serious competition with the Soviet Union and the defense industry needed money and had to operate with urgency, limit unnecessary regulations, and maximize production capacity and innovation.

In April 1975, Denys Overholser, a 36-year-old mathematician and radar specialist at Skunk Works who had graduated from Oregon State University, stumbled across a dense, virtually impenetrable monograph on electromagnetic waves by Pyotr Ufimtsev, the chief scientist at Moscow's Institute of Radio Engineering. The title was a mouthful: "Method of Edge Waves in the Physical Theory of Diffraction."[39] Overholser took a particular interest in Ufimtsev's analysis near the end of the monograph, where his mathematical calculations predicted the reflection of electromagnetic waves from two-dimensional and three-dimensional objects. Overholser was floored. He had a strong hunch that Ufimtsev's work represented a potential breakthrough in stealth technology for aircraft and other systems because it provided insight into how to reduce radar signatures.[40] Ironically, Ufimtsev was ignored by his Soviet peers, who were indifferent to his wave theory work. "Senior Soviet designers were absolutely uninterested in my theories," he later recalled.[41] But Overholser saw the value of his work and sprinted to the office of Ben Rich, who had recently replaced Kelly Johnson as director of Lockheed Skunk Works following the latter's retirement.

"Ben," Overholser began excitedly in Rich's office in the barnlike Building 82 at Skunk Works, "this guy has shown us how to accurately calculate radar cross sections across the surface of the wing and at the edge of the wing and put together these two calculations for an accurate total."[42]

Rich sat stone faced, not entirely comprehending what Overholser was saying. A radar beam is an electromagnetic field, and the amount of energy reflected from the target determines its visibility on radar. Boeing's B-29 Superfortress, which was so critical for strategic bombing of the Japanese mainland during World War II, looked like a flying barn on radar screens and was easy to spot. So was Lockheed's B-52 bomber, F-15 fighter, and B-70 bomber.

"Ufimtsev has shown us how to create computer software to accurately calculate the radar cross section of a given configuration, as long as it's in two dimensions," Overholser continued. "We can break down an airplane into thousands of flat triangular shapes, add up their individual radar signatures, and get a precision total of the radar cross section."[43]

Overholser's hunch was that Skunk Works could build an airplane that was invisible to modern radar by computing the radar cross sections of an airplane and dividing the plane into a series of flat triangles—what Skunk Works' engineers called "faceting."

"If I understand you," Rich replied, still somewhat puzzled, "the shape of the airplane would not be too different from the airplane gliders we folded from looseleaf paper and sailed around the classroom behind the teacher's back."[44]

And so stealth was born at Skunk Works. Rich gave Overholser three months—half the time Overholser requested—to create computer software based on Ufimtsev's formula for a program that Skunk Works called Echo I. Overholser reported back with stunning results.

Handing Rich the diamond-shaped sketch of what would be code-named Have Blue and eventually become the stealth F-117 Nighthawk, he said, "Meet the Hopeless Diamond."

"How good are your radar-cross-section numbers on this one?" Rich asked.

"Pretty good," Overholser replied with a confident grin. Then he paused briefly and prodded, "Ask me, 'How good?'"

"How good?"

"This shape is one thousand times less visible than the least visible shape previously produced at Skunk Works."

"Whoa!" Rich answered in utter disbelief. "If we made this shape into a full-size tactical fighter, what would be its equivalent radar signature... as big as what? A Piper Cub, a T-38 trainer? What?"

Overholser shook his head. "Ben," he protested, "understand, we are talking about a *major, major*, big-time revolution here. We are talking *infinitesimal*."

"Well, what does that mean? On a radar screen it would appear as a... what? As big as a condor, an eagle, an owl, a what?"

"Ben," Overholser said with a great belly laugh, "try as big as an eagle's *eyeball*."[45]

It was a remarkable development. Rich, Overholser, and the team at Skunk Works benefited from an environment at Lockheed that supported innovation and limited oversight and regulation. After all, the first of Kelly Johnson's 14 rules was that the "Skunk Works manager must be delegated practically complete control of his program in all aspects."[46] Rich and his team pushed forward. But they faced at least three serious hurdles in developing Have Blue, one of the most secretive U.S. aircraft ever produced up to that point.

The first was convincing the Department of Defense to fund the research and development. They benefited from an increasingly competitive landscape with the Soviet Union, which had reached nuclear parity with the United States and had, according to some U.S. estimates, a 3:1 advantage in conventional assault weapons, including armored personnel carriers, main battle tanks, and artillery pieces.[47] The United States needed to spend more money on defense and move faster in the acquisitions process to produce systems that could give them an edge over the Soviets. But Rich quickly discovered that DARPA had already invited Northrop, McDonnell Douglas, and three other companies to compete to build a stealth airplane. Lockheed had been shut out.

With help from the CIA, whose leadership was willing to reveal Lockheed's previous sensitive programs to Department of Defense officials at DARPA, Rich and his team were eventually allowed to compete. And they won—big. As Overholser recalled, "Our diamond was ten times less visible than [Northrop's] model. We achieved the lowest radar cross sections ever measured."[48] Stealth was critical since the Soviet Union had developed increasingly sophisticated surface-to-air missile systems, such as the S-200 (what NATO called the SA-5 Gammon), and started exporting them to Syria, Poland, and other countries.[49] U.S. aircraft that had to fly against these air defense systems risked being destroyed.

A second hurdle was convincing Lockheed to move forward. Johnson was emphatically *not* a believer in Have Blue. "Ben Rich," he said after looking at one of the initial sketches of the stealth fighter, "have you lost your goddam mind? This crap will never get off the ground." Johnson had officially retired after reaching Lockheed's mandatory retirement age, but he continued as a paid consultant at Skunk Works. He thought the future was about missiles, not stealth or any other manned aircraft.[50] "You're wasting your time," he chastised Rich. "This is like chasing a butterfly in a rain forest because in the end the government won't invest big dollars in stealth, when for the same money they can invest in new missiles."[51] But Johnson came around when he saw the results. And so did Lockheed.

The third hurdle was building a workable stealth aircraft during the development phase of Have Blue. The engineering feat was exceptional for Rich, Overholser, and other members of the Lockheed team, such as Ed "Baldy" Baldwin, Alan Brown, and Dick Scherrer. They worked out of Building 82 in Burbank and developed an aircraft with a faceted shape made from two-dimensional flat surfaces, a noncircular tail pipe to decrease the infrared signature, radar-absorbing composite materials and shields to minimize engine and exhaust noise, and special additives to prevent exhaust contrails. The airplane could not go supersonic or have an afterburner, since speed created surface heating that would be identified by enemy radar. Skunk Works engineers stripped Have Blue of any electronic device that could be picked up by air defense systems, and they muffled the engines to prevent unwanted noise. The final aircraft, the F-117 Nighthawk, was extraordinary. It was virtually invisible to enemy radar and negated Moscow's massive investments in air defense systems.[52]

By the time of Operation Desert Storm, the F-117 stealth tactical fighter was ready for prime time. It was used sparingly during the U.S. invasion of Panama in 1989, but it would soon get the spotlight in Iraq. The initial idea and development had come from the pioneering private sector, not the government. "We were great innovators, rule benders, chance takers, and when appropriate, corner cutters," said Rich of Skunk Works. It was U.S. innovation at its best. The same was true of U.S. advances in precision-guided technology and weapons systems, such as the Paveway and Maverick bombs.

Yet it was still unclear what new concepts of operation might come from the evolution in precision-guided weapons and stealth technology, which were initially designed to offset Soviet advantages. Operation Desert Storm provided more clarity—a lot more clarity.

The U.S. plan for the air component of Desert Storm, which was led by the Special Planning Group (colloquially referred to as "the Black Hole"), focused on an "inside-out" campaign. Planners designed the initial air strikes to damage a broad range of targets that would cascade throughout other sectors. Black Hole planners hoped that strikes against specific targets—such as Iraq's electricity grid, certain areas of the air defense system, and the telecommunications sector—would spread throughout the system.[53] To conduct the air campaign, however, the U.S. Air Force needed a lot more precision-guided bombs. Most of the bombs stored in theater were dumb bombs and dated back to the Vietnam War. Over the course of the campaign, the United States transported more than 300,000 tons of bombs—with a heavy focus on precision-guided bombs—to the theater.[54] U.S. Central Command's theater objectives for the war were relatively straightforward:

- Target Iraq's political and military leadership, including command-and-control infrastructure.
- Achieve and sustain air superiority.
- Cut and destroy Iraq's military supply lines.
- Destroy Saddam Hussein's Republican Guard forces.
- Liberate Kuwait.[55]

Iraq's air defenses were formidable. They included four air defense sectors providing the country with overlapping surface-to-air missile and anti-anticraft artillery coverage. The Iraqi Air Force had late-generation French and Soviet fighters, including three squadrons of advanced MiG-29 fighters. Iraq's integrated air defense system, code-named KARI, was based in Baghdad. After Moscow, KARI had the world's second highest concentration of air defenses.[56] The air campaign, code-named Instant Thunder, focused on attacking the heart of Iraqi defenses.

Phase I, which began on January 17, 1991, targeted Iraq's integrated air defenses and other strategic targets, including television and telecommunications sites. It was led by Lockheed's stealth F-117s. The F-117s achieved an extraordinary success rate, hitting 23 targets out of 33 bombs dropped. The U.S. Air Force's Gulf War Air Power Survey concluded that "the F-117s that had executed the first strikes on *downtown Baghdad* had needed no [suppression of enemy air defenses] or fighter support to attack their targets—against a fully functioning defense system."[57] The F-117s were followed by 52 Tomahawk missiles, which struck Iraqi leadership, chemical, and electrical power targets in and near Baghdad. In addition, F-15Es conducted strikes on Scud missile sites, supported by F-15Cs and F-14s ready to attack Iraqi fighters brave enough to put up a fight. A range of other aircraft, such as F/A-18s and A-6s, accompanied by EA-6B jammers, continued suppression of enemy air defense missions (Figure 3.1).[58]

Over the first 24 hours of the war, an astounding 700 combat aircraft from the United States, the United Kingdom, France, and Saudi Arabia conducted sorties against targets in Iraq and Kuwait.[59] They relied on several precision-guided weapons, such as Maverick and Paveway II missiles. Mavericks were particularly useful against Iraqi surface-to-air missile sites, tanks, electric power plants, and aircraft parked on Iraqi airfields.[60] The first night of attacks seriously degraded Iraq's air defenses, and Iraq's integrated air defense system no longer operated as an integrated system. The U.S. Air Force's *Gulf War Air Power Survey* concluded, "Maverick missiles (over 5,000 expended by air force aircraft) also made a major contribution to destruction of Iraqi armor."[61] In addition, F-111F and other aircraft dropped a total of 4,493

FIGURE 3.1 Day 1 of Operation Desert Storm, 3:20 a.m. to 4:30 a.m.[62]

GBU-12 Paveway IIs against Iraqi tanks, artillery pieces, and other targets.[63]

GBU-12 Paveway II laser-guided bombs were so lethal against Iraqi armor, particularly those from Republican Guard units, that tank crews stopped living in their vehicles, which severely decreased the readiness of both crews and equipment.[64] One U.S. pilot noted, "[T]he 500-pound GBU-12 would totally destroy a tank, and it was not uncommon to see the turret flipping away looking like a big lollipop."[65] One Iraqi general recalled, "During the Iran war, my tank was my friend because I could sleep in it and know I was safe. During this war my tank became my enemy, none of my troops would get near a tank at night because they just kept blowing up."[66] F-111Fs eventually flew 664 "tank plinking" missions and destroyed approximately 1,500 tanks, other mechanized vehicles, and pieces of artillery over the course of Desert Storm.[67]

During Phase II of the war, the air campaign focused on suppressing Iraqi air defenses in the Kuwait theater of operations and gaining overall air supremacy over Kuwait. With the suppression of enemy air defense campaign accomplished, U.S. and other coalition aircraft were able to operate relatively safely at medium and high altitudes. Among the coalition air forces only one U.S. Navy F/A-18 around Baghdad was lost, courtesy of a MiG-25. But Iraq lost 33 fixed-wing aircraft, for a 5:1 ratio, an enormous improvement over the 2:1 ratio during the Vietnam War.[68] During Phase III, coalition aircraft aggressively targeted the Iraqi Army in what was termed "preparation of the battlefield."[69] By February 24, the air campaign had reduced the combat effectiveness of Iraqi units in the Kuwaiti theater of operations by roughly 50 percent—a stunning achievement.[70] Phase IV was the ground campaign, supported by air power. It began on February 24 and lasted only 100 hours.

By all accounts, Operation Desert Storm was a major success. The U.S.-led coalition defeated the Iraqi Army within six weeks and with minimal losses. And the U.S. Air Force's *Gulf War Air Power Survey* concluded, "[T]he most impressive operational achievement of the Gulf War was the successful battle for air control, fought, and largely won, in the opening days of Desert Storm. That air battle, against the Iraqi air defenses, broke the enemy's capacity to defend himself from the blows that would fall throughout the remainder of the war."[71] Only about 8 percent of munitions (7,400 out of 84,000 tons) dropped during Operation Desert Storm were precision-guided weapons because the stockpiles were limited, but they were responsible for 75 percent of the major damage to Iraqi targets.[72] A U.S. Defense Science Board study concluded that the effectiveness of air operations dramatically improved during Operation Desert Storm from previous wars such as Vietnam, noting that the "Gulf War experience showed that for many types of targets, a ton of PGMs [precision-guided munitions] typically replaces 12–20 tons of unguided munitions on a tonnage per target kill basis."[73] As one U.S. commander summarized, the precision campaign placed Iraq in the position of a "tethered goat, being pounded to death from beyond its reach."[74]

The combination of stealth and precision was lethal. Nearly all the F-117 weapons were precision-guided, and each F-117 generally carried two laser-guided, 2,000-pound GBU-27 Paveway III bombs. In contrast, most of the F-16 weapons dropped dumb bombs. Because of their greatly reduced vulnerability to radar-directed fire, F-117s were used in night operations to attack heavily defended targets, such as command-and-control centers, air defense radar, and military production facilities. Moreover, F-117s flew only 2 percent of the sorties during the air campaign, but they struck 50 percent of the strategic targets and achieved a success rate of roughly 80 percent.[75] In terms of precision targeting, two raids of 300 B-17 bombers during World War II with 3,000 bombs could not achieve what two F-117s did with only four bombs during Operation Desert Storm.[76]

There was considerable debate about whether the integration of precision-guided weapons, stealth technology, and air power was actually *revolutionary*. Secretary of Defense William Perry wrote shortly after the war, "In Operation Desert Storm the United States employed for the first time a new class of military systems that gave American forces a revolutionary advance in military capability." He continued, "[L]aser-guided bombs, laser-guided missiles and infrared-guided missiles were dramatically more effective and caused far fewer civilian casualties than the area bombing that characterized previous wars."[77] Andrew Krepinevich likewise concluded in an influential study for the Department of Defense's Office of Net Assessment that U.S. military operations in Iraq were revolutionary: "This revolution is being driven primarily by advances in microelectronic technologies that vastly increase our ability to gather, process, and disseminate information; support the development and employment of advanced precision-guided conventional munitions; and permit major advances in simulations techniques."[78]

But while the U.S. military victory was impressive, there were several important caveats.

First, Operation Desert Storm was a lopsided victory. The United States enjoyed an extremely favorable situation. It deployed a military force that was trained, equipped, and sized to fight the Soviet Union around the globe, received diplomatic and military support from virtually every major power (including a range of European militaries that sent ground and air forces), and selected the time of its air and ground operations.[79] "Knowledgeable observers," remarked military historian Eliot Cohen, should be "skeptical that a revolution had taken place."[80] These realities shouldn't distract from what were clear military victories, but the United States was not facing the Red Army in Eastern Europe during the height of the Cold War.

Second, some arguments overstated the role of air power. Air strikes were critical in weakening Iraqi forces, but the United States still needed ground forces to defeat the Iraqi military and retake territory in Kuwait and Iraq. The same argument surfaced later in the decade in the Balkans, where some argued that air power predominantly won the wars.[81] Again, these arguments exaggerated the role of air power. In the Kosovo war, for example, NATO's threat of a ground invasion, Serbian concerns about regime stability, and Serbia's failure to secure Russia's support played significant roles in coercing Serbian leader Slobodan Milošević to withdraw his forces from Kosovo.[82] As Cyril Falls, a British military historian and journalist, noted in his 1953 book *A Hundred Years of War, 1850–1950*, "Observers constantly describe the warfare of their own age as marking a revolutionary breach in the normal progress of methods of warfare. Their selection of their own age ought to put readers and listeners on their guard.... It is a fallacy, due to ignorance of technical and tactical military history, to suppose that methods of warfare have not made continuous and, on the whole, fairly even progress."[83]

Consequently, it is highly debatable—and likely false—that Desert Storm was a veritable revolution in military affairs. But it was still a remarkable achievement in military power just as the main U.S. competitor, the Soviet Union, disintegrated. The United States made extraordinary strides in such areas as precision-guided weapons and stealth thanks to the work of innovative engineers such as Word, Rich, and Overholser. "Prior to 1991, two separate, leap-ahead military technologies had matured enough to offer an order-of-magnitude breakthrough," remarked David Deptula, who was one of the main planners for Desert Storm's air campaign. "The first was low-observable (i.e. stealth) technology, and the second was the development of precision munitions."[84] It may not have been a true revolution in military affairs, but Marshall and other individuals were perceptive in noting that "long-range precision strike [was] becoming the dominant operational approach," changing warfare itself.[85]

In addition, the crucial technological developments for Desert Storm—such as precision-guided munitions and stealth—came out of an environment in the late 1970s and 1980s in which U.S. policymakers urgently focused on offsetting Soviet capabilities. While the private sector developed stealth technology, Brown, Perry, and others in the Carter administration grasped the importance of stealth and provided money and high-level support to convert a relatively small project into a major weapons program.[86] The Reagan administration accelerated many of these programs, increased the defense budget, and operated with a determination to maximize defense production. Under the leadership of Defense Secretary Weinberger, the Pentagon deployed Lockheed's stealth F-117 fighter in early 1981 and supported the research, development, and production of Northrop's stealth B-2 bomber.[87] By the time the Bush administration launched Desert Storm, the technology and concepts of operation were already in place.

But would this wartime environment persist? Companies were about to find out.

4

The Last Supper

Regulations grow at the same rate as weeds.
—NORMAN AUGUSTINE, chairman of Martin Marietta

We expect defense companies to go out of business.
—WILLIAM PERRY, Deputy Secretary of Defense

AT PRECISELY 7:32 P.M. ON the night of December 25, 1991—eight months after the end of Desert Storm—the Kremlin lowered the red Soviet hammer-and-sickle flag and replaced it with the tricolor white, blue, and red flag of prerevolutionary Russia.[1] There was no organized ceremony, only the ringing of chimes from Spassky Tower and a tirade from a solitary Soviet war veteran standing in Red Square. Journalist Serge Schmemann penned a poignant obituary of the collapsing country in the *New York Times*: "Conceived in utopian promise and born in the violent upheavals of the 'Great October Revolution' of 1917, the union heaved its last in the dreary darkness of late December 1991, stripped of ideology, dismembered, bankrupt and hungry—but awe-inspiring even in its fall."[2]

With the collapse of the Soviet Union, Norman Augustine, who was chairman of the defense company Martin Marietta, sensed that the defense industrial base was in for a wild ride. "The handwriting was on the walls," he said. "There was to be a peace dividend."[3] Augustine initiated an internal assessment within Martin Marietta about the implications of a declining defense budget, including the possibility of mergers and acquisitions with other defense companies. Raised in Colorado, Augustine graduated from Princeton University with a B.S.E. in aeronautical engineering. His senior thesis was titled "Preliminary Design for a Supersonic Trainer." In 1958, Augustine was hired as a research engineer at Douglas Aircraft Company, where he went on to become a program manager and chief engineer. In 1965, he served in the Office of the Secretary of Defense as assistant director of defense research and engineering, and he later returned to the Defense Department to become undersecretary of the army and acting secretary of the army. He joined Martin Marietta in 1977 as vice president of technical operations and was later elected CEO and chairman.

Everywhere Augustine looked he saw efficiency decimated by armies of auditors, mountains of unnecessary government regulations, and far too many managers—actually micromanagers—holding too many meetings and demanding too much bureaucracy and paperwork. "I'd make speeches and write articles about the evils of bureaucracy," he lamented. "Everyone would nod yes, and promptly forget what I said."[4] So he turned to the art of hyperbole. One night he mused about the future costs of new military aircraft. He worried that the exponential growth in the cost of building high-technology military aircraft would shrink the number that the government could afford.

And so law 16 was born, one of 52 laws Augustine jotted down to cover every area of business. "In the year 2054, the entire defense budget will purchase just one aircraft," he wrote, somewhat tongue-in-cheek. "This aircraft will have to be shared by the Air Force and Navy 3-1/2 days each per week except for leap year, when it will be made available to the Marines for the extra day."[5] Lockheed Skunk Works' Kelly Johnson routinely quoted Augustine's law 16 in his belief that unmanned platforms, including missiles, would replace manned aircraft.[6] Augustine also despised regulations, which he believed stifled innovation, creativity, and efficiency and which some organizations and government agencies viewed as a substitute for sound management judgment. Too many regulations were insidious in the defense sector, he believed, especially for procurement. And thus emerged law 49: "Regulations grow at the same rate as weeds."[7]

Augustine's assessment of the future of the defense industry was prophetic. The Soviet Union collapsed, its once vaunted defense industrial base began to crumble, and the United States was the indisputable global military power. The rise and fall of the great powers began a new era as the international landscape shifted from a bipolar system led by the United States and the Soviet Union to what U.S. journalist Charles Krauthammer referred to as the "unipolar moment." As Krauthammer argued, the United States was "the only country with the military, diplomatic, political and economic assets to be a decisive player in any conflict in whatever part of the world it chooses to involve itself."[8]

Yet with the end of the Soviet Empire, the United States returned to a peacetime environment. The defense industrial base did not need to operate with the same sense of urgency, and there was a strong impetus to consolidate, save money, and cut the defense budget—which declined by over 11 percent between 1992 and 1996.[9] What's more, Secretary of Defense Les Aspin and Deputy Secretary of Defense William Perry convened a remarkable dinner of defense industry executives in the fall of 1993 at the Pentagon, which became known as "the Last Supper." Perry told the group that the administration was cutting the defense budget and they needed to consolidate. The chief executives listened, and the number of major defense companies plummeted from 107 in 1990 to a half dozen or so by the end of the decade.[10]

While the collapse of the Soviet Union surprised many analysts, the system—including the Soviet defense industry—had been in a tailspin for several years.

Soviet gross national product was stagnant, shortages of basic consumer goods were endemic, and rationing was widespread. A World Bank study bluntly concluded that Soviet economic growth was "the worst in the world by the end of the Cold War, after controlling for investment and human capital."[11] The Soviet Union's planned economic system was disastrous for long-run economic growth. The country faced a low elasticity of substitution between capital and labor, which caused declining returns to capital to become particularly severe.[12] One major drag on the economy was the massive spending on defense, which undermined productivity. Soviet defense spending rose from 2 percent of GDP in 1928 to as high as 16 percent by the 1980s.[13] According to some economic assessments, defense spending above roughly 6 to 7 percent can seriously—and negatively—impact economic growth.[14] Consequently, the Soviet Union's 16 percent spending on defense as a percentage of GDP was a major drag on its economy.

The Soviet defense industry had historically been shielded from the bottlenecks and shortages that plagued the Soviet economy. The Military Industrial Commission controlled defense industrial output and ensured that even scarce supplies went to defense production facilities. In addition, the defense industry produced a wide range of nondefense goods, including equipment for the agricultural sector and railroad industry, washing machines, vacuum cleaners, automobiles, and other consumer goods. By the end of the 1980s, however, President Mikhail Gorbachev's economic reforms and the rampant economic chaos throughout the country had undermined the defense sector's traditional insularity and increased its vulnerability to economic problems. Consequently, defense was caught up in the Soviet Union's economic crisis in at least two ways. High defense spending had a negative impact on economic growth, and the economy's failures gutted the defense industry.

In December 1988, Gorbachev cut defense procurement and the size of Soviet military forces, leading to a decline in military orders. Weapons factories began to suffer serious cash flow problems. The country's deteriorating financial situation undermined the government's ability to help even defense plants remain solvent. As one CIA assessment concluded, the result was that "many defense-industrial facilities are desperately seeking solutions—including Western financial commitments—to stem a hemorrhage of their best workers and to stave off insolvency."[15]

The Chelyabinsk Tank Plant ceased tank production in 1991, and a growing number of factories shed workers. Soviet weapons production decreased dramatically in 1989, 1990, and 1991.[16] Soviet military expenditures dropped from $350 billion in 1988 to $60 billion in 1992.[17] The number of tanks produced at Soviet factories plummeted from 1,300 in 1990 to 675 in 1992, artillery production declined from 1,900 to 450, military aircraft production dropped from 600 to 170, and

Soviet Weapons System	1990	1992
Tanks	1,300	675
Artillery	1,900	450
Military Aircraft	600	170
Submarines and Major Combatants	20	8

FIGURE 4.1 Soviet production of selected weapons systems, 1990 and 1992.[18]

submarines and major surface combatant production decreased from 20 to 8 (Figure 4.1). In addition, the Soviet defense industrial base lost two significant capabilities to Ukraine with the dissolution of the Soviet Union: the shipyard at Nikolayev (now Mykolaiv) near the Black Sea and the Antonov production plant in Kyiv.[19]

The collapse of the Soviet industrial base left the United States as the sole remaining superpower. Compared to the U.S. defense budget of $282 billion in 1992, the defense budgets of the United Kingdom ($42 billion), France ($35 billion), and Germany ($33 billion) were tiny. So were those of Japan ($36 billion) and China ($22 billion).[20] The United States was the sole remaining superpower, and its 1992 defense budget of $282 billion was still larger than the defense budgets of all major powers *combined* (Figure 4.2).[21] The United States was now clearly the world's only superpower.

The U.S. military's rapid defeat of Iraqi forces during the First Gulf War also had a profound impact on foreign leaders.[22] For example, Chinese leaders were acutely aware that the PLA military was woefully unprepared should war arise. Desert Storm made the gap clear. China lacked sophisticated technology and, as Chinese leader Jiang Zemin warned in March 1991 in a quote borrowed from Stalin, "[B]ackwards technology means being in a passive position and taking a beating."[23] In December 1992, PLA leadership began a formal analysis of China's military strategy. Within a month, the PLA had established a new strategic guideline that the Central Military Commission adopted in early January 1993. As one PLA leader explained, China's goal would be "winning local wars that may occur under modern technology, especially under high-technology conditions."[24]

Country	GDP (Billions of Dollars)	Defense Budget (Billions of Dollars)
United States	$5,946	$282
United Kingdom	$1,048	$42
France	$1,271	$35
Japan	$3,666	$36
Russia	$400[1]	$47[2]
China	$434[3]	$22[4]
Germany	$1,775	$33

FIGURE 4.2 GDP and defense expenditures of the major powers, 1992.[25]

Notes: [1] Represents gross national product.
[2] Represents defense expenditures. Russia's 1992 official defense budget was $40 billion.
[3] Represents gross national product.
[4] Represents defense expenditures. China's 1992 official defense budget was $7 billion.

Yet precisely because of the preponderance of U.S. power and the collapse of the Soviet Union, the U.S. defense budget—and defense industry—were now in jeopardy. That was the reality of a peacetime environment.

During the 1992 presidential election campaign, Bill Clinton outlined a plan called "New Covenant" to establish a "leaner" government. One component was slashing the defense budget. On December 12, 1991, for example, Clinton gave a speech at Georgetown University arguing, "[W]e can and must substantially reduce our military forces and spending, because the Soviet threat is decreasing and our allies are able to and should shoulder more of the defense burden."[26] The United States still faced a range of threats, such as disorder in the Soviet Union, weapons of mass destruction, tensions in the Korean Peninsula and Middle East, and instability in Yugoslavia. But the main U.S. global competitor was now a shell of itself. Clinton proposed cutting defense spending by over a third by 1997.[27] "The end of the Cold War," he reiterated at the Democratic National Convention in July 1992, "permits us to reduce defense spending... [and] plow back every dollar in defense cuts into building American jobs right here at home."[28]

Clinton's secretary of defense, Les Aspin, and deputy secretary of defense, William Perry, began implementing a major defense cut and urging a consolidation of the defense industry. One of the most important drivers of the cuts was the administration's Bottom-Up Review, which was led by John Deutch, undersecretary of defense for acquisition and technology, and Bill Lynn, director of program analysis and evaluation at the Pentagon, among others. The main objective of the Bottom-Up Review was to fundamentally reexamine U.S. defense strategy, plans, force structure, modernization, and programs following the dissolution of the Soviet Union. The review noted that the United States needed to move away from a defense strategy focused on countering a global Soviet threat to fighting and winning two major regional conflicts, against Iraq and North Korea. A decrease in the threat environment meant a smaller force structure (including cuts to the active-duty forces of the army, navy, and air force); a reduction in military headquarters, bases, and other defense infrastructure; decreases in civilian personnel levels; and ultimately a smaller defense budget. The military also no longer needed the same number of systems and platforms—such as aircraft, ships, and main battle tanks—required during the Cold War. Overall, the Bottom-Up Reviewed estimated that the Defense Department would save nearly $100 billion between 1995 and 1999 because of these adjustments.[29]

For Deutch, there were three motivating factors for consolidation: the main U.S. adversary was now gone, there would consequently be a major decline in the defense budget, and the Pentagon could not afford such a large defense industrial base.[30] There were other financial concerns, including budget deficits. By the mid- and late 1980s, Congress had been putting pressure on the White House to balance the nation's budget. Senators Phil Gramm (R-TX), Warren Rudman (R-NH), and Fritz Hollings (D-SC) spearheaded two major balanced budget acts that set annual targets for the deficit and required spending cuts if projected deficits exceeded them.

Deutch concluded that if the industrial base was properly sized during the 1980s, when there was heightened competition with the Soviets, the defense industry had to decrease by as much as 40 percent in the 1990s to keep up with declining defense budgets. It was therefore necessary to decrease defense assets in both private and public sectors.

The Department of Defense would concentrate on decreasing physical assets, such as property, equipment, and production factories. "If assets were not reduced," Deutch argued, "smaller defense budgets would mean unit costs would rise, inevitably placing downward pressure on profit margins available to industry." And "if returns on capital reasoned," he reasoned, defense companies that were "essential to a strong defense infrastructure would be in trouble, and this was not in the interest of the nation, [Department of Defense], or stockholders."[31] Consequently, the Pentagon began four rounds of closures to bases and government-owned shipyards, weapons depots, and laboratories as part of the Base Reduction and Consolidation process. Despite supporting the need to save money, various members of Congress still fought these closures, especially in their own districts, because they translated into fewer jobs. Nevertheless, the Pentagon aided workers in the defense sector by assisting with the adjustment costs of consolidation, which opponents often referred to as "payoffs for layoffs."[32]

With the Defense Department focused on slashing the defense budget and cutting its physical assets, Pentagon leaders also set in motion a major consolidation of the private sector.

On May 18, 1993, Aspin welcomed roughly two dozen chief executive officers of the largest U.S. defense companies to a secretive—and cryptic—dinner at the Pentagon. "I received an invitation to the dinner," said Norm Augustine, who found himself seated next to Les Aspin in room 3E912 in the Pentagon.[33] Augustine joked that in the peacetime environment after the Cold War, the industry's new strategy for survival was "Mutual Assured Starvation." He explained, "There may only be one airplane, but everyone will share in it: Company A will build the vertical tail, Company B the left horizontal tail, Company C the right horizontal tail, and so forth."[34] Augustine then asked Aspin the question that was on everyone's mind: "Les, this is awfully nice of you to invite us all to dinner, but why are we here?"

"Well, in about 15 minutes, you're going to find out," Aspin responded. "You probably aren't going to like it."[35]

After dinner, the group assembled in a room next to the secretary of defense's office. Aspin welcomed everyone and then turned to Perry to

		Number of Suppliers	
		Current	Future
Aircraft	Bombers	3	1
	Fighters	5	2.5
	Helicopters	4	2
Space	Ballistic Missile Defense	6	2
	Expendable Launch Vehicles	3	2
	Satellites	5	2.5
	Rocket Motors	5	2
Shipbuilding	Aircraft Carriers	1	1
	Submarines	2	1
	Surface Combatants	5	2
	Auxiliary/Amphibious	7	3
	Shipyards	8	4
Tracked Vehicles	Tanks	1	1
	Armored Personnel Carriers	2	1
Missiles	Strategic	1	1
	Tactical	8	4

FIGURE 4.3 Department of Defense industrial base review, 1993.[36]

walk through a presentation on a screen at the front of the room. With the end of the Cold War, Perry argued, there was a "peace dividend" that provided the government an opportunity to cut defense spending and divert those funds to domestic programs.[37]

"The budget was not only down," Perry explained, "it was going to go down further."[38]

He then showed a chart listing major areas of the defense sector—such as aircraft, space, shipbuilding, tracked vehicles, and missiles—and outlined roughly how many specific types of platforms and systems the Department of Defense would be able to keep in business with a declining budget.[39] For example, the chart showed that the number of companies making bombers needed to decrease from three to one, helicopters from four to two, ballistic missile defense from six to two, surface combatants from five to two, and tactical missiles from eight to four (Figure 4.3).

It was a grim chart. Perry told the group that the government had no intention of paying for rising overhead costs as their factories disappeared, particularly if companies attempted to preserve their headquarters and corporate aircraft fleets.[40] Indeed, it made little sense to have companies in a peacetime environment with half-full factories, insufficient funds to invest in research and development, massive overhead, and high costs.[41] Yet it also made little sense for Pentagon officials to engineer consolidation of the industry, Perry said. That decision would be up to each CEO, board, and shareholders, who were in a much better position to decide what was best for their company. The market would determine the shape and scale of defense consolidation. At the end of the meeting Perry summed up the Pentagon's message to industry: "There are too many companies.... We can't afford it. But we aren't going to decide which companies have to go. You need to decide that."[42]

Augustine's jaw dropped: "I was stunned, for really two reasons. One, it pointed to how fragile our defense industrial base was going to become. But there was another factor that to me was also important, that in those areas there would not be competition. I happen to be a strong believer in competition. The free enterprise system, I think, has served our country well. And apparently we were in such a financial position where we weren't going to be able to afford that in some areas."[43]

Augustine turned to the executives on his right and left and said, "One of us is not going to be here next year."[44] A few days later, a newspaper reporter asked Augustine for a comment about the mysterious dinner. "It was the Last Supper," he blurted out.[45] And so the name stuck.

Companies were not entirely on their own. Undersecretary Deutch introduced a series of rules for sharing savings from consolidation between the Pentagon and industry. In addition, the Defense Science Board created a task force to address the antitrust issues raised by defense consolidation.[46] Still, companies had several choices in this market: buy other firms to grab a larger share of a shrinking defense market, diversify by adding or expanding their commercial business side, sell off many of their defense companies and assets since they were generating a high cash value, or leave the defense business altogether and focus on the commercial sector.

Nearly all the diversified Fortune 500 firms—including IBM, General Electric, General Motors, Ford, Chrysler, Honeywell, Texas Instruments, and Westinghouse—sold their defense subsidiaries and exited the defense industry because of what they saw as a declining market. So did a chunk of high-technology companies, such as California Microwave, GTE, IBM, Lucent, Magnavox, and Phillips. The primary buyers were those firms more dependent on defense. Other high-technology companies, such as Hewlett Packard, 3-M, and Corning, declined to participate in key defense research and development projects, though they continued to sell their commercial products to the Defense Department. They were generally turned off by the complexity of U.S. government acquisition rules, including excessive regulation, specialized accounting, and propriety rights.[47]

Under Augustine's leadership, Martin Marietta started making deals—eventually combining all or part of 17 major companies. Augustine's company bought the defense and space business of General Electric Aerospace Company and General Dynamics Corporation's rocket division. "We had a three-ring binder with an overview of potential companies to buy," he said. "Our goal was to buy healthy companies and pay a fair price."[48] General Electric Aerospace merged with Martin Marietta. In 1995, Martin Marietta merged with Lockheed, which itself had acquired General Dynamics' jet fighter division. The new mammoth defense company, Lockheed Martin, then bought the defense business of Loral Corporation, a collection of military contracting firms assembled over the years by Wall Street dealmaker Bernard Schwartz. Lockheed Martin's acquisition of Loral established it as the world's largest defense electronics firm, one of the few growing areas of military contracting. While only 1 percent of U.S. defense contracts were devoted to electronics during World War I, and 10 percent during World War II, the number grew to 35 percent during the Vietnam War and 45 percent by 1997.[49]

During this wild merger period, a fake press release made its way around the Washington, DC, defense community. It announced that one of the next consolidation dominoes would be Lockheed Martin's acquisition of the U.S. Air Force. When asked by a senior Department of Defense official to comment on the press release, Augustine quipped,

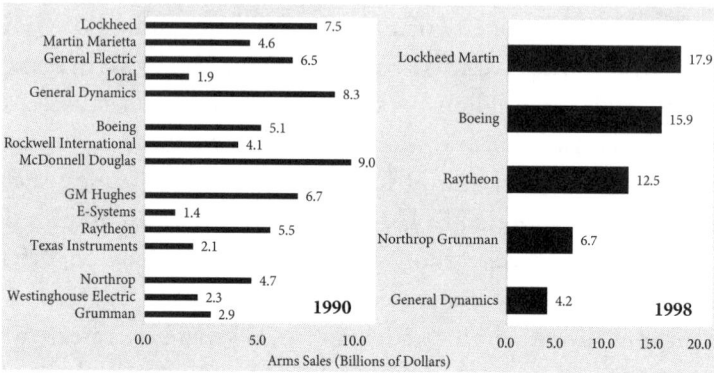

FIGURE 4.4 Example of the consolidation of the U.S. defense industry in the 1990s.[50]

"We looked into the possibility, but your present owner has too much debt on the books."[51]

Augustine wasn't the only aggressive buyer. Boeing bought Rockwell's aerospace and defense units in 1996 and then merged with McDonnell Douglas in 1997 to become a behemoth. Raytheon gobbled up Dallas-based E-systems in 1995, Texas Instruments' defense business (including its Paveway missiles) in 1997, and Hughes Aircraft Company (including its Maverick missiles) from General Motors in 1997. Northrop bought Grumman Aerospace in 1994 and the defense division of Westinghouse Electric Corporation in 1996 to become Northrop Grumman.

By the end of the 1990s, several giants dominated the U.S. defense industrial base—Boeing, Lockheed Martin, Raytheon, and Northrop Grumman—along with several other major players, such as General Dynamics and Litton (Figure 4.4).[52] Consolidation was inevitable after the Last Supper. Defense companies saw 50 percent of their market disappear by 1997, and defense procurement decreased by 60 percent in constant dollars between 1989 and 1997. Only about one-quarter of the 120,000 companies that once supplied the Department of Defense served in that capacity. The others shut down their defense lines of business or dissolved altogether.[53] In addition, the Department of Defense cut back on federal funding for defense research and development.[54] So did companies. Between 1994 and 1999, the percentage of sales on independent research and development by defense firms decreased from 4.1 to 2.9. Since sales were declining rapidly, total independent research and development was a smaller percentage of a smaller number.[55]

The defense industry borrowed money to make these acquisitions, and its collective debt level rose dramatically, from $15 billion in 1993 to $43 billion in 1999. In the second quarter of 2000, for example, Lockheed Martin had a debt-to-equity ratio of 175 percent because of the large number of acquisitions it made during the consolidation period. The debt-to-equity ratio represents the amount of long-term debt a company uses to finance its assets relative to the value of shareholders' equity. During the same period, Lockheed Martin's bond rating fell from A to BBB–, and Raytheon's went from AA to BBB–.[56] The defense industry consolidations also had a major impact on employment, which fell by half a million people between 1990 and 1995.[57]

The U.S. military services took a huge hit as well. The navy reduced its fleet size from 550 ships in 1987 to just over 320 by 1999. Many surface ships were mothballed in the mid-1990s before the end of their scheduled service lives.[58] The air force cut back from 37 wings to 12 active fighter-wing equivalents. It sent a growing number of aircraft to storage at Davis-Monthan Air Force Base in the Arizona desert—appropriately named "the boneyard"—well before the end of their combat service.[59] Overall, the procurement of major weapons systems—including ships, aircraft, and tanks—declined dramatically.[60] Between 1990 and 2000, the number of companies that produced weapons systems dropped from 8 to 3 for aircraft, from 8 to 3 for surface ships, from 13 to 3 for tactical missiles, and from 6 to 3 for tactical wheeled vehicles (Figure 4.5).[61]

Eventually, the consolidation of the U.S. defense industry slowed down. The Departments of Justice and Defense became increasingly worried about the creation of defense monopolies and anticompetitive practices. The quintessential example was Secretary of Defense Bill Cohen's decision to block a merger between Lockheed Martin and Northrop Grumman. "I had a handshake deal with Kent Kresa at Northrop," said Augustine. Kresa was the CEO of Northrop and a former employee of DARPA. With Perry's support, Lockheed and Northrop began developing plans for the merger. But in 1998,

Platform	Number of Companies (1990)	Number of Companies (2000)
Fixed-wing Aircraft	8	3
Launch Vehicles	6	3
Rotorcraft	4	3
Satellites	8	6
Strategic Missiles	3	2
Submarines	2	2
Surface Ships	8	3
Tactical Missiles	13	3
Tactical Wheeled Vehicles	6	3
Tracked Combat Vehicles	3	2

FIGURE 4.5 Number of U.S. companies for selected military platforms, 1990 and 2000.[62]

Department of Defense officials invited Lockheed and Northrop senior executives to the Pentagon, where top Justice and Defense officials explained that they were going to kill the deal; there were too many antitrust concerns.[63] Sure enough, in March 1998 the Justice Department sued Lockheed to stop its proposed $11 billion acquisition of Northrop Grumman, which Lockheed eventually abandoned.[64]

Led by Cohen, senior Department of Defense officials worried that the Lockheed-Northrop merger would stifle competition for critical systems and components in such areas as radar for military aircraft, sonar for surface ships and submarines, and electronic warfare systems. Attorney General Janet Reno announced, "This merger would cost the taxpayer and take the competitive wind out of the sails of innovation in the production of many critical systems that protect our fighting men and women."[65] While understandable in many respects, it was a shock to Lockheed and Northrop executives who had spent countless hours and conducted thousands of meetings on a deal that had been blessed by the Pentagon. The Defense and Justice decision to kill the Lockheed-Northrop merger was not an isolated incident. In 2001, for example, General Dynamics canceled its $2.1 billion merger agreement with Newport News Shipbuilding after the Justice Department sued to block the acquisition. General Dynamics, which had already bought the Electric Boat nuclear submarine facility, was the only other shipyard capable of building nuclear submarines.[66]

By the end of the decade, Wall Street had pummeled defense companies because of the declining number of mergers and acquisitions, low profits, and high debt problems. Lockheed Martin's stock price plummeted from nearly $60 per share in mid-1998 to under $20 in the closing days of 1999. Boeing lost a third of its market value between April and September 1998. Raytheon's stock plummeted 43 percent in one day during the fall of 1999. Northrop Grumman ended the decade trading at $59 a share, far below the $139 it reached in early 1998.[67] As a blistering *Wall Street Journal* article concluded in December 1999, "Some of the defense industry's biggest players, including Lockheed Martin and Raytheon, are struggling. Eight years of consolidation has left these companies with large debt loads, low stock prices and weak earnings. Pentagon and industry officials have questioned whether these weakened giants can make the necessary research investments to maintain a U.S. technological edge."[68]

The decade after the Last Supper was a roller-coaster ride for the defense industrial base, and there were numerous questions about the wisdom of defense consolidation.

The list of grievances was long. Some protested that Pentagon leaders should have prevented some of the large primes from gobbling up mid-size defense companies.[69] More defense firms would have increased competition and innovation. Perry even had second thoughts. "The trend toward fewer and larger prime contractors has the potential to affect innovation, limit the supply base, pose entry barriers to small, medium, and large businesses, and ultimately reduce competition—resulting in higher prices to be paid by the American taxpayer," he concluded. "We would have been better off with more, smaller firms than with a few large ones."[70] Others criticized Pentagon leaders for failing to inform companies when consolidation was over. Lockheed was blindsided by the Pentagon's decision to block the Lockheed-Northrop merger with little warning. As Deutch lamented, "The absence of a clear signal ending the consolidation policy is unfortunate because it left several defense firms stranded on a different course."[71]

Still others believed that the Pentagon underestimated the value of stock prices and the financial impact on defense companies, which were saddled with a mountain of debt and little or no ability to surge production in the future. As John Hamre, who was deputy secretary of defense from 1997 to 1999, noted:

> The immediate problem with consolidation was that we had to monetize 'good will' on the books of companies that were sold. Good will is the difference between what the stock price says the company is worth, and what the tangible asset value of the company is worth. Suddenly, companies were sold, and that good will had to be borne by the acquiring companies as debt. This forced a ruthless process of cutting any costs that the government would not allow in forward pricing rates. So we eliminated a lot of production capacity.[72]

By 2000, the U.S. defense industrial base was in turmoil. The assets of numerous defense companies significantly decreased, profit margins declined, debt rose, and government outlays were still flat for defense investments. The result for many of these companies was a decline in earnings, credit ratings, cash flow, and profitability. Both companies and talented workers fled the defense sector, and those companies that remained had to reduce expenditures on internal research and development and other efforts to innovate.[73]

However, the biggest problem was not consolidation. Instead, it was the creeping regulations in U.S. acquisition policy, which impacted the timelines for major programs. A Department of Defense Inspector General report at the end of the decade concluded that the timelines for major defense acquisition programs had notably increased. In 1960, a typical acquisition took seven years (or 84 months) from beginning the research and development to achieving initial operating capability. By 1996, a similar acquisition took 11 years (or 132 months) from start to finish.[74] U.S. acquisition policies gutted any incentives for defense companies to retain surge capacity for a war. "We adopted 'lowest cost, technically compliant' as the guiding principle," said Hamre. "Primes and suppliers would not get paid for retaining surge capacity—unused tooling, unused factory spaces. Defense companies had to defend margins in order to support stock prices and bond ratings. So any infrastructure not immediately tied to revenue contracts was eliminated."[75]

While there are legitimate questions about how consolidation occurred during the 1990s, the reality is that it was necessary, though imperfect in its implementation. The United States was in a peacetime environment following the collapse of the Soviet Union. The unipolar moment had arrived. There was no longer a need for a large defense budget and, consequently, no need for as many companies to produce airplanes, ships, tanks, and other systems. The U.S. military also had a huge stockpile of relatively modern weapons and did not need to buy more for at least a decade or two.[76] Consolidation saved the government money, including $3 billion alone from Lockheed Martin.[77] As Augustine put it, "Les [Aspin], Bill [Perry], and John [Deutch] had it right, given the public's unwillingness to support high defense spending under the then prevailing geopolitical circumstances. But next time I am invited to dinner at the Pentagon, I hope they provide Rolaids along with the dessert."[78]

The United States seemed invincible. What could go wrong? It turned out that no one had bothered to tell Osama bin Laden and his small band of al-Qa'ida terrorists, who took aim directly at the U.S. homeland.

5

Drone Warfare and the Legacy of 9/11

Yes, we have slain a large dragon, but we live now in a jungle filled with a bewildering variety of poisonous snakes. And in many ways the dragon was easier to keep track of.
—Jim Woolsey, CIA director

My golden rule is to always buy straw hats in the winter.
—Neal Blue, CEO of General Atomics

THE CIA AND U.S. MILITARY had a hot lead on Taliban leader Mullah Muhammad Omar.[1] It was October 7, 2001, one month after the al-Qa'ida terrorist attacks in the United States. A sleek 27-foot-long MQ-1 Predator drone with the tail number 3034, designed and produced by General Atomics, was tracking a convoy of three vehicles and motorcycles moving toward the Afghan city of Kandahar on a clear, starlit night.[2]

"The convoy profile fits Taliban leadership, Sir," said Brigadier General Jeff Kimmons to General Tommy Franks, the head of U.S. Central Command. They were sitting in the sensitive compartmented information facility at U.S. Central Command headquarters in Tampa, Florida, which had a video link to Predators flying in Afghanistan.

A duty officer from the CIA's Directorate of Operations then piped in from CIA headquarters, which also had a video link. "General," he said, "this target has all the characteristics of a leadership convoy. You have armed lead and trail vehicles. And the pickup in the middle is a dual cab. That could be Mullah Omar's personal vehicle."[3]

The Predator flying over the target was different from previous ones flown in Bosnia, Kosovo, Afghanistan, and other countries by the CIA and U.S. military. It was armed with two air-to-surface, 30-pound Hellfire missiles.[4] Secretary of Defense Donald Rumsfeld and CIA Director George Tenet had agreed that U.S. Central Command retained operational control over CIA activities in Afghanistan and the broader theater of war, including this Predator.[5] Captain Scott Swanson was the pilot in command of the Predator and sat in a ground control station in a parking lot at CIA headquarters in Virginia. He was supported by Master Sergeant Jeff Guay, the sensor operator, who handled the targeting laser.[6] They were operating under a sensitive CIA covert action program that was hunting al-Qa'ida, Taliban, and other targets in Afghanistan.

The convoy arrived at 4:35 a.m. in Kandahar City and sped through its vacant streets. The vehicles suddenly stopped at a series of two- and three-story buildings and mud-block walled compounds. Several silhouetted figures slipped into one of the compounds, and U.S. officials decided to pounce.

"Valid target for Hellfire," said Navy Captain Shelly Young, U.S. Central Command's senior Judge Advocate General, who concluded it was legal to fire.[7]

But they waited too long. U.S. Air Force General John Jumper, who was watching the events unfold from a Predator link in the Pentagon, was apoplectic. "What are they waiting on?"[8] The darkened figures jumped back into their vehicles carrying several large containers, likely shoulder-fired missiles. Roughly an hour later the convoy stopped again, at a compound that included a courtyard and several buildings. CIA and military officials vehemently disagreed on whether there was a mosque at the compound.[9] The Predator had less than an hour left of fuel to stay on the target, and Franks had an idea.

"Can you take out one of the sedans parked near the wall?" Franks inquired. "Maybe that will persuade the people to leave the mosque and give us a shot at the principals."[10]

Back at CIA, Swanson, the Predator pilot, needed to move the drone into position to fire the missiles. After he was cleared to fire, Swanson took a deep breath and whispered under his breath, "Oh Lord, please don't let me screw up."[11]

"Ten, nine, eight," Swanson announced. "Two, one, launch!" Swanson pulled the trigger on his joystick, and the Predator launched a Hellfire missile.[12]

"Weapon away," he said. It was then up to Guay, the sensor operator, to keep the crosshairs on the target.[13]

For the next 20 seconds, everyone held their breath, then there was a blinding flash of light on their video screens. Swanson watched in disbelief. "The screen was filled by a bright white bloom of light," he recalled. "As the bloom dissipated, we saw an object move quickly across the screen, flailing like a ragdoll tossed in the air. It was a body, twisting and contorting and glowing from the heat of the blast."[14] Luminous figures then began streaming out of the building and running in all directions, seemingly unaware they had been hit from a drone loitering overhead. Those images would forever remain burned into Swanson's memory.[15]

It was a remarkable moment in the history of the U.S. defense industrial base: the first strike *ever* in combat by a U.S. drone.[16] The peacetime environment of the 1990s and the legacy of the Last Supper had partially shifted to a wartime environment against terrorist groups. Unlike World War II and the Cold War, however, the U.S. government focused on developing and producing systems and platforms to fight terrorist groups—not great powers. While the defense budget temporarily increased, the urgency from the government was to produce mine-resistant ambush-protected (MRAP) vehicles, technology and systems to counter roadside bombs, and drones—not major platforms for great power war. Perhaps the preeminent example was the General Atomics MQ-1 Predator.

Much like in previous decades, the research, development, and production of the Predator came from a synergy between the private sector and the government. Engineers and business leaders—such as Neal and Linden Blue, Abe Karem, and General Atomics engineer Tom Cassidy—were instrumental in creating and shaping the design and production of drones. A range of individuals at CIA and the Department of Defense—such as CIA Director Jim Woolsey, Under Secretary of Defense John Deutch, and personnel in the U.S. Air Force's Big

Safari office—recognized the importance of drones, outlined requirements, provided the key elixir (money), and developed new concepts of operation.

But the research, development, and eventually production of the Predator did not happen overnight.

One of the earliest examples of drone research and development was the Kettering Bug during World War I. Developed by Charles Kettering and built by Dayton-Wright Airplane Company in Dayton, Ohio, the Kettering Bug was designed to take off from a dolly-and-track system and strike ground targets up to 75 miles away. But it was never used during the war, in part because U.S. officials were skeptical about its reliability when carrying explosives over Allied forces.[17] During World War II, the U.S. Army Air Forces converted some worn-out B-17s and B-24s, armed with weapons, into automatically piloted aircraft that could crash into targets. "If you can get mechanical machines to do this," said Hap Arnold, commanding general of U.S. Army Air Forces, "you are saving lives at the outset."[18] However, this use of an aircraft made it much closer to a missile than a drone like the Predator, which could loiter over targets, collect intelligence, and strike if required.

Top-secret research and design efforts continued during the 1950s and 1960s. U.S. Strategic Air Command used the Lightning Bug, developed and produced by Ryan Aeronautical, to collect intelligence on Chinese air defenses, China's nuclear program (Beijing detonated its first nuclear weapon in October 1964), and other targets. But the early versions of the Lightning Bug were largely a bust. One assessment concluded, "The unit's initial performance was dismal. . . . Numerous single-point failures haunted drone operations. The first seven missions resulted in only two reels of film and a number of lost air vehicles, with most flights demonstrating poor navigational accuracy. Drone damage on recovery was a persistent problem. Very quickly the unit was down to a few operating air vehicles and the program was in trouble."[19]

Around this time, Kelly Johnson and his team at Lockheed Skunk Works proposed an offshoot of the SR-71 Blackbird, a drone called D-21, for reconnaissance missions over China.[20] It was 44 feet long, looked like an oversized manta ray, could reach speeds around Mach 4 (over 3,000 miles per hour), and was launched by a specially designed Boeing B-52 bomber. The D-21 had the lowest radar cross section of any platform ever constructed at Skunk Works.[21] In all, Lockheed produced 38 D-21 and D-21B drones, and the air force flew several of them over China to photograph the Lop Nor nuclear test site.[22] But the Department of Defense ultimately canceled the program because of the D-21's exorbitant costs, repeated technological challenges, a fatal accident in February 1965 following a collision with an M-12 high-altitude aircraft, and the government's growing use of satellites for imagery collection.[23] In one of the more lighthearted moments in the history of the program, a D-21 experienced a guidance failure in November 1969 that kept it flying across China until it ran out of fuel and crashed in Siberia. The KGB eventually seized the drone—or what was left of it. Several years later, a CIA agent visiting Skunk Works plopped a panel on the desk of Ben Rich, who had taken over for Johnson.

"Ben, do you recognize this?" he asked, with a smile.

"Sure I do," Rich replied, identifying it as a panel from the D-21's engine mount. "Where did you get it?"

"Believe it or not, I got it as a Christmas gift from a Soviet KGB agent," responded the CIA case officer. "He told me this piece was found by a shepherd in Soviet Siberia."[24]

Despite the D-21's failures, the United States eventually employed drones on the battlefield during the Vietnam War for limited missions, such as bomb damage assessment and other reconnaissance missions. One study concluded, "Drone operations in the Vietnam War proved to be a valuable complement to Air Force manned tactical reconnaissance assets, providing information impractical to get using manned platforms."[25] The United States and other countries, such as Israel, also used drones as decoys. Unmanned research and development programs continued during the 1970s and 1980s. One of the most interesting was the Boeing Condor, which was made of carbon-fiber materials and had an astonishing 200-foot wingspan (twice the length of the Lockheed U-2). Supported by the U.S. Navy and DARPA, Boeing designed the Condor as a long-endurance, high-altitude drone, though the Department of Defense ultimately canceled the program because of high costs.[26]

There were several key takeaways from this early period of drone research and development. First, there were clear champions in the military, CIA, and industry for drone research and development. As early as 1956, Air Force Major General David Baker remarked, "We can readily see that except for certain types of missions, the manned combat aircraft will become technically obsolete in the future." But he added a caveat: "[W]e cannot predict the time at which this will happen. In the interim we must continue to advance as rapidly as possible in the quality of our manned aircraft."[27] Second, there were still huge downsides. One was the exorbitant cost of drone programs. In 1975, for instance, the army awarded Lockheed a contract to design a drone for artillery targeting, called the MQM-105 Aquila, but canceled the program after spending $1 billion for little in return.[28] In addition, drones usually underperformed, especially compared to manned aircraft and stand-off weapons like cruise missiles.[29] Finally, the necessary technologies to produce drones at scale—such as composite materials, microprocessors, and digital flight controls—had not been invented or were far too expensive.[30]

Yet drones still had massive potential. It would take a particularly innovative engineer to design a cheap drone that could fly for long periods at high altitudes without crashing. Abe Karem was just the person.

Abraham E. Karem was born in Baghdad, Iraq, on June 27, 1937. After the creation of the state of Israel following World War II, Karem's father moved his wife and four sons—including Abe—to Israel. Karem was obsessed with technology for as long as he could remember. As a child, he tore off the back of a large radio and pulled out each of the vacuum tubes, searching for the mysterious voice speaking from inside the device. He was destined to be an engineer. "What motivates me from the time I was a kid—call it technology, call it whatever—it was play. By the age of eight, I knew I'm going to be a mechanical engineer. And oh my God, by the age of 13 or 14, I fell in love with aeronautics. At 14, I started building model aircraft. Within two years, I was the instructor in the [high school] aero club."[31]

He graduated from Technion, the Israel Institute of Technology in the coastal city of Haifa, with an aeronautical engineering degree and joined the Israeli Air Force in 1961. He then worked at Israel Aircraft Industries (later called Israel Aerospace Industries), which designed and produced military and commercial aircraft for the Israeli government. Karem rapidly moved his way up the corporate ladder. He was bright, but could also be arrogant, implacable, and sometimes excruciatingly difficult to get along with. "He was known as a brilliant engineer," one study summed up, "but he was also known for *knowing* he was a brilliant engineer."[32] He was fiercely independent and detested working for others, especially those he considered inferior to him in technological prowess and acumen.

In early 1974, Karem left Israel Aircraft Industries and started his own company, Matos ("aircraft" in Hebrew), to design, develop, and produce drones and other aircraft. His departure from Israel Aircraft Industries was one of the first indicators of his maverick streak, but it also highlighted that he was a much better engineer than a businessman. Over the next three years, he made exactly *zero* sales to the Israeli Air Force. It didn't help that his former employer had vowed to destroy his business. "Abe, we all love you," said a vice president from Israel Aircraft Industries before Karem departed. "We owe you a lot. But we had a meeting about you forming your own company, and we decided we are going to crush you."[33]

With no sales and few prospects, a frustrated Karem and his wife, Dina, picked up and left for the United States. Karem initially accepted a position with a small defense company in Los Angeles named Developmental Sciences, which was doing work for DARPA. But the unbridled Karem needed to run his own company, so he quit and founded Leading Systems. Karem's company would initially be headquartered at his home—his garage, to be precise—so he needed to go house hunting. Dina quickly realized they had very different priorities. "I'm looking for a house with a garage attached," she told him. "You're looking for a garage with a house attached."[34] The couple found a garage Abe liked, attached to a house that Dina wanted, in Hacienda Heights, a suburb east of Los Angeles. The garage had 600 square feet of floor space, which by 1981 was stuffed with tools, computers, and handmade molds to fabricate aircraft parts from lightweight composites such as fiberglass and carbon epoxy.[35]

Leading Systems produced a drone named Albatross, which was intended to be a technology demonstrator. Karem borrowed money from his family to develop and build the first prototype, which cost less than $100,000.[36] It weighed a mere 200 pounds; was made mostly of mahogany plywood, spruce, urethane foam, and fiberglass; and could carry a camera in its nose. DARPA funded the Albatross's flight tests, in part because the aircraft could stay aloft for a stunning 56 hours.[37] The drone's exceptional performance led DARPA in 1985 to contract with Leading Systems to develop a larger endurance drone. Named Amber, it cost roughly $300,000 to build (still a meager price compared to some drone programs that cost well over 100 times that amount), was radio controlled, and could be configured to take off and land like conventional aircraft or fold its wings and stabilizers for launch by rocket from a canister.[38] It could also stay aloft for more than 30 hours and land safely, which piqued the interest of the CIA.[39] Karem built a conventional runway-launched version of Amber, called GNAT-750, that was bigger, heavier, and less capable than Amber, with a two-stroke Rotax 532 engine.[40]

By 1988, Karem had high hopes for selling large numbers of Amber drones to the U.S. Navy. But neither the navy nor any other military service was ultimately interested in purchasing Ambers. At the time, Congress froze funding for drone programs and created the Joint Program Office to consolidate drone development. DARPA transferred Amber to the office, which promptly canceled it.[41] It didn't help that Karem's business acumen had not improved. "I could not control Abe Karem," complained Lieutenant Colonel Joseph Thomas, a marine corps aviator who oversaw the Amber program for the Joint Program Office. "I couldn't control Abe's burn rate, and I was running out of money."[42]

Navy personnel also found Karem difficult to work with. According to Frank Pace, his deputy at Leading Systems, Karem refused to partner with anyone, including a larger company. "He didn't really want to team," said Pace. "He didn't want anybody to tell him what to do."[43] In September 1989, Leading Systems owed a bank loan of almost $5 million, which Karem couldn't pay, and Leading Systems filed for bankruptcy the next month. In November, the Joint Program Office sent the six Ambers to a storage warehouse—more of an aircraft graveyard—at Naval Air Weapons Station China Lake in the western Mojave Desert.[44]

But Karem and Leading Systems were not entirely dead. Neal and Linden Blue, who owned General Atomics, bought the assets of Leading Systems, including its jigs, tooling, and airframes.[45] General Atomics, which had been working on research and development of drones, hired Karem and eight of his workers.[46] It was a gamble for General Atomics to purchase the assets of Leading Systems and merge it with their own drone program. After all, the military and Congress had little appetite to fund drone programs, as the recent experience with Amber indicated. But Neal Blue had a hunch that the time would soon be ripe for drones.

"My golden rule is to always buy straw hats in the winter," he said. It sure looked like winter in 1991, but Neal and Linden Blue's gamble would eventually pay off.

In early 1993, Linden Blue's phone rang. It was Jim Woolsey, director of Central Intelligence, who asked whether General Atomics could work with the CIA to develop an advanced version of Amber.

"Jim, we'll give you whatever you need," said Blue.[47]

Blue's gamble of buying straw hats—or drones, in this case—when few wanted them now looked like a brilliant move. The Balkans had erupted into war following the breakup of Yugoslavia. The United States and other NATO countries initiated a series of air missions—such as Operation Sky Monitor and Operation Deny Flight—to enforce compliance of a series of no-fly zones following allegations of Serbian war crimes. But the United States had a significant information gap that frustrated President Bill Clinton. U.S. intelligence agencies had a difficult time finding Serbian artillery used to bomb civilians in Sarajevo, including through a combination of U.S. satellites (which were limited to only a few minutes each day), human spies, and manned surveillance aircraft.[48] General Atomics had what the CIA wanted: a drone that could potentially loiter over targets for prolonged periods and conduct intelligence, reconnaissance, and surveillance missions. And the Blue brothers could not have been happier.

Neal and Linden Blue were the sons of a real estate investor, James E. Blue, and the state's first female treasurer, Virginia Neal Blue. Their parents were active Republicans with strong pro-business and anticommunist views, as well as a flare for adventure. Between his sophomore and junior years at Yale, Neal went on a 10-week, 17-country trek to Europe and Asia to interview people living near the Iron Curtain. Neal and three other Yale students—George Morgan Browne Jr., Charles White Trippe, and Henry G. Von Maur—documented their travels in a series of colorful dispatches published in the *New York Times*.[49] Among the most interesting adventures was in Afghanistan and Pakistan, countries where—a half century later—the brothers' MQ-1 Predator would conduct the first U.S. drone strike. "A few miles from the highway, the tightly knit tribes are extremely powerful," Neal and his travel companions wrote in one *New York Times* travel log. "Even in the larger cities such as Peshawar, the tribesmen stroll through the streets carrying rifles. A glance at their long knives and war axes made it easy to believe their reputation as among the fiercest warriors in the world."[50]

As teenagers, Neal and Linden flew a tiny plane over the Andes, a daring feat that earned them the cover of *Life* magazine with the title "The Flying Blue Brothers."[51] Their company, General Atomics, was remarkably innovative. Unlike most defense companies, which were publicly owned and beholden to shareholders, General Atomics was privately held. "It allowed us to be quicker and spend more money on independent research and development than other companies, not just focus on the bottom line," explained Linden.[52] It also helped that two of their main customers were willing to move fast. One was the CIA, which bought several GNAT-750s and used them in Bosnia in 1993 and 1994.[53] The other was a highly classified, quick-reaction aircraft modification program named "Big Safari," which was located at Wright-Patterson Air Force Base in Ohio. While the military services and much of the Pentagon often moved glacially slowly on new defense programs, the CIA and Big Safari had minimal oversight, limited paperwork, and a strong desire to quickly produce platforms for operational use. "Their willingness to move fast was essential to innovation," said Neal.[54]

It also helped that the program had two major backers in the Pentagon. One was Admiral David Jeremiah, vice chairman of the Joint Chiefs of Staff, who supported drone research, development, and production—despite skepticism from the air force and navy.[55] Another was John Deutch, under secretary of defense for acquisition and technology. "John Deutch was very important to the creation of the Predator," said Neal Blue. "He understood how to work the system. If you were going to do something with unmanned systems, you had to go around the Pentagon bureaucracy."[56] Deutch wanted a drone—or unmanned aerial vehicle (UAV), as it was sometimes called—to fly 500 miles from its launch point, loiter over a target area for at least 24 hours at altitudes between 15,000 and 25,000 feet, carry some 400 to 500 pounds of sensors, and transmit imagery using satellites while airborne.[57] As Deutch lamented at the time:

> No system exists which can provide continuous all-weather coverage of world wide targets. National Sensors cannot provide long dwell coverage of small mobile targets. Existing theater airborne assets are limited by endurance of less than 8–12 hours, limited numbers, and possible loss of aircrew over hostile areas. There is no endurance UAV currently funded. No long range endurance UAV will be available to military commanders until the year 2000. Ground based systems cannot operate in denied and or hostile areas without the possibility of loss or capture of personnel. In order to meet the above requirement, the Joint Staff has identified an urgent need for the capability of an Endurance Unmanned Aerial Vehicle (UAV) system.[58]

The CIA and several offices in the Department of Defense were now in sync in developing and producing a long-range, high-endurance drone. The Blue brothers, Karem, and several others at General Atomics, such as Tom Cassidy, went to work on what would eventually become the Predator. Cassidy was a retired rear admiral who commanded at Top Gun and flew roughly 6,000 hours during his 34-year career in the navy. "Tom Cassidy was invaluable to the development and production of Predator," said Neal Blue. "He was truly innovative in the creation of the Predator."[59]

In just six months, Cassidy, Karem, and others at General Atomics extended the GNAT-750's fuselage and wings, and they installed a new engine. General Atomics also achieved a historic accomplishment: the use of a satellite communications link between the ground station and drone, which gave the GNAT-750 a substantially greater range and payload. It used commercial satellite data links for control and imagery transmission. To make room for the satellite antenna, Karem and other engineers gave the aircraft a nose job, adding a big upward bulge. They also added heavier landing gear and a wing chord that measured 43.25 inches at the root.

In 1994, Karem quit General Atomics after clashing with several of its leaders, including Cassidy.[60] It was time for the maverick to move on. The General Atomics team held a competition among the engineers for the name of the new drone, and Cassidy had the winner: "Predator."[61] It was now time to go public. On October 19, 1994, Tom Brokaw announced on *NBC Evening News* that the U.S. Department of Defense had successfully tested a high-tech unmanned aircraft called the Predator.[62] It was time to go operational.

The United States used Predators extensively in Bosnia and based them out of a remote airfield in Albania. They were flown by a team managed by the navy's Joint Program Office for Unmanned Aerial Vehicles and provided imagery of targets on the ground.[63] Admiral Leighton "Snuffy" Smith, who was commander of U.S. Naval Forces Europe, concluded that "the inherent value of UAVs is the ability to fly in areas where putting manned vehicles would be unacceptable due to risk or operational considerations." He congratulated the Predator team for "extended surveillance of heavy weapons withdrawal from the Sarajevo area, reconnaissance operations during Deliberate Force, and confirmation of warring factions' compliance with UN mandates."[64] The Predator also flew missions in Operation Southern Watch in Iraq in 1998 and Operation Allied Force in Serbia in 1999.

With the CIA and air force demonstrating the value of drones, the logical—though controversial—next step was arming them. In May 2000, Air Force General John Jumper, head of Air Combat Command, announced his decision to weaponize the Predator with the support—if not the prodding—of senior General Atomics executives.[65] As Neal Blue explained, "Tom Cassidy thought it would be useful to arm the Predator and leaned on General Jumper."[66] Initially, Jumper's plan had nothing to do with the CIA's growing intelligence-collection campaign against al-Qa'ida operatives. Instead, Jumper simply wanted to provide a weapon to attack what he called "fleeting targets." As he wrote in an Air Combat Command cable, the U.S. military needed to move to "the next logical step for USAF UAVs using Predator—weaponizing UAVs."[67]

Jumper's project to arm the Predator faced two potential roadblocks. One was gaining congressional approval for a new program, which turned out to be relatively easy. The other was determining whether it was *legal* to arm the Predator and use it to strike targets—including humans. The State Department's general counsel initially concluded that an armed Predator was illegal since the U.S.-Soviet Intermediate Nuclear Forces Treaty of 1987 banned ground-launched cruise missiles.[68]

In response, Jumper sent an email in late September to the air force chief of staff, General Mike Ryan, arguing, "[W]e should not allow this opinion to stand or to ripen for any length of time." Jumper believed that arming the Predator was crucial for "the tactical level of warfare" and would also "save lives and allow us to react to those targets most sensitive to Joint Commanders." He signed the email, "Your Junk Yard Dog."[69] Under Secretary of Defense Jacques "Jack" Gansler agreed, saying the Department of Defense's Compliance Review Groups had reviewed the current air force plans to weaponize the Predator and "found the planned activity in compliance with" the Intermediate Nuclear Forces Treaty, Strategic Arms Reduction Treaty, and Treaty on Conventional Armed Forces in Europe.[70] CIA Director Tenet also agreed, arguing that it was vital to have the capability to track and target Osama bin Laden and his key lieutenants.[71]

The White House eventually concurred. On July 11, 2001, Deputy National Security Advisor Stephen Hadley sent a memo telling CIA Deputy Director John E. McLaughlin, Deputy Defense Secretary Paul Wolfowitz, and Vice Chairman of the Joint Chiefs of Staff General Richard Myers that the White House wanted to deploy Predators "capable of being armed" to Afghanistan by September 1, 2001.[72] That same day, the air force legislative liaison office sent 10 key members of Congress a letter reporting that $2 million was being transferred from other programs in order "to complete the Hellfire demonstration." The money would be used, the letter said, "to modify two more Predator aircraft to develop useable tactics, techniques and procedures for weapons delivery from UAVs."[73] The real purpose of the reprogramming was to provide armed Predators for a potential mission to kill bin Laden and potentially other senior al-Qa'ida leaders.

On September 11, 2001, al-Qa'ida terrorists launched their attacks on New York and Washington. A week later, an air force team assembled at CIA headquarters in Langley, Virginia, to help set up the Predator program. The Department of Defense issued official orders forming Detachment 1, Air Combat Command, Pentagon, on September 18, 2001, with no explanation of the unit's mission. Also known as the Air Combat Command Expeditionary Air Intelligence Squadron, the unit was based in a double-wide mobile home hidden by trees on the CIA campus and flew armed Predators over Afghanistan and elsewhere from first one—and later two—ground control stations parked next to the trailer.[74]

After the first Predator strike on October 7, 2001, which targeted senior Taliban leaders, the CIA and U.S. military launched an intense drone campaign. CIA drone strikes killed Pakistan Taliban leader Nek Mohammad Wazir in June 2004 and al-Qa'ida leader Hamza Rabia in December 2005, both in Pakistan.[75] By 2007, however, it was increasingly clear that these strikes were not weakening al-Qa'ida, which retained the intent and likely the capabilities to strike the U.S. homeland. A classified National Intelligence Estimate darkly warned in 2007, "We judge the U.S. Homeland will face a persistent and evolving terrorist threat over the next three years. The main threat comes from Islamic terrorist groups and cells, especially al Qa'ida, driven by their undiminished intent to attack the Homeland and a continued effort by these terrorist groups to adapt and improve their capabilities."[76]

Even as the United States struggled against al-Qa'ida, the U.S. defense industrial base surged to help the military and intelligence community combat terrorist and insurgent groups.

The U.S. defense budget rose courtesy of the wars in Iraq and Afghanistan, from $320 billion in 2000 to $558 billion in 2006.[77] The defense budget as a percentage of GDP also grew, from 3.1 in

2000 to 4.0 in 2006.[78] The increase included supplemental budget items—primarily operations and maintenance costs for Iraq and Afghanistan—that reached $189.3 billion in 2008.[79]

Several examples highlighted the surge capacity of the industrial base for the war on terrorism. One was with drones. General Atomics ramped up the production of Predators and other drones, along with ground control stations and associated systems. Production jumped from a handful of Predators in 2001 to over 250 in 2007, and Predators flew in over 145 combat missions and over 300,000 flight hours in Afghanistan, Iraq, and other battlefields.[80] General Atomics also surged production of Predators and other drones for a growing number of foreign countries—including Italy, the United Kingdom, and Turkey—that were desperate for drones because of their intelligence, surveillance, reconnaissance, and strike capabilities.

A second example was the production of MRAPs. In the spring of 2007, Secretary of Defense Robert Gates was increasingly frustrated with the military's inability to protect soldiers from improvised explosive devices, or IEDs. In Iraq, for example, roughly 80 percent of U.S. military casualties came from IEDs. Perhaps the most dangerous were explosively formed penetrators, shaped charges with a concave end that sent a molten copper slug through targets like armored vehicles and then created a deadly spray of hot metal. On April 19, Gates read an article on MRAPs written by Tom Vanden Brook in *USA Today* which noted that "in more than 300 attacks since last year, no Marines have died while riding in new fortified armored vehicles the Pentagon hopes to rush to Iraq in greater numbers this year."[81] The article discussed the V-shaped hulls of the MRAP, which deflected the force of IED explosions. Yet as Gates angrily discovered, lower-level U.S. Army and Marine Corps initiatives to develop and produce MRAPs had languished in the Pentagon bureaucracy. No senior Pentagon officials wanted to spend billions of dollars to buy them, and the military services did not want to spend procurement dollars on a vehicle that was not part of their long-term acquisition plans.

On May 2, Gates met with the secretaries of the army and navy, Deputy Secretary of Defense Gordon England, Chairman of the Joint Chiefs of Staff Peter Pace, and several others to accelerate the money, scope, and speed of MRAP procurement. "Every delay of a single day costs one or more of our kids his limbs or his life," Gates stated emphatically.[82] Congress agreed to support urgent MRAP production and provided billions of dollars. Gates then gave the MRAP program legal priority over other military and civilian programs so that the military could acquire essential components for production, such as axles, tires, and special steel. Gates also set aside a range of bureaucratic hurdles to ensure rapid production. Ultimately, the Pentagon purchased roughly 27,000 MRAPs, which saved countless limbs and lives, for a total cost of nearly $40 million. Casualty rates in MRAPs were 75 percent lower than in Humvees and about 50 percent lower than in Abrams main battle tanks, Stryker armored fighting vehicles, and Bradley fighting vehicles.[83] But MRAP production still required an enormous push from the secretary of defense. "As usual in a huge bureaucracy, the villains were the largely nameless and faceless people—and their leaders—who were wed to their old plans, programs, and thinking and refused to change their ways regardless of circumstances," Gates later wrote. "Time and again I would have to tackle the damnable peacetime mindset inside the Pentagon."[84]

A third example was the massive effort to counter IEDs. Terrorist and insurgent groups in Iraq and Afghanistan conducted an increasingly aggressive campaign against U.S. and other international forces using a wide range of IEDs, from simple pressure plates to more sophisticated remote-controlled models. In response, the U.S. Department of Defense created the Joint Improvised Explosive Device Defeat Organization—a mouthful of a name. Its main goal was to find and deploy technology to help troops find IEDs on the battlefield. Examples included the Thor, a backpack-like radio that jammed radio-controlled IEDs; metal detectors that troops used to search for bombs; handheld mine and explosive detectors; and helium-filled aircraft called aerostats (which looked like large balloons) that hovered over bases overseas and collected information.[85]

Gates also established the Counter-IED Task Force, co-chaired by Ashton Carter, under secretary of defense acquisition, technology, and logistics, and General Jay Paxton, director of operations for the Joint Staff.[86] Much like with the MRAPs, Gates had to fight the Pentagon's bureaucracy to produce counter-IED technology. At one point, he ripped into senior officials from the Joint Improvised Explosive Device Defeat Organization: "Your agency has lost its sense of urgency. Money is no object. Tell me what you need."[87] With Gates's aggressive efforts, the defense industrial base surged to produce other capabilities to counter IEDs, including small robots, handheld command-wire devices that could detect IEDs, electronic warfare kits, demining devices that could be mounted on a tank or armored personnel carrier, and explosive trace detectors.[88]

As even these successful cases highlighted, there were underlying problems with the U.S. defense industrial base. The Defense Science Board, an independent advisory board for the Department of Defense, warned that U.S. defense companies were significantly decreasing their independent research and development budgets, which could jeopardize innovation; the U.S. defense industrial base was less agile and innovative than other industrial sectors; resources needed to be shifted from weapons platforms, such as ships, planes, and tanks, to information technology and software; and there was inadequate planning for the future of the defense industry as customers moved toward 21st-century equipment and systems.[89] As the Defense Science Board cautioned, "The Defense Industrial Base is increasingly isolated from the broader domestic and the global economy. It is less agile and innovative than it once was. The industrial base operates under a unique set of rules and regulations that deters industry providers. Also, there are an increasing number of barriers that prevent access to non-U.S. sources of technology. As the [Department of Defense] undergoes transformation, access to non-U.S. sources of technology will be vital to maintaining state-of-the-art capabilities within the enterprise."[90]

With rapid changes in technology and information, warfare was evolving in such areas as precision weapons, unmanned systems, network-centric operations that linked sensors to shooters, command and control, and navigation (including satellite-based global positioning systems). But sometimes the military was way off the mark. Gates killed the army's future combat systems, a modernization program involving vehicles, electronics, and communications with a ballooning projected cost of between $165 billion and $200 billion and an acquisition cycle time of 139 months.[91] A growing number of influential voices, such as Under Secretary Gansler, predicted that the U.S defense industrial base was increasingly unprepared for these changes.[92]

As Gansler noted tongue-in-cheek, "[E]verybody seemed happy to live in this Alice in Wonderland world, and no one chose to look behind the mirror."[93] But with the counterterrorism campaign struggling and al-Qa'ida plotting attacks on the U.S. homeland, something had to change.

For some U.S. officials, such as Director of Central Intelligence Mike Hayden and Assistant Secretary of Defense for Special Operations and Interdependent Capabilities Mike Vickers, the United States had to think and act differently: "What we needed was an industrial-style covert war strategy that we could largely conduct on our own, with only general Pakistani buy-in required," concluded Vickers.[94] The George W. Bush administration came up with a new plan that combined far more intense Predator strikes with cross-border special operations raids to take away al-Qa'ida's safe haven in Pakistan's Federally Administered Tribal Areas. The goal was to achieve what Vickers called "escalation dominance" over al-Qa'ida—to escalate the conflict in a range of ways that would be disadvantageous to al-Qa'ida and other groups.[95]

Inside war zones, the United States would focus on special operations and other ground forces. Outside war zones, the United States would rely on the Predator as the principal instrument for warfare. But there weren't enough drones. Conducting an effective campaign would require more Predators—a lot more—for intelligence, surveillance, reconnaissance, and strike. In August 2007, the United States had three Predator orbits in Pakistan. By the summer of 2008, Vickers and other policy leaders had increased the number to eight.[96]

There were also several critical policy changes. The first was shifting to unilateral operations, which meant informing Pakistan about U.S. strikes but not asking Islamabad's leaders for approval. U.S. officials were increasingly concerned that Pakistan and its Directorate for Inter-Services Intelligence (ISI) were providing aid to some terrorist and insurgent groups, including the Afghan Taliban and the Haqqani Network, an insurgent group which had strong links with the Afghan Taliban and al-Qa'ida. Admiral Mike Mullen, chairman of the Joint Chiefs, would later testify before a U.S. House Armed Services Committee that the Haqqani Network was a "veritable arm" of Pakistan's Inter-Services Intelligence Agency.[97] Pakistan could not be trusted with sensitive information on U.S. operations, U.S. officials believed, because they worried that the ISI might pass it on to groups or individuals the United States was targeting.

Another policy change was to expand Predator operations to include "signature strikes," which involved targeting individuals where the exact identity of the individuals was not certain, but intelligence strongly indicated that they were involved in terrorist activity. Signature strikes were controversial. As the nongovernmental organization Amnesty International argued, "In an armed conflict, individuals are entitled to a presumption of civilian status, which the practice of signature strikes may effectively deny, leading to direct attacks on civilians and disproportionate civilian casualties, in violation of international humanitarian law."[98] That didn't bother Abe Karem, who argued that the United States went to extraordinary lengths to limit civilian casualties against terrorists who were trying to kill as many civilians as possible. The United States, he said, spent "hours and hours with very good sensors to identify the target and try to minimize collateral damage."[99]

The final change was to significantly expand the number of al-Qa'ida senior leaders on the U.S. target list and to add several groups: the Haqqani Network; the Tehreek-e-Taliban Pakistan, whose objective was to establish an extreme version of Islamic law in parts of Pakistan and cooperated with al-Qa'ida; and the Commander Nazir Group, a group led by Maulvi Nazir that also cooperated with al-Qa'ida. The U.S. goal was to target their operational planners, facilitators, and trainers with Predators.[100]

U.S. officials had two overall objectives with this evolving approach. The first was the "operational defeat" of al-Qa'ida, which meant that the group would have no ability in the Afghanistan-Pakistan border region to conduct terrorist attacks against the U.S. homeland and other major targets. The second was "strategic defeat," in which al-Qa'ida largely collapsed as a functioning organization and its ideology was largely rejected.[101] After U.S. forces killed al-Qa'ida leader Abu Musab al-Zarqawi in 2006, General Stanley McChrystal brought in contractors to analyze how Joint Special Operations Force units were using the Predator in Iraq. One of their primary contributions was to flesh out a concept of operations, which McChrystal coined "find, fix, finish, exploit, analyze."[102] As McChrystal explained, "You understand who or what is a target, you locate it, you capture or kill it, you take what intelligence you can from people or equipment or documents, you analyze that, and then you go back and do the cycle again, smarter."[103]

U.S. forces first identified a target based on human, signals, or other types of intelligence (find). Intelligence agencies, including the National Security Agency and CIA, were critical in collecting and analyzing intelligence. U.S. forces kept targets under constant surveillance, including developing a pattern of life (fix). Next, U.S. forces either killed or captured the target with ground units or aircraft (finish). They then secured items with intelligence value, from computers and detainees to intercepted phone calls (exploit). Finally, U.S. forces leveraged the information to better understand the adversary, including its strengths and weaknesses, for further action (analyze).[104]

The Predator and subsequent drones, such as the MQ-9A Reaper, were helpful in all these phases, along with other capabilities such as night vision goggles, communications equipment, and precision-guided weapons.[105] In fact, the Predator was *so helpful* that it allowed U.S. special operations forces to conduct more operations with far fewer soldiers—from an average of 100 soldiers per operation to roughly 20.[106] Over time, U.S. special operations forces also evolved the Predator to fit their needs, including adding sensor packages and intelligence collection capabilities. "The Predator became central to our operations, and it actually changed our doctrine," McChrystal asserted.[107]

In addition to the Predator and other capabilities, U.S. forces leveraged a growing amount of intelligence collected by the CIA, National Security Agency, National Geospatial-Intelligence Agency, and other U.S. and partner intelligence agencies. The National Security Agency had developed a major intelligence innovation called the Real Time Regional Gateway, or RT-RG for short, which was a data processing and data mining system. It merged established sources of signals intelligence with information gathered from other sources, such as special operations raids, satellite images, and on-the-ground situation reports from forces on the battlefield. RT-RG reduced the time needed to provide intelligence to the warfighter from days to hours or even minutes.[108]

Based on this evolving concept of operations and advanced systems, the United States conducted a lethal campaign against al-Qa'ida and other groups led by General Atomics drones—the legacy of Karem, the Blue brothers, and Cassidy. In January 2008, U.S. strikes killed Abu Layth al-Libi, Sulayman al-Jaza'iri, and Abu Khabab al-Masri—all senior al-Qa'ida leaders. During the final months of 2008, the United States conducted nearly 30 Predator strikes in the Afghanistan-Pakistan border region, which killed eight senior al-Qa'ida leaders. CIA Director Hayden quipped, "[W]e were eight for 08."[109] The United States conducted more attacks in the last five months of 2008 that it had in the previous four years *combined*.

The pace of drone strike continued to escalate over the next several years, and the number of Predator orbits rose to 22 by the summer of 2011.[110] Most were for the campaigns in Afghanistan, Pakistan, and Yemen, though the United States occasionally used ground forces for some operations, such as the killing of bin Laden in May 2011.

In Yemen, the most significant U.S. target was Anwar al-Awlaki, a U.S. citizen. He had been involved in several terrorist attacks and plots in the United States, including the November 2009 Fort Hood attack by Nidal Hasan and the December 2009 Northwest Airlines attack by Umar Farouk Abdulmutallab.[111] The United States conducted nearly 50 Predator strikes in 2012 in Yemen against al-Qa'ida in the Arabian Peninsula operatives, such as Fahd al-Quso, who had been a key plotter in the attack against the USS *Cole* over a decade earlier.[112] Between 2011 and 2015, the United States conducted more than 100 Predator strikes in Yemen against al-Qa'ida in the Arabian Peninsula, likely preventing another major terrorist attack in the United States.[113]

By 2012, the United States had seriously weakened—though not eliminated—al-Qa'ida across the globe. As one U.S. intelligence assessment concluded, al Qa'ida "losses, combined with the long list of earlier losses since [counterterrorism] operations intensified in 2008, lead us to assess that core al-Qa'ida's ability to perform a variety of functions—including preserving leadership and conducting external operations—has weakened significantly." It added that "al-Qa'ida's losses are so substantial and its operating environment so restricted that a new group of leaders, even if they could be found, would have difficulty integrating into the organization and compensating for mounting losses."[114]

The U.S. defense industrial base had surged to produce specific counterterrorism capabilities, such as MRAPs, counter-IED systems, and drones. The research, development, and production of drones—including the MQ-1 Predator—had taken years and involved synergy between the commercial sector and the government. It had been, to a great extent, the result of inventive thinking, persistence, and plenty of failures and frustration by Abe Karem, Linden and Neal Blue, Tom Cassidy, and others. What huge defense companies had failed to do, a small group of innovative engineers and entrepreneurs succeeded in doing. "It's not always the size of the dog in the fight," said Karem, "it's the size of the fight in the dog."[115] A new concept of operations had also emerged that combined advanced technology and analysis to target adversaries, characterized as find, fix, finish, exploit, analyze.[116] The role of the private sector was critical. Engineers and business leaders worked closely with CIA and Defense Department personnel, such as Jim Woolsey and John Deutch, and personnel at Big Safari.

But the wartime environment of the decade after September 11, 2001, was limited, and Defense Secretary Gates remained frustrated with the "peacetime" mentality within the Pentagon acquisitions system.[117] The priority of the defense industrial base was to produce systems and platforms to fight small terrorist groups—not great powers like China and Russia. This meant that there was not a national revitalization of the defense industrial base to broadly maximize production capacity, minimize unnecessary regulations, provide incentives to the private sector for innovation, and streamline acquisition and contracting for the defense sector. It was narrowly focused on counterterrorism capabilities.

In fact, Defense Secretary Rumsfeld had called for a broader transformation of the U.S. defense industrial base: "The war on terrorism is a *transformational* event that cries out for us to rethink our activities, and to put that new thinking into action."[118] For

Rumsfeld, transformation required exploiting new information technology to improve defense business practices, developing new joint warfighting concepts, and reforming the acquisition process.[119] But his efforts largely failed. As William Perry and Ashton Carter wrote in the journal *National Interest*, "To a remarkable degree, the 50 percent increase in the [Department of Defense] baseline since 9/11 has gone to funding the program of record on 9/11 (i.e., the weapons that were already in the pipeline on 9/11)."[120] Pentagon leaders talked a good game about transforming the military and strengthening the defense industrial base, but their spending practices were still stuck in the past. Rumsfeld's transformation never took place.[121]

Nevertheless, the United States was still the dominant global power. But would that status continue? China had just selected a new leader, Xi Jinping, who put the country on a new course and vowed to make China a major military and defense industrial power.

6

Xi Jinping and the Third Offset

Realizing the great rejuvenation of the Chinese nation is the greatest Chinese dream of the Chinese nation in modern times.
—Xi Jinping, president of the People's Republic of China

The necessity that America be in the lead in software-enhanced systems and AI is something people understand but they don't understand it enough. And whoever has the nuclear equivalent to software will define the world order, and I don't think anyone in America or in the West will be particularly happy if that's not us.
—Alex Karp, CEO of Palantir

ON NOVEMBER 15, 2012, ONLY two weeks after his appointment as general secretary of the Chinese Communist Party (CCP), Xi Jinping led the Politburo Standing Committee on a trek to Beijing's impressive National History Museum.[1] The museum, which sits on the eastern side of Tiananmen Square, is a subtle mixture of ancient and modern. It had recently reopened, after architects from the German firm Architekten von Gerkan, Marg und Partner merged two separate museums that had occupied the space since 1959: the Museum of the Chinese Revolution and the National Museum of Chinese History. The Grand Forum, which welcomed visitors, was decked in granite and cherrywood cladding, with bronze doors, coffered ceilings, and a large bas-relief socialist-realist-style mural. The centerpiece attraction was the "Road to Rejuvenation" exhibit. It began by detailing China's dark century of humiliation at the hands of foreign aggressors, and then it shifted to the nation's virtues in overcoming adversity through the Chinese Communist Revolution and the creation of the People's Republic of China.

With this symbolic backdrop, Xi made a dramatic speech titled "The China Dream." He explained that while the Chinese nation had "suffered very gravely after the beginning of the modern era" from foreign powers—triggering such events as the Boxer Rebellion—the Chinese people had never surrendered. He then turned to the future. "What is the Chinese dream?" he asked rhetorically. The answer was simple: the restoration of the great Chinese nation. Xi's dream—and the dream of all of China, in his view—was to revive China's status as an economic and military power under the leadership of the CCP. But he warned that this would not be accomplished without a mighty struggle: "Our historical task of fighting for the great rejuvenation of the Chinese nation is glorious and arduous and requires generation after generation of us Chinese to unwaveringly make common efforts."[2] One of the most important aspects of Xi's "China dream" was building military power, including reinvigorating the country's woeful defense industrial base.

Xi was intent on revitalizing China as a great power. Over the previous century, Germany, Japan, the United Kingdom, France, the United States, and the Soviet Union had been great powers. But not China. Xi's "China dream" did not go unnoticed in Washington. Robert Work, the chief executive officer at the Center for a New American Security, a U.S. think tank, believed that China under Xi could be a serious competitor and a great power. The strategic landscape shifted after September 11, 2001, from the peacetime environment of the Last Supper years to a wartime environment against terrorists.

Now there was a question about whether the international landscape was shifting to a wartime environment against great powers. China had begun to invest in precision-guided munitions, long-range ground-based fires, battle networks, and air defense capabilities in ways that were designed to mitigate U.S. military advantages and challenge U.S. power projection in Asia. An alarmed Work, who would soon become the U.S. deputy secretary of defense, believed the United States needed to counteract China through what he and Secretary of Defense Ashton Carter eventually referred to as "the third offset." The initiative involved the utilization of advanced technologies—such as artificial intelligence, machine learning, and unmanned systems—to potentially offset Chinese and Russian capabilities.[3]

Over at the CIA's recently created nonprofit investment corporation, In-Q-Tel, Chris Darby also grappled with the nature of the challenge. "The U.S. can compete and win," said Darby, "but we will need to fill the gaps in U.S. policy and investment, then do what we do best: innovate and deliver."[4] Thanks to the pioneering thinking of Ruth David and Joanne Isham, the CIA had created In-Q-Tel in 1999 to better leverage commercial technology. To do this, CIA Director George Tenet explained, the spy agency had to "swim in the Valley"—Silicon Valley, that is.[5] In-Q-Tel did not have the scope or resources to revitalize the industrial base, but the newly established organization did present an opportunity to better connect the government to the private sector.

Once again the private sector was in the lead, though synergy between the private sector and government was crucial for innovation. There were tectonic changes afoot in the U.S. commercial sector that impacted the defense industry. U.S. companies, such as Palantir, charged forward in the investment, research, development, and production of software and advanced technology with applications for the defense and intelligence communities. Instead of providing military hardware—such as the B-29, U-2, F-117, Paveway, or MQ-9—Palantir provided *software* that the U.S. military and intelligence community could use on the battlefield. One of the most significant Palantir software programs was Gotham, which synthesized a hodgepodge of data for U.S. government agencies and turned it into usable products for intelligence analysts and warfighters. Palantir was led by a new generation of visionary entrepreneurs and engineers: Alex Karp, Akash "Aki" Jain, and Stephen Cohen.

But the United States would have to move fast. China was beginning to wake up after a century of slumber.

Exactly 100 years before Xi's "China Dream" speech, the last Chinese emperor, Puyi, abdicated the thrown in 1912, ended the Qing dynasty, and catapulted China into the dark ages. After several decades of CCP rule, Xi was committed to making China a major power and to achieve the "Chinese dream of rejuvenation of the Chinese nation" in several ways.[6]

First, Xi moved to solidify his grip on power, including maintaining uncontested CCP rule at home. Under Chinese leader Hu Jintao, political power had fragmented among CCP officials. Societal discontent rose, resulting in Hu's focus on establishing "stability maintenance," or 维稳. But disenchanted workers, farmers, and urban migrants engaged in a growing number of demonstrations, some of which exceeded 100,000 protesters.[7] As Susan Shirk argued in her book *Overreach*, "China's top leaders became progressively weaker over time—from Mao to Deng to Jiang Zemin to Hu Jintao—as the political system evolved from personalistic dictatorship to more institutionalized collective leadership."[8] Xi was acutely aware of the Soviet Union's collapse two decades before, which ended the country's run of four decades as a global superpower. He put intense pressure on officials to prove their loyalty, centralized decision-making, tightened the party's grip on power, and developed a personality cult around himself. His comprehensive reform plan, which he released in late 2013, called for intensified societal surveillance and a clampdown on free expression.[9]

Second, Xi focused on building China's economic power. For Chinese leaders, economic power was important for many reasons, not least because a country cannot develop a powerful military if it lacks the money and technology to build a strong defense industrial base and equip, train, and modernize its forces.[10] Xi vowed to counter slowing economic growth by encouraging consumer spending and removing barriers to farmers migrating to towns and cities.[11] He was open to doing business with Western companies and to importing Western technology.

Some Chinese leaders before Xi, such as Mao Zedong, had largely been averse to foreign technology. U.S. export restrictions made it difficult for China to acquire advanced semiconductor equipment from the United States, and Chinese companies could not produce many advanced components. But that didn't stop Mao from adding his own self-inflicted embargo and denouncing his political rivals for infecting China's chip industry with foreign components.[12] Instead, Mao urged support for the "independent and self-reliant development of the electronic industry."[13] During the 1980s and 1990s under Deng Xiaoping, Hu Yaobang, Zhao Ziyang, Jiang Zemin, and Hu Jintao, China was far behind such global leaders as the United States in the domestic development and production of technology—including technology relevant to the defense industry.[14] But Xi was committed to changing China's competitiveness in an attempt to jump-start China's economy.

Xi also announced an ambitious development strategy, the Belt and Road Initiative, that used infrastructure investments to expand China's political, economic, and military power.[15] It was extraordinary in its scope and vision. Xi's goal was to create a vast network of railways, highways, energy pipelines, maritime trade routes, and ports to connect China with the rest of Asia, Europe, the Middle East, and Africa. The "belts" referred to the network of land routes that connected China to other countries in Asia, the Middle East, Africa, Russia, and Europe. The "roads" referred—somewhat confusingly—to the maritime routes, including ports, that connected Chinese seaports to countries in the South China Sea, Indian Ocean, South Pacific, and Mediterranean Sea. Over time, China used its economic assistance to pressure foreign governments to adopt favorable policies on such issues as a "One China" policy for Taiwan, crackdowns in Hong Kong, the status of Tibet, control of islands in the South China Sea, and the plight of Uyghurs in western China.[16]

Third, Xi committed to reforming and modernizing the Chinese military and defense industrial base.[17] Following the Politburo's eighth collective study session in July 2013, Xi explicitly noted that it was a top priority to make China a "superpower."[18] Expanding Chinese military power, including naval power, was an important part of his desire for a "great national rejuvenation" and for the PLA to become a world-class military by 2049.[19]

An important aspect of modernizing China's military was building a stronger and more resilient defense industrial base. For example, the PLA Navy ramped up efforts to build surface combatants, submarines, patrol craft, drones, and other platforms and systems. A 2014 assessment by the U.S. Office of Naval Intelligence concluded, "The People's Republic of China (PRC) has continued to modernize its military, providing the PLA(N) with increasingly modern multipurpose platforms such as the LUYANG III-class destroyers and the JIANGDAO-class corvettes."[20] Xi inherited an industrial base that was adapted from the Soviet Union's command economy model, which included top-down central planning and the pursuit, wherever possible, of technological self-sufficiency. The Communist Party of China maintained tight control of decision-making, including in the research, development, and production of nuclear weapons, missiles, space-based capabilities, aircraft, navy surface and subsurface vessels, and other major weapons systems. The state operated under a central planning regime with close adherence to official orders and five-year plans.[21]

The major workhorses of China's industrial base were a series of colossal state-owned enterprises, many of which had dozens of subsidiaries, subcontractors, and subordinate research institutes.[22] Unlike U.S. defense contractors, the largest Chinese defense companies were state-owned enterprises, and they produced almost all major Chinese military platforms.[23] The Chinese government established these firms in the 1980s and 1990s as the CCP carved up its old Stalinist command economy into distinct enterprises.[24] Above the state-owned defense enterprises sat a centralized, top-down structure—including the Central Military Commission and the CCP—that drove central planning and oversaw the research, development, acquisition, and production of weapons systems, dual-use components, and other defense equipment.[25]

The country's defense strategy also evolved under Xi. China's 2013 *Science of Military Strategy*, which incorporated the views of influential strategists at China's Academy of Military Science, outlined the country's growing interest overseas through a concept of "forward defense."[26] It concluded that China needed to expand its battlespace beyond national borders to increase the country's strategic depth.[27] In addition, the *Science of Military Strategy* emphasized that modern war now included five major domains: land, sea, air, space, and information. China needed to be a leader in *all* of these. In one of the first signs that the Chinese defense industrial base was improving, the PLA successfully tested a hypersonic glide vehicle, the WU-14.

In the summer of 2014, the PLA's strategic guidelines advanced and emphasized the role of "informatization" in warfare.[28]

"Informatization" (信息化) referred to the transition from the industrial age to the information age caused by the development and use of information technology.[29] The following year, China's defense white paper explained that warfare was significantly changing and required a shift in PLA preparations to focus on "winning informatized local wars."[30] This meant that China needed to focus on developing such weapons as medium- and long-range missiles for precision strike, drones, space-based assets, and cyber capabilities.

To leverage commercial technology for military purposes, Xi developed a program of "military-civil fusion" (军民融合). This involved developing and acquiring dual-use technology for military purposes and deepening reform of the national defense science and technology industries.[31] In many ways, the concept of military-civil fusion was not new. Every leader since Mao had outlined the need to leverage commercial capabilities to support the PLA. However, Xi elevated the concept of military-civil fusion as essential to developing military power.[32] He was motivated by the reality that the private sector—not the military—was responsible for creating society's most transformative technologies, even in China. To bridge the gap in defense research and defense capacity, China needed to retain its top-tier engineering and managerial talent.

An important part of building China's power was competing with the United States. Xi was not the first Chinese leader to view the United States as the country's chief rival, but he became increasingly assertive in criticizing the United States. One of Xi's speeches to the CCP Central Committee cast relations with the West as a Cold War–type ideological contest between socialism and capitalism.[33] In a speech in May 2014, Xi called for an end to "external blocs" and an end to—or at least a downgrading of—U.S. alliances in Asia.[34] Chinese documents were progressively blunt. The 2013 *Science of Military Strategy* painted a dark view of competition with the United States. It argued that "Western nations led by the United States [are] carrying out strategic encirclement against our country."[35] It claimed that the United States was aggressively trying to integrate China into a U.S.-led international order, balance against Chinese power in the Pacific, and control the world's major strategic channels and natural resources.[36]

Despite Xi's ambitions, however, China still lagged behind the United States in military and economic power. But it was beginning to catch up.

The United States remained the world's only superpower in terms of military, economic, and technological capacity. In 2014, the United States still enjoyed a significant advantage in defense spending over every other major power, and its defense budget remained greater than all the major powers combined. The United States also spent more than every other major power on defense research and development, including 13 times as much as China.[37] In such domains as land, maritime, air, cyber, and space capabilities, the United States remained the dominant military power.[38] Dartmouth professors Stephen Brooks and William Wohlforth concluded that, "compared to any previous era except the years between 1991 and the early 2000s, the overall gap in the military realm remains unprecedented in modern international relations."[39]

Despite U.S. preponderance, however, the gap between the United States and China was shrinking. For instance, China moved into second place among major powers in defense expenditures. In 2004, China spent a paltry 10 percent on defense compared to the United States, but it jumped to 33 percent by 2014.[40] China also expended nearly three times more than Russia on defense in 2014, nearly four times more than France and the United Kingdom, and nearly five times more than Germany and Japan (Figure 6.1). In addition, while Russia did not possess the growing capabilities of China, it still fielded air defenses of such density and sophistication that U.S. forces would likely face severe challenges in a war. A growing number of classified and unclassified U.S. wargames and simulations in the European and Asian theaters also concluded that U.S. forces could lose the next war.[41]

A second area was economic capacity. Despite Xi's ambitions, China's economy lagged behind that of the United States. U.S. gross domestic product was nearly double the size of China's and was over 36 percent of the total GDP of the major powers. China's GDP per capita was also a paltry $7,646, significantly smaller than every other major power except for India. The United States remained the world's

Country	Defense Expenditures (Billions of Dollars, Current Prices)	Percentage of World Defense Expenditures	Defense Expenditures Percentage of GDP	Defense R&D Expenditures (Billions of Dollars, Current Prices)	Defense R&D as a Percentage of Total Government Allocations for R&D
United States	$647.8	36.5%	3.7%	$46.1	41.0%
China	$182.1[1]	10.3%	1.7%[1]	—	—
Japan	$46.9	2.6%	1.0%	$1.6	4.4%
Germany	$44.7	2.5%	1.2%	$1.3	3.8%
Russia	$84.7	4.8%	4.1%	—	—
France	$53.1	3.0%	1.9%	$1.2	6.6%
Britain	$67.0	3.8%	2.2%	$2.5	16.9%
India	$50.9	2.9%	2.5%	—	—
Brazil	$32.7	1.8%	1.3%	—	—

FIGURE 6.1 Defense expenditures of the major powers, 2014.[42]

Note: [1] Represents SIPRI estimates.

Country	GDP (Billions of Dollars, Current Prices)	Percentage of World GDP (Current Prices)	GDP Per Capita (Current Prices)	Productivity (GDP Per Hour Worked, Dollars, Current Prices)
United States	$17,608	22.1%	$55,264	$68.2
China	$10,524	13.2%	$7,646	–
Japan	$4,897	6.1%	$38,523	$44.5
Germany	$3,890	4.9%	$48,036	$63.6
Russia	$2,049	2.6%	$14,024	$26.5
France	$2,857	3.6%	$44,616	$64.2
United Kingdom	$3,066	3.8%	$47,468	$56.2
India	$2,039	2.6%	$1,560	–
Brazil	$2,456	3.1%	$12,601	–

FIGURE 6.2 Economic indicators of the major powers, 2014.[43]

largest, richest, and most economically productive economy in the world. Nevertheless, China's economic ascent put it in a class by itself among the other major powers, and China's share of global GDP grew dramatically, from 4.5 percent in 2000 to 13.2 percent in 2014 (Figure 6.2).[44]

A third area was technology, which is important in part because of the nature of modern weapons. Again, the United States remained the preponderant technological power. It had the highest gross expenditures on research and development of any country in the world, along with highly developed infrastructure. In addition, the United States was by far the leading source of innovative technologies, and its $105 billion

Country	High-Technology Exports (Billions of Dollars, Current Prices)[1]	Gross Domestic Expenditure on R&D (Billions of Dollars, Current Prices)	Number of Science and Engineering Doctoral Degrees Awarded	Number of Researchers in R&D Per Million People	Number of Science and Engineering Publications
United States	$175.9	$477.0	39,682	3,837	434,412
China	$653.8	$346.3	34,103	1,104	385,101
Japan	$107.4	$169.6	7,357	5,353	105,287
Germany	$215.6	$109.6	14,912	4,305	108,118
Russia	$10.4	$40.4	24,522	3,087	44,779
France	$120.6	$60.6	10,023	4,282	73,314
United Kingdom	$76.0	$60.4	14,271	4,286	99,811
India	$18.3	–	14,163	215[2]	91,832
Brazil	$8.8	–	9,124	888	52,367

FIGURE 6.3 Science and technology indicators of the major powers, 2014.[45]

Notes: [1] High-technology exports are products with high research and development intensity, such as aerospace, computers, pharmaceuticals, scientific instruments, and electrical machinery.
[2] Represents 2015 data.

receipts of royalty and license fees were roughly four times greater than Japan's, which had the second highest amount. China was a huge importer of these technologies and exported less than $1 billion.[46] Nevertheless, China began to close the gap in some areas. China's gross domestic spending on research and development rose from $25 billion in 2000 to roughly $346 billion in 2014, while the United States increased spending from $260 billion to $477 billion during the same period. China was nearly at parity with the United States in the number of scientific and engineering doctoral degrees, having 34,103 compared to 39,682 in the United States (Figure 6.3).[47]

Despite its preponderance of military, economic, and technological power, however, the U.S. defense industry continued to struggle in at least two areas. First, technology-savvy people generally migrated to companies in Silicon Valley and other areas that focused on the consumer sector, not the defense sector. Second, companies that once considered sharing their cutting-edge technologies with the government now enjoyed an era of easy venture capital financing, with none of the inconveniences of doing business with the government.[48]

Indeed, the U.S. government's inability to appeal to talented innovators in the private sector came, in part, from its antiquated procurement process, which reflected a peacetime mentality and often appeared tailor-made to *inhibit innovation*. Although the U.S. government plowed money into DARPA and the national laboratories, such as Lawrence Livermore and Los Alamos, commercial companies blanched at oppressive government regulations. Far too many firms, both big and small, were deterred by the costs of complying with the Federal Acquisition Regulation, or FAR, the set of rules regarding government procurement, including for defense.[49] The FAR and Department of Defense Acquisition Regulations contained over 16,000 pages of text and hundreds of pages of appendices—a monstrosity that stifled flexibility and innovation.[50] An exasperated Jacques Gansler, former under secretary of defense for acquisition, technology, and logistics, remarked that the focus of government regulations "is on compliance rather than on results" and that excessive regulation "discourages government contracting personnel from applying management flexibility as they interpret the steps that should be taken in the interests of efficiency and effectiveness."[51]

As the U.S. defense industry struggled and Xi set China on a crash course to modernize the military, there was a glimmer of hope of U.S. innovation. It did not come from the Pentagon, but rather from the CIA.

Many of the CIA's senior leaders, including Director Tenet and the head of the Science and Technology Directorate, Ruth David, believed that the U.S. intelligence community lacked access to the latest and most advanced technology. Private industry had considerably outpaced the U.S. intelligence community and the Department of Defense in innovation and the development of cutting-edge technology. David had received her master's and PhD in electrical engineering from Stanford University. She began her career at Sandia National Laboratories in Albuquerque, New Mexico, and in 1995 moved to the CIA to become deputy director for science and technology. She and her deputy at CIA, Joanne Isham, went to Tenet with a plan for the CIA to better leverage technology developed in the private sector and harness the innovation of entrepreneurs.[52] As David argued, in the past the intelligence community was at the front edge of technology in such sectors as space. But that was no longer the case. "In the information age... the marketplace is being driven by commercial entities, by private business," she said. The challenge for the CIA was "to be continually playing catch-up and trying to anticipate future technological changes and their impacts on the business of intelligence."[53]

Tenet, David, and Isham's solution was to create In-Q-Tel in 1999 to serve as the strategic investment arm of the CIA.[54] It would go on to become a good example of synergy between the government and the private sector. By the time of Xi's emergence, In-Q-Tel was led by the Chris Darby, who had taken over as chief executive officer in 2006 after serving as vice president at the technology company Intel.[55]

The In-Q-Tel experiment was a massive departure for the CIA. Tenet reached out to Lockheed Martin's retired CEO Norman Augustine, who had been involved in the Last Supper, to help create a private, independent, nonprofit corporation that would use CIA money to facilitate the acquisition of new technologies.[56] "I have a problem," Tenet explained in a phone call to Augustine. "Information is an important part of the CIA. But the leading edge of technology is no longer at the CIA. It is in places like Silicon Valley and Boston. In addition, companies don't like talking to us."[57]

The organization was initially named In-Q-It. The "In" stood for intelligence, the "Q" for the fictitious engineering outfit in the James Bond movies, and the "It" for information technology. After a trademark dispute, however, the CIA settled on In-Q-Tel.[58] CIA leaders envisioned In-Q-Tel as an integrator of commercial technologies that focused on identifying promising products and early-stage companies, making it more of a strategic investor than a venture capital fund.[59] In-Q-Tel also provided an opportunity for the U.S. intelligence community to communicate the requirements of its customers directly to the commercial sector.[60] For Augustine and Darby, the brilliance of In-Q-Tel was that it did not follow the lumbering government procurement rules, including FAR. In-Q-Tel could move quickly in getting companies under contract, and it was designed to leverage commercial sector innovation.[61] While small, it was a quintessential rat-catching organization. It wasn't always smooth sailing, though, since CIA bureaucrats routinely tried to regulate In-Q-Tel.

Early on, Darby lamented that the In-Q-Tel investment process was not as effective as it could be. The investment teams typically identified a handful of interesting companies and provided capital to them, but too few would ultimately solve a problem that the government needed to answer. Another limitation was In-Q-Tel's focus on the United States—especially Silicon Valley. Since technological advances occurred across the globe, In-Q-Tel needed to broaden its scope and develop an overall strategy. Darby developed an "architectural approach" in investing, which involved identifying challenges that U.S. intelligence agencies faced in war zones and other areas, finding capabilities to address those challenges, and *then* investing in companies that were developing—or could develop—those capabilities. "In any In-Q-Tel document," said Darby, "we could explain where a company fits into the architecture."[62] Darby and In-Q-Tel personnel also examined the company's leadership: "Who are the individuals leading this team? Are they credible? Do they have domain expertise? Do we have reason to believe that they can deliver and be successful?"[63]

Finally, they looked at the financing and economic health of the company. Over time, roughly 10 percent of In-Q-Tel's investments were outside the United States, and In-Q-Tel opened offices in London and Sydney.[64] The reality was that some of the best companies and research were not in the United States but in Europe, Asia, or Latin America. The Universidad Nacional de Córdoba in Argentina, for example, had an outstanding cyber security program. Understanding foreign markets also provided an insight into what U.S. adversaries, such as China and companies like Huawei, were doing.

In-Q-Tel invested in a wide range of businesses, including some that made satellites and satellite components, developed artificial intelligence, analyzed data, built drones and other autonomous platforms, engaged in cybersecurity, translated languages, and evaluated chemical compounds. A major goal was to assess which emerging technologies could help solve intelligence challenges either now or in the future. Darby, who graduated from the University of Western Ontario, used an ice hockey metaphor that the NHL legend Wayne Gretzky learned from his father, Walter: "I skate to where the puck is going to be, not where it has been."[65] For Darby, this meant analyzing where the market was going and trying to get ahead of it. "It is also about shots on goal," he believed. "We were only taking a few shots per year, but we needed to take a lot more" and invest in more companies.[66]

After identifying a promising company, In-Q-Tel had two primary tools for developing a relationship. One was a "work program" transaction, in which In-Q-Tel entered an arrangement with a promising company and provided between $500,000 and $3 million. In-Q-Tel generally structured this relationship as a development and licensing agreement, and the company worked to adapt its technology to the needs of the CIA or another government agency. The second tool was an equity-only "seed" investment. It was much smaller—between $250,000 and $500,000—and In-Q-Tel typically received a small equity stake and status as a board observer. These direct equity investments provided an opportunity to better understand the technology; if it turned out to be promising, the company might get additional funding.[67] Each dollar In-Q-Tel invested in a company was generally matched by up to $28 from somewhere else. The In-Q-Tel board was initially reluctant to support seed investments because they were worried about throwing away government money. But Darby helped convince them, partly because In-Q-Tel was successful in converting seed funds into work program deals.[68]

In-Q-Tel's initial results were good, but there were challenges. For example, In-Q-Tel invested in Forterra Systems, a 3D graphics software company, but the Silicon-based firm failed to attract commercial interest and sold off pieces of the company.[69] Investors in Forterra, including In-Q-Tel, incurred losses. Some media outlets and investors raised conflict-of-interest concerns, noting that In-Q-Tel funded businesses on several occasions that had financial links to an In-Q-Tel trustee.[70] Others criticized companies that worked with In-Q-Tel as fronts for the CIA.[71] But these challenges tended to be outliers. According to a *Washington Post* investigation, "In interviews with more than a dozen current and former CIA officials, congressional aides, venture capitalists that have worked with it and executives who have benefited from it, no one disputed that what began as an experiment in transferring private-sector technology into the CIA is working as intended."[72]

In-Q-Tel's support to companies was relatively small, and it could not—and was never intended to—serve as a juggernaut for the U.S. industrial base. But its ability to move quickly to identify and fund promising technologies and companies was an important development and a major improvement over the slow and inflexible contracting and acquisition processes in the defense sector. In-Q-Tel was also willing to take risks and even fail in some investments, a sign that the U.S. government could potentially move more expeditiously in a wartime environment. There were several big successes. One was In-Q-Tel's support to the cybersecurity firm FireEye, which became a dominant player in the cyber market. Another was MongoDB, one of several big data companies that In-Q-Tel supported. Still another was investment in the software company Palantir, led by Alex Karp.

Karp, with his salt-and-pepper corkscrews of frizzy hair and penchant for tai chi, cross-country skiing, and shooting guns, was in many ways the antithesis of a tech CEO. He had no background in computer science or business and worked out of a barn in New Hampshire when he wasn't on the road. After graduating from Haverford College outside of Philadelphia and then Stanford Law School—the latter of which he referred to as "the worst three years of my adult life"—Karp made his way to Germany to study under Jürgen Habermas, one of the world's foremost philosophers and social theorists.[73] Though he had a falling-out with Habermas, Karp slogged through his dissertation and received a PhD in neoclassical social theory from Goethe University. But he wasn't cut out to be an academic. When he inherited money from his grandfather he began investing in start-up companies and stocks. He was extremely successful—so successful, in fact, that he set up the Caedmon Group to invest money for high-net-worth individuals after word circulated that "this crazy dude was good at investing."[74]

The eccentric Karp had a brilliant mind, and a group of individuals led by Peter Thiel (one of Karp's Stanford Law School friends), Joe Lonsdale, Nathan Gettings, and Stephen Cohen were impressed with his knack for quickly understanding complex issues and translating them to non-engineers. Together they established Palantir in 2003, with Karp as CEO. In-Q-Tel provided Palantir two rounds of investment totaling nearly $2 million.[75] By 2015, as Xi set China on a crash course to great power status, Palantir was valued at a whopping $20 billion and was one of the most valuable private companies in tech.[76]

From its start, Palantir was unusual. The name itself came from J. R. R. Tolkien's *Lord of the Rings* novels. In the fictional land of Middle-earth, a palantir was an indestructible orb, or seeing stone, used for communication and intelligence gathering. It allowed the holder to peer across vast distances and to see parts of the past and future.

From the beginning, a primary goal of Palantir was to fuse massive amounts of information that were often held on different platforms. Unlike Boeing, Lockheed, Texas Instruments, and General Atomics, Palantir was not trying to sell the U.S. Department of Defense or CIA *hardware*, such as the B-29, U-2, Paveway, or MQ-9. Instead, it offered something different: *software* to help fuse data, conduct analysis, and solve problems. Karp, Thiel, and Palantir's other founders initially had several ambitions for the company.

One was to produce software that could help keep the country safe from terrorism and other national security threats. A second ambition was to prove that there was a technological solution to the dual—and often conflicting—dilemma of balancing security and civil liberties.[77] A third was to make sense of an exponentially increasing amount of data. As Google's CEO Eric Schmidt observed, government agencies and companies were drowning in information. "There were five exabytes of information created by the entire world between the dawn of civilization and 2003," Schmidt remarked. "Now that same amount is created every two days. No wonder we are so overloaded."[78] (An exabyte is 1 billion gigabytes, roughly equivalent to the amount of information from a pickup truck filled with books.)[79] Thiel had helped develop fraud-recognition software at PayPal. Now he, Karp, and others wanted to translate that software into identifying terrorist activity and stopping extremists before they could strike.

Palantir had an interesting business concept, at least in theory. But it had a serious problem early on: a paucity of customers and skepticism from some U.S. investors. Several American venture capitalists were allergic to the company. Michael Moritz, chairman of the venture capital firm Sequoia Capital, was patently uninterested, even allegedly doodling through an entire sales pitch. A senior executive from Kleiner Perkins, another Silicon Valley–based venture capital firm, lectured Karp and others about the inexorable failure of their company.[80] More broadly, venture capital firms and other private investors were deeply hesitant to invest in the defense sector. Most recoiled at the antiquated and suffocating government procurement process, while others had moral quandaries about investing in a sector that produced weapon systems that could kill people.

But the CIA's In-Q-Tel was interested and provided two rounds of investment.[81] "They were clearly top-tier talent," recalled former In-Q-Tel executive Harsh Patel. "The most impressive thing about the team was how focused they were on the problem . . . [of] how humans would talk with data."[82] Thanks to In-Q-Tel and a budding relationship with the U.S. intelligence community, Palantir was off and running.

Palantir's primary software program for the national security community was Gotham, a nod to the fictional city that was home to the superhero Batman. Using strategic algorithms, Gotham synthesized data that an organization collected—such as intelligence reports, phone numbers, emails, databases of cyber threat actors, and imagery—which are often mismatched, formatted differently, and siloed in separate databases.[83] Gotham acted as a centralized operating system and allowed customers to integrate, manage, secure, and analyze data—including real-time data—with the goal of improving the information picture for intelligence analysts and operators. It could detect anomalies in the data and suggest courses of action. Palantir engineers could also parachute—or "forward-deploy"—into the offices of clients to customize data and programs through visualized maps, organizational structures, histograms, link charts, and other outputs.[84] The uses were nearly infinite, from understanding and targeting terrorist organizations to identifying malign Iranian, Chinese, and Russian activities around the globe.[85]

Synergy between the CIA and Palantir was crucial. In its formative years, In-Q-Tel was Palantir's primary patron and the CIA was its main customer, alpha-testing and evaluating its software. Engineers were critical. One was Akash "Aki" Jain, a Stanford graduate with a degree in computer science and one of the first engineers hired by Thiel. Another was Stephen Cohen, an engineer who had worked at Thiel's hedge fund Clarium Capital Management and had written code since he was a teenager. They traveled together from Palo Alto to the CIA with an updated version of their software program. CIA analysts, who referred to Cohen as "Two Weeks" because he trekked to the CIA roughly every two weeks, tested out the software and offered feedback. Cohen and Jain would then fly back to California to make changes. Jain estimated that from 2005 to 2009, he and Cohen made roughly 200 trips to Virginia.[86] They were motivated, in part, by the pursuit of technological superiority, including artificial intelligence. "We know we have an immediate competitor (China), but how will we know if—and when—we have won?" Jain wrote. "For the U.S. to position itself in a place of technological strength for decades to come, we must create systems that allow for steady, continuous, and trustworthy progress on AI."[87]

With the CIA's imprimatur, word of Palantir's growing abilities spread.[88] A distinctive Palantir culture took shape in Karp's iconoclastic image. Its Palo Alto headquarters, which it called "the Shire" in reference to the area of Middle-earth inhabited by Tolkien's hobbits, featured a conference room that the company turned into a pit of giant plastic balls.[89] Employees dubbed its Washington office Rivendell after a valley in Middle-earth that was home to elves. Karp was sometime called Papa Karp or Daddy Karp.

Not everyone loved Palantir's software. In 2016, Palantir sued the army in the U.S. Court of Federal Claims—and won—for an unlawful procurement solicitation for the army's next iteration of its Distribution Common Ground System-Army, or DGCS-A.[90] Palantir convincingly argued that its data management product, Gotham, did exactly what DCGS-A was trying to do and came at a lower cost, even though the army opted for a more expensive proposal that was years away from effective deployment.[91]

Palantir's software marked a significant technological innovation. Gotham was effective in helping the CIA, military, FBI, and state and local law enforcement agencies fuse voluminous amounts of data on terrorist and other activity, conduct analysis, and take preventative action.[92] For example, the military used Gotham to help locate IEDs in Afghanistan and Iraq. "It's like plugging into the Matrix," remarked one U.S. Special Forces soldier deployed to Afghanistan.[93]

Gotham and other Palantir software programs were a good example of the kind of "breakthrough technologies" that Secretary of Defense Chuck Hagel and Deputy Secretary Robert Work were aiming to identify, develop, and field as part of a new concept they were formulating called "the third offset."[94]

Before coming to the Pentagon as deputy secretary of defense, Work had been the chief executive officer at the Center for a New American Security, a Washington think tank, and he had also served as under secretary of the navy. Concerned primarily about Xi and China's acceleration, Work wanted to *offset* Chinese—and to some degree Russian—capabilities. The third offset, as Work referred to it, was a "combination of technology, operational concepts, and organizational constructs—different ways of organizing our forces—to maintain our ability to project combat power into any area at the time and place of our own choosing."[95] It came on the footsteps of the first offset (the effort in the 1950s under President Eisenhower to counter Soviet conventional superiority in Europe by building up nuclear weapons) and the second offset (the effort in the 1970s spearheaded by Harold Brown and William Perry to counter Soviet nuclear weapons by developing stealth, precision-guided munitions, and other technology and concepts of operation).

In developing the third offset, Work was worried about three challenges. The first was the tyranny of distance and time. Almost any major war would involve deploying U.S. forces to—and fighting in—the backyard of one of its major adversaries, most likely China or Russia. "How do we get there and how do we arrest power projection when we are not in the theater ready to fight?" asked Work. "That is a tough problem."[96] U.S. wargames highlighted serious concerns about the ability of the United States to quickly move forces to Eastern Europe or the Taiwan Strait in case of Russian or Chinese invasions.[97]

The second challenge was that China and Russia were making progress in achieving parity with the United States in some areas, such as theater-level battle networks, precision-guided munitions, and long-range, ground-based fires. Work was primarily concerned about China, which he assessed was trying to achieve military technical parity with the United States. China had developed the DF-21D, an anti-ship ballistic missile with a range of nearly 1,000 miles dubbed the "carrier killer," which posed a serious threat to U.S. surface ships—including aircraft carriers—in the Pacific.[98] Work was also troubled by Russian progress. "It's modernizing a military that was in steep decline through the 1990s and the early 2000s," he concluded in 2015. "Its naval and air units are operating at a pace and an extent that hasn't been seen in quite some time, to include a large increase in trans-oceanic and global military operations."[99] Russia's defense industrial base was aided by a strong arms export market. Russia accounted for 27 percent of global arms exports between 2009 and 2013, second only to the United States at 29 percent.[100] Russian defense companies produced a wide range of platforms and weapons systems, such as an aircraft carrier (the *Gorshkov*, which was renamed the *Vikramaditya*) to India, fighter aircraft, surface-to-air missile systems, and transport helicopters.

President Vladimir Putin was also becoming more aggressive. In February 2014, Russian intelligence and special operations forces—sometimes referred to as "little green men"—illegally seized and then annexed Crimea from Ukraine.[101] Two months later, in April, Russia began military operations in Eastern Ukraine. In 2015, Russia launched an air campaign in Syria to help President Bashar al-Assad regain territory that had been seized by the Islamic State and other insurgent groups. Work assessed that Russian units in Syria were more effectively conducting long-range conventional strikes and employing advanced sensors enabled by small unmanned aircraft systems.[102] Work's view that the United States had to increasingly worry about China and Russia as strategic competitors ran counter to the conventional wisdom of many policymakers in the second Obama administration, who remained focused on terrorism.[103]

The third challenge was that China and Russia were increasingly investing in cyber, space and counterspace, and electronic warfare capabilities.[104] "When you add those three together," said Work, "you have anti-access/area-denial capabilities, making it hard to get into the theater, making it hard to maintain freedom of action."[105] The solution for the United States, therefore, was to identify and develop the right technologies and operational concepts to move from rough parity with China and Russia to a position of advantage. To jump-start the third offset, Secretary Hagel wrote an influential memorandum under the heading "The Defense Innovation Initiative." He warned, "[W]e are entering an era when American dominance in key warfighting domains is eroding." In this competitive security environment, the United States needed "to identify a Third Offset strategy that puts the competitive advantage firmly in the hands of American power projection over the coming decades." Consequently, the U.S. military needed to accelerate innovation in several areas, including "breakthrough technologies and systems that sustain and advance the capability of U.S. military power."[106]

Work and Hagel's thinking was shaped by a Defense Science Board Summer Study, which concluded that the Department of Defense "must accelerate its exploitation of autonomy—both to realize the potential military value and to remain ahead of adversaries who also will exploit its operational benefits."[107] The study convinced Work that autonomy and artificial intelligence had to be key components in any effort to offset Chinese and Russian developments and provide U.S. combat systems with greater range and dispersal capabilities.[108] Artificial intelligence could be used to augment critical warfighting systems, such as command and control, surveillance, reconnaissance, and targeting systems.[109]

In addition, the United States needed to invest in new space capabilities, advanced sensors, missile defense, cyber capabilities, and a range of promising technologies: unmanned underwater systems, advanced sea mines, high-speed strike weapons, advanced aeronautics, electromagnetic rail guns, and high-energy lasers.[110] Work concluded, "The coin of the realm during the Cold War was armored brigades, mechanized infantry brigades, multiple launch rocket system battalions, self-propelled artillery battalions, tactical fighter squadrons, among others. Now, the coin of the realm is going to be learning machines and human-machine collaborations, which allow machines to allow humans to make better decisions; assisted human operations, which means bringing the power of the network to the individual; human-machine combat teaming; and the autonomous network."[111]

However, these capabilities were being developed in the commercial sector—not in the traditional defense industry—by companies like

Palantir, making it important to increase government-commercial synergy. By this time, the top five U.S. technology companies (which included Amazon, Apple, and Google) spent roughly 10 times the amount of research and development per year as the top five U.S. defense companies (Lockheed Martin, Boeing, Northrop Grumman, Raytheon, and General Dynamics).[112] Consequently, Work pushed forward on several fronts, or "lines of effort," as he called them, that involved a partnership between the deputy secretary of defense (Work), vice chairman of the Joint Chiefs of Staff (General Paul Selva), and deputy director of national intelligence (Stephanie O'Sullivan). They established the Advanced Capabilities and Deterrence Panel, which developed seven lines of effort.

The first was encouraging the under secretary of defense for policy to develop a new strategic approach for countering China and Russia. A second line of effort was pressing the military services to develop new warfighting operational concepts, such as the navy's Distributed Maritime Operations and the air force's Agile Combat Employment concept.[113] The goal was to create warfighting concepts that could more effectively operate against an adversary—especially China—that had an ability to strike the United States with long-range precision weapons. The third was developing innovative technologies, such as space, artificial intelligence, and autonomous capabilities, which became the third offset. As Work argued, "China's long-term goal was technological superiority. The offset was to get ahead of them."[114]

The fourth line of effort was wargaming. "I established the Wargaming Incentive Fund to revitalize wargaming and provide funding throughout the department," Work explained, to test operational concepts and capabilities in wargames.[115] One example was Persistent Hobgoblin, a series of wargames the Department of Defense ran involving China and the United States to better develop and refine organizational constructs and operational concepts. The fifth line of effort was information management, including assessing when to reveal sensitive defense capabilities and when to conceal them. "We should reveal capabilities in some cases to deter adversaries," Work believed, "and conceal them in others to ensure warfighting advantage."[116] The sixth was to establish closer coordination between the Department of Defense and the U.S. intelligence community, as well as to encourage the intelligence community to collect more information on Chinese and Russian capabilities—a shift from the nearly singular U.S. intelligence focus on counterterrorism. The seventh line of effort was to create stakeholders for this new direction outside of the Department of Defense, particularly in the White House and Congress. Work needed their support for a broad-based effort to reestablish U.S. "overmatch," which involved possessing overwhelming military advantages over an adversary.[117]

"Together," Work believed, "these seven lines of effort could help the U.S. maintain superiority."[118] Work also helped establish several sensitive initiatives to give the United States a competitive advantage: Project Maven, a pathfinder program to demonstrate the battlefield potential for artificial intelligence and autonomy; the Special Program Missile Defeat, which included a range of high-altitude sensors, distributed ground sensors, and other capabilities to identify and destroy incoming missiles before and after their launch; the Joint Interagency Combined Space Operations Center (which later became the National Space Defense Center) to increase the U.S.'s ability to detect and defend against threats to the country's space systems; and a range of efforts to strengthen nuclear command, control, and communications.[119]

In addition, Ashton Carter, who succeeded Hagel as secretary of defense, established the Defense Innovation Unit Experimental—which eventually became simply the Defense Innovation Unit, or DIU—in 2015 in Silicon Valley to accelerate the military's adoption of commercial technology. The idea was for DIU to partner with organizations across the Department of Defense, from the military services to combatant commands, to quickly prototype and field advanced commercial products that addressed national security challenges. Key focus areas included artificial intelligence and machine learning, autonomy, cyber, human systems, energy, and space.[120] Carter modeled DIU, in part, on In-Q-Tel.[121] Carter and Work also supported the Strategic Capabilities Office, led by Will Roper, which produced some innovative capabilities. For example, the office transformed the navy's Standard Missile-6 from a defensive surface-to-air weapon into a missile that could offensively strike and destroy enemy ships at extended ranges.[122]

Work, Carter, and other U.S. officials had to move quickly because Xi was beginning to flex his muscles in Asia.

Over a matter of weeks in early 2015, U.S. intelligence analysts from the National Geospatial-Intelligence Agency examined disturbing satellite images. Clusters of Chinese vessels at Mischief Reef busily dredged white sand by sucking it up from the sea bed and pumping it onto the formerly undeveloped reef. It looked like they were building a military base. China replaced the few dilapidated fishing shacks on stilts with an airfield, control tower, aircraft hangars, and radar installations. Chinese amphibious warships, capable of holding 500 to 800 troops, began to patrol the reef's southern flank.[123] In case anyone had questions about the true nature of Mischief Reef, China then added HQ-9B surface-to-air missile systems and YJ-12B anti-ship cruise missile systems.[124]

Mischief Reef was only the beginning. China used hundreds of dredgers and barges to transform other atolls (coral islands that consist of a reef surrounding a lagoon) and reefs into military bases: Subi Reef, Hughes Reef, Gaven Reefs, Fiery Cross Reef, Cuarteron Reef, and Johnson South Reef. One of the most impressive dredgers was the *Tian Jing Hao*, a hulking 2,400-ton ship that was over 400 feet long and armed with a terrifying set of revolving teeth that could excavate 4,500 cubic meters of sand per hour. It was eventually replaced by the *Tian Kun Hao*—dubbed the "magic island maker"—an even larger Chinese-built dredging vessel that was 460 feet long and could excavate 6,000 cubic meters of sand per hour.[125]

The story was similar across the South China Sea. On Fiery Cross Reef, roughly 200 miles west of Mischief Reef, China created an island 9,850 feet long and 985 feet wide with a harbor capable of docking warships and a runway that could support military aircraft. Other islands across the Spratlys now had military barracks, fuel depots, anti-aircraft and anti-missile systems, and high-frequency radar installations. They served as important logistics hubs for the PLA across the South China Sea. Over time, China placed anti-ship cruise missiles, long-range surface-to-air missiles, sensors, electronic warfare capabilities, space-based systems, and signals intelligence platforms on these outposts.[126]

In addition, China claimed sovereignty over *all* these islands, ignoring the long-standing claims of its neighbors.

In 2015, Chinese leaders announced "Made in China 2025," a national strategic plan to develop Chinese industry and become a leader in advanced technologies, such as artificial intelligence, quantum computing, and robotics.[127] In language reminiscent of Paul Kennedy's *The Rise and Fall of the Great Powers*, Made in China 2025 concluded, "Since the start of industrial civilization in the mid-eighteenth century, the history of the rise and fall of world powers and the struggle of the Chinese nation have repeatedly proven that without a strong manufacturing industry, there will be no prosperity for the country and nation."[128] The guiding principle of Made in China 2025 was to put China on the path to becoming an industrial—including a *defense* industrial—global power.

But China had work to do. Contracts between the PLA and the country's massive state-owned enterprises were simplistic and perfunctory, without clear technical obligations. China's General Armaments Department (which became the Equipment Development Department) attempted to reform the PLA pricing structure to allow for other pricing models and to control costs.[129]

China also began to improve its research, development, and acquisition process. It had previously taken decades for China to produce high-end military platforms and systems. For example, China's J-20 stealth fighter aircraft, which was produced by Chengdu Aerospace Corporation and nicknamed "The Mighty Dragon," spent roughly nine years in preliminary research and another decade in technology and engineering development. In addition, the Xi'an Aircraft Industrial Corporation labored for 17 years to produce the Y-20 large military transport aircraft, with eight years in preliminary research and nine years in development. Both aircraft were high-priority programs with substantial backing from the highest levels of the CCP and PLA. However, China tried a different approach with the J-15 carrier-based fighter. It accelerated preliminary research over a two- to three-year period and then moved quickly to production. There were some trade-offs, including identifying and fixing a range of design problems. But China shrank the research, development, and acquisition process for the J-15 to roughly a dozen years—an impressive feat.[130] As one study by

University of California–San Diego professor Tai Ming Cheung concluded, "Major technological progress is taking place across virtually the Chinese defense industry's entire spectrum from traditional sectors such as aerospace and sea power to the newer domains of space, information technology, and cyber. This is steadily narrowing the defense technological gap with the U.S."[131]

China also turned to joint ventures and other investments to grow its organic research and development capacity.[132] Its defense industry had previously focused on a "copy-replace" model, which emphasized reverse-engineering U.S. or other technology over foundational research and development work.[133] But China began to fix this deficiency by increasing its national spending on research and development at a compound annual growth rate of almost 15 percent between 2010 and 2016.[134] This increase also coincided with a rise in the size of the Chinese workforce and the number of Chinese research and development institutions.[135]

Despite some progress, the Chinese defense industrial base struggled in several areas. For example, Chinese defense companies suffered from significant bloat and debt.[136] State-owned enterprises dominated each of the major defense industry's sectors, and a long-established system of compartmentalization meant there was little crossover between sectors. Contracts were single-sourced for the majority of military equipment, with only non-combat-related contracts undergoing a formal bidding process.[137] Oversight was predominantly administered by military representatives, who were active-duty officers stationed in factories and research institutes across the country. Quality testing was often insufficient or only partially carried out.[138] Corruption was endemic in the defense industry.[139] The design of Chinese defense contracts did little to encourage transparency and accountability. The language of contracts was simplistic and superficial, without clear technical or schedule obligations.[140] China also struggled in a range of other areas. One was engines for military aircraft, including China's fifth-generation aircraft. China could not mass-produce high-performance aircraft engines and was forced to rely on second-rate Russian engines.[141]

Finally, China still relied on espionage and the theft of intellectual property for weapons development, which helped it remain competitive but ensured that it was several years behind cutting-edge systems and technologies. For example, Chinese government spies obtained confidential information about some of the U.S. Department of Defense's most advanced weapons systems and platforms, including the F-35 Lightning II—the next-generation U.S. stealth fighter.[142] More broadly, China stole hundreds of gigabytes of sensitive data and targeted companies in such fields as aviation, space, satellites, manufacturing, pharmaceuticals, oil and gas exploration and production, communications, computer processors, and maritime systems.[143] Su Bin, a Chinese Canadian businessman, assisted PLA officers in their efforts to steal trade secrets regarding the U.S. C-17, F-22, and F-35 aircraft. This espionage campaign included more than 630,000 files—totaling more than 65 gigabytes—on the C-17 aircraft. Such theft allowed China to evade the costs, both in time and money, to modernize its systems. For a sense of the scale of the investments that went into the three aircraft targeted during the Su case, the U.S. government spent more than $100 billion over more than three decades to modernize these airlift and fighter systems.[144]

To ramp up its defense industry, China pursued a dual-track strategy of stealing defense technology from the United States and other countries and improving its own defense industrial base and increasing innovation. As Xi recognized, the world was increasingly competitive—and China needed to use virtually all means to get ahead.

In January 2017, Xi stepped onto the stage at the World Economic Forum in Davos, a ski resort nestled in the Swiss Alps. The audience included a highly curated group of elites from around the world, composed of government ministers, industry titans, academics, and royalty—including Palantir's Karp. Xi was the first Chinese leader ever to address the forum. He spoke softly and said that while "some people blame economic globalization for the chaos in our world," he wished to pursue "a well-coordinated and inter-connected approach to develop a model of open and win-win cooperation." He then quoted a Chinese adage: "Victory is ensured when people pool their strength; success is secured when people put their heads together."[145] In many ways, it was a heartwarming talk that promoted peaceful cooperation, not competition.

But only months before, Xi had given a very different and much more combative speech to a domestic audience in China. He ripped into foreign powers that had "trampled on" China, causing the nation to sink "into a miserable situation of poverty and weakness." But that was in the past, he promised; now China was on the trajectory of becoming a great power—and perhaps a truly *global* power. Using warlike language, he said that China "must promote strong alliances" against the United States and its defense industry, "assault the fortifications of core technology research and development," and "compose shock brigades and special forces to storm the passes."[146] Xi was committed to catching up—and surpassing—China's chief rival.

Yet China still lagged behind the United States. Ultimately, the power gap between the United States and China undermined the effectiveness of Carter and Work's third offset. Neither China nor Russia possessed significant military advantages over the United States—at least not yet. The United States enjoyed a preponderance of military power. This reality made the situation in 2015 fundamentally different from the first and second offsets, when the Soviet Union had considerable advantages that the United States needed to offset or risk losing deterrence. For example, since the Soviet Union possessed a major advantage in conventional military capabilities in the 1950s in Europe, President Eisenhower expanded the U.S. nuclear arsenal and developed a doctrine of massive retaliation to deter a Soviet invasion of Western Europe. But it was unclear what Carter, Work, and others needed to offset and what the United States specifically needed to develop, though they were attempting to prevent the Chinese from achieving technological superiority. By the time Work stepped down as deputy secretary of defense in July 2017, it was clear that there would be no veritable offset. In many ways, it was a decade ahead of its time.

Still, there was a small but growing number of individuals in the United States—including Carter and Work—cognizant that the peacetime environment among the great powers was coming to an end. U.S. government officials needed to operate less like regulators and more like rat-catchers by increasing the capacity, flexibility, surge capability, and innovation of the industrial base. The commercial sector was already there. The CIA had made some progress with Tenet, David, Isham, and others establishing In-Q-Tel as a nonprofit investment company that could help the government harness private-sector innovation. Over at Palantir, Karp, Jain, Cohen, and others were at the forefront of developing advanced software for the military and intelligence community.

There was also a growing number of areas—such as space—where the private sector was rapidly outpacing the U.S. government in ways that were fundamentally changing the defense industry. And SpaceX's indomitable and quirky Elon Musk was at the forefront of these changes.

7

Private Capital and the Space Age

Sending this tweet through space via Starlink satellite.
—Elon Musk, CEO of spacex

The threats the United States faces from its strategic competitors have grown substantially. At the same time, the environment is being shaped by a rapidly growing commercial space sector, which is cultivating an ecosystem of innovation and reducing barriers to entry to deliver new, operationally relevant capabilities.
—*U.S. Space Force Commercial Space Strategy*

IN JUNE 2018 ELON MUSK, THE chief executive officer of SpaceX, flew to Seattle to fire the entire leadership team of Starlink, his satellite-based internet service company that was a subsidiary of SpaceX.[1] By this time, space had turned into a hugely profitable business, generating $300 billion in annual revenue.[2] Musk had designed Starlink to provide internet service from satellites operating in low Earth orbit, roughly 342 miles (or 550 kilometers) from the Earth's surface. "It would be like rebuilding the Internet in space," Musk bragged. "The goal would be to have a majority of long-distance Internet traffic go over this network."[3]

But Starlink was having serious problems and Musk was irate. He was trying to compete with OneWeb and Canada's Telesat to be first to market with a satellite-based service. Starlink's satellites were too large, too expensive, and too slow to manufacture. To be profitable, Musk figured that he needed to produce satellites at one-tenth of the cost and as much as 10 times faster. But he sensed little urgency from the Starlink team, a cardinal sin. Something had to change—and fast. He brought with him eight of his senior SpaceX rocket engineers, including a whiz kid named Mark Juncosa. These engineers knew little about satellites, but they all understood how to solve engineering problems and, perhaps more important, how to work for Musk.[4]

Over the next three years, SpaceX sent almost 2,000 Starlink satellites into low Earth orbit, and its internet service was available in 14 countries.[5] Starlink also had significant military potential. The electronic warfare, offensive cyber, and space capabilities of China, Russia, and other major powers were improving dramatically. Using Starlink, however, militaries could maintain Internet connection despite an adversary's use of electronic warfare and offensive cyber operations.[6] The private sector was increasingly interested in the possibilities of space. Among SpaceX's earliest investors was Founders Fund. Led by venture capitalist Peter Thiel, who had funded Palantir, Founders Fund initially invested $20 million in Space X.[7] SpaceX and Starlink were on the cutting edge of a revolution in space, which involved a massive shift in space-based capabilities from the government to private companies. "The commercial space age is here," trumpeted Matthew Weinzierl and Mehak Sarang from Harvard Business School. "For the first time in human history, humans accessed space via a vehicle built and owned not by any government, but by a private corporation with its sights set on affordable space settlement."[8] And the United States was the dominant power.

Musk could move much more nimbly than most of the defense sector, which was operating in a peacetime environment with slow and overly bureaucratic contracting systems, excessive regulations, and little urgency. He developed the "algorithm" to maximize production, which included several steps: question every requirement, delete any part or process if feasible, simplify and optimize, accelerate the cycle time, and automate.[9] Musk pushed his employees to produce satellites and rockets with urgency and minimize excessive requirements. Musk—and the space sector more broadly—were also able to take advantage of a profound development in the defense sector: venture capital and private equity firms had become major players in the defense industrial base, spearheading a growing amount of innovation.

During the Cold War, much of the defense-related funding for the private sector—including companies based in Silicon Valley and along Route 128 in Massachusetts—came from the Department of Defense, especially from DARPA and similar organizations. Kelly Johnson's Skunk Works at Lockheed Martin, Abe Karem's Leading Systems, and MIT, Stanford, Carnegie Mellon, and the California Institute of Technology received DARPA funding to produce drones, stealth technology, computers, and countless other technologies and weapons systems. But that changed dramatically beginning in the 2010s. The United States was able to retain a competitive advantage as a great power in the defense sector with the growing role of venture capital and private equity firms. They poured vast amounts of money into start-ups and established companies that developed space and cyber capabilities, artificial intelligence, quantum computing, autonomous platforms, and a wide array of other software in the defense sector.

Never in U.S. history had private capital invested in defense companies like this. Venture capital investment in defense technology start-ups skyrocketed from $1.9 billion in 2013 to $7.5 billion in 2017 and $40.5 billion in 2021.[10] In comparison, DARPA's entire budget in 2022 was a mere $3.9 billion—more than 10 times smaller than venture capital defense investments.[11] Big name venture capital firms included Andreessen Horowitz, Founders Fund, Sequoia Capital, Lux Capital, General Catalyst, and Shield Capital. Private equity investment in the defense sector also soared, led by the Carlyle Group, Veritas Capital, Arlington Capital partners, and other firms. The number of private equity deals involving defense companies swelled from less than $2 billion in 2010 to over $14 billion in 2021.[12]

Once again, the private sector was ahead of the government. Space—an increasingly important domain of warfare among the great powers—was symptomatic of this change. U.S. companies, such as SpaceX and its subsidiary Starlink, charged forward in the research, development, and production of space capabilities that had significant applications for the U.S. defense industrial base. Flush with cash from venture capital firms and contracts from NASA, SpaceX was led by a new generation of visionary entrepreneurs and engineers, such as Musk, Juncosa, and Gwynne Shotwell. As senior U.S. government officials in the space sector recognized, synergy between the private sector and government was essential to stay competitive with great powers like China.[13]

But the profound shift in space did not happen overnight. It transpired over several decades, and SpaceX was in a prime position when it did occur.

During the Cold War, space was dominated by governments, particularly the United States and the Soviet Union. In the United States, the Eisenhower administration established the National Aeronautics and Space Administration, or NASA, in 1958, the year after the Soviets launched Sputnik 1. Three years later, the Department of Defense created the National Reconnaissance Office to design, construct, launch, and operate satellites.[14] For the rest of the Cold War, the U.S. military and intelligence community relied on their own satellites for imagery intelligence, though the private sector had been launching satellites at least since the 1960s.[15]

NASA then suffered two major NASA disasters—the tragic explosions of the *Challenger* in 1986 and the *Columbia* in 2003. President George W. Bush's Commission on Implementation of United States Space Exploration Policy published a stinging criticism of NASA and recommended that "NASA's role must be limited to only those areas where there is irrefutable demonstration that only government can perform the proposed activity."[16] The U.S. government eventually canceled the space shuttle program, which formally ended in August 2011. "The failure of NASA to find a replacement for the shuttle for 30 years shattered the idea of NASA being in charge," said Bretton Alexander, an executive at Blue Origin, a U.S. space company founded by Jeff Bezos, and former White House space official. "When the shuttle was retired, it created this void that allowed NASA to look to the commercial sector."[17] There were several private sector visionaries—with money—willing to invest in space. One was Musk.

Musk grew up in Pretoria, South Africa, to a South African father and a Canadian mother. At a young age he developed an affinity for computers and entrepreneurship, creating a video game at the age of

13, which he named Blastar, and selling it to the computer magazine *PC and Office Technology*. The game appeared in the 1984 issue of the magazine with a short introduction by Musk: "In this game you have to destroy an alien space freighter, which is carrying deadly Hydrogen Bombs and Status Beam Machines."[18] Musk left South Africa and briefly attended Queen's University in Kingston, Ontario, eventually landing at the University of Pennsylvania, where he received a bachelor's degree in physics and economics. While he showed flashes of brilliance, Musk was also wildly eccentric and, at times, downright childish. He had a teenage tendency to live-tweet his time in the bathroom. "Just dropping some friends off at the pool," he once tweeted to his 66 million followers.[19] The proclamation came not long after announcing that half of his tweets were "made on a porcelain throne" because "it gives me solace."[20]

Musk had been interested in space since his childhood, building small rockets and reading books on space. After being ousted as the CEO of PayPal in 2000, he turned his focus to space exploration. But Musk was shocked to find on NASA's website no clear plans for a human mission to Mars.[21] He founded the company SpaceX in May 2002, for which he was CEO and chief engineer. His goal was to send humans to Mars. But creating SpaceX was excruciatingly difficult. Its first rocket, the Falcon 1, launched in 2006, did not reach Earth orbit. The second and third launches also failed to get rockets into orbit. Facing personal bankruptcy, Musk was in a bind for a fourth attempt.

His deus ex machina came from a group of investors, including Thiel, from the venture capital firm Founders Fund. Thiel and Musk knew each other well. They had merged their respective online payment companies—Musk's X.com and Thiel's Confinity—to form PayPal. During the merger negotiations, Thiel let Musk drive his $1 million silver McLaren F1 sports car with 627 horsepower. Musk pulled into the fast lane on a highway in Silicon Valley and floored the accelerator. The rear axle promptly broke and the car spun around and slammed into an embankment. Both emerged unscathed, and Musk proudly said, "At least it showed Peter I was unafraid of risks."[22] Despite the incident, Thiel, intrigued by SpaceX, agreed to a conference call with Musk.

"At one point I asked Elon whether we could speak to the company's chief rocket engineer," recalled Thiel, "and Elon replied, 'You're speaking to him right now.'"[23] Thiel was not impressed. But one of his colleagues at Founders Fund, Luke Nosek, saw an extraordinary opportunity in the commercial space sector. "I argued that what Elon was trying to do was amazing," said Noske, "and we should be part of it."[24] Thiel and Founders Fund agreed to provide $20 million to SpaceX in 2008 and, in return, secured a 10.4 percent minority stake in the company.[25]

By this time, the U.S. government was increasingly willing to allow private companies to compete for public sector contracts in space. For example, the Commercial Orbital Transportation Services, a NASA program that coordinated the development of vehicles that could deliver cargo to the International Space Station, offered companies fixed-price agreements to help resupply the International Space Station.[26] In addition to SpaceX, a growing number of companies—such as Blue Origin (founded by Jeff Bezos of Amazon), OneWeb (founded by Greg Wyler), and Virgin Galactic (founded by Richard Branson and Burt Rutan)—jumped into the space business.[27] They performed a growing range of missions, including launching people and payloads into space (what they called "space access"), conducting remote sensing (scanning the Earth and measuring its reflected and emitted radiation), and enhancing communications. Investments in start-ups rose from less than $500 million per year between 2001 and 2008 to roughly $2.5 billion by 2015.[28]

In 2014, Musk jumped into the military space market and sued the U.S. Air Force after it awarded a contract for launching military satellites—without opening the contract to competition—to United Launch Alliance, a joint venture of Lockheed Martin and Boeing. "This is not SpaceX protesting and saying these launches should be awarded to us," Musk insisted. "We're just saying these launches should be competed. If we compete and lose, that's fine. But why would they not even compete it? That doesn't make sense."[29] SpaceX eventually dropped the lawsuit after the U.S. Air Force agreed to expand the number of competitive opportunities for launch services.[30]

In January 2015, Musk announced the creation of a new division of SpaceX named Starlink to develop a satellite-based internet service. He explained, "Internet revenue is about one trillion dollars a year. If we can serve three percent, that's $30 billion, which is more than

NASA's budget."[31] Musk based Starlink in Redmond, Washington, not far from Microsoft's headquarters. His vision was to send satellites into low Earth orbit to improve the latency of the signals. "Latency" refers to the amount of time it takes data to go from one point to another and then back again. Generally measured in milliseconds, latency for Starlink indicated the amount of time it took for a packet (or set of data) to move from a Starlink router to a satellite and back, often called "round trip time."[32]

For Musk, an internet-based service using satellites in low Earth orbit had some advantages over satellites in geosynchronous orbit, which operated roughly 22,000 miles above the Earth. For example, satellites in low Earth orbit had better latency than those in geosynchronous orbit because their round-trip time was shorter. However, Starlink's beams could not cover nearly as much ground because of the low altitude of its satellites, so Musk needed more satellites. A lot more.

Juncosa was an interesting choice to lead Starlink after Musk fired most of the leadership team.[33] He looked more like a gangly surfer from Southern California than an engineer. Juncosa also talked like one, with a vocabulary sprinkled with "dude" and "like." But he was just what Musk needed. Musk typically preferred two types of people to work for him. The first were the "Red Bulls," who were full of vim and vigor, much like the energy drink. The second were the "Spocks," who were quiet, measured, and nerdy, much closer to the fictional character from the *Star Trek* franchise. Juncosa fit squarely into the Red Bull category.[34] He was trained as an engineer, with a Bachelor of Arts in Economics and a Master's in Systems Engineering, both from Cornell. He was not a great student, but he was a solid engineer and developed an affinity for designing and manufacturing cars as part of Cornell's Formula One racing team.[35]

One of Juncosa's best qualities was his ability to work for—and with—Musk, including a ruthless determination to maximize productivity that was fundamentally different from the peacetime mentality of Pentagon contracting and acquisitions bureaucrats. "Elon kept hammering at us to eke out a tiny percent more efficiency by chilling down the fuel more and more," recalled Juncosa in describing their work on Falcon 9, SpaceX's reusable, two-stage rocket designed to transport people and payloads into Earth orbit. "It was ingenious, but it was giving us a real pain in the ass." A few times Juncosa pushed back, saying Musk's demands would present challenges with valves and leaks. But Musk was unrelenting. "There is no first-principles reason this can't work," he said. "It's extraordinarily difficult, I know, but you just have to muscle through."[36] Musk was looking for every possible way to cram more power into Falcon 9 without substantially increasing its mass or size. And his vision was correct.

Juncosa was also a workaholic and demanded a lot from his staff. "A normal work day at best contains eight hours of meetings, a few hours to respond to emails," Juncosa summed up. "It all blurs together. The only time to shut out the world is when I exercise, surf, take a shower or sit on the toilet. That's when new solutions surface."[37]

And Starlink needed solutions fast.

When Juncosa took over Starlink, he threw away the existing design, went back to first principles, and questioned everything. The goal was to make the simplest communication satellite that could work. One point of friction was the satellite's antennas, which were on a separate structure from the flight computer. The engineers argued that the antennas had to be thermally isolated from one another. Juncosa wasn't convinced. When told that the antennas might overheat, Juncosa asked to see the test data. "By the time that I asked 'Why?' five times," he recalled, his engineers threw up their hands and said "maybe we should just make this one integrated component."[38] By the end of Starlink's design process, Juncosa had helped create a satellite that was notably cheaper, and the Starlink team could stuff more than twice the number of satellites into the nose cone of a Falcon 9.

Since World War II, the United States had numerous innovative teams in the defense sector: Wellwood Beall and his colleagues at Boeing; Kelly Johnson and his Skunk Works comrades; and the Blue brothers, Abe Karem, and Tom Cassidy at General Atomics. Musk, Shotwell, Juncosa, and their teams at SpaceX and Starlink were only the most recent. Shotwell had joined SpaceX in 2002 and eventually became the president and chief operating officer. Born and raised in Illinois, she graduated from Northwestern University with a Bachelor of Science in Mechanical Engineering and a Master of Science, also from Northwestern, in Applied Mathematics. Musk liked Shotwell's engineering prowess and bluntness.

Musk and his team operated according to five principles—or commandments, as Musk referred to them—called "the algorithm," that emphasized efficiency and the elimination of unnecessary regulations. The first was to question each requirement no matter who established it. "You should never accept that a requirement came from a department, such as from 'the legal department' or 'the safety department,'" Musk demanded. Requirements could undermine productivity and efficiency. The second commandment was to delete unnecessary parts or processes in the production line, even if "you may have to add them back later." The goal was to cut needless bureaucracy. The third was to simplify and optimize parts and processes—or eliminate them if they shouldn't exist. The fourth commandment was to accelerate cycle times. "Every process can be speeded up," he declared. The goal was to expedite the rate of production. The fifth and final commandment was to automate where feasible. Overall, Musk developed the algorithm out of "a maniacal sense of urgency," which was his core operating principle to maximize production rates.[39]

In May 2019, Juncosa and his team launched a batch of 60 satellites into orbit from Cape Canaveral Air Force Station in Florida, a staggering feat for an industry used to a small number of satellites that took years to develop and produce.[40] When Starlink became fully operational in October, Musk went on Twitter and bragged, "Sending this tweet through space via Starlink satellite." Starlink had considerable commercial value in providing broadband internet to populations across the globe, including to rural and underdeveloped areas without substantial internet access. It was sometimes slower and more expensive than other providers and connection types, and its service could be impacted by inclement weather. But it had high-speed potential, no contract requirements, and low latency.

Starlink also had massive—though largely untapped—military utility. Both Russia and China had the ability to jam transmission links and, at least temporarily, take down the communications networks of other countries. A U.S. Defense Intelligence Agency assessment around this time concluded, "Russia's world-class electronic warfare forces support denial and deception operations and allow identification, interception, disruption, and, in combination with traditional fires, destruction of adversary command, control, communications, and intelligence capabilities."[41] With so many satellites in low Earth orbit, Starlink provided militaries with significant resiliency by allowing terminals on the ground to connect to multiple satellites at once. It was also user friendly, highly mobile, and relatively secure.

More broadly, space—including commercial space—had a huge military and intelligence value for governments. Space-based assets were critical for collecting intelligence on sensitive programs and activities of foreign governments, such as their nuclear weapons and missile programs; tracking weather; conducting secure communications; and assisting with the navigation of missiles, rockets, and other stand-off weapons.[42] Innovative thinkers like Musk and Juncosa were front and center. Walter Isaacson, Musk's biographer, noted that Musk had an innate "compulsion to aim high, act impulsively, take wild risks, and accomplish amazing things—but also to blow things up and leave smoldering debris in his wake while cackling maniacally."[43]

In the age of space, however, Musk's instincts were visionary, and space was altering the defense industrial base.

By 2021 space was booming, and the space economy was valued at $469 billion, up 9 percent from the previous year.[44] Venture capital firms—Seraphim Capital, TechStars, Space Capital, Sparx Space Frontier Fund, Data Collective, Promus Ventures, Founders Fund, and many others—led the way. Even the CIA's In-Q-Tel provided funding to some space start-ups. Space ventures attracted more than $15 billion in financing in 2021, crushing the previous record of $7.7 billion set in 2020. The year 2021 broke records in several other categories. There were 241 start-up deals in the space sector, up 48 percent from 2020; the average deal size was $64 million, up 35 percent from the previous year.[45] One market analysis summed up, "Private investors continue to pour large amounts of capital into start-up space ventures, shattering previous records as increasing numbers of investors fund more recipients with larger average deal sizes."[46] Private funding also poured into the space sector from so-called angel investors—wealthy individuals and families, such Amazon's Jeff Bezos. Some private equity firms, corporations, and banks also invested in space companies.[47]

The result of private investment was impressive: the number of commercial satellites in operation more than doubled, from 1,381 in 2015 to 3,371 by the end of 2020. This jump was virtually all from Starlink. And satellites were smaller and cheaper. In 2011, there were only 39 "smallsats"—satellites that weighed less than 600 kilograms. But that number jumped to 338 in 2017 and 1,202 in 2020, thanks in large part to Starlink as it sent small satellites into space at historic numbers.[48] Once the size of a garbage truck and costing as much as $1 billion each, some satellites had even shrunk to the size of a microwave. They cost a fraction of their predecessors and could be mass-produced in factories or, in some cases, in a garage or college classroom.[49] In fact, costs to low Earth orbit dropped from $65,400 per kilogram for NASA's space shuttle to launch the Hubble Space Telescope, to $8,100 per kilogram for Atlas V to launch one government satellite, to $2,600 per kilogram for SpaceX's Falcon 9 to launch 50 Starlink satellites. With SpaceX's Starship, Musk's goal was to reduce launch costs even further to $200 per kilogram and eventually to $10 per kilogram.[50]

The private sector—and its capacity for innovation—had become an essential part of the Department of Defense's space program. As the Pentagon's *Commercial Space Integration Strategy* bluntly noted, "The commercial space sector's innovative capabilities, scalable production, and rapid technology refresh rates provide pathways to enhance the resilience of national security space architecture and strengthen deterrence." Because of "the expansion of the commercial space sector and the proliferation of space capabilities," the report concluded, "the Department will benefit by making commercial solutions integral—and not just supplementary—to national security space architecture."[51] Reliance on commercial space and public-private partnership was now essential to the U.S. military in over a dozen mission areas, from command and control to electromagnetic warfare, missile warning, nuclear detonation detection, positioning, navigation, and intelligence, surveillance, and reconnaissance.[52]

Space was also a growing arena for great power competition, in part because it was an increasingly important enabler of a country's economic and military power. The United States was the most dominant country in space on both the commercial and military sides, thanks in part to the role of the commercial sector. By 2022, the United States had 3,415 satellites orbiting the Earth—6 times more than China, 7 times more than the United Kingdom, 20 times more than Russia, 39 times more than Japan, and 58 times more than India.[53] The United States also dominated the smallsat market, followed by China, Russia, Japan, and India (Figure 7.1).[54] But other countries were pressing ahead.

China was a fast-moving challenger, as Xi Jinping pushed his country to develop commercial, intelligence, and military space capabilities.[55] "To explore the vast cosmos, develop the space industry and build China into a space power is our eternal dream," Xi wrote in the country's white paper, *China's Space Program: A 2021 Perspective*.[56] China conducted 52 successful space launches in 2021 and landed its Zhurong rover on Mars, becoming the second country ever to land and maneuver a vehicle on the Martian surface. More broadly, China developed increasingly robust space capabilities, such as advanced positioning, navigation, and timing; satellite communications; missile warning; intelligence, surveillance, and reconnaissance; and geolocation.[57] Its

Country of Operator/Owner	Number of Satellites Orbiting Earth
United States	3,415
China	535
United Kingdom	486
Multinational	180
Russia	170
Japan	88
India	59
Canada	56

FIGURE 7.1 Number of satellites in orbit, by country, 2022.[58]

BeiDou global navigation satellite system, similar to GPS in the United States, included 35 positioning, navigation, and timing satellites.[59]

Russia was a slightly different matter. While it inherited a successful Soviet program, it struggled in some areas of space. Its version of GPS, the Global Navigation Satellite System, was overseen by its civil space agency, Roscosmos. But the bedrock of Russian space capabilities was in Soviet-era technology and infrastructure. One analysis of Russian space capabilities concluded, "In a nutshell, Russia's space program has a shortage of competent and highly qualified staff, obsolete facilities and technology, and weak leadership."[60] Nevertheless, Russia still maintained a large network of reconnaissance, communications, and navigation satellites. It also integrated its space services into its weapons and command-and-control systems, allowing Moscow to identify, track, and target U.S. satellites in the event of war.[61]

The United Kingdom, France, and several other European countries had major space capabilities, though notably smaller than the United States had. Within the European Union, member states largely pursued their own national space programs, though they often coordinated through the European Space Agency. India, Iran, North Korea, Australia, Israel, Canada, Japan, and South Korea, among others, also had space-based capabilities.

China and Russia developed robust counterspace capabilities. Some of these weapons could strike a satellite directly or detonate a warhead near a satellite or ground station, destroying or severely impacting its ability to function. For example, China and Russia could launch direct-ascent, anti-satellite weapons from Earth and strike a satellite in orbit. In addition, China and Russia could conduct attacks on ground stations that were responsible for the command and control of satellites or the relay of satellite mission data to users. In November 2021, Russia tested a direct-ascent anti-satellite weapon.[62]

In addition to direct attacks, some countries developed anti-satellite weapons that could destroy or degrade the functioning of satellites or ground stations without making physical contact. For example, China and Russia could use lasers to blind the sensors on satellites or cause components to overheat. High-powered microwave weapons could disrupt a satellite's electronics or cause permanent damage to electrical circuits and processors in a satellite. A nuclear device detonated in space could create a high-radiation environment and an electromagnetic pulse that would have indiscriminate effects on satellites in affected orbits. China, Russia, and several other countries developed cyber capabilities to intercept data or insert false or corrupted data in a satellite system, including destroying the capabilities of computer systems. These cyber attacks could target ground stations, end-user equipment, and the satellites themselves.[63]

The U.S. government's *State of the Space Industrial Base* report bluntly warned, "Strategic competition in space remains a paramount concern—China continues to compete toward a strategic goal of displacing the U.S. as the dominant global space power economically, diplomatically and militarily by 2045, if not earlier."[64] But space was only one of many areas the private sector was expanding into, and a growing number of venture capital firms took notice. The defense industrial base was in the process of a tectonic shift.

Venture capital investments in the defense sector exploded by 2021. According to an assessment from the research firm PitchBook, "VCs are increasingly investing in companies that are developing innovative technologies to help the U.S. military keep pace with emerging threats."[65] Such companies as Founders Fund, which provided funding to SpaceX, began to invest in start-up companies that developed satellite imagery, artificial intelligence, space technology, cyber security, and autonomous platforms such as drones. It was a striking development since most venture capital firms had previously eschewed the defense sector.

Venture capital itself was nothing new in the U.S. economy. Before World War II, J. P. Morgan, the Rockefellers, and the Vanderbilts invested in private companies, though venture capital was mostly the domain of wealthy individuals. By the 1960s, such investors as Arthur Rock made a profession of venture capital. The son of Jewish immigrants, Rock cut his teeth on his father's small candy store in Rochester, New York; earned an MBA at Harvard Business School; worked in the corporate finance department at Hayden, Stone & Company in New York; and then established a San Francisco–based venture capital firm in 1961 with his new partner, Tommy Davis—appropriately named

Davis & Rock. In 1968, Rock bankrolled the technology company Intel.

But the benefit of venture capital firms was heavily debated. Intel's co-founder, Gordon Moore, coined the term "vulture capital" and warned that venture capital firms could pick companies clean.[66] As one assessment concluded, "Semiretired millionaires who routinely arrived late for pitch meetings, they'd take half your company and replace you with a CEO of their choosing—if you were lucky."[67] But venture capital could also be a lifeline to companies and provide funding essential for innovation.

In simple terms, venture capital firms attempted to locate, finance, and profit from promising start-up companies.[68] They raised money from individual investors, investment banks, and other financial institutions for one- or two-year timelines—a lightning-fast period of time compared to the slow regulatory and peacetime mindset within the Department of Defense. Funding typically came in stages or rounds, such as seed funding, series A, series B, and series C. The goal of venture capital firms was to make money—lots of it. In order to play such an influential role, investors usually took large equity positions in their companies and exerted substantial control. But success could be elusive. In many cases, venture capital investments failed—and investors expected many of them to fail. The hope was to finance a "unicorn"—a start-up company valued at over $1 billion.[69] Some venture capital firms, such as Andreessen Horowitz, could invest in 15 start-ups each year after listening to thousands of pitches. Of those, perhaps two-thirds might eventually fold, three or four might financially prosper, and one *might* become a unicorn.[70]

For decades, venture capital firms stayed away from the defense sector. But that began to change by the end of the 2010s. There were 848 venture capital deals in 2021 in defense technology—nearly five times larger than the 184 deals in 2013. The value of those deals also skyrocketed, from $1.9 billion in 2013 to $40.5 billion in 2021—roughly 21 times larger (Figure 7.2).[71] The trend lines over the decade showed a steady increase in the deal count and deal value of venture capital investment as firms became increasingly willing to invest in space technology, autonomous platforms, and other areas with commercial *and* defense applications. Thiel and some other venture capitalists averred

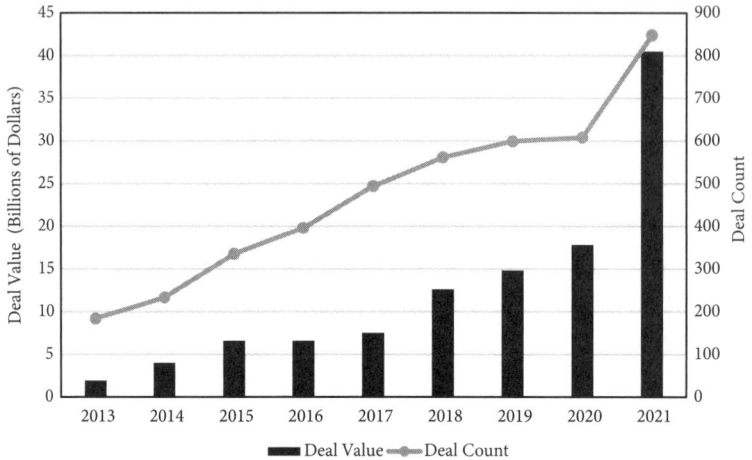

FIGURE 7.2 Venture capital investment in defense companies, 2013–2021.[72]

that investing in defense technology could strengthen U.S. national security and reduce the possibility of wars like those in Afghanistan and Iraq by helping the U.S. military and intelligence community develop more targeted responses. "If we can pinpoint real security threats," Thiel explained, "we can defend ourselves without resorting to the crude tactic of invading other countries."[73]

Big venture capital firms such as Sequoia Capital and Andreessen Horowitz led the charge in investing in the defense sector. Other major firms, such as Lux Capital, General Catalyst, Shield Capital, Accel Partners, and Founders Fund, also invested in defense start-ups. In addition, several big defense contractors created their own venture capital funds: Lockheed Martin launched Lockheed Martin Ventures, and Raytheon established Raytheon Ventures. As investors expected, many start-ups went out of business. In some cases, the start-ups lacked a sound business plan. In other cases, the Defense Department failed to recognize the innovation occurring in the private sector or couldn't move its stifling bureaucracy and peacetime mentality fast enough.

Andreessen Horowitz's Katherine Boyle asserted, "Time is running out with Silicon Valley [for the Department of Defense]." Boyle had come to Andreessen Horowitz after serving as a partner at the venture capital firm General Catalyst, and after being a general assignment reporter at the *Washington Post*. She noted, "After five years of [the Department of Defense] saying 'we want to work with the best start-ups,' we have, at most, two years before founders walk away and private capital dries up. And many, many start-ups will go out of business waiting for [the Department of Defense] to award real production contracts." As Boyle recognized, Defense Department officials talked a good game in claiming that they wanted to work with start-ups. But in practice, the Pentagon couldn't shake its peacetime mindset. The answer, she argued, was to "award production contracts to the most important start-ups with the teams who've proven they can build" and to change the culture of Pentagon procurement. "Procurement officers are punished for betting on a young startup," she said. "Incentivize the procurement officers to work with venture-backed startups that can build needed capabilities for the warfighter.[74] For Boyle and many others, the main problem in the U.S. defense industrial base was *not* a lack of cutting-edge companies that could develop and produce essential matériel for warfighters. Instead, it was a business climate and procurement system that made it far too difficult for start-ups and other outsiders to secure contracts.

Some venture capital gambles did pan out. These included SpaceX, Palantir, Anduril (which produced autonomous platforms and advanced technology), Shield AI (artificial intelligence–powered systems and technology), HawkEye 360 (geospatial analytics), Skydio (drones), and Epirus (electronic warfare and advanced electronics).[75] Several of them—such as SpaceX, Anduril, and Palantir—became unicorns that were valued at over $1 billion.

Yet venture capital was not the only area where the private sector increasingly invested in defense, reshaping the U.S. defense industrial base. Private equity was another.

The modern private equity industry developed in the late 1970s and was pioneered by New York–based investment company Kohlberg Kravis Roberts & Company.[76] Unlike venture capital funds, which focused on start-ups, private equity firms raised funds from financial institutions, pension funds, insurance companies, endowments, and wealthy individuals to acquire and then sell *established* companies.[77] Following an acquisition, private equity managers endeavored to add value to a portfolio company by reorganizing the firm, cutting costs, and attempting to improve operations. After reforms and reorganization were complete, a private equity firm typically sought to make a return on its investment by selling the portfolio company. Sales of portfolio companies—often referred to as "exits"—generally were made to another company or to another private equity firm. Consequently, private equity firms had a "buy to sell" business model: they purchased companies with the intent of selling them within a limited period, such as four to five years.[78]

Unlike public companies, private equity firms in the United States were not registered with the governmental financial watchdog, the Security and Exchange Commission, and were not required to publish annual reports on or submit financial statements for any of the companies in their portfolios.[79] Before 2000, private equity firms were generally not interested in the defense market compared to other sectors because they (correctly) perceived defense as a closed shop dominated by a small number of primes, such as Lockheed Martin, Raytheon, Boeing, and Northrop Grumman.[80]

By the 2010s, however, the number of private equity acquisitions of defense firms had skyrocketed. Between 2004 and 2009, there was an average of 67 deals per year. But that number doubled over the next decade, averaging 120 deals per year between 2015 and 2021.[81] Investors also went after larger defense companies. Prior to 2010, private equity firms generally bought small or midsize companies. By 2021, however, firms were involved in deals for companies of all sizes. The median size of a deal in 2000 was $50 million; by 2021, the median had jumped to nearly $350 million (Figure 7.3).[82] Private equity firms gobbled up companies in such sectors as cyber, intelligence, additive manufacturing, defense electronics, space, drones, and sensors.[83]

By 2021, numerous private equity firms were active in the defense sector. Some of the larger ones were the Carlyle Group, Veritas Capital, Arlington Capital Partners, and Stellex Capital Management. These firms bought established companies in a wide range of defense sectors. For example, Veritas Capital and Evergreen Coast Capital acquired Cubic Corporation, a San Diego-based defense electronics company, for $3.0 billion.[84] The private equity firm KPS Capital Partners purchased a controlling stake in AM General, which produced Humvees—the

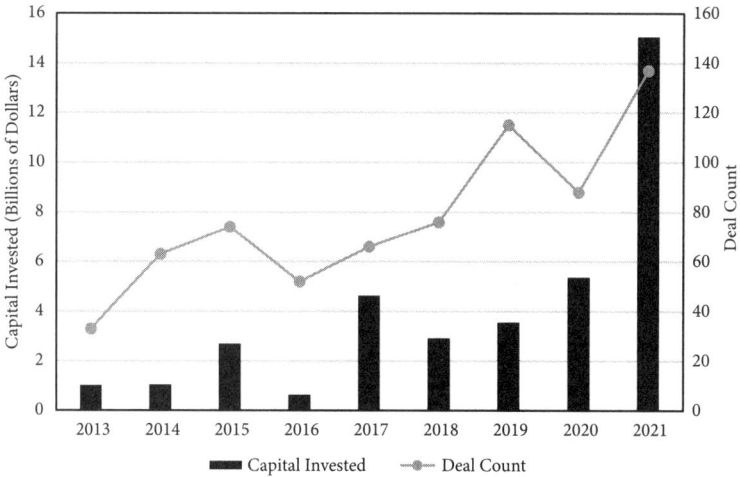

FIGURE 7.3 Private equity deals in the defense sector, 2013–2021.[85]

light, four-wheel-drive trucks used by the U.S. military, most recently in the wars in Iraq and Afghanistan.[86] The result was a major increase in private sector investment in space, autonomous platforms, cyber, electronic warfare, and software.

———

By 2021, there was a major shift in private investment in defense—especially in the United States—led by venture capital and private equity firms. What explains this phenomenon? There were several factors.

First was the Pentagon's growing interest in technologies that had both military *and* commercial applications. For many investors and non-defense companies, the scope of what "defense" meant began to broaden. Following the collapse of the dot-com bubble in the early 2000s, institutional investors turned to private equity funds to diversify their portfolios. This inflow of capital caused private equity to expand into new fields.[87] But many investors were wary of defense, since they refused to invest in companies that produced weapons systems that could potentially kill people. A range of big technology companies felt the same way.

Google employees revolted in 2018 against their company's involvement in the Department of Defense's Project Maven. Google had significant capabilities to offer the U.S. military since Project Maven used imagery and other information collected by U.S. government drones and other platforms to detect individuals (such as terrorists) and objects (such as terrorist infrastructure), track their movement, and, in some cases, pass the information to platforms such as drones. As U.S. Deputy Secretary of Defense Robert Work summarized, "the Department of Defense must integrate artificial intelligence and machine learning more effectively across operations to maintain advantages over increasingly capable adversaries and competitors."[88]

Google initially became involved in Project Maven in September 2017, providing artificial intelligence and machine learning expertise. But a chunk of Google's workforce strongly objected. A scathing letter to Google's CEO, Sundar Pichai, signed by thousands of Google employees, declared, "We believe that Google should not be in the business of war."[89] The signatories expressed alarm that participating in Project Maven contravened the company's motto "Don't Be Evil" and would devastate its reputation and undermine public trust. "Building this technology to assist the U.S. Government in military surveillance—and potentially lethal outcomes—is not acceptable," the letter concluded.[90] Faced with a corporate revolt, Google cut ties with Project Maven. But the company still worked for the Pentagon under new "AI Principles" and ethical guidelines, which explained that Google would not work on "weapons or other technologies whose principal purpose or implementation is to cause or directly facilitate injury to people."[91]

With the Department of Defense's growing interest in software and high-tech systems, technologies that had both a commercial *and* a defense function were more palatable to venture capital and private equity investors. Space, software, cyber, artificial intelligence, autonomous platforms, quantum, and sensor technologies all had commercial and military uses.[92] Defense itself was changing dramatically. The massive amount of digital data collected from satellites, drones, surveillance, cameras, social media costs, and other types of sources motivated Pentagon planners to find new ways of analyzing information.[93]

The U.S. Department of Defense became more amenable to private-sector involvement even if too many Pentagon officials operated in a peacetime mindset. To begin with, the Pentagon encouraged vetted sources of private capital to enter the national security marketplace in reaction to bids by foreign companies—particularly from concerning countries such as China—in the defense supply chain.[94] In addition, the department's byzantine acquisition practices were slowly evolving, although not quickly enough. One feature that had long spooked investors was the reality of long-term contracts set up between suppliers and the companies that put together the end products. Contracts often had 20- or 30-year life cycles. While this model sometimes led to steady cash flows, it did not guarantee rapid profits and clashed with the traditional model, in which investors wanted to exit at a premium after four or five years. By 2021, companies involved in cutting-edge technology of interest to the Pentagon had a chance of a shorter return on investment.[95]

Another reason for the jump in venture capital and private equity investment was that great power competition had replaced terrorism as the primary concern of the U.S. government. Russia was engaged in a brutal war in eastern Ukraine after illegally seizing Crimea, and China had turned several reefs in the South China Sea into military bases. Great power competition was alive and well, and the U.S. Department of Defense needed help in developing cyber, space, intelligence, and other capabilities to deal with the rising threats. The Donald Trump administration's 2018 *National Defense Strategy* unambiguously argued that "inter-state strategic competition, not terrorism, is now the primary concern in U.S. national security."[96] Venture capital and private equity firms took notice. So did the companies they were investing in.

Yet despite the surge in venture capital and private equity investment in the defense sector, some were strongly opposed to this type of funding.

U.S. Senator Elizabeth Warren was concerned that the rise in private capital created a cadre of greedy modern-day war profiteers. She cautioned that private investment "makes President Eisenhower's warning about the military-industrial complex seem quaint" and that "war profiteering is not new, but the significant expansion risks advancing private financial interests at the expense of national security."[97] Warren's concerns were not unprecedented. During President Franklin

Roosevelt's defense buildup before and during World War II, U.S. Secretary of Interior Harold Ickes, Secretary of War Henry Stimson, Assistant Attorney General Thurman Arnold, and elites such as newspaper columnist Walter Lippmann blasted the administration for supporting policies that, in their view, lined the pockets of rich executives and big businesses.[98]

But Warren's comments were largely a misreading of history, even of Eisenhower. As chief of staff of the army, Eisenhower believed that the U.S. defense industry played a pivotal role in winning World War II.[99] While Eisenhower as U.S. president warned about the "unwarranted influence" of the defense industry, his New Look strategy accelerated the buildup of missiles and other advanced electronics.[100] The Soviet Union's launch of Sputnik 1 had shown Eisenhower—and the world—how far behind the United States was in some areas of advanced technology. In fact, Eisenhower supported a strong and vibrant defense industrial base to protect the nation from external threats. The comments in his 1961 farewell address were focused on the future—not the present—and a recognition that the establishment of a large military establishment required scrutiny by the U.S. population.[101] An "alert and knowledgeable citizenry," he argued, was important to ensure "the proper meshing of the huge industrial and military machinery of defense . . . so that security and liberty may prosper together."[102]

Other skeptics worried about excessive private sector influence—and even corruption—in the Department of Defense. One *New York Times* investigative piece noted, "[T]he close ties between venture capital firms and Defense Department decision makers have . . . put a new twist on long-running questions about industry access and influence at a time when the Pentagon is under pressure to rethink how it allocates its huge procurement budget."[103] The investigative report argued that a growing list of former senior Department of Defense officials—such as former secretary of defense Mark Esper, former secretary of the army Ryan McCarthy, and former head of the Pentagon's Defense Innovation Unit Raj Shah—were using their connections in the military to work for venture capital firms and cash in on the potential to sell weapons systems to the Pentagon. In fact, the *New York Times* identified over 50 former Pentagon and national security officials who had left the government in the previous five years and were now working for venture capital or private equity firms in the defense sector.[104]

For Senator Warren, current and former Pentagon officials were "too cozy with private investment firms," raising numerous questions about possible corruption and federal ethics infractions.[105] James Fallows, a national correspondent for the *Atlantic Monthly* magazine, warned about "the corrupting effect on the uniformed military by their alliance with contractors."[106] Despite these concerns, however, there was nothing illegal or fraudulent about the vast majority of this activity. In fact, it was generally helpful to have individuals that knew both the government and private sector because they could bridge the gap between the two sides.

Still others were concerned that the venture capital and private equity bubble might burst. Some evidence suggested that private equity investment in defense companies raised the risk of bankruptcy for acquired companies.[107] Private equity investors typically structured their acquisitions as leveraged buyouts. In a leveraged buyout, a private equity firm might finance 60 to 90 percent of the acquisition of a company by using debt capital. The debt was often placed on the acquired company's balance sheet, and the acquired company was responsible for servicing this debt.[108] What's more, private firms operated with less regulatory and investor oversight compared to publicly traded companies. In some cases, the result was a downgrade for defense contractors owned by private equity firms.[109] Yet there was not a major uptick in defense bankruptcies caused by private equity investment, making this concern somewhat exaggerated.

Many of these objections were simply the latest iteration of long-standing concerns about strong defense budgets and worries—often mistaken—about the excessive influence of a greedy and nefarious "military-industrial complex."[110] These fears came from all sides of the political spectrum. As one *New York Times* writer summarized, "It is not a stretch to believe that the armaments industry—which profits not only from domestic sales but also from tens of billions of dollars in annual exports—manipulates public policy to perpetuate itself."[111] Similarly, Ron Paul, a Republican congressman, railed against "blank checks to the military-industrial complex" that, he argued, did not actually make the United States more secure.[112]

Despite these objections, venture capital and private equity money continued to pour into the defense sector and, in most cases, was helpful in developing the U.S. defense industrial base.

By 2021, the private sector had spearheaded multiple innovations in the defense sector. SpaceX and Starlink led the way in space. Elon Musk eventually expanded these efforts to create Starshield, a business unit of SpaceX with satellites in low Earth orbit that provided space capabilities to U.S. intelligence agencies, such as the National Reconnaissance Office.[113] As China tried to close the military gap with the United States, it was the commercial sector—enjoying synergy with the government—that gave the United States an advantage in competition among the great powers. In space, the United States remained the dominant global power with potent space and counterspace capabilities, though China emerged as the second most capable space nation.[114]

In a fitting tribute, *Time* magazine christened Elon Musk Person of the Year in 2021. "This is the man," *Time* wrote, "who aspires to save our planet and get us a new one to inhabit: clown, genius, edgelord, visionary, industrialist, showman, cad; a madcap hybrid of Thomas Edison, P. T. Barnum, Andrew Carnegie and Watchmen's Doctor Manhattan, the brooding, blue-skinned man-god who invents electric cars and moves to Mars."[115] Yet 2021 was not just the year for SpaceX, Starlink, and Musk's ultimate quest to colonize Mars. Venture capital and private equity had arrived in the defense sector, and they were driving innovation.

How would the systems these companies developed perform on the battlefield? The world was about to find out thousands of miles from Silicon Valley in Ukraine.

8

The New Cyber Wars

> Our huge advantage is the private sector. I mean, this is what we have learned from Russia-Ukraine. Being able to leverage the private sector, being able to work with the private sector, being able to understand what the private sector is doing is tremendously important.
>
> —GENERAL PAUL NAKASONE, director of the National Security Agency

> We really have been closely involved [in Ukraine] in a way that I frankly would never have imagined when I started at Microsoft 28 years ago in what I really think of as the frontlines of this cyber war.
>
> —BRAD SMITH, Microsoft CEO

RUSSIA'S BRUTAL INVASION OF UKRAINE began several hours *before* ground forces stormed across the Russian and Belarusian borders on February 24, 2022.[1] Cyber actors from Russia's Main Intelligence Directorate, the GRU, launched a cyberweapon called FoxBlade, a Trojan horse wiper malware. The GRU used FoxBlade to infiltrate over 19 government and private sector entities across Ukraine and attempted to take down Ukraine's critical infrastructure—from the electricity grid to the financial system—by erasing, or "wiping," data on targeted computers.[2] The GRU unit involved in the cyber attack was Military Unit

74455, a cyber warfare group that U.S. officials referred to as Sandworm and that was well known to cyber experts.[3] Earlier that month, a U.S. intelligence report had warned that Russia was highly capable in cyber operations and remained "a top cyber threat as it refines and employs its espionage, influence, and attack capabilities."[4]

In response to Sandworm's attack, the Microsoft Threat Intelligence Center acted quickly. The center was located over 5,400 miles from Kyiv, in Redmond, Washington—not far from Elon Musk's SpaceX development facility—and led by engineer John Lambert. Microsoft software detected FoxBlade in Ukrainian systems. More than 40 percent of Russia's destructive attacks were aimed at organizations in Ukraine's critical infrastructure, such as its electricity grid.[5] Microsoft executives immediately reached out to the Ukrainian government and provided technical advice on steps to combat the malware. In addition, Microsoft engineers updated virus detection systems to detect and block FoxBlade from proliferating across computer networks in Ukraine and around the globe.[6] Tom Burt, Microsoft's corporate vice president, contacted Anne Neuberger, the White House's deputy national security advisor for cyber and emerging technologies, who suggested they alert governments in Europe. Before midnight in Washington on February 23, Microsoft was in touch with senior officials in Poland, the Baltic states, and other European countries about Russian cyber operations.[7] The war in Ukraine had begun.

FoxBlade was only the start of Russian cyber operations. Between February 23 and April 8, 2022, Microsoft's Threat Intelligence Center identified nearly 40 separate GRU attacks that permanently destroyed files in dozens of Ukrainian organizations.[8] In response, Microsoft established a secure line of communication with Ukrainian cyber officials to ensure a rapid response and to help Ukrainian government agencies and companies defend against future attacks.[9] In addition, Microsoft helped shift 16 Ukrainian government ministries and numerous Ukrainian corporations from local servers to cloud platforms, protecting their computer services from Russian attack and earning the company a peace prize from Ukrainian President Volodymyr Zelensky. "Big tech support Ukraine," affirmed Ukrainian Vice Prime Minister Mykhail Federov. "We are grateful to have you on the light side of digital. Microsoft stands for truth and for peace."[10]

Microsoft was not alone. The outbreak of conflict in Ukraine was a clear indication that the United States faced an evolving wartime environment that pitted Ukraine on one side, along with the United States and its European and Asian backers, and Russia on the other side, aided by China, Iran, and North Korea. The war in Ukraine was also the latest example of synergy in the defense industrial base between the private sector and the government. Companies like Microsoft were essential to the development of capabilities—including cyber capabilities—used by the Ukrainian government on a battlefield that ranged from Kyiv and other cities to the cyber and space domains. The private sector was led by such individuals as Microsoft chief executive officer Brad Smith and engineer John Lambert. As a Microsoft analysis concluded, "Unlike the traditional threats of the past, cyber defenses rely on a unique level of public and private collaboration. . . . The private sector, particularly technology companies, are on the front lines of cyber and information attacks."[11]

The role of Microsoft and other cyber companies highlighted the evolution of the cyber domain in the defense industrial base. Air, land, and sea had long been important domains of warfare. But space and cyberspace became increasingly important domains for the great powers. While Russia was a serious cyber threat to the United States, a 2022 U.S. intelligence assessment concluded that "China's cyber pursuits and export of related technologies increase the threats of attacks against the U.S. homeland, suppression of U.S. web content that Beijing views as threatening to its control, and the expansion of technology-driven authoritarianism globally."[12] It continued that the People's Liberation Army and other Chinese agencies were investing in sophisticated cyber capabilities to conduct offensive attacks, collect intelligence, and influence operations against the United States, including its critical infrastructure.

With the great powers expanding their cyber capabilities, the war in Ukraine was a serious test of cyber offense and defense—as well as air, land, naval, and space capabilities. Ukraine's struggles with Russian cyber operations started well before the February 2022 invasion. And Lambert had been preparing for this fight for years.

Lambert lived by a simple motto: "You never know where your journey will take you. Stick with it. You might just be surprised where you end up."[13]

Lambert's life passion for computers began when his parents, who were both accountants, bought an IBM personal computer. "That PC started my journey in programming," he recalled.[14] At Brother Martin High School in New Orleans, he took a computer class from Brother Neal Golden, who encouraged Lambert to compete in local computer programming competitions. "I remember our team of four being beaten by a team of just two people from a rival school. How could fewer people solve all the same problems we had in less time?" he wondered. "Their success taught me a powerful lesson in teams and collaboration."[15] It was an experience that would come in handy later in life when dealing with Russian cyber attackers.

Following graduation from Tulane University with a bachelor's degree in computer science, Lambert joined IBM as a software engineer. After nearly three years at IBM, he moved to Microsoft in 2000 to become lead program manager in the Microsoft Windows Security Group. It was an era when software engineers grappled with such computer worms as Blaster, Sasser, Code Red, and Nimda. Some of these worms were deadly. The Nimda virus, which some computer experts called "one of the worst bugs in history," used five different infection vectors to rip through computers running on Windows 95, 98, 2000, and Windows NT.[16] Nimda clogged computer servers and slowed down traffic on countless corporate networks and infected thousands of home personal computers. Blaster was a computer worm that burrowed through internet connections and crippled thousands of machines using Microsoft's Windows 2000 and XP operating systems.[17]

Lambert discovered that he loved the security side of computer science. "I switched from shipping products to finding security bugs in them," he recalled.[18] And he turned out to be extremely good at it. So good, in fact, that in 2014 he founded and managed the Microsoft Threat Intelligence Center to defend Microsoft and its customers against adversary threats. "I set it up because organizations face threat actors, not threats," said Lambert.[19]

Over the next several years, Microsoft Threat Intelligence Center became the *corps d'elite* of cyber security units, with a growing number of cyber attacks by major powers. Russia's GRU Sandworm unit was active, including conducting a December 2015 attack that temporarily took down part of Ukraine's power grid, the 2017 NotPetya cyber attack that caused massive damage across the globe, cyber attacks against the 2017 French presidential election, and the brazen cyber attack at the opening ceremony of the 2018 Winter Olympics in Pyeongchang, South Korea. In response to Sandworm's operations, the U.S. Department of Justice referred to the Russian GRU unit as engaging "in a global campaign of hacking, disruption and destabilization, representing the most destructive and costly cyber-attacks in history."[20]

Sandworm's NotPetya attack was particularly destructive. Russian attackers started to develop NotPetya in December 2016, when they released the "Moonraker worm," which could self-proliferate across networks and disrupt systems through data encryption.[21] By May 2017, the GRU had figured out how to compromise its key target, the Ukrainian software firm Intellect Services, which produced the popular M.E.Doc accounting software.[22] Before deploying NotPetya, the GRU had propagated a newly developed piece of malware called "XData" through this server. XData infected 134 victims and caused some minor disruptions, but it did not significantly affect Ukraine.[23] The GRU deployed NotPetya, propagated it to M.E.Doc clients using a compromised software update on June 22, and activated it across all infected machines on June 27. NotPetya self-proliferated across networks from all affected machines before executing a disk encryption program that irreversibly destroyed all data on targeted computers.[24] "NotPetya spread in an uncontrollable way," said Lambert. "It was a really destructive attack."[25]

Orchestrated by Russian military intelligence, NotPetya was the most damaging cyber attack in history up to that point. It disabled an estimated 500,000 computers in Ukraine alone and decreased Ukraine's gross domestic product by approximately 0.5 percent in 2017.[26] It also had a massive global impact. The malware infected the computer systems of organizations in 65 countries, including companies in the United States, United Kingdom, France, Estonia, Germany, Australia, and even Russia itself.[27]

But NotPetya was only the beginning.

By this time, cyberspace had become an increasingly contested domain of warfare by the great powers and a crucial part of their defense industrial bases. It was a wartime environment on cyber platforms. Organizations across the globe spent a stunning $150 billion per year on cyber security.[28] The U.S. military developed significant cyber capabilities centered on the National Security Agency and U.S. Cyber Command. The U.S. cyber security budget was over $17 billion, of which the National Security Agency received roughly $10 billion.[29] According to a report by Harvard University's Cyber Project, the United States was the world's dominant cyber power, followed by China and then Russia.[30] The United States had particularly robust offensive cyber capabilities, giving it the ability to disrupt, degrade, and destroy an adversary's critical infrastructure (such as its energy sector, financial system, electricity grid, and water system), command-and-control capabilities, computers, information systems, and weapons systems.

Other great powers also had offensive cyber capabilities. U.S. intelligence agencies concluded that Chinese organizations such as the PLA's Unit 61398 were "capable of launching cyber attacks that would disrupt critical infrastructure services within the United States, including against oil and gas pipelines and rail systems."[31] China was a global leader in cyber surveillance and censorship at home and abroad, and Chinese agencies routinely conducted espionage and disinformation campaigns. Russia was also highly capable—as Lambert and others at Microsoft were acutely aware—and posed a serious threat to critical infrastructure, such as underwater cables and industrial control systems, in the United States and allied countries.

Iran and North Korea too had notable offensive cyber capabilities. One U.S. intelligence assessment summarized, "Iran uses increasingly sophisticated cyber techniques to conduct espionage; it is also attempting to deploy cyber attack capabilities that would enable attacks against critical infrastructure in the United States and allied countries."[32] Iran had targeted U.S. casinos, dams, the power grid, and financial institutions like Bank of America, JPMorgan Chase, and the New York Stock Exchange. It developed destructive malware through one of its state-sponsored hacking groups, Elfin. One example was "Shamoon," malware that deleted files from an infected computer and then wiped the computer's master boot record (a critical part of a computer's storage device that boots before the operating system loads), making it unusable. Iran also conducted aggressive cyber attacks against foreign parliaments, government agencies, and companies. North Korea too posed a serious threat with capabilities to launch ransomware campaigns against healthcare organizations and other critical infrastructure targets.[33]

As global powers raced to build cyber capabilities, Microsoft and other private sector actors faced growing challenges in the lead-up to the Russian invasion of Ukraine. One of Lambert's biggest tests came in November 2020, when an analyst at the cybersecurity company FireEye (which had received In-Q-Tel support and later changed its name to Mandiant) detected something unusual. While examining sign-in logs for the prior day, the analyst noticed that a user had signed in from an unregistered device. The analyst called the user and asked a simple question: "Did you register a different device?" The answer—an unequivocal no—set off an aggressive global hunt that Microsoft and other cyber experts traced back, yet again, to the Russian government.[34] The Mandiant analyst informed colleagues, including Charles Carmakal, Mandiant's senior vice president and chief technology officer, of the unusual activity. At 9:00 p.m., Carmakal reached out for help. "We didn't want to do it alone because we knew that we'd be able to gain more speed by pulling in an organization that is highly capable—has smart people, has really strong intelligence and could help us investigate it," Carmakal explained.[35]

That organization was Microsoft. Over time, Lambert and his team at the Microsoft Threat Intelligence Center had developed extraordinary telemetry capabilities, which involved collecting data from Microsoft hardware and software and sending it back to Microsoft so that engineers could identify and fix problems. Microsoft also used sensors and "web crawlers"—programs that visited webpages, downloaded their content, and processed information—to constantly scan the internet and look for threatening cyber actors and their activity. In addition, Microsoft developed powerful machine learning and artificial intelligence tools to analyze data and process billions of requests across millions of webpages.[36] When Microsoft assessed that a country, such as Russia, targeted or compromised an organization or individual, it delivered a "nation-state notification" directly to the customer.[37]

In response to the call from FireEye, Microsoft established a global threat hunting campaign in the Microsoft Threat Intelligence Center. "From information we learned in collaborating with [FireEye]," explained Lambert, "we took those leads, and we started turning those over in our data sets. And we understood the scope started to grow very quickly from that."[38] Lambert and others at Microsoft realized that the supply-chain attack extended well beyond one security company. The attackers used advanced tactics, techniques, and procedures. They never used the same IP address across organizations, even changing IP addresses every time the group reentered the same organization's network. According to Lambert, the attackers were "sophisticated and stealthy in the sense that they took a lot of effort to silo how their operations looked and presented to a victim to be very different victim to victim."[39] That meant that traditional markers—including hashes, file names, and IP addresses—were less helpful for tracking the attacker's path.[40]

After conducting a wide range of analysis, including examining 50,000 lines of SolarWind's code, Microsoft and FireEye engineers were confident that the perpetrators were *not* from the GRU. Instead, they were from the Russian Intelligence Service, or SVR, Russia's main external spy agency. They were part of a group that cyber experts called "Nobelium," also known by such names as Advanced Persistent Threat 29, Cozy Bear, and The Dukes.[41] The attack involved a complex cyber kill chain, a series of steps that began with reconnaissance and continued through the exfiltration of data and other types of attacks.

Microsoft investigators discovered that Russian attackers had attached malware to a software update from SolarWinds, a company based in Austin, Texas, that made network monitoring software. Russia hackers had secretly modified the source code of SolarWind's Orion network management software.[42] The malicious code then penetrated deep into the network of client organizations through legitimate software updates from SolarWinds, allowing it to bypass multiple layers of security and providing Russian attackers with immediate high-level permissions. "You got a sense that this attacker could start in hundreds of customer networks, very deep into them with elevated rights," said

Lambert. "When you realize how many enterprise customers and government departments use [SolarWinds], you knew that this attacker had achieved a place to have major impact, across the globe."[43]

As Microsoft eventually discovered, Russia's SolarWinds supply-chain attack gave Russia the ability to spy on and disrupt more than 18,000 computer systems across the globe, including in the U.S. Departments of Treasury, Commerce, State, and Defense.[44] In tandem with government agencies, such as the U.S. National Security Agency, Microsoft and other companies used advanced telemetry and additional methods to identify and counter the Russian attack. Private sector capabilities were crucial.

In March 2021, analysts at the Microsoft Threat Intelligence Center concluded that Russian-linked cyber actors might be prepositioning for a war because they began to ramp up attacks against Ukraine. To Lambert, Russian activities appeared aimed at securing persistent computer access to collect intelligence and facilitate future destructive attacks.[45] "It was an act of intimidation," he said. "The cyber operations were largely intended to have a psychological impact. Psychological operations are an important part of the Russian playbook."[46] As Russian forces began to build up near the Ukrainian border in April 2021, Microsoft analysts watched Nobelium—the Russian actor from the SVR involved in SolarWinds—launch a large-scale phishing attack in Ukraine.[47]

In mid-2021, Microsoft observed Russian cyber actors targeting supply-chain vendors in Ukraine and across the globe to secure access and preposition themselves for future attacks against Ukraine and NATO countries. A GRU unit, referred to by cyber experts as "Cadet Blizzard," compromised the computer network of an information technology firm that established resource management systems for Ukraine's Ministry of Defense and organizations in Ukraine's communications and transportation sectors. At the same time, the SVR's Nobelium attempted to access information technology firms serving government customers in NATO member states.[48]

Russian cyber attacks against Ukraine persisted over the rest of 2021. In August, a Russian cyber unit referred to by Microsoft experts as "Aqua Blizzard"—this time from the Federal Security Service (FSB),

Russia's domestic intelligence agency—launched a spear phishing campaign to access the accounts of Ukraine-based foreign military advisors and humanitarian workers.[49] Another Russian actor, nicknamed "Forest Blizzard," from the GRU's Military Unit 26165, attempted to compromise defense-related organizations in Ukraine.[50] More broadly, Russian cyber actors tried to gain persistent access to a large pool of government and nongovernment organizations that included Ukrainian defense, the defense industrial base, foreign policy, national and local administration, law enforcement, and humanitarian organizations.[51]

Microsoft analysts watched with growing alarm in early 2022 as Russia's cyber assault increased in intensity. Lambert explained, "At the beginning of January, before the outbreak of the war, we saw a wave of attacks designed to create fear by defacing websites or leaking gigabytes of information about residents."[52] Russian cyber actors launched wiper malware attacks against Ukrainian organizations with increasing intensity. These efforts suggested that Russian actions in Ukraine had entered a destructive phase that could further escalate. The Russian actor Cadet Blizzard, from the GRU, launched WhisperGate malware that deleted selected file extensions and then manipulated the master boot record to render targeted machines inoperable in Ukraine.[53]

While Ukrainian cyber defense had improved dramatically over the previous decade thanks to years of countering Russian cyber operations and help from organizations such as Microsoft, Ukraine still had vulnerabilities. The Ukrainian government operated exclusively on servers situated in major government buildings. These locations were vulnerable to Russian cruise and ballistic missile attacks, and their physical destruction could paralyze the work of the country's leadership. With help from Microsoft and other private sector firms, such as Amazon Web Services, the Ukrainian minister of digital transformation and colleagues in the parliament decided on February 17, 2022, to transfer local servers to information-processing centers across Europe.[54] Amazon Web Services also moved massive quantities of information from Ukrainian ministries, educational institutions, and private sector companies to Amazon data centers outside the country.

The timing was impeccable. Less than a week later, Russia invaded Ukraine.

Following the opening salvo of cyber attacks, Russia's conventional invasion began in the early hours of February 24, 2022, when the Russian military deployed electronic warfare systems against Ukrainian air defense radar. These electromagnetic disruptions were followed by an opening salvo of missile strikes against Ukrainian air defenses.[55] It was clearly a wartime environment as the conflict moved from cyberspace to the physical battlefield in Ukraine. Russia's airborne forces spearheaded the invasion, with help from the 9th Directorate of the Fifth Service of the FSB. The Russian military conducted the initial stage of the invasion along several axes.

In the north, Russian forces pushed toward Kyiv from Belarus, led by units from the Central Military District, including the 29th, 35th, and 36th Combined Arms Armies. In the northeast, Russian forces invaded west toward Kyiv from Russian territory, led by units from the Western Military District, including the 41st Combined and 2nd Guards Combined Arms Armies. Russian forces from the Western Military District moved toward such Ukrainian cities as Sumy and Kharkiv, including the 1st Guards Tank Army and 20th and 6th Combined Arms Armies. In the southeast, Russian forces from the Southern Military District pushed toward Luhansk, Donetsk, and Mariupol along the Sea of Azov. In the south, Russian forces from the Southern Military District and Russian Airborne Forces (VDV) moved from Crimea northwest toward Kherson, Mykolaiv, and Odesa, as well as north and east toward Melitopol, Berdyansk, and Mariupol (Figure 8.1).[56]

In the northern front, a company-size element of the VDV attempted an airborne seizure of Hostomel Airport, approximately 40 kilometers outside of Kyiv, to establish a base capable of rapidly transporting Russian matériel to the outskirts of the Ukrainian capital. This assault ultimately failed because of staunch Ukrainian defenses.[57] Meanwhile, follow-on forces advancing southward from Belarus were disrupted by Ukrainian defensive efforts. Russian advances were often unsupported by artillery, and ground forces did not attempt a series of combined-arms breakthroughs and exploitations, as Russian doctrine dictated.[58] Russian troops had likely not conducted adequate exercises of the invasion before the war, many soldiers did not even know they were going to Ukraine until the last minute, and the FSB had wildly unrealistic assessments that the Ukrainian population would either rise up

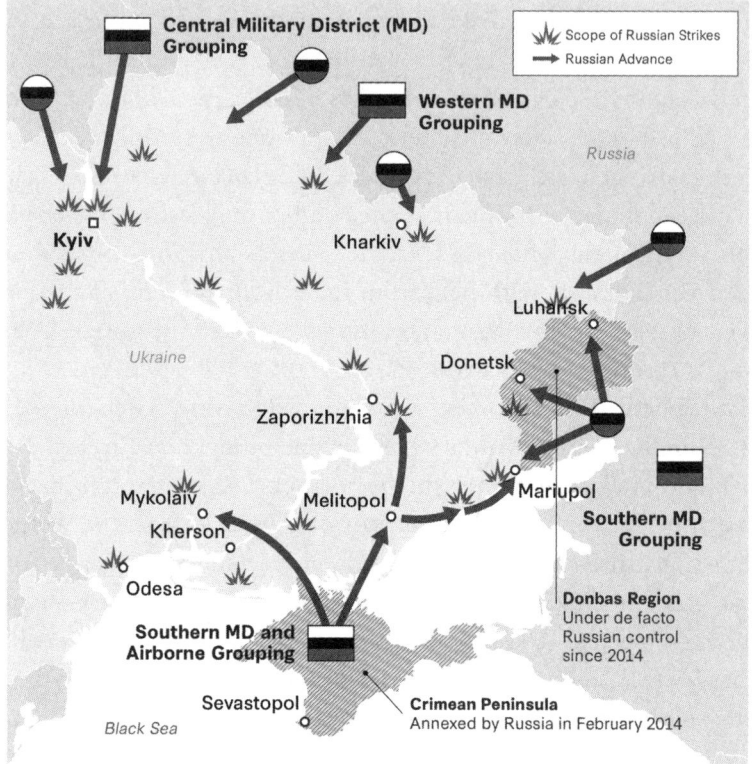

FIGURE 8.1 Russian invasion of Ukraine.[59]

against the government of President Zelensky or else would be cowed into submission.[60]

By contrast, Russian forces along the southern axis of advance made notable gains during the opening phase of the invasion. Elements of Russia's 42nd Motor Rifle Division, as well as some VDV elements, captured Kherson on February 25.[61] Russian forces also advanced along the coast of the Sea of Azov, beginning a siege of Mariupol on February 24 and capturing Melitopol on March 1. Ukrainian forces waged a protracted urban defense in Mariupol, which was gradually weakened by intensive Russian artillery shelling throughout April that culminated in a Ukrainian retreat to the Azovstal steel plant, where forces held out until they were overrun by a Russian advance in May 2022.[62]

The initial Russian invasion plan, which was heavily influenced by the FSB, was likely designed to seize Kyiv and other major urban centers in a blitzkrieg operation, forcing the capitulation of the Zelensky government and possibly clearing the way for the installation of a pro-Russian regime.[63] Russian forces deployed some of their most capable formations, such as the 1st Guards Tank Army, away from Kyiv and left insufficient forces in reserve. This approach strained Russian logistical capacities and left supply lines vulnerable, limiting the ability of Russian forces to regroup and make further thrusts toward the key targets of Kyiv and Kharkiv.

Facing the compounding difficulties of a logistics breakdown and a stalled advance to Kyiv, Russian political and military authorities reoriented the invasion around the eastern and southern axes of advance. By April 6, Russian forces had completely withdrawn along the northern axis of advance, removing forces from the outskirts of Kyiv and the city of Chernihiv.[64] On April 19, Russian Foreign Minister Sergey Lavrov announced that the "next phase" of the Russian invasion would focus on the "complete liberation" of the Donetsk and Luhansk oblasts in eastern Ukraine.[65] That same day, Russian missile and artillery forces struck hundreds of targets, primarily in the Donbas, as Ukrainian military officials claimed to repel seven different Russian thrusts against the line of contact.[66]

Russian offensive efforts in the south and east were uneven. While Russian forces advancing along the coast of the Sea of Azov secured control of a land bridge from Rostov-on-Don to Crimea, forces in the Donbas made only limited gains against determined Ukrainian defenses. By the end of April, Ukrainian forces had fought Russian forces to a standstill near Izyum in the Kharkiv oblast, including elements of the elite 1st Guards Tank Army.[67] Russian offensive efforts were hampered by the declining availability of Russian forces. U.S. defense officials assessed that the number of Russian battalion tactical groups had declined by 18 percent between late February and late April 2022.[68] British officials further assessed that by mid-May the Russian military had lost one-third of the total ground combat forces it had committed to the invasion in February.[69]

Ukraine's successes in preventing the capture of Kyiv and the collapse of the government and military were impressive. When the war began,

Russia had nearly five times as many military personnel as Ukraine, a defense budget 11 times larger, an economy almost eight times larger, and significantly better military capabilities.⁷⁰ Yet Russia's preponderance of power failed to deliver it a swift victory on the battlefield.

While Russian and Ukrainian forces battled across the country, Russian actors linked to the GRU, SVR, and FSB conducted multiple cyber attacks utilizing such malware as FoxBlade, Industroyer2, WhisperGate, SonicVote, CaddyWiper, DesertBlade, and FiberLake.⁷¹ The malware was designed to overwrite data and render machines unbootable, delete information, and destroy critical infrastructure. Russian-linked hackers used several common intrusion techniques, such as exploiting public-facing, web-based applications; sending spear phishing emails with attachments or links; and stealing credentials and using valid email accounts.⁷²

In response, Microsoft and other companies worked closely with the Ukrainian government to protect critical infrastructure, such as energy companies, from cyber attack. Microsoft provided emergency tips on cyber threats to the Ukrainian government and other countries and companies and countered attacks once they occurred. But the Russians kept coming. After countering a destructive malware family that Microsoft called WhisperGate, one of the next set of wipers dropped a note that said, "[T]he gate is still whispering."⁷³

In March 2022, Russia's Sandworm unit from the GRU conducted a wiper malware attack against a shipping company based in the western Ukrainian city of Lviv. Microsoft Defender, an antivirus software, detected and then blocked the malware using a suite of artificial intelligence models scanning for cyber threats across the company's network and cloud.⁷⁴ Microsoft and the Ukrainian government took several other measures in response to Russian attacks. One was the utilization of technology that Microsoft acquired the year before from a cyber security company named RiskIQ.⁷⁵ The technology identified and mapped attack surfaces, including devices that were unpatched against known vulnerabilities and susceptible to attack.⁷⁶ As Lambert explained, Microsoft used the technology from RiskIQ "to scan the Ukrainian government's network from the outside, and see what vulnerabilities attackers could see. The government then went ahead and closed up the breaches."[77] Microsoft also made available its Azure cloud computing platform and Office365 family of software.[78] The response highlighted a close synergy between Microsoft and the Ukrainian government.

In addition, Lambert and the Microsoft Threat Intelligence Center discovered that Russian malware could be countered by turning on a feature in Microsoft Defender, an antivirus software component of Microsoft Windows, called "controlled folder access." This feature required information technology administrators to access devices across their organization. The Ukrainian government passed emergency legislation that allowed Microsoft to remotely turn on the controlled folder access feature on devices throughout the country, including government devices. Microsoft could then ensure that only trusted apps could access protected folders, which was effective at blocking wiper attacks.[79]

Microsoft kept in close touch with cyber officials from the United States, NATO, and the European Union.[80] Before the war, U.S. Cyber Command had sent roughly 40 people to work with Ukraine to strengthen its cyber defenses, including through "Hunt Forward" teams. These teams included operators that sat alongside Ukrainian cyber experts to identify and mitigate malicious cyber activity on Ukrainian networks.[81] The combined cyber defense efforts of the Ukrainian government, private sector, and Ukrainian partners such as the United States were instrumental in blunting Russian cyber attacks. Russian military planners had hoped to use cyber warfare to blind Ukraine's command and control, cause chaos in its computer systems and communication networks, and undermine its ability to fight effectively.[82] But these efforts failed.

Lambert and his Microsoft Threat Intelligence Center had operated around the clock to help defend Ukraine from Russian cyber attacks. All of Russia's chief spy agencies—the GRU, SVR, and FSB—had launched aggressive cyber attacks against Ukrainian critical infrastructure, government, and civilian targets. Russia's goal was straightforward: to overthrow the Ukrainian government. Cyber tools were an important part of Russian operations, along with land, navy, air force, and space capabilities.

There were several takeaways. One was the increasing weaponization of cyber by major powers. Several U.S. adversaries—such as China, Russia, Iran, and North Korea—continued to develop their cyber capabilities, which had become an important part of their defense industrial bases. China and Russia had the most sophisticated capabilities, using malware, ransomware, interactive intrusion (in which adversaries mimicked expected user and administrator behavior), and other techniques to target governments, the private sector, and critical infrastructure networks. Russia would not be the last major power to use cyber as part of a conventional military campaign. As Lambert and others at Microsoft recognized, China had significant offensive cyber capabilities, including from such hacking groups as Volt Typhoon, and it would likely use these capabilities in a conflict in Taiwan, the South China Sea, or the East China Sea.

A second takeaway was the critical role played by the private sector in the cyber domain. "The turf of technology is the private sector," said Lambert, "and technology is made by the private sector."[83] This reality allowed companies like Microsoft to effectively aid Ukraine in response to Russian cyber attacks. "From an early stage, we gave Ukraine threat alerts. . . . We thought that the chance of us reaching [Ukrainian officials] was maybe 10 percent, but in practice 90 percent of the time we were able to contact them, give them the information directly and see how they took the information and use it to repel the attackers from their network. This happened daily."[84] Unlike such domains as air, land, and sea, cyberspace is owned and operated to a great extent by companies. This made the war in Ukraine fundamentally different from previous wars in the cyber domain, and it pulled in the private sector as a key part of the industrial base.

A final lesson was the limitation of offensive cyber. Some policymakers and analysts had predicted that cyber operations would revolutionize warfare by crippling adversary command, control, communications, computers, intelligence, surveillance, and reconnaissance capabilities.[85] The logic was that cyber operations could have strategic effects for at least three reasons: information technology enabled unrivaled operational speed compared to conventional warfare, the internet's design facilitated anonymity, and the cyber arena's global scale allowed actors to disrupt or damage targets at a massive scale.[86] However, the war in Ukraine suggested that cyber operations fall short of some arguments that cyber is a "game changer" in war, especially against states with substantial defensive capabilities. In Ukraine, Russian offensive cyber operations failed to significantly blind Ukrainian command-and-control efforts or threaten critical infrastructure for a prolonged period. Russian agencies conducted cyber attacks and utilized electronic warfare against Ukrainian targets, including destructive wiper attacks on hundreds of Ukrainian government and critical infrastructure systems.

But these attacks did not significantly impact the Ukrainian will or ability to fight. With the aid of Microsoft and other entities, Ukraine was able to blunt Russian operations. "Those who expected cyber would be an important part of a Russian victory in Ukraine were wrong," Lambert said.[87] Countries still needed armies to control territory, along with air, naval, and space-based capabilities. "Cyber doesn't wear boots" and can't conquer territory. "Cyber can provide an advantage, but it can't determine the outcome."[88] One broad lesson for future warfare is that the effects of offensive cyber operations may be fleeting against a major power with significant cyber defenses—unless exploited quickly and in combination with other tools.

Cyber was only one component of a much broader conflict in Ukraine that evolved into the largest conventional land war in Europe since World War II.

9

Slava Ukraini

Our weapons have been used in Ukraine since the second week of the war, and we are sanctioned by Russia and China.
—Palmer Luckey, cofounder of Anduril

Production is deterrence.
—William Laplante, U.S. Under Secretary of Defense for Acquisition and Sustainment

UKRAINE HAD BLUNTED RUSSIA'S INVASION and was now ready for offense.[1] In September 2022, the Ukrainian military conducted two major offensive operations. One was in Kharkiv oblast in eastern Ukraine; the other was in Kherson in the south. The Russian military was overstretched trying to stabilize a front that was nearly 1,000 miles long with an exhausted force and auxiliary units, including soldiers from the Luhansk and Donetsk People's Republics and the Rosgvardia, or National Guard. Russian morale was low; many units were severely understrength in Kharkiv, some at 25 percent strength; and Russia had not prepared formidable defenses.[2] Over the fall of 2022, the Ukrainian military retook roughly 4,600 square miles of territory in Kharkiv and nearly 4,000 square miles in Kherson.[3] It was an amazing military success against a notably larger military.

While Ukrainian forces continued to fight Russia throughout the rest of 2022 and over the next several years, they were not alone. U.S.

and foreign defense companies—including the big primes—provided hardware and software to Ukraine for offensive and defensive operations under the banner "Slava Ukraini" (Glory to Ukraine), a symbol of resistance to Russian aggression. Ukraine received air defense systems and munitions, such as Raytheon (RTX) Patriot air defense batteries, HAWK air defense systems, and PAC-2 missiles; artillery, such as Lockheed Martin's Army Tactical Missile System, Guided Multiple Launch Rocket System, and High Mobility Artillery Rocket System (HIMARS); cruise and ballistic missiles, such as the Boeing Harpoon and Raytheon (RTX) AIM-9M Sidewinder; ammunition, such as General Dynamics 155mm artillery rounds; ground vehicles, such as Abrams tanks and Stryker armored fighting vehicles produced by General Dynamics; and fighter aircraft, such as the Lockheed Martin F-16.[4] Northrop Grumman agreed to manufacture weapons inside Ukraine, making it the first U.S. company to take that step.[5]

An army of smaller U.S. and Western companies—AeroVironment, Aevex Aerospace, Amazon Web Services, Anduril, Google, Mandiant (FireEye), Maxar, Palantir, Planet Labs, SpaceX, Starlink, Zoom, and many others—provided critical software and hardware to the Ukrainian government. These companies were involved in securing sensitive government data on the cloud, using artificial intelligence and machine-learning systems to collect and analyze battlefield data, providing satellite communication to frontline forces, and manufacturing drones, loitering munitions, and other weapons systems.

One of the most innovative of these companies was Anduril, whose eccentric cofounder, Palmer Luckey, was distinguishable by his flamboyant Hawaiian shirts, flip-flops, and mullet hairstyle. "Never judge people for their body or what they wear!" he once tweeted. "Look at the fat techbro in his stupid hawaiian shirt."[6] As the war in Ukraine raged on, it became increasingly clear to Luckey and other entrepreneurs that the United States was in a wartime environment and needed a wartime industrial base. "We've seen for years that this shift away from counterinsurgency and back to superpower conflict was going to be what we needed to focus on," Luckey observed. "We've been putting all of our effort into things that are relevant to conflict or to preventing conflict with great powers like Russia and China."[7] In addition to Ukraine, war broke out in the Middle East after Hamas launched a surprise attack on October 7, 2023, against Israeli communities near the Gaza Strip, pulling into the war the United States, Iran, Hezbollah in Lebanon, the Houthis in Yemen, and others. Yet the U.S. defense industrial base struggled to keep up with these wars. With some exceptions—such as the surge in production of 155mm artillery rounds, Javelin antitank weapons systems, and Stinger man-portable air-defense systems—there was little urgency, insufficient money, and too many regulations.

The peacetime mentality of far too many U.S. government officials was maddening to Luckey.

As a child, Palmer Luckey was homeschooled by his mother in Long Beach, California, and, at 13, his entrepreneurial imagination was inspired by Donald Trump's book *The Art of the Deal*.[8] At the spirited age of 16, Luckey designed and constructed virtual reality headsets—including a 90-degree field of view and low latency—in his parents' garage. In 2012, still only 20, he launched a company, Oculus VR, which developed virtual reality technology, including a headset for virtual reality games. Facebook acquired his company in 2014 for $2 billion, though he was fired two years later for what he says was a $9,000 donation to Nimble America, a pro-Trump group that paid for an advertisement criticizing Hillary Clinton.[9] But Luckey was undeterred. He was inspired by the Japanese anime character Seto Kaiba, an innovative and rich video game entrepreneur. "You said technology has limits," Luckey frequently said, quoting Seto Kaiba. "Wrong."[10]

In 2017, the millennial trifecta of Palmer Luckey, Brian Schimpf, and Trae Stephens founded Anduril. Stephens was at the venture capital firm Founders Fund, which supported SpaceX, and Brian Schimpf was the former director of engineering at Palantir. Luckey had a head start, as he told Stephens when they first discussed starting a defense company. "I'm actually building a ramjet in my swimming pool," Luckey told him, referring to a jet engine that is used for high-speed supersonic or hypersonic systems such as missiles.[11] Together, they attempted to turn the strategy of run-of-the-mill defense contractors on its head. While most companies conducted research and development *after* responding to a request for proposal from the U.S. Department of Defense, Anduril's approach was to build first *and then sell*. Anduril's founders also shied away from focusing only on software, as Palantir and some other start-ups did, instead combining software and hardware. "We found that selling software was incredibly difficult. There's almost a moral aversion to paying software margins inside of the [Department of Defense]," explained Stephens. "Our focus was putting the thing we know [the Department of Defense] really needed, which was the software system and autonomy capability, and wrapping it in metal because it is significantly easier for the customer to buy metal than it is to buy software."[12]

Anduril was unusual in several other ways. Its name came from the sword used by Aragorn, one of the heroes of Tolkien's *Lord of the Rings*. Luckey was also obsessed with Dungeons & Dragons; his 1980s-designed home in Los Angeles featured a coffee table with a map of his Dungeons & Dragons campaign in which he played a wizard named Nilrim V. He had a fascination with owning military-grade vehicles, including a Mark V special operations boat that U.S. Navy Seals used for insertion and extraction operations, a U.S. Marine Corps Humvee, and half a dozen helicopters (including a UH-60 Black Hawk).[13] But breaking into the defense world was difficult, since, as Luckey saw it, the Pentagon's convoluted procurement rules were rigged in favor of the large prime contractors. Luckey joked that Anduril had to hire more lawyers and lobbyists than engineers.[14] Nevertheless, a growing number of venture capital firms were willing to invest in Anduril and its vision.[15] Luckey, Stephens, and Schimpf raised an initial seed round led by Founders Fund. After a year of gaining traction, Anduril raised additional money, with Founders Fund again leading the round. Several other venture capital firms, such as SV Angel and Human Capital, also joined.

For Luckey and others at Anduril, autonomous platforms were the future of warfare. "Fifty years from now the seas are going to be transparent. The skies are going to be transparent. We're going to know where every sub is, every airplane is," said Luckey. "So then it's a matter of: who's going to make enough stuff to beat the other guy's stuff."[16] By 2019, Anduril had landed several contracts with the Department of Defense and the Department of Homeland Security, the latter to help secure the southern and northern U.S. borders with sentry towers that could detect incursions. Anduril's valuation broke the $1 billion threshold during its series B round in late 2019. The round was, once again, led by Founders Fund, with additional funding from Andreessen Horowitz and other venture capital firms. In July 2020, Anduril raised another $200 million, which it used to expand research and development capabilities. Along the way, Anduril acquired several start-ups, such as Dive Technologies and Area-I, which produced autonomous aerial drones.[17]

One of Anduril's biggest draws for military and homeland security agencies was its family of autonomous systems, powered by the Lattice open software platform, a "battlefield operating system" that fused together information from multiple sources, constructed a real-time picture, and pushed relevant information to operators on the ground, in ships, and on aircraft. Lattice used artificial intelligence and computer vision to depict a view of the battlefield that could interact with a computer, tablet, or virtual reality headset. Lattice also served as the foundation for Anduril's hardware systems, such as drones, surveillance towers, and other sensor systems. One of the main benefits of Lattice was that it allowed Anduril to easily make changes at any time to one of its products, such as software, subsystems, or the overall hardware. One of Anduril's demonstration videos showed a Sentry Tower (one of the company's surveillance towers which combined long-range radar with artificial intelligence processing) detecting an enemy drone, processing the information through Lattice, using electronic warfare capabilities to disrupt the drone's control link, and dispatching a small, high-speed drone to destroy the enemy drone.[18]

Some of Anduril's most important hardware were Anvil, a counter-drone system deployed on the ground to target enemy drones; Ghost, an autonomous drone that could be assembled in roughly three minutes and could fly silently for an hour; Altius, a drone with four models that could deploy from air, land, and sea for up to 15 hours (and that Anduril later exported to Ukraine); Dust, a ground-based sensor that could detect people and objects; and Dive-LD, an underwater autonomous vehicle that could collect intelligence and conduct other missions at up to 6,000 meters under water.[19] Anduril's revenue soared: it generated $5 million in 2018, $29 million in 2019, $67 million in 2020, and $150 million in 2021—with a valuation of nearly $5 billion.[20] It would go on to raise $3.7 billion in venture capital funding by 2024.[21]

In addition to major defense contractors, which Luckey said produced "old legacy zombie programs," Anduril faced competition from a handful of start-ups funded by venture capital firms.[22] One was Shield AI, which developed artificial intelligence-powered drones and technology.

The war in Ukraine was a boon for Anduril and other Western companies that were part of a defense industrial base that included cyber, space, software, electronic warfare, and drones—not just fighter aircraft, tanks, and artillery.

In the early days of the war, Moscow conducted several attacks against Viasat KA-SAT modems to disable satellite services in Ukraine.[23] The attacks impacted 5,800 wind turbines in Germany, rendering them unable to communicate because of issues with their satellite communication. Russia utilized a type of malware called AcidRain, which was designed to wipe modems and routers.[24] Russia also targeted Ukraine's internet and communications network with missile and cyber attacks. Perhaps most concerning, the Ukrainian military's command-and-control system was crippled. Senior Ukrainian officials desperately appealed to Elon Musk for help.

"While your rockets successfully land from space—Russian rockets attack Ukrainian civil people!" tweeted Ukrainian Prime Minister Mykhailo Federov, tagging Musk's Twitter handle. "We ask you to provide Ukraine with Starlink stations."

Musk obliged. But how would he get the equipment quickly to Ukraine?

"We have the U.S. military looking to help us with transport, State has offered humanitarian flights and some compensation," SpaceX's Gwynne Shotwell informed Musk in an email. "Folks are rallying for sure."

"Cool," Musk responded. "Sounds good."[25]

With help from the U.S. government, Musk and his team began shipments to Ukraine through Poland. Musk asked for regular updates from his staff.

"Russia took offline a bunch of Ukraine communications infrastructure today, and a number of Starlink kits are already allowing Ukraine

Armed Forces to continue operating theater command centers," one SpaceX email updated Musk. "These kits can be life or death, as the opponent is now focusing heavily on comms infrastructure. They are asking for more."

When Ukrainians encountered problems with Starlink because of problems with the electricity grid—a major target of Russian cyber and missile attacks—Musk had a solution. "Let's offer to ship some field solar+battery kits," he said in an email. "They can have some Tesla Powerwalls or Megapacks too."[26]

Overall, SpaceX sent network terminals, thousands of dish antennas, battery kits, and other equipment to Ukraine, which provided Ukrainians with satellite-based internet connectivity. Many of the Starlink kits donated to Ukraine included a 23-inch-wide receiver dish that needed to be mounted outside, as well as a cord that connected to a simple router that projected a Wi-Fi internet signal.[27] By October 2022, SpaceX had forked over $80 million of its own money for Starlink terminals, equipment, and services in Ukraine.[28]

Starlink was crucial for a Ukrainian military at war. One Ukrainian commander quipped, "[F]ighting without Starlink service at the front line is like fighting without a gun."[29] It enabled soldiers to collect intelligence and conduct fire support operations against Russian positions.[30] Ukrainian drones relied on Starlink to launch strikes against forward-deployed Russian forces.[31] Starlink helped blunt Russia's attempts to jam signals, block the internet, and undermine Ukrainian command-and-control capabilities. Ukrainian soldiers were master innovators, real-life versions of the television character MacGyver, whose intellect, improvisation, and innovative solutions secured his way out of sticky situations in the 1980s television series. For example, some Ukrainian troops strapped Starlink user terminals to drones involved in strike operations.[32]

Musk was not alone in providing tech support to Ukraine. Ukrainian soldiers frequently communicated through videochat software, such as Google Meet and Zoom. Anduril and Luckey provided cutting-edge hardware, software, technical support, and training to the Ukrainian military. One example was Anduril's Altius drone. "It's a drone that fires out of a tube into the air and then unfolds itself—extends its wings, extends its tail, unfolds the propeller—and kind of transforms itself into a small airplane," explained Luckey. "We have versions of it that can carry up to a 30-pound warhead. So you've got a lot of punch in this thing."[33]

Palantir and its CEO, Alex Karp, offered software that helped Ukrainian forces fuse intelligence and other information. In fact, Karp took a secret trip to Kyiv in June 2022 and visited Zelensky, becoming the first major Western chief executive officer to meet with the embattled Ukrainian president. Karp told Zelensky he was ready to open an office in Kyiv and deploy Palantir's software to support Ukrainian defense and team up with Zelensky "in ways that allow David to beat a modern-day Goliath."[34] *Time* magazine ran a cover story on Ukraine as a laboratory for artificial intelligence and warfare, with the unabashed title "The First AI War: Palantir and Other Tech Giants Are Building the Future of Battle in Ukraine."[35]

Eventually, more than a half-dozen government agencies, including the Ministry of Defense and Ministry of the Economy, used Palantir software. The Ukrainian military used Palantir's AI-enabled software to analyze satellite imagery, drone footage, intelligence from military units, and open-source data for a wide range of purposes, from conducting military operations to compiling information on war crimes, identifying land mines, and resettling internally displaced persons. Palantir hired Ukrainian engineers who could adapt its software for the war effort and trained government officials to use a tool called MetaConstellation, which used commercial data (including satellite imagery) to give a near real-time picture of a given battle space. Palantir's software integrated that information with commercial and classified government data, including from allies, which allowed military officials to communicate enemy positions to commanders on the ground.[36]

In addition, companies lined up to sell drones and drone components for use on the battlefield. One was Turkey's Bayraktar TB-2, a medium-altitude, long-endurance drone, which was extensively used in the early phase of the war. The private sector company Baykar manufactured the TB-2, led by its innovative chairman and chief technology officer, Selcuk Bayraktar, an engineer who had received master's degrees from the University of Pennsylvania's Department of Electrical and Systems Engineering and the Massachusetts Institute of Technology.[37] The TB-2 performed a range of intelligence, surveillance, reconnaissance, and strike missions. The United States also provided Ukraine with several loitering munitions—one-way "suicide" drones intended to locate and destroy a target—such as the tube-launched Switchblade 300 and 600 made by the U.S. company AeroVironment and the long-endurance tactical Phoenix Ghost manufactured by the California-based Aevex Aerospace. Over time, Ukraine developed its own drones, which it used to conduct short-range strikes against Russian ground units in Ukraine and long-range strikes against targets in Russia—including against Russian bombers during Operation Spider's Web in June 2025.[38]

With private sector assistance, the Ukrainian military developed a new concept of operations that involved using drones in combined arms warfare—the blending of infantry, direct and indirect fire, aviation, and other joint capabilities to achieve political and military objectives.[39] Ukraine was hardly the first country to use drones in warfare. But Ukraine's and Russia's employment of drones in multiple missions and integration of them into targeting complexes was novel.[40] Ukraine and Russia utilized drones to conduct several types of missions as part of combined arms warfare.

First, Ukraine used drones for intelligence, surveillance, and reconnaissance missions to monitor Russian activity and facilitate battlefield awareness. The sensors on some Ukrainian drone platforms could record videos and collect signals intelligence and other information for operational use by ground and air forces. These capabilities allowed drones to be useful for battle damage assessment.[41] Second, Ukraine used drones to identify targets for artillery and aircraft.[42] For example, Ukrainian ground forces used forward-deployed drones to detect Russian infantry units. Ukrainian soldiers then distributed the information to command-and-control centers, which passed it on to units operating 122mm howitzers and other artillery systems.[43] Third, Ukraine utilized drones for strike missions, including against Russian land and maritime targets.[44] Fourth, Ukraine utilized drones for information operations, such as showing successful strikes and placing them—overtly or covertly—on social media platforms such as Twitter, Telegram, and TikTok.[45] Fifth, the Ukrainian military used drones for numerous other missions, such as electronic warfare and counterdrone activity.

With help from private sector companies and organizations such as Aerorozvidka, a Ukrainian nongovernmental organization that helped the government with drones and aerial reconnaissance, Ukrainian forces utilized software packages developed and deployed by volunteers. One example was Kropyva, an intelligence mapping and artillery software populated by information from drones and other sources.[46] Forward-deployed tactical units downloaded the software and continuously updated it on handheld tablets and computers. Kropyva allowed Ukrainian units to plot both enemy and friendly positions. It used short-wave and digital radio stations compatible with NATO security communications standards and was relatively easy to use.[47]

Thanks in part to aid from the commercial sector, Ukrainian forces mounted a strong defense against invading Russian forces and conducted limited offensive operations. Western government assistance was critical. Over the first year of the war, U.S. military assistance topped $20 billion and included hundreds of weapons systems and munitions, from M142 High Mobility Artillery Rocket System launchers to Javelins.[48] This assistance—along with training, intelligence, and other Western aid—helped Ukraine defend itself from invading Russian forces and provided it with the tools to retake some territory in Kharkiv, Kherson, Donetsk, Luhansk, and other oblasts. Russia failed to achieve its political and military objectives—at least in the short term. The Ukrainian government did not fall, its population united to fight invading Russian forces, and NATO expanded to include Finland and Sweden. It was not the result Putin had wanted. What's more, Russian soldiers were dying in extraordinary numbers.

Russia suffered more combat deaths in Ukraine in the first year of the war than in all the Soviet and Russian wars since World War II *combined*.[49] Russian combat fatalities climbed to between 200,000 and 250,000 total killed between February 2022 and June 2025 (Figure 9.1). Russian fatality rates per year in Ukraine were roughly 33 times larger than in Russia's war in Chechnya, 40 times larger the Soviet Union's war in Afghanistan, and 87 times larger than Soviet fatalities in Hungary in 1956. No Soviet or Russian war since World War II even came close

War	Dates	Russian Forces Killed or Missing (Regular and Irregular)
Korea	1950–1953	120
Hungary	1956	669
United Arab Republic (Egypt)	1962–1963, 1969–1972, 1973–1974	21
Yemen Republic	1962–1963	1
Algeria	1962–1964	25
Vietnam	1965–1974	16
Mozambique	1967, 1969, 1975–1979	6
Czechoslovakia	1968	96
Sino-Soviet Border Conflict	1969	58
Angola	1975–1979	7
Ethiopia	1977–1990	34
Afghanistan	1979–1989	14,000–16,000
Chechnya (First and Second Wars)	1994–1996, 1999–2009	12,000–25,000
Georgia	2008	64
Ukraine (Crimea and Donbas)	2014–February 2022	6,000–7,000
Syria	2015–2023	264
Ukraine	February 2022–June 2025	200,000–250,000

FIGURE 9.1 Number of Russian and Soviet soldiers killed or missing in selected wars, 1946–2025.[50]

to Ukraine in fatality rates. Total Russian casualties reached 1 million killed and wounded by the summer of 2025.[51]

Although Russian fatalities in Ukraine paled in comparison to the Soviet death rate in World War II, the political context was entirely different. On June 22, 1941, Adolf Hitler launched Operation Barbarossa, Germany's invasion of the Soviet Union, despite reaching a nonaggression pact two years before.[52] World War II was a war of survival, and the Soviet Union suffered nearly 10 million military fatalities and another 14 million civilian fatalities over the course of the war.[53] But Russia's 2022 invasion of Ukraine was a war of choice against a country that posed no meaningful threat to Russia's survival.

Despite Russian losses, U.S. aid to Ukraine laid bare a dark reality: the U.S. defense industrial base was in worse shape than most government officials and experts had anticipated. One way to gauge the effectiveness of a defense industrial base is to assess how it supports a country during war. Ukraine should have been a relatively easy case for the United States because the U.S. military was not actually fighting in Ukraine. Instead, the United States was providing aid to the Ukrainian military. But the U.S. defense industrial base was wholly unprepared to support a protracted conventional war and was not suited for an international landscape fundamentally shifting from counterterrorism to great power competition.

Battlefield consumption rates in Ukraine placed a significant strain on the U.S. defense industrial base. Since many of the weapons systems and munitions came directly from U.S. inventories, U.S. assistance depleted stockpiles for training, future contingencies, or other operational needs. For example, the quantities of Javelins anti-missile systems the United States transferred to Ukraine through late August 2022 represented seven years of production at fiscal year 2022 rates.[54] The number of Stingers the United States transferred to Ukraine was roughly equal to the total number built for *all* non-U.S. customers in the previous 20 years.[55] One of the most lethal weapons the United States sent was the 155mm howitzer, which fired high-explosive ammunition weighing about 100 pounds each and able to hit targets nearly 20 miles away. By December 2022, the U.S. military had provided Ukraine with up to 1,004,000 rounds of 155mm ammunition, significantly shrinking the availability of 155mm rounds in storage.[56] Because of the limited availability of 155mm howitzers and ammunition, the U.S. military began sending 105mm howitzers and ammunition instead.[57]

The problem of depleted stockpiles was not uniform. In some instances—such as M113 armored personnel carriers and 105mm howitzers—the amounts given to Ukraine were relatively small compared to U.S. inventories and production capabilities. But in other cases—such as Javelins, Stingers, 155mm howitzers and ammunition, and counterartillery radar—U.S. inventories were low (Figure 9.2).

Senior U.S. defense officials, such as Under Secretary of Defense for Acquisition and Sustainment William LaPlante, publicly acknowledged industrial base challenges and outlined steps to help fix them.[58] U.S. Army officials, such as Secretary of the Army Christine Wormuth and Assistant Secretary of the Army for Acquisition, Logistics and Technology Doug Bush, committed to tripling the production of 155mm shells over the next few years.[59] In late 2022, the U.S. Army awarded a $431 million contract for full-rate production of High Mobility Artillery Rocket Systems to support the U.S. Army and several U.S. partners overseas.[60] But the U.S. defense industrial ecosystem overall was slow to respond. As a U.S. Department of Defense study

System	Manufacturer	Status of Production Line	Number Committed to Ukraine	Status of U.S. Inventory
Javelin anti-armor systems	Raytheon (RTX)/ Lockheed Martin	Active	Over 8,500	Low
Stinger anti-aircraft systems	Raytheon (RTX)	Semi-active	Over 1,600	Low
155mm howitzers	BAE Systems and other manufacturers	Semi-active	142	Low
155mm artillery rounds	General Dynamics and other manufacturers	Active	Up to 1,004,000	Low
Excalibur precision-guided 155mm rounds	Raytheon (RTX)	Active	4,200	Medium
Counter-artillery radars	Raytheon (RTX)	Active	Over 50	Low
M113 armored personnel vehicles	BAE Systems	Closed	200	Medium
105mm howitzers	Rock Island Arsenal	Closed	36	Medium
Harpoon coastal defense systems	Boeing	Active	2	Medium
High Mobility Artillery Rocket Systems	Lockheed Martin	Active	38	Medium
105mm artillery rounds	BAE Systems and other manufacturers	Active	180,000	High
Small arms ammunition	Various manufacturers	Active	Over 104,000,000	High

FIGURE 9.2 Selected U.S. weapons systems and munitions provided to Ukraine, February–December 2022.[61]

Notes: "High" means that there was significant U.S. inventory currently available for the system or munition despite exports to Ukraine. "Medium" means that there was some U.S. inventory still available for military requirements, such as operational plans, though the stockpiles were depleting. "Low" means that there was limited inventory available for U.S. military requirements, such as operational plans, and the limited numbers were creating risk.

concluded, one difficulty was the "onerous business processes and regulations" in which Department of Defense accounting requirements and other actions "impos[ed] uncompensated additional costs compared to more profitable commercial procurement opportunities."[62] Years of acquisition policy and peacetime mindset prioritized efficiency and cost control over speed and capacity. It turned out that Secretary of Defense Robert Gates's frustration with the "damnable peacetime mindset inside the Pentagon" during the U.S. wars in Afghanistan and Iraq was still a problem.[63]

There were three final lessons for the U.S. defense industrial base from the war in Ukraine. The first was a stark reminder that the United States was in a wartime environment; a conventional war with one or more major powers was a real possibility. After 9/11, the United States fought terrorists and insurgents in Afghanistan, Iraq, Somalia, Yemen, and other countries. These conflicts were not conventional wars against major powers. However, the Russian invasion of Ukraine demonstrated that artillery, air defense systems, tanks, armored personnel vehicles, and other weapons systems were critical to fighting—and winning—conventional wars. They didn't involve just drones and other unmanned systems, artificial intelligence, and additional emerging technologies. Competition and conflict between major powers required a robust U.S. and allied industrial base, which did not exist—at least not yet.

A second lesson was that big defense companies were still critical because they produced platforms and systems essential to deter major powers and—if deterrence failed—to fight and win conventional wars. Ukraine's military had an insatiable appetite for tanks, infantry fighting vehicles, helicopters, fighter aircraft, artillery, air defense systems, and munitions. They included a wide range of systems: the General Dynamics Abrams tank, Boeing Ground Launched Small Diameter Bomb, Lockheed Army Tactical Missile System, Lockheed Guided Multiple Launch Rocket System, and joint Lockheed and Raytheon (RTX) Javelin. In Asia, the U.S. military also needed nuclear-powered submarines, bombers, fighter aircraft, ships, space-based systems, and long-range missiles for deterrence and warfighting against China. Lockheed Martin, Raytheon (RTX), Northrop Grumman, Boeing, General Dynamics, Huntington Ingalls Industries, and others were still important.

In the Middle East, Israel used a range of U.S. systems against Hamas, Hezbollah, Iran, and other Iran-backed groups. For example, Israel flew Boeing F-15s and Apache helicopters, as well as Lockheed Martin F-16s and F-35s. The Israeli Air Force deployed Raytheon (RTX) Sidewinder air-to-air systems and Advanced Air-to-Air Missiles and Standard Missile-3 interceptors; Boeing GBU-31 Joint Direct Attack Munitions and GBU-39 Small Diameter Bombs; General Dynamics Mk82 500-pound bombs, MK84 2,000-pound bombs, and 30mm ammunition; and Lockheed Martin Hellfire missiles. In addition, the

Company	Defense Revenue (Millions of Dollars)	Major Systems and Platforms
Lockheed Martin	$64,650	F-35 Lightning II, F-22 Raptor, Black Hawk helicopter, MGM-104 Army Tactical Missile System, Guided Multiple Launch Rocket System, M142 High Mobility Artillery Rocket System, PAC-3 Missile, AGM-158 Joint Air-to-surface Standoff Missile, Terminal High Altitude Area Defence system
Raytheon (RTX)	$40,600	MIM-104 Patriot surface-to-air missile system, Javelin antitank missile (with Lockheed Martin), BGM-109 Tomahawk land-attack cruise missile, SM-2 missile, SM-3 missile, SM-6 missile, Naval Strike Missile, AIM-9X Sidewinder missile, MK54 lightweight torpedo, PAC-2 missile, RIM-162 Evolved SeaSparrow Missile
Northrop Grumman	$35,197	B-2 bomber, B-21 Raider bomber, LGM-35 Sentinel intercontinental ballistic missile system, RQ-4 Global Hawk, EA-6B Prowler, Orbital ATK
General Dynamics	$33,651	Virginia-class submarine, Columbia-class submarine, Ohio-class submarine, Arleigh Burke–class destroyer, Abrams main battle tank, Stryker armored fighting vhicle
Boeing	$32,684	AH-64 Apache helicopter, E-7 Airborne Early Warning and Control, B-52 bomber, B-1B Lancer, C-17 Globemaster III, F-15EX, Harpoon missile, LGM-30G Minuteman III missile, Small Diameter Bomb

FIGURE 9.3 Top five U.S. defense companies, 2024.[64]

United States deployed Lockheed Martin's Terminal High Altitude Area Defense missile defense system to Israel, which supplemented Israel's own Iron Dome, David's Sling, Arrow 2, and Arrow 3 air defense systems.[65] In an attempt to deter regional escalation of the war, the United States also deployed carrier strike groups to the Middle East, including aircraft carriers, guided-missile cruisers, and destroyers built by Huntington Ingalls Industries and General Dynamics, as well as fighter jets, electronic warfare aircraft, surveillance planes, helicopters, and defense systems produced by Lockheed Martin, Raytheon (RTX), Boeing, Northrop Grumman, and other companies (Figure 9.3).

A third lesson was that conventional war could be *protracted*, and the defense industrial base might need to develop and produce substantial volumes of munitions and equipment over a sustained period. As William Knudsen recognized during World War II, militaries need massive amounts of matériel during prolonged conflicts. "We are here to help you," said Knudsen during meetings with defense companies, "and all we ask in return is that you give us speed and more speed. We need every machine running at full speed."[66] The effort to deploy, arm, feed, and supply forces was a monumental task, and the consumption of equipment, systems, vehicles, and munitions required a large-scale industrial base for resupply.[67]

There was no better indication of the need for a strong industrial base than to turn to developments in China. Xi Jinping and China were hard at work building a defense industrial base thousands of miles away from the Ukrainian battlefield. Not only did China continue to rise as a great power, but Xi's defense industrial base was now on a wartime footing.

10

China's Wartime Footing

> The PRC has continued the most extensive and rapid buildup since World War II.
> —Admiral John C. Aquilino, commander of U.S. Indo-Pacific Command

> China is preparing for a war and specifically for a war with the United States.
> —Frank Kendall III, U.S. Secretary of the Air Force

IN OCTOBER 2024, THE PEOPLE'S LIBERATION Army Eastern Theater Command held a massive military exercise around Taiwan, deploying 125 aircraft and 34 naval vessels—including the *Liaoning* aircraft carrier, cruisers, and numerous other ships—that surrounded Taiwan and several of its outlying islands.[1] Code-named "Joint Sword-2024B," the Chinese exercise was in response to Taiwan's celebration of National Day, when Taiwanese President Lai Ching-te remarked that China had no right to represent Taiwan and declared his commitment to "resist annexation or encroachment" (Figure 10.1).[2] The red boxes and circles in the figure, which were produced by the PLA's Eastern Theater Command, showed the location of PLA drills during Joint Sword-2024B. The Japanese Maritime Self-Defense Forces deployed the destroyer *JS Kirisame*, which shadowed the PLA Navy carrier strike group. The Japanese Air Self-Defense Force also scrambled fighter aircraft in response to the *Liaoning*'s launch of fighter jets.³

This aggressive behavior was not isolated. In May 2024, the PLA orchestrated a series of exercises around Taiwan termed Joint Sword-2024A, which followed the inauguration of Taiwan's eighth president, Lai Ching-te. In April 2023, China conducted a belligerent set of exercises around Taiwan, following a meeting between U.S. Speaker of the House Kevin McCarthy and Taiwanese President Tsai Ing-wen at the Ronald Reagan Presidential Library in Simi Valley, California.⁴ East of Taiwan, the PLA Navy deployed the *Shandong* aircraft carrier, which launched 620 sorties from J-15 fighter jets and other aircraft.⁵ Once again, PLA forces encircled Taiwan and simulated a blockade and potential invasion.⁶ U.S. military officials were deeply alarmed about

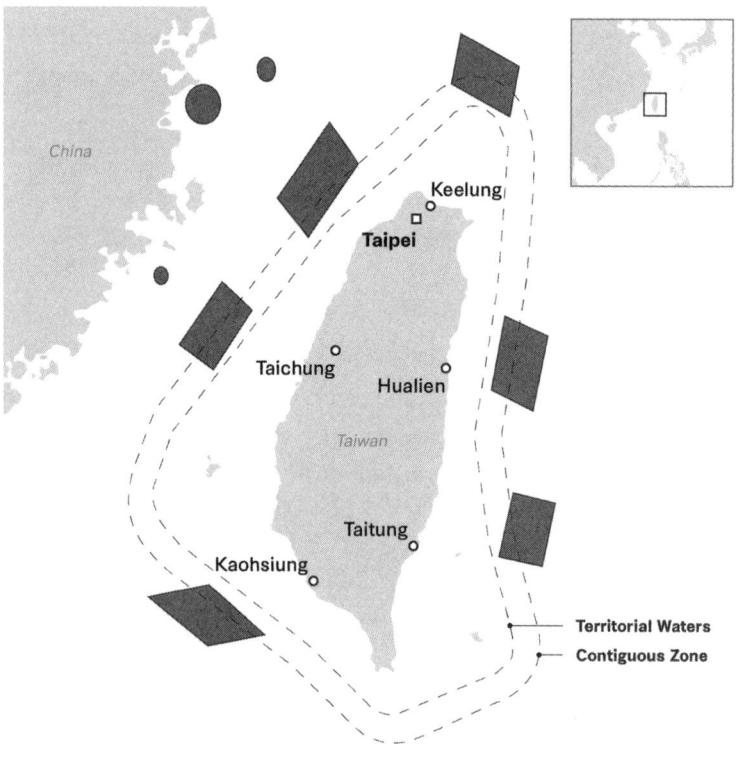

FIGURE 10.1 PLA exercises during Joint Sword-2024B, October 2024.⁷

the military exercises, which were unprecedented in their scale and scope.

In August 2022, after U.S. Speaker of the House Nancy Pelosi visited Taiwan, the PLA had launched another massive exercise that strongly suggested how China could—and perhaps would—conduct military operations against Taiwan. According to the PLA, its forces were preparing for a possible future "blockade, sea target assault, strike on ground targets, and airspace control operation."[8] On August 4, 2022, the PLA fired multiple Dongfeng-15 short-range ballistic missiles into waters to the east, northeast, and southeast of Taiwan.[9] Five of the missiles landed in the waters of Japan's exclusive economic zone (EEZ), an area in which Japan has exclusive rights regarding the exploration and use of maritime resources, provoking outrage among Japanese officials. "To have five Chinese missiles fall within Japan's EEZ like this is a first," said a visibly angry Nobuo Kishi, Japan's defense minister. "We have protested strongly through diplomatic channels."[10] Together, this series of PLA actions was bellicose and indicative of China's preparation for possible war. As Admiral Samuel Paparo, commander of U.S. Indo-Pacific Command, warned, "Beijing's aggressive maneuvers around Taiwan are not just exercises—they are dress rehearsals for forced unification."[11]

China was not only a great power; it was becoming a formidable military challenger of the United States. The weapons systems and platforms used by China in the exercises—from aircraft carriers and modern fighter aircraft to missiles and drones—showed that China was rapidly developing and producing weapons systems needed to fight a war. China had achieved technical parity with the United States in many areas. In blunt terms, China's defense industrial base was on a wartime footing—a stark contrast to a U.S. defense industry that was on a peacetime footing. Naval vessels played an important role in the exercises, thanks to China's shipbuilding prowess. The country had become the world's largest shipbuilder, with a military and commercial shipbuilding capacity that was roughly 230 times larger than the United States.[12] By 2025, China's defense industrial base produced fighters at a faster rate than the United States, more than doubled its inventory of ballistic and cruise missiles, increased the number of satellites launched by 50 percent, developed a stealth bomber, and doubled its nuclear warhead inventory.[13] In addition, China had become notably faster—as much as five to six times faster—than the United States in acquiring weapons systems.[14]

While China faced challenges with its hulking state-owned enterprises, the country had advanced in some areas—including emerging technology. At the center of its technology campaign was Ren Zhengfei, founder of the telecommunications giant Huawei. Under Ren's leadership, Huawei played an important role in China's growing defense industrial base and military-civil fusion strategy, and it showed that some Chinese companies could innovate in such emerging technologies as artificial intelligence and quantum computing.

Ren was, in many ways, the Chinese version of Alex Karp or Palmer Luckey. He had a legendary work ethic, which was epitomized by the image for one of his global advertising campaigns: a photograph of a ballet dancer's two feet, one in an elegant satin shoe and the other that was bare, bruised, and bandaged. It captured Ren's ethos and symbolized the extraordinary struggle required for success. The caption appropriately read, "The journey is hard. And joyful."[15] Ren was perhaps better dressed than Luckey, preferring crisply tailored jackets, slacks, and an unbuttoned collar with no tie. He had few hobbies, though when pressed, he confided that he had a fondness for British tea and reading.[16] Huawei's telecommunications equipment—including routers, switches, modems, and base stations—formed the backbone of the world's mobile internet and rivaled Apple and Samsung in the numbers of phones sold. The company provided other types of technology infrastructure, from undersea fiberoptic cables and artificial intelligence to chips and cloud computing, making Huawei a critical part of the emerging technology side of China's defense industrial base.[17]

Born in 1944 to high school teachers in rural Zhenning County, Guizhou Province, Ren was the oldest of seven children. He and his family survived the famine during Mao's Great Leap Forward, and he spoke regularly of being toughened by poverty. "In retrospect," he recalled, "the material hardships, as well as the mental trials and tribulations, were an opportunity for us to get mature later in our lives."[18]

After graduating from Chongqing Institute of Civil Engineering and Architecture in 1963, Ren joined the PLA as an engineer. He served for nearly a decade, until the PLA discharged him in 1983 during a massive decommissioning wave.[19]

He then moved into a cramped apartment in Shenzhen, a fishing village near Hong Kong that had just been registered as a special economic zone and would eventually balloon into a metropolis.[20] Ren saw an opportunity to import telecommunication switches, the equipment that connected one caller to another. With nearly $6,000 in start-up capital, he began importing telecommunication gear from Hong Kong.[21] When his partners across the border realized he was making a profit by reselling their equipment, they cut him off. In response, Ren decided to build his own equipment just as China was opening up to the global economy. And so began Huawei. "I founded Huawei when China was shifting from a planned economy to a market economy," he said. "Not only people like myself, but even the most senior government officials, did not have the vaguest idea of what a market economy was. It seemed it was hard to survive."[22]

In 1990, Huawei started its own research and development effort, which mostly focused on building switching equipment.[23] Ren had been influenced by Western, particularly U.S., business practices and the American work ethic. "This nation's practical, indomitable spirit of working hard is worth learning for us," he penned in a 1994 article titled "Notes from a Trip to America." "The space shuttle, large-scale silicon wafers, super-large computers, super-miniature terminals, developed and excellent telecommunication equipment, and testing instruments were created by the hard work of the American people."[24]

In 1997, Ren brought a group of Huawei executives to tour the United States, visiting companies such as HP, IBM, and Bell Labs. They left convinced of the importance of research and development, as well as an effective management organization and culture. They were keenly interested in U.S. business practices to manage supply chains, anticipate customer demand, develop top-notch marketing, and sell products worldwide.[25] Ren was also impressed with the West's open and free exchange of ideas. "Academic freedom is the foundation of innovation," he declared. "The freedom to have different academic ideas and to study whatever you want is very important. Undoubtedly, the U.S. has the world's most innovation-friendly environment."[26] Ren was, of course, correct. The political liberties and freedom to exchange ideas were central to U.S. innovation. Neither Kelly Johnson, Alex Karp, Elon Musk, Gwynne Shotwell, nor Palmer Luckey could have said it any better.

Ren built Huawei by embracing foreign competition from its earliest days. His business model took concepts pioneered abroad, produced quality versions at lower cost, and sold them to the world, allowing him to grab international market share from multinational companies.[27] In 2000, Ren slowly began to expand Huawei's business overseas, starting in Africa, the Middle East, and South Asia. He moved on to Europe, working with such companies as the United Kingdom's Vodafone and British Telecom.[28] Ren instituted a hard-charging spirit—or "wolf culture," as he called it.[29] In the company's early years, Huawei representatives crisscrossed China peddling the company's telephone switches to post offices. Huawei allegedly provided mattresses to employees so they could take naps while working late nights. Some company employees kept telecommunications services running during a terrorist attack in Mumbai, an earthquake in Algeria, and subzero temperatures in Siberia, while others braved freezing cold and exhaustion providing mobile coverage to climbers on Mount Everest.[30] "Sacrifice is a soldier's highest cause," trumpeted a saying on the wall at Huawei's Shenzhen headquarters. "Victory is a soldier's greatest contribution."[31]

Along the way, Huawei had some help. It benefited from Chinese government assistance, including support from the local government in Shenzhen, state-owned banks, and the central government in Beijing. Huawei had access to as much as $75 billion in Chinese government support through grants, credit facilities, tax breaks, and other types of aid.[32] The company also benefited from preferential buying contracts and subsidies from Chinese state-owned entities, governing agencies, and Communist Party bodies.

To stay competitive, Huawei was likely involved in intellectual theft. In January 2003, the U.S. company Cisco sued, alleging that Huawei had copied Cisco's software code and violated several of its patents. They settled out of court.[33] In 2017, a Seattle jury awarded T-Mobile $4.8 million in damages after the company accused two Huawei workers of stealing part of a smartphone-testing robot named Tappy at T-Mobile's lab in Bellevue, Washington.[34] In 2019, the U.S.

Department of Justice indicted Huawei and charged it with theft of trade secrets, attempted theft of trade secrets, wire fraud, and obstruction of justice. As part of the investigation, the FBI obtained emails which indicated that Huawei offered bonuses to its employees based on the value of information they stole from companies around the world.[35]

Nevertheless, no quantity of intellectual property was sufficient to build a business as successful as Huawei. The company developed efficient manufacturing processes that drove down costs and built products that customers saw as high-quality. Huawei's spending on research and development was also world leading.[36] Yet Ren was not really a capitalist. He once acknowledged that if there was a conflict between the interests of Huawei and the Chinese Communist Party, he would unfalteringly "choose the CCP whose interest is to serve the people and all human beings." He likewise noted, "Huawei's culture is the culture of the Chinese Communist Party, and to serve the people wholeheartedly means to be customer-centric and responsible to the society."[37]

While he was impressed with U.S. innovation and business practices, Ren nevertheless viewed the United States as China's main competitor and a declining power. "The U.S. is the most powerful country in the world," he acknowledged. "It used to maintain order as the 'World Policeman.' . . . However, the U.S. destroyed this mechanism itself. Everyone no longer believes that the U.S. is looking to maintain order in the world, or that the USD is the most reliable reserve currency."[38]

What made Ren particularly valuable for China—including the PLA—in its competition with the United States was Huawei's position at the forefront of emerging technologies, such as artificial intelligence, quantum computing, chip production, cloud computing, 6G, and consumer electronics.[39] As part of military-civil fusion (军民融合), in which China encouraged closer integration of military and civilian industries, Huawei technology was used in high-end weapons systems, from missiles to air defense systems.[40] Huawei also provided China with the capability to collect intelligence in the U.S. homeland, including intercepting sensitive Defense Department communications around U.S. military bases.[41] U.S. officials took notice of

Huawei's ties to the PLA and other Chinese government agencies, and the United States blacklisted Huawei and tagged it as one of China's most important military companies.[42]

Huawei was a private company, not a hulking state-owned enterprise, and Ren pioneered a U.S.-style employee stock ownership plan there. This structure and ethos made Huawei globally competitive, even innovative. Yet Ren and Huawei were, in many ways, crowded out by China's mammoth state-owned enterprises.

China's defense industrial base was a serious competitor of the United States, producing a growing number of surface and subsurface vessels, aircraft, missiles (including those capable of carrying nuclear warheads), space-based capabilities, and land systems.[43] China's gigantic economy, second only to the United States in overall GDP but larger than the United States in purchasing power parity, was the foundation of China's defense industrial base. Its economy struggled because of a deepening property crisis, gloomy consumer confidence, trillions of dollars in local government debt, a deflationary spiral, rising youth unemployment, and an aging society.[44] Nevertheless, China continued to pour money into its defense industry.

Beijing's massive state-owned enterprises were at the core of its industrial base with the support of technology companies like Huawei. China's centralized power and decision-making allowed the government to establish a unified strategy, set priorities, and align government actions in ways the United States and other Western governments could not do.[45] The government could reliably forecast and plan future defense spending, and the government could direct university-based research to prioritized science and technology areas.[46] In addition to state budget allocations, some Chinese defense companies also acquired financial investments. One of the most important ways was through "asset securitization," in which companies raised funds through the domestic stock market and investors.[47]

Four of the world's top 10 largest companies as measured in combined defense and nondefense revenue were Chinese enterprises, including the top two companies (Aviation Industry Corporation of

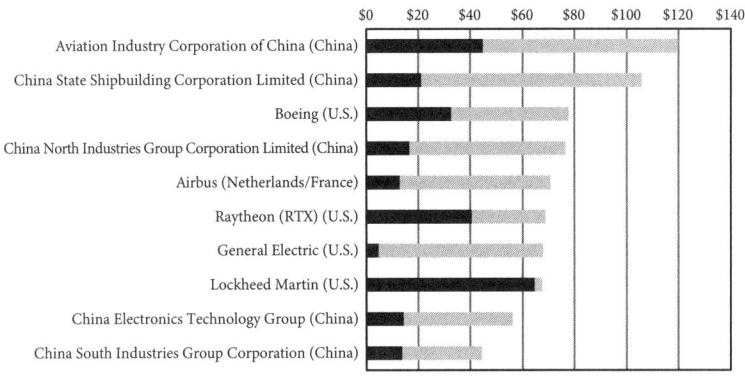

FIGURE 10.2 The 10 largest defense companies globally by total revenue, 2024.[48]

China and China State Shipbuilding Corporation Limited). This ranking was a huge change from a decade earlier, when there were *zero Chinese companies* in the entire list of the world's top 100 defense companies. In defense revenue alone, China had five companies in the top 12, also up from zero a decade earlier.[49]

Aviation Industry Corporation of China (AVIC, total revenue of $119.8 billion) manufactured fighter, bomber, transport, and rotary-wing aircraft; China State Shipbuilding Corporation Limited ($105.8 billion) produced surface ships; China North Industries Group Corporation Limited ($76.6 billion) produced ground combat vehicles, main battle tanks, small arms, and other land warfare capabilities; China Electronics Technology Group ($56.1 billion) produced electronic and other equipment; and China South Industries Group Corporation ($44.4 billion) produced land warfare capabilities. In terms of total revenue, Chinese companies were major players, even compared to Western giants such as Boeing at $77.8 billion, Airbus at $70.8 billion, Raytheon (RTX) at $68.9 billion, General Electric at $68.0 billion, Lockheed Martin at $67.6 billion, and General Dynamics at $42.2 billion (Figure 10.2).[50]

Like much of the Chinese government, these defense companies were shrouded in secrecy. There was little publicly available information about their inner workings, including on such challenges as corruption, inefficiency, the workforce, and supply chain. The same was true of China's system of *guanxi*—the network of social relationships used to facilitate management, business deals, and party direction—which was wholly opaque to outside observers and, frankly, to many inside China.[51] Nevertheless, the available information indicated that Chinese defense companies grew in leaps and bounds.

Unlike in Western countries, the primary duty of state-owned enterprises was not to support shareholders but rather—as Ren acknowledged on numerous occasions—to serve the Chinese Communist Party.[52] Tan Ruisong, former chairman of the AVIC, perhaps said it best when he acknowledged that "being absolutely loyal to the Party, bearing the original intention of serving the country in mind, and keeping in mind the mission of making the armed forces powerful have been the political responsibilities that we have consistently upheld."[53]

To manufacture weapons systems, Chinese defense companies heavily relied on an absorptive model in which firms stole or otherwise acquired foreign military and dual-use technology and incorporated it into the design and development of products. Chinese companies reverse-engineered foreign platforms and weapons systems—such as fighter aircraft, ships, and missiles—and produced their own variants.[54] This approach significantly reduced the amount of time and money China needed to invest in research and development, testing, and integration.[55] China was able to fast-track some platforms, such as the Type 052D *Luyang III*-class guided-missile destroyer and J-15 fourth-generation fighter.[56]

Over the previous decade, the PLA also markedly enhanced its research, development, and acquisition process, allowing it to produce advanced platforms in such difficult areas as carrier-based aviation, hypersonics, and propulsion systems.[57] China's acquisition process had five general steps: a feasibility study to determine the technical requirements for a new system, project design, engineering and development of the new system, experiment and design finalization that included increasingly difficult tests, and batch production (if a system passed all of these steps).[58] It took China on average less than 7 years to deliver an operational capability, compared to 16 years for the United States.[59] "It's really impressive," said U.S. Under Secretary of Defense for Acquisition and Sustainment William LaPlante in discussing China's defense industrial base. "They've developed . . . really good high-end capability in numbers. So, they've done the development, and the development has been pretty continuous and not just one thing. They place multiple bets. We don't do that. We . . . very rarely will place multiple bets and . . . [have] three different development activities going on. We used to do that. We don't do that."[60]

China had caught up to—and even surpassed—the United States in some areas. For example, China had more principal surface combatants, active ground forces, main battle tanks, and artillery systems than the United States, though the United States was still dominant in such areas as aircraft carriers, submarines, fourth- and fifth-generation aircraft, and nuclear weapons (Figure 10.3). Still, the main storyline of China's defense industrial base was clear: China was catching up to the United States in all military domains—maritime, land, air, space, and cyber—and building a force to deter and fight the United States if necessary.

In addition to building military hardware, China focused on building its network-centric warfare capabilities to fight a joint campaign against the United States. For example, the PLA developed a concept called "multi-domain precision warfare" (多域精确战). The concept was designed to improve the PLA's ability to fight a war by leveraging a command, control, communications, computers, intelligence, surveillance, and reconnaissance network; rapidly coordinate firepower using artificial intelligence, big data, and other emerging technologies; and identify and exploit U.S. vulnerabilities.[61] The concept of multi-domain precision warfare was, in some ways, similar to the U.S. Defense Department's notion of combined joint all-domain command and control, which focused on building data architecture to fuse information from sensors across multiple domains—such as air, space, land, and maritime—and make that information rapidly available to warfighters and decision-makers.

Taken together, China's production of major weapons systems indicated that it was specifically preparing for a war *with the United States*. Perhaps the main beneficiary of China's defense industrial growth was the PLA Navy.

Category	Variable	China	United States
Defense Sector	Total defense spending	$350–$500 billion[1]	$880 billion
	Military personnel	2,035,000 (3,045,000 including reserves, paramilitary personnel)	1,326,050 (2,132,750 including reserves)
Maritime	Principal surface combatants (hulls)	151	122
	Principal surface combatants (tons displacement)	781,850	2,026,499
	Nuclear attack submarines	6	52
	Diesel attack submarines	46	0
	Total subsurface displacement	240,216	708,935
Air	Fifth-generation aircraft	200	816
	Fourth-generation aircraft	1,865	2,536
	Bomber aircraft	209	140
Land	All active ground forces personnel	1,000,000	623,550
	Combined arms brigades/brigade combat teams	75	24
	Main battle tanks	4,700	2,640
	Other armored fighting vehicles	6,304	11,137
	Artillery systems	9,722	6,443
Nuclear Forces	Air-launched warheads	20	988
	Land-based warheads	318	800
	Sea-based warheads	72	1,920

FIGURE 10.3 Chinese and U.S. military capabilities, 2024.[62]

Note: [1] This range of Chinese defense spending was reached following author interviews with senior U.S. government officials and a review of such analyses as U.S. Department of Defense, *Military and Security Developments Involving the People's Republic of China* (Washington, DC: Office of the Secretary of Defense, U.S. Department of Defense, 2024), xi; *Commission on the National Defense Strategy* (Santa Monica, CA: RAND, July 2024); M. Taylor Fravel, George J. Gilboy, and Eric Heginbotham, "Estimating China's Defense Spending: How to Get It Wrong (and Right)," *Texas National Security Review* 7, no. 3 (Summer 2024): 40–54; Mackenzie Eaglen, *Keeping Up with the Pacing Threat: Unveiling the True Size of Beijing's Military Spending* (Washington, DC: American Enterprise Institute, August 8, 2024); Josh Rogin, "The U.S. Military Plans a 'Hellscape' to Deter China from Attacking Taiwan," *Washington Post*, June 10, 2024. Rogin used estimates from U.S. Indo-Pacific Command.

China had become the world's largest shipbuilder by a significant margin, led by the China State Shipbuilding Corporation. It had the capacity to build 23 million tons of vessels, compared to less than 100,000 tons in the United States at shipyards run by General Dynamics, Huntington Ingalls Industries, and other companies.[63] According to U.S. Navy estimates, a single Chinese shipyard—such as Changxing Island located on China's east coast along the East China Sea—had more military and commercial capacity than all U.S. shipyards *combined*.[64] The PLA Navy's growth made it the largest navy in the world, though not necessarily the most powerful. It produced a wide range of naval combatants, such as submarines, surface combatants, and unmanned systems; gas turbine and diesel engines; and shipboard weapons and electronic systems.[65]

The PLA Navy had been growing larger since at least 2006, with major advances in several categories: an increase in corvette construction since 2014, the completion of the aircraft carrier *Shandong* and the Type 003 carrier *Fujian*, and the construction of eight Type 055 destroyers since 2019.[66] The *Fujian* design featured an electromagnetic catapult launch system rather than a "ski ramp" for aircraft launches, allowing for more comprehensive air operations and making it more capable than the *Liaoning* and *Shandong*.[67] The *Fujian* could deploy up to 70 aircraft, including J-15 fighters and Z-9C anti-submarine helicopters.[68] The PLA Navy also continued developing Type-096 and Type-095 nuclear-powered submarines.[69]

The PLA Navy still trailed the U.S. Navy in several indicators of military might. China had more ships than the United States, but they were smaller.[70] The aggregate displacement of the PLA Navy's surface warships was a little more than a third that of the U.S. Navy. The PLA Navy was capable of carrying roughly half as many missiles as the U.S. Navy, indicating a relative disadvantage in firepower.[71]

But China's naval gap with the United States had dramatically closed. Chinese shipbuilding facilities had been expanding for years, with Changxing Island shipbuilding base growing to approximately 11.5 square kilometers by 2024, about 64 percent larger than China's historic Jiangnan Shipyard.[72] Nor was Changxing alone. China had dozens of commercial shipyards that were significantly larger than the biggest U.S. shipyards in size and throughput. Many of these shipyards were used for both military and civilian construction, meaning that China could surge its military shipbuilding capacity more readily than could the United States. The result was that China could produce far more ships than the United States.

China's defense industrial base also made startling advances in aircraft production.

The United States operated the world's largest and most advanced fleet of fifth-generation fighter aircraft and bombers, led by Lockheed Martin (with the F-35 and F-22 fighters) and Northrop Grumman (with the B-21 bomber). But China was catching up. Established in 1951, AVIC, China's largest aviation defense company, produced virtually all of China's domestic fighter, bomber, transport, reconnaissance, drone, and training aircraft, as well as helicopters. It oversaw a vast network of 86 laboratories and applied research centers, and it had hundreds of subsidies and more than 100 overseas entities.[73] The PLA had produced over 3,150 total aircraft, excluding training aircraft and drones. This number included 2,065 fourth- and fifth-generation combat aircraft, more than doubling the 800 China operated in 2017. Among these aircraft were 200 fifth-generation Chengdu J-20 heavy multi-role fighter aircraft.[74] While the United States was still ahead, with over 3,352 fourth- and fifth-generation fighters, including 816 Lockheed Martin F-22s and F-35s, China was close behind. In addition, China significantly increased its production of drones, which it began to use in exercises around Taiwan, as well as manned-unmanned teaming.[75] In 2024, China North Industries Group unveiled a new kamikaze drone with a range of 124 miles and a cruising speed of 90 miles per hour.[76]

China also made significant advancements in its space, cyber, and electronic warfare programs, which were managed by the PLA. Space was critical, led by China Aerospace Science and Technology Corporation and China Aerospace Science and Industry Corporation Limited. In 2023 alone, China conducted 67 space launches—the most in its history.[77] As individuals like Elon Musk, Mark Juncosa, and Gwynne Shotwell spearheaded U.S. space research and development, China continued to push forward in such areas as Long March rockets, global navigation satellite system capabilities, and intelligence, surveillance, and reconnaissance. China also continued to develop its counterspace capabilities. It fielded jamming and directed energy systems, demonstrated direct-ascent antisatellite capabilities, and tested technologies relevant to on-orbit counterspace weapons systems.[78]

The PLA maintained both fixed and mobile electronic warfare systems that could interfere with satellite communications links, global navigation satellite system signals, and synthetic aperture radar intelligence-gathering satellites. China also possessed growing cyber capabilities. As one U.S. military assessment concluded, "The PRC is advancing its cyberspace attack capabilities and has the ability to launch cyberspace attacks—such as disruption of a natural gas pipeline for days to weeks—in the United States."[79]

What's more, China modernized its intercontinental ballistic missile forces, putting it on pace to possess more than 1,000 operational nuclear warheads by 2030.[80] The broader Chinese missile arsenal was formidable, and it consisted of a rapidly growing ballistic missile stockpile and a variety of cruise missiles.[81] China also fielded its first missile with a hypersonic glide vehicle, the DF-17. In contrast, the United States struggled to field hypersonic missiles.[82] To achieve these results, Chinese companies such as China Aerospace Science and Technology Corporation and China Aerospace Science and Industry Corporation Limited expanded their facilities and hired more workers (Figure 10.4).[83]

The PLA Army was the world's largest ground force. China had more ground forces and operated more main battle tanks and artillery pieces than the United States. Led by China North Industries Group Corporation and China South Industries Group Corporation, China's

Defense Industrial Base Manufacturing Areas	Parent State-owned Enterprise	Manufacturing Activity
Land warfare, ground forces	China North Industries Group Corporation Limited China South Industries Group Corporation	Ground combat vehicles, main battle tanks, infantry fighting vehicles and soldier equipment, small arms and light weapons, ordnance
Air warfare, air forces	Aviation Industry Corporation of China	Fixed-wing combat, transportation, bomber aircraft, rotary-wing aircraft
Naval warfare, sea forces	China State Shipbuilding Corporation Limited	Frigates, corvettes, destroyers, and cruisers; submarines (diesel and nuclear-powered); aircraft carriers; dock landing ships
Electronic warfare, electronic equipment	China Electronics Technology Group Corporation	Drones, radars, computing resources, other military electronics
Space warfare, space forces	China Aerospace Science and Technology Corporation	Surface-to-air missile systems; intelligence, surveillance, and reconnaissance systems; drones, ballistic missiles, space launch vehicles
Nuclear warfare, nuclear facilities	China National Nuclear Corporation	Nuclear reactors, nuclear weapons

FIGURE 10.4 Major Chinese defense companies and their products.[84]

production capacity increased in nearly every PLA ground system category: main and light battle tanks, armored personnel carriers, infantry fighting vehicles, integrated air and missile defense systems, unmanned ground systems, multiple rocket launchers, and other artillery systems.[85]

Yet the PLA suffered from what some called "peace disease" (和平病), a lack of combat experience since the 1979 Sino-Vietnamese War.[86] In that war, the PLA performed poorly and suffered from weak leadership, lackluster coordination between units at the tactical level, antiquated weapons and logistics equipment, and inadequate training and readiness.[87] With no major combat experience for nearly 50 years, PLA soldiers, equipment, and doctrine were not battle-tested. Nevertheless, China's growing air, space, and missile capabilities posed a major threat to U.S. forces operating in the Indo-Pacific region, as well as to U.S. partners such as Japan, Taiwan, Australia, and South Korea.

China possessed thousands of missiles, some of which—like the JL-3 submarine-launched ballistic missile—could strike the U.S. homeland.[88] Others could strike U.S. bases throughout the Indo-Pacific, including aircraft, runways, ships, fuel and munitions storage sites, ports, command-and-control facilities, and other infrastructure at such locations as Okinawa and Guam. China's suite of anti-ship ballistic missiles also posed a serious risk to U.S. surface ships in the region. As a suite of wargames conducted by the U.S. government and research institutions indicated, PLA forces could cause massive damage to the U.S. military in a war.[89] In one wargame that included 24 separate iterations of a Chinese amphibious invasion of Taiwan, "[t]he United States and its allies lost dozens of ships, hundreds of aircraft, and tens of thousands of servicemembers. Taiwan saw its economy devastated. Further, the high losses damaged the U.S. global position for many years."[90]

Despite these impressive gains, however, China still had problems in its defense industrial base.

Overall, China's defense industry faced at least four main weaknesses.

First, China relied on massive state-owned enterprises with convoluted and sprawling organizational structures, which undermined efficiency, competition, and innovation.[91] Huawei was an exception, but Xi Jinping failed to fully appreciate and effectively leverage the innovative contribution that companies like Huawei could make to his country's defense industrial base. For most of China's defense companies, there was little competition to win major weapons systems and defense equipment.[92] Factories that failed to fulfill contracts on time often evaded serious consequences. Most contracts, which were typically awarded as single sources, were built on a "cost-plus" model imported from the Soviet command economy and did not incentivize state-owned enterprises to keep costs down and improve efficiency.[93] Cost-plus contracts guaranteed 5 percent profit for contractors on top of their incurred costs, which provided little incentive for firms to innovate or improve efficiency in their operations because higher costs translated to higher profits.[94]

In fact, China's entire defense contracting process was outdated. Contracts were generally vague and failed to clearly outline contractual obligations for companies or performance goals, such as quality, pricing, and schedules.[95] In addition, the PLA's acquisition and procurement system was plagued by inefficiencies, which stemmed from state-owned enterprises that were infamous for their lack of innovation and hierarchical bureaucracies.[96] As University of California–San Diego professor Tai Ming Cheung summarized, China's defense industry is "cumbersome, risk-averse, and results in a lack of strong ownership that is critical to ensure that projects are able to succeed in the thicket of bureaucratic red tape and cut-throat competition for funding."[97]

China's industry generally lacked the contributions of a robust private sector and had fewer innovators like Kelly Johnson at Lockheed, Alex Karp at Palantir, John Lambert at Microsoft, Palmer Luckey at Anduril, and Elon Musk, Mark Juncosa, and Gwynne Shotwell at Space X. There were some exceptions, of course. One was Ren Zhengfei and Huawei, whose status as a private company—not a state-owned enterprise—allowed it to be leaner and more innovative. By 2024, Huawei was, by far, the number one company in the world in patent applications filed, 6,494, ahead of South Korea's Samsung (3,924), the United States' Qualcomm (3,410), and Japan's Mitsubishi Electric (2,152).[98] It spent $23 billion on research and development in 2023, more than Intel Corporation ($16 billion) and Samsung

Electronics ($19.8 billion) but less than world leaders like Alphabet (Google) ($45.4 billion), Apple ($30.0 billion), and Microsoft ($27.2 billion).[99] Huawei was also the world's largest seller of the components that made up the telecommunications network and internet, as well as a major global player in consumer gadgets such as smartphones. But Huawei was not the norm, making it a lost opportunity for Xi. His focus on state-owned enterprises—not private companies like Huawei—and his support for the Chinese Communist Party's creeping reach into companies were counterproductive to innovation.

Second, corruption plagued China's defense industrial base.[100] The opacity of the Chinese Communist Party made it difficult to determine whether the investigations were truly driven by an effort to root out corruption or a way to punish political opponents.[101] China oversaw a range of corruption investigations within the defense sector.[102] It removed at least 15 high-ranking military officers and defense industry executives between July and December 2023, such as Minister of National Defense Li Shangfu.[103] Several major defense companies, including in China's shipbuilding industry, faced corruption scandals.[104] Overall, corruption in China was high, according to multiple corruption indices compiled by such organizations as the World Bank and Transparency International.[105] And corruption within the PLA itself was historically widespread, including around promotions.[106] After all, the courts in China did not represent an independent branch of government but were, in essence, an instrument of the Chinese Communist Party.[107]

Third, China struggled with supply-chain vulnerabilities. Its diesel submarine fleet relied to some extent on German engines.[108] The PLA imported advanced aircraft engines and radar, traditionally from Russia.[109] Many of AVIC's J-20 fighters employed Russian Saturn AL-31 engines, and versions of the Shenyang FC-31 jet fighter used Russian RD-93 engines.[110] China depended on high-end chips and integrated circuits, but Chinese-manufactured chips were of lower quality than those produced abroad, and U.S. export control regulations limited China's access to the expertise, equipment, and export markets required to rapidly advance its chip industry.[111]

China's defense industrial base was dependent on importing some manufacturing equipment. Chinese-made machine tools often performed worse than foreign tools, contributing to low rates of domestic machine tools in high-tech industries such as aerospace.[112] The result was that high-end manufacturing still depended on foreign equipment, most of which came from Germany, Japan, South Korea, and Taiwan.[113] China was also dependent on importing several types of critical minerals and metals from overseas: iron and ferroalloy metals, such as niobium, cobalt, and chromium; nonferrous metals, such as beryllium; precious metals, such as rhodium, platinum, and palladium; and industrial minerals, such as boron and zirconium.[114]

Still, China began to decrease its dependence on foreign parts and equipment over time. It steadily reduced its arms imports. Especially notable were the decreases in aircraft imports after major investments in weapons development programs in the mid-2000s.[115] China attempted to lessen its dependence on foreign aircraft engines by producing indigenous engines using novel techniques and acquiring foreign firms such as Germany's Thielert Aircraft, the United States' Continental Aerospace Technologies and Superior Air Parts, and Canada's Diamond Aircraft Industries.[116]

A fourth weakness was that China faced adverse demographics, such as an aging population and low birth rates, which impacted the defense industrial base.[117] Its workforce was aging at a time when its fertility rate was below replacement levels and declining. Its labor force was projected to shrink over the next two decades, raising questions about whether its defense industrial base would be able to attract and retain talent in the future.[118] According to one report, a third of recent Chinese graduates quit their first job within six months of graduation because of unmet career expectations.[119] China also faced a lack of skilled personnel in the defense industry.[120]

These challenges—inefficient state-owned enterprises, corruption, supply-chain vulnerabilities, and unfavorable demographics—impacted the quality of some weapons systems produced by the Chinese industrial base. For example, China struggled to design specialized sound-absorbing coatings, deal with vibration-suppression issues created by steam turbines, and decrease the sonar signature of its hull designs.[121] Some of China's reverse-engineered platforms were inferior to the originals on which they were based.[122] The PLA also struggled to use some of its weapons systems and platforms.

One example was anti-submarine warfare. China attempted to improve its capabilities in this area, but the PLA struggled to consistently find submarines in deep water.[123] The acoustic properties of water made it difficult to detect enemy submarines. Anti-submarine warfare required joint intelligence collection platforms because of the complexities of the maritime environment, the size of the area that needed to be covered, and the overall mission to find, fix, track, target, and potentially engage enemy submarines. Numerous PLA Navy ships lacked organic sensors, such as towed-array and variable-depth sonar systems, and the PLA did not have sufficient helicopters and fixed-wing maritime patrol and reconnaissance aircraft for anti-submarine warfare.[124]

China certainly had its weaknesses. But it was a rising great power, and its defense industrial base was on a wartime footing.

"It's time to pick up the guns, mount the horses and go into battle," trumpeted Ren at an internal Huawei meeting.[125] He was referring to business, of course. But it was a theme he continued to advocate in competition with the United States and U.S. companies. In a memorandum the following year to Huawei employees, he pushed them to reach their sales targets in a competitive market and to go into "battle mode" against other firms, including those in the United States. "If you cannot do the job, then make way for our tank to roll," he warned. "And if you want to come on the battlefield, you can tie a rope around the 'tank' to pull it along, everyone needs this sort of determination!"[126]

China had emerged as a major competitor in emerging technologies, and its broader defense industrial base was able to churn out weapons systems at mass and scale. As its military exercises around Taiwan highlighted, China could bring together air, naval, space, and cyber capabilities to project power. Admiral John Aquilino, Commander of U.S. Indo-Pacific Command, bluntly remarked that "the PRC has continued the most extensive and rapid buildup since World War II."[127]

Beijing was committed to building capabilities for a specific purpose: to deter and, if necessary, to fight the United States.

Back in the United States, the defense industrial base did not operate with the same urgency or purpose—and certainly did not operate on a wartime footing. And U.S. deficiencies were becoming increasingly obvious.

11

Empty Bins in a Wartime Environment

> The U.S. defense industrial base (DIB) is unable to meet the equipment, technology, and munitions needs of the United States and its allies and partners. A protracted conflict, especially in multiple theaters, would require much greater capacity to produce, maintain, and replenish weapons and munitions.
> —U.S. Commission on the National Defense Strategy

> China continues to pursue unprecedented military modernization and increasingly aggressive behavior that threatens the U.S. homeland, our allies, and our partners.
> —Admiral Samuel J. Paparo, commander of U.S. Indo-Pacific Command

IT IS D-DAY.[1] CHINA'S PLA breaks the serenity of an early morning in Taiwan with a surprise air and missile attack that decimates the bulk of Taiwan's navy and air force. PLA Navy vessels then encircle Taiwan, quickly set up a blockade, and interdict all ships and aircraft attempting to reach—or leave—Taiwan. Tens of thousands of PLA soldiers cross the Taiwan Strait using a mixture of amphibious ships—including landing ship, tanks—and civilian roll-on, roll-off ships as PLA air assault and airborne troops land behind Taiwan's beachheads. The fighting is intense and China runs into difficulties attempting to seize Taiwan as U.S. Virginia-class submarines, B-21 stealth bombers, and F-35 and other aircraft—with help from Japan's Self-Defense Forces—strike China's amphibious fleet.

The costs are staggering for all sides. The United States and Japan lose dozens of ships (including multibillion-dollar U.S. aircraft carriers), hundreds of fifth-generation aircraft, and thousands of servicemembers—and more if the war expands into other theaters. These losses damage the U.S. and Chinese economies for many years. Taiwan's military is severely degraded—and possibly defeated—on an island that has been partially reduced to ruin. China too suffers substantial destruction. The PLA Navy is in shambles, the core of its amphibious forces is broken, and tens of thousands of soldiers are killed or prisoners of war.[2]

These were the results of a series of wargames organized by the Center for Strategic and International Studies, a nonpartisan research institution based in Washington, DC. Like any wargame or analysis, these wargames provided a perspective—but only one perspective—on what might happen in a war between the United States and China. Who wins or loses depends, in part, on several factors: How quickly does the United States enter the war? How well do Taiwan's military and civilians fight? How capable is the PLA, including in performing a complex amphibious landing and in combined arms and joint operations? What other countries, such as Japan, South Korea, Philippines, Australia, and Russia, enter the war? Does the war expand into other theaters, such as Europe, the Korean Peninsula, or Middle East? Answers to these and other questions provide insight into the war's outcome.

Yet there is one constant across virtually all unclassified and classified wargames and analyses on great power war: the U.S. defense industrial base is not prepared for a protracted war. The U.S. military consistently runs out of long-range precision munitions, such as the Long-Range Anti-Ship Missile (LRASM), and faces significant logistics challenges, including fuel, spare parts, food, and other equipment.[3] "Amateurs talk strategy. Professionals talk logistics," U.S. General Omar Bradley is credited as saying.[4]

On munitions, the U.S. military exhausted its inventory of LRASMs within the *first week* of a Taiwan conflict in the Center for Strategic and International Studies wargame and ran out of Joint Air-to-Surface Standoff Missile-Extended Range missiles after a month. Taiwan used up its entire inventory of Anti-Ship Cruise Missiles after a week. It would be very difficult to sustain a fight without these weapons.[5] LRASMs are particularly useful in a Taiwan Strait conflict because of their ability to strike Chinese naval forces from outside the range of Chinese air defenses. Chinese defenses are likely to be formidable—especially in the early stages of a war—and would prevent most aircraft from moving close enough to drop short-range munitions. U.S. bombers, such as the B-21, would generally employ LRASMs because they can fire them outside the range of Chinese missiles. But the problem is not just a shortfall of munitions. The production timelines for producing advanced munitions can be two years or more, so there are no quick solutions.[6]

These and other concerns about the industrial base are not new. Policymakers, analysts, and various national commissions have expressed alarm about the U.S. defense industrial base—including munitions stockpiles—for years.[7] As the bipartisan, congressionally appointed Commission on the National Defense Strategy bluntly concluded in 2024, the defense industrial base is "currently unable to produce the weapons, munitions, and other equipment and software needed to prepare for and engage in great power conflict."[8] Despite repeated calls for change, there has been limited progress.

This chapter argues that based on China's rise as a great power and growing collaboration with Russia, Iran, and even North Korea, the U.S. defense industrial base is unprepared to deter future conflict or—if deterrence fails—to fight and win a protracted war against one or more major powers. Despite a history of innovation, the U.S. industrial base today cannot respond at speed and scale—and with sufficient flexibility—to meet the needs for deterrence and warfighting. An appreciation of the challenge facing the United States first requires a review of the rise and fall of the defense industrial bases of the great powers.

At the beginning of World War II, Germany and the Soviet Union led the great powers in defense production at $6 billion and $5 billion, respectively, with Britain, France, Japan, Italy, and the United

States lagging behind.[9] Hitler spearheaded rearmament and aggressively pushed his defense industry to produce aircraft, ships, tanks, and other weapons systems and platforms at a torrid pace. Yale historian Paul Kennedy wrote, "With a political culture bent upon war and conquest and a political economy distorted to the extent that by 1938 52 percent of government expenditure and a massive 17 percent of gross national product was being poured in armaments, Germany had entered a different league from any of the other western European States."[10] In 1938, Germany spent more on arms than Britain, France, and the United States *combined*. Over the course of World War II, however, the U.S. industrial base was critical in providing the U.S. and allied militaries what they needed to fight—and win—a protracted war against Germany and Japan.

By the end of World War II, the landscape had shifted dramatically. The defeat of Nazi Germany and Imperial Japan decimated their respective industrial bases—and their countries more broadly. The United States and the Soviet Union emerged as the dominant global military powers, and their defense industries produced massive amounts of aircraft, tanks, ships, and nuclear weapons. In 1950, for example, U.S. and Soviet defense expenditures were $14.5 billion and $15.5 billion, respectively. No other country was even close. In 1970, the United States spent $77.8 billion on defense and the Soviet Union spent $72.0 billion. Once again, no other power came near spending those amounts: West Germany spent $6.1 billion, France $5.9 billion, the United Kingdom $5.8 billion, Italy $2.4 billion, and Japan $1.3 billion.[11] A wartime U.S. industrial based was essential in fighting wars, such as Korea, and deterring others, such as the Soviet Union during the second offset.

In 1991, the Soviet Union collapsed, leaving the United States alone atop the world. That same year, precision strike, stealth, and other advancements in the defense industrial base helped the United States defeat Iraqi forces during Operation Desert Storm. After September 11, 2001, advancements in unmanned systems—especially Predator—were critical for U.S. counterterrorism operations in Pakistan, Libya, Yemen, Iraq, and Afghanistan.

But beginning in 2012, Xi Jinping began to rebuild China's economy. A decade later, China certainly faced the serious economic challenges of youth unemployment, a troubled real estate market, high government

Country	GDP (Billions of Dollars, Current Prices)	Percentage of World GDP (Current Prices)	GDP Growth
United States	$27,358	26.1%	2.7%
China	$17,662	16.9%	4.6%
Japan	$4,213	4.0%	0.9%
Germany	$4,457	4.3%	0.2%
Russia	$1,997	1.9%	3.2%
France	$3,032	2.9%	0.7%
United Kingdom	$3,345	3.2%	0.5%
India	$3,572	3.4%	6.8%
Brazil	$2,174	2.1%	2.2%

FIGURE 11.1 Economic indicators of the major powers, 2023.[12]

debt, and adverse demographics. But China's economy continued to grow. Its GDP was second only to that of the United States and well above that of every other major power (Figure 11.1). China's science and technology advances were also impressive. China had more high-technology exports than the United States ($770 billion vs. $160 billion), nearly as much expenditure on research and development, more science and engineering doctoral degrees (43,399 vs. 41,701), and more science and engineering publications (898,949 vs. 457,335).[13]

Based on these developments, China's military made significant advances as Xi poured money into his country's defense industrial base. The United States still had the largest defense budget, but China was closing the gap. In 2000, the U.S. defense budget was 12 times the size of China's.[14] By 2025, China's defense budget was likely between 40 and 60 percent of the size of the U.S. defense budget, and catching up.[15] China likely underreported—and perhaps significantly underreported—its defense spending. Its defense budget in yuan bought substantially more in China than the equivalent amount of dollars in the United States because wages and other costs were notably lower in China. Average wage incomes in China were roughly one-fifth of those in the United States. For example, a truck driver in the United States earned a beginning salary of $40,000 per year, compared to only $7,400 for a Chinese truck drive. The result was that China's overall defense budget was roughly 60 percent higher than the dollar equivalent suggested.[16]

Country	Defense Spending (Billions of Dollars, Constant 2022 Prices)	Active Armed Forces	Estimated Reservists
United States	$880	1,326,000	807,000
China	$350–500	2,035,000	510,000
Russia	$126	1,100,000	1,500,000
India	$83	1,476,000	1,155,000
United Kingdom	$69	144,000	71,000
Germany	$61	181,000	35,000
France	$57	204,000	37,000
Japan	$52	247,000	56,000
Brazil	$21	367,000	1,340,000

FIGURE 11.2 Selected military indicators of the major powers, 2023.[17]

No other major powers were close: India spent $83 billion, Japan $51 billion, and Brazil a lowly $21 billion. European defense budgets were also relatively low, at $69 billion for the United Kingdom, $61 billion for Germany, and $57 billion for France (Figure 11.2). These numbers raised serious questions about the ability of European militaries to fight a major war. Rob Johnson, director of the U.K. Ministry of Defense's Office of Net Assessment, lamented that U.K. armed forces could not "defend the British homelands properly" and were unprepared for "conflict of any scale," including a conventional war. "In any larger-scale operation, we would run out of ammunition rapidly.... Our defenses are too thin, and we are not prepared to fight and win an armed conflict of any scale."[18]

China's growth was particularly disturbing because of its deepening cooperation with a coalition that included Russia, Iran, and North Korea. China provided significant dual-use components to Russia, whose defense industrial base was on a wartime footing, to wage war in Ukraine. Examples of assistance included semiconductors and microelectronics for use in Russian weapons systems; parts for fighter jets; drones; engines for drones and cruise missiles; parts for mobile radar units used on S-400 antiaircraft missile systems; and other components and systems. Iran provided drones, artillery shells, ammunition, and Fateh-110 short-range ballistic missiles to Russia. In response,

Russia supplied Iran with Su-35 multi-role fighter jets, Mi-28 attack helicopters, and S-400 air defense systems, as well as aid to Iran's space and missile programs. North Korea sent artillery rounds (including 152mm and 122mm rounds), rocket short-range ballistic missiles, other munitions, and soldiers to Russia. In return, Russia supplied North Korea with advanced technology for satellites, nuclear-powered submarines, and ballistic missiles.[19] In short, there was growing defense industrial cooperation between this coalition of countries.

In addition to military and dual-use cooperation, China, Russia, Iran, and North Korea coordinated in other ways. For example, China and Russia conducted roughly 100 joint military exercises between 2017 and 2024 in a growing number of geographic areas, such as Asia, Europe (including the Mediterranean), the Middle East, the Arctic, and Africa.[20] China and Russia agreed to what they termed a "no limits" friendship in February 2022, and then they reaffirmed their partnership in February 2025.[21] In 2021, Iran signed a 25-year cooperation agreement with China that promised hundreds of billions of dollars in economic and technical cooperation. In June 2024, Russia and North Korea signed a "Treaty on Comprehensive Strategic Partnership," which committed the countries to mutual military and other assistance if the other was invaded.[22] In January 2025, Russia and Iran signed a 20-year pact that formalized close ties between the two countries.[23]

In light of China's rise as a great power and growing collaboration with Russia, Iran, and North Korea, U.S. defense spending was historically low as a percentage of gross domestic product and total federal outlays.[24] For comparison purposes, the United States spent roughly 3 percent of GDP on defense in 2025. The U.S. defense budget peaked at 14 percent of GDP during the Korean War. It was between 9 and 11 percent during President Eisenhower's New Look policies in the 1950s, between 8 and 9 percent during Presidents Kennedy and Johnson's Flexible Response period in the 1960s, and over 6 percent during President Reagan's defense buildup in the 1980s.[25]

After the collapse of the Soviet Union and the end of the Cold War, defense budgets dramatically decreased to 3 to 4 percent in the absence of a major conventional threat and following Secretary of Defense Les Aspin and Deputy Secretary of Defense William Perry's Last

Supper in 1993. The U.S. defense budget briefly crept above 4 percent during the surges in Afghanistan and Iraq, although the money went to wartime operations and not to revitalizing the defense industrial base. Nevertheless, defense budgets shortly fell back into the 3 percent range.[26]

Yet the international landscape changed dramatically in the early 2020s, with Russia's invasion of Ukraine, active wars in the Middle East, and serious tensions in the Taiwan Strait and Korean Peninsula. Dartmouth College professors Stephen Brooks and William Wohlforth argued that the United States remained the globe's dominant power, though the gap was closing with China. "Yes, the United States has become less dominant over the past 20 years," they contended, "but it remains at the top of the global power hierarchy."[27] While true, many of the traditional measures of U.S. military and economic might—such as defense expenditures and GDP—masked a disturbing reality: the U.S. defense industry, the bedrock of U.S. military might, lacked the capacity to meet the military's production needs in a world in which China was a rising great power and cooperating with Russia, Iran, and North Korea.

The rest of this chapter outlines some of the most significant challenges faced by the U.S. defense industrial base, beginning at the top of the U.S. government.

Revitalization of the U.S. defense industrial base and broader defense ecosystem has historically required leadership, prioritization, and a sense of urgency from the president of the United States. During World War I, for example, President Woodrow Wilson established the War Industries Board to coordinate the purchase of war matériel for the military.[28] Leadership from the top has been important because the defense industrial base is much bigger than just the military. Numerous entities beyond the Department of Defense play important roles in the defense industrial base, including the Departments of State, Commerce, and Treasury; Congress; and the private sector. In fact, the growing role of commercial technology in modern defense systems has increased the role of nondefense agencies and organizations in the industrial base.

Yet there is no major body today that serves as an executive agent for the president with the power and authority to break bureaucratic logjams and coordinate across departments and agencies. Government departments, members of Congress, companies, and other actors have competing interests, priorities, and authorities.[29] In the United States, the president plays a particularly important role in providing strategic guidance and leadership. As professors Morton Halperin and Priscilla Clapp concluded in their work on bureaucratic politics, "The president stands at the center of the foreign policy process in the United States.... In any foreign policy decision widely believed at the time to be important, the president will almost always be the principal figure determining the general direction of actions."[30]

Presidential leadership has been essential during critical periods of U.S. history to strengthen—or consolidate—the defense industrial base. Since World War II, Roosevelt, Truman, Eisenhower, and others created institutional bodies to advise the president and coordinate across government agencies and the private sector, issue directives, and even plan, direct, and control industrial mobilization (Figure 11.3).

In May 1940, a year and a half before Pearl Harbor and the U.S. entry into World War II, a perceptive President Roosevelt created the National Defense Advisory Commission to help coordinate various segments of the defense industrial base. It was led by Bill Knudsen, the president of General Motors, and six other titans of industry.[31] When Knudsen asked Roosevelt at the first meeting who was head of the group, Roosevelt responded that, as president of the United States, he was.[32] Roosevelt's point was that a major revitalization of the defense industrial base required the weight—and oversight—of the president. Indeed, his strategic guidance was essential to mobilization *before* the United States was involved in World War II.

The National Defense Advisory Commission eventually gave way to the War Production Board, which supervised production for the remainder of World War II. The War Production Board provided overall direction for wartime production, oversaw the evolution of companies from peacetime to wartime production, and prioritized materials and services.[33] Since the country was at war, the War Production Board also rationed such commodities as gasoline, heating oil, metals, rubber, paper, and plastics.

Defense Industry Body	U.S. President	Years	Responsibilities
National Defense Advisory Commission	Franklin D. Roosevelt	1940–1941	Advise the president on better coordinating key parts of the defense industrial base, including production, raw materials, employment, farm products, transportation, price stabilization, and consumer protection.
Office of Production Management	Franklin D. Roosevelt	1940–1942	Coordinate the procurement and production of armaments and equipment, including the conversion of industry from civilian to defense production.
War Production Board	Franklin D. Roosevelt	1942–1945	Exercise general direction over war procurement and production; determine the policies, plans, and procedures of federal departments regarding procurement and production; establish priorities in the distribution of materials and services; and prohibit nonessential production.
Civilian Production Administration	Harry Truman	1945–1947	Oversee the transition from wartime to peacetime production, including expanding the production of materials in short supply and granting priority assistance to breaking bottlenecks that impede the reconversion process.
Office of Defense Mobilization	Harry Truman	1950–1958	Plan, coordinate, direct, and control all wartime mobilization activities of the U.S. government.
Office of Defense and Civil Mobilization	Dwight D. Eisenhower	1958–1973	Coordinate military, industrial, and civilian mobilization. The office was later renamed the Office of Civil and Defense Mobilization, Office of Emergency Planning, and then Office of Emergency Preparedness.

FIGURE 11.3 President–led defense industry bodies since World War II.

President Truman abolished the War Production Board in October 1945, but he switched gears when the Cold War began.[34] He established a cabinet-level Office of Defense Mobilization in 1950 to plan, coordinate, direct, and control all defense industrial production.[35] He also established the National Security Resources Board to mobilize natural resources and the scientific community to meet the nation's growing military demands.[36] In addition, Truman signed the Defense Production Act on September 8, 1950, which authorized the president to force companies to prioritize defense production, set aside price ceilings, and expand private and public production capacity during the Korean War.[37] In 1958, President Eisenhower stood up the Office of Defense and Civil Mobilization to coordinate military, industrial, and civilian mobilization. The office was later renamed the Office of Civil and Defense Mobilization, Office of Emergency Planning, and then Office of Emergency Preparedness. President Reagan spearheaded a major defense buildup and continued the second offset investments in stealth, precision strike, and other capabilities.[38] In developing a strong defense, Reagan explained, it was necessary to "maintain our strength in order to deter and defend against aggression—to preserve freedom and peace."[39] While the United States was not at war with the Soviet Union, a revitalization of the defense industry was critical to strengthen deterrence and ensure that the Red Army did not send forces across the Fulda Gap along the border of East and West Germany.

These institutional bodies and presidential initiatives were important during periods of heightened strategic competition and wars. But they are missing today. There are several additional challenges.

One challenge is an anachronistic contracting and acquisitions system that has made it difficult for innovative small and medium-size companies, as well as some of the most advanced technology companies, to sell to the Department of Defense. U.S. and allied military power has unfortunately been defined by an increasingly smaller number of exquisite and extremely expensive platforms and weapons systems. But since winning a protracted war—and deterring a war from the beginning—generally requires the ability to produce weapons and equipment in mass, it is critical to build lower cost, mass-producible, and precision-strike systems. Some have called the current age of warfare the era of "precise mass."[40] In addition, modern warfare has evolved to include weapons and systems enabled by artificial intelligence, autonomous vehicles, ubiquitous sensors, modern software, and other advanced capabilities.[41]

Government officials and experts have long called for defense acquisition reform. One Department of Defense study bluntly warned, "Major defense programs continue to take ten years or more to deliver less capability than planned, often at two to three times the planned cost."[42] Jacques Gansler, who was at the center of the Pentagon's acquisition program as under secretary of defense for acquisition, technology, and logistics, bitterly complained that the defense acquisition process was far too slow, inflexible, and risk-averse. "This entire process tends to take ten to fifteen years for weapon systems, and during that time technologies change, requirements change, and quantities and budgets change," he objected. "The program goes through constant revisions (a typical program goes through thousands of changes during this period), and many changes in personnel (senior government people rarely stay on a program for the entire process)."[43] While this prolonged period might be fine for peacetime, it is not sufficient for a wartime environment.

A 2024 Government Accountability Office study that reviewed 108 defense acquisition programs concluded that the Department of Defense "remains alarmingly slow in delivering new and innovative weapon system capabilities, even as national security threats continue to evolve."[44] Would-be companies that want to deal with the Pentagon, including start-up companies with venture capital funding, must comply with the dizzying Federal Acquisition Regulation, which includes the policies and procedures for acquisitions by U.S. executive departments and agencies. They also have to deal with the Defense Federal Acquisition Regulation Supplement, rules and regulations established by the Department of Defense to make sure that contractors and subcontractors follow specific cybersecurity best practices to protect sensitive information.

It is no wonder that numerous companies in the commercial sector, including venture capital and private equity firms, have shied away from the defense sector. Many *want* to work with the Department of Defense or the U.S. intelligence community. But they have little interest in trekking through a byzantine contracting and acquisition system and are deterred by the heavy regulatory burden and the limited financial upside. These companies often support the government's mission and are unstintingly patriotic but have little patience for contracting and acquisition processes that takes too long, are far too uncertain, and are maddeningly opaque. Many are concerned about the "Valley of Death," a phenomenon faced by start-ups trying to do business with the Department of Defense. The term refers to the precarious journey in which a company transitions from a prototype or commercially available product to a Department of Defense contract. Many start-ups trying to do business with the Pentagon never make it from prototype to contract because of the mismatch in timelines between raising capital and securing a contract. Start-ups typically raise venture funding on timelines of one to two years, while the Defense Department often operates on an acquisition cycle of three to five years—or more. A few, such as Palantir and Anduril, have succeeded. But most fail.[45]

Commercial companies are also concerned that the Department of Defense will attempt to seize their intellectual property. Trae Stephens, one of Anduril's founders along with Palmer Luckey and Brian Schimpf, quipped that far too often the department asks companies to "turn over your source code." He continued, "It's crazy. We're literally doing to our companies in America what we're criticizing the Chinese for doing to their companies and to our companies when we enter that market."[46]

The outcome of such a convoluted contracting and acquisition process is that companies with broad commercial interests and expertise have generally not received significant Department of Defense funding, despite the explosion of venture capital and private equity investment. Companies with little or no commercial business accounted for 61 percent of the Department of Defense's major programs by value in 2024—a major increase from 6 percent at the end of the Cold War. If one includes companies whose only commercial business was in aerospace, such as Boeing or Textron, the percentage jumped to 86.[47] That means that only 14 percent of the Department of Defense's major programs went to commercial companies that served defense and other markets. Ford Motor Company, Kodak, and a large number of other companies sold off their defense businesses long ago, following the Last Supper.

The paucity of companies with both defense *and* commercial units that have won major defense contracts raises serious questions about the future of innovation. After all, some of the most successful innovations in the U.S. defense sector came from companies that served both the defense and nondefense markets, such as Boeing, SpaceX, Microsoft, and Palantir. In a few cases, such as Lockheed's Skunk Works, innovation came from a traditional defense company with a patently nontraditional unit that worked autonomously from the rest of the company. As Kelly Johnson explained at the time, "The ability to make immediate decisions and put them into rapid effect is basic to our successful operation. Working with a limited number of especially capable and responsible people is another requirement." But Johnson was deeply concerned about whether large companies would allow such innovative units in the future. "I fear that the way I like to design and build airplanes one day may no longer be possible," he worried. "I see the strong authority that is absolutely essential to this kind of operation slowly being eroded by committee and conference control from within and without."[48]

A second challenge is shortfalls of key defense systems, such as munitions. As wargames and analyses demonstrated, the U.S. military has too few munitions and other systems for a protracted war, which undermines both deterrence and warfighting. The dilemma for the government is to try to match the *production rate* of defense systems with the *consumption rate* in a possible protracted war.[49] This is more an art than a science, since it requires estimating the possible timelines and munitions usage in a future war: Will a possible conflict between the United States and China over Taiwan be short or long? Will it spread to other theaters? What types of munitions and weapons systems will be required? Numerous variables impact the duration and geographic expanse of wars.[50] But it would be prudent to plan for longer, rather than shorter, wars.

The problem is that it is difficult to establish stockpiles quickly. It takes an average of 8.4 years to replace the inventories for major defense acquisition programs at surge production rates.[51] Missiles, space-based systems, and shipbuilding face the longest replacement times. It can also take roughly two years to produce numerous types of advanced missiles, such as the Patriot Advanced Capability-2 and -3 air and missile defense system, Tomahawk Block V, Joint Air-to-Surface Standoff Missile, and Precision Strike Missile. These lead times are generally to deliver the *first* missiles, not the *last* ones in a production order (Figure 11.4). Filling inventories requires sustained multiyear investment as well as accurate projections of the rate of use. Missile obsolescence, tooling, and sub-tier capacity have not been a priority and are a major constraint.

In addition, it can take at least 18 to 24 months to implement investments in some factories to develop capacity to meet surging demands.[52] There are also potential challenges in expanding some facilities, such

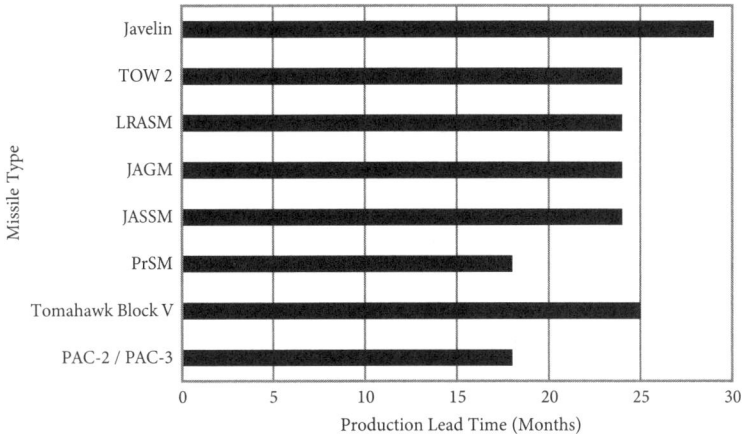

FIGURE 11.4 Selected munitions production timelines.[53]

Notes: LRASM: Long Range Anti-ship Missile; JAGM: Joint Air-to-ground Missile; JASSM: Joint Air-to-surface Missile; PrSM: Precision Strike Missile; PAC-2 / PAC-3: Patriot Advanced Capability (PAC)-2 and PAC-3.

as munitions assembly plants, since companies are required to have sufficient standoff distance—or "quality distance"—between the plant and surrounding area to protect civilians from accidental explosions. Building a larger plant can involve purchasing additional land, securing permits, buying additional insurance, and taking other steps.[54] All of this takes time and money.

A third challenge is a fragile supply chain. There is limited production of key components, such as solid rocket motors, processor assemblies, castings, forgings, ball bearings, microelectronics, and seekers for munitions.[55] There are also long lead times for some types of equipment, such as engines and generators. Dependence on a small number of companies—or even a single source—leaves the United States highly vulnerable to supply disruption.

In addition, the United States is overreliant on single or foreign sources for some components and materials.[56] China dominates the advanced battery supply chain across the globe, such as lithium hydroxide, electrolyte, lithium carbonate, anodes, and cathodes.[57] China also controls—or partially controls—the global market for several types of raw materials used in the defense sector: iron and ferroalloy metals, such as vanadium and molybdenum; nonferrous metals, such as gallium, germanium, tellurium, antimony, and arsenic; and industrial minerals, such as graphite.[58] The Department of Defense depends on foreign governments, including China, for large cast and forged products, which are utilized in some defense systems.[59] Finally, China controls global refining for some critical minerals, such as lithium, cobalt, nickel, and natural graphite.

To illustrate Western vulnerabilities, China imposed export curbs on gallium, germanium, and antimony in 2024 citing "national security concerns."[60] Antimony is used in defense equipment, such as night vision goggles, ammunition, explosive formulations, nuclear weapons production, infrared sensors, and semiconductors.[61] In 2025, China imposed export restrictions on several rare earth metals—samarium, gadolinium, terbium, dysprosium, lutetium, scandium, and yttrium—critical for U.S. weapons systems, such as Virginia-class submarines, F-35 fighter jets, Tomahawk land attack cruise missiles, and Predator drones.[62] However, China is also vulnerable in some areas of the defense sector and needs to import cobalt, chromium, tantalum, beryllium, lithium, rhodium, platinum, boron, and zirconium.[63]

Smaller companies that serve as suppliers to large companies are also at risk. Many operate on narrow profit margins, which makes them susceptible to cyclical defense demands and changes in the defense budget. These challenges undermine the ability and willingness of some small suppliers to remain in the defense market.[64]

A fourth challenge is with the workforce. The U.S. labor market is unable to provide enough workers with the right skills to meet the defense demands of today and tomorrow. Hiring and retention are both problematic.[65] Skills in short supply range from software engineers to welders. Under Secretary of Defense William LaPlante argued, "[T]he workforce in many ways is the most stressing element right now, both talented workforce, in terms of writing software, engineering, but also the workforce that does the production and is conversant in advanced production, whether it's additive or subtractive manufacturing."[66] The causes of workforce problems are varied, such as the high cost of living near factories and shipyards, stiff competition from other sectors, and insufficient training from trade and vocational schools.

Shipyards are particularly problematic. Some skill sets, such as nuclear welding, are difficult to acquire outside of U.S. Navy procurement. But the workforce shortage is widespread in such areas as engineers, electricians, pipefitters, shipfitters, and metalworkers.[67] In 2024, the navy acknowledged that the first Constellation-class guided-missile frigate (FFG-62) would be at least a year late because of workforce shortfalls at Fincantieri's Marinette Marine shipyard. The Wisconsin shipyard was short several hundred workers, including welders.[68] In 2022, the navy ended the fiscal year short 1,200 workers across its four shipyards. As the head of Naval Sea Systems Command remarked, hiring and retaining skilled workers in government repair yards and private sector shipbuilding is the navy's top strategic challenge across the enterprise.[69] In addition, construction of the Block V version of the Virginia-class fast-attack submarine was at least two years behind schedule because of workforce constraints and other factors.[70] And some Arleigh Burke-class guided-missile destroyers were two to three years behind schedule.[71]

A final challenge is defense industrial cooperation with allies. Since the end of the Cold War, the United States has fought with allies in every major military operation, from Bosnia and Kosovo to Afghanistan and Iraq. There are always problems working with allies, from differing interests and domestic constraints to interoperability. But it is virtually impossible to conceive of the United States fighting a war against China, Russia, or Iran alone. "There is only one thing worse than fighting with allies," Winston Churchill noted in April 1945, "and that is fighting without them."[72] Integration with allied defense industries is an important component of cooperation. Partnership in the defense industry can include such arrangements as co-development, co-production, co-sustainment, second-sourcing, and licensed production. Yet there have been significant obstacles to cooperation with allies.

One challenge is with foreign military sales, in which the United States sells defense articles and services to foreign countries.[73] When an eligible foreign government wants to purchase or acquire a U.S. defense system or service, it begins with a letter of request, or LOR. The foreign government submits the LOR to the United States and, following approval of the transfer, the United States responds with a letter of offer and acceptance, or LOA. The time it takes to prepare an LOA can vary based on such factors as the foreign government involved, the defense system or service requested, and the overall complexity of the sale. It can be fast for routine items, but time consuming for others. After that, the defense item needs to be produced.[74]

There has been some progress in improving the foreign military sales process.[75] Nevertheless, the entire process—from initial discussions to LOR, LOA, production, and modifications—is too long: an average of 18 months.[76] There is also no real accountability in the foreign military sales system. The Department of State statutorily owns it, but execution largely falls to the Department of Defense and is split among the military services and several Department of Defense agencies. No one is held accountable for strategic success or failure. Partner and ally requests for U.S. systems can go unanswered for months or even years. Foreign military sales programs are executed under a U.S. government contract negotiated and awarded by a U.S. military service contracting officer on behalf of the foreign military sales partner. The Department of Defense contracting community is understaffed. Foreign military sales contracts are sometimes given a low priority by contracting officers, who look first to support U.S. service personnel, then to contracts to support innovation for next-generation capabilities for U.S. service personnel, and then to foreign military sales. In addition, staffing constraints, technological limitations, and the increasing complexity of systems can slow the rate at which transactions are approved if there is a major increase in foreign military sales.[77]

Another challenge is technology transfer review policies and procedures—including the International Traffic in Arms Regulations (ITAR)—for foreign military sales and direct commercial sales.[78] ITAR is the U.S. regulation that controls the manufacture, sale, and distribution of defense and space-related articles and services.[79] ITAR and other regulations are designed to prevent the transfer of sensitive technology to adversaries and, in some instances, to signal disapproval to foreign countries for their actions.[80]

The United States has a long-standing exemption for Canada and can transfer some unclassified defense material and services without an export license. This exemption is limited, and companies sometimes avoid using the exemption because they are worried about the consequences of ITAR violations. Exports to Canada of classified and more sensitive material and services still require a license.[81] In addition, AUKUS—the security pact initiated between Australia, the United Kingdom, and the United States to cooperate on sensitive technologies, including nuclear-powered submarines—led to some technology-sharing changes. The United States agreed in 2024 to exempt Australia and the United Kingdom from a range of defense technologies, such as munitions, sensors, and propulsion systems.[82]

In the past, the United States occasionally made exceptions to technology transfers. But these outliers have generally required major foreign policy priorities, such as countering the Soviet Union's growing capabilities in the 1960s or aiding Ukraine following Russia's 2022 invasion. In 1963, the United States and United Kingdom signed the Polaris Sales Agreement, which allowed the United States to export Polaris missiles, launch tubes, fire control systems, and relevant technologies to the United Kingdom to build and maintain its submarine-based nuclear weapons systems.[83] U.S. and other NATO officials had become increasingly concerned about the Soviet Union's nuclear and conventional capabilities and their impact on the military balance in Europe.[84]

Despite a strong strategic rationale today because of competition with China, Russia, Iran, North Korea, and other adversaries, the United States has failed to make significant progress in reducing export barriers with its closest allies and partners.[85] Even for close allies, there are notable delays, confusion, and unpredictability with the U.S. technology transfer process—a sign of a peacetime, not a wartime, mindset.[86]

For example, U.S. delays held up a routine upgrade on sonar systems for U.K. Royal Navy submarines for several months, while another U.K. submarine had to wait months to be serviced by a cleared contractor until the U.S. Department of State authorized an export-controlled component. One analysis concluded that "months went by waiting for a license that just added cost and risk to an ally's military capability."[87]

More broadly, the United Kingdom spent a shocking *$500 million each year*—almost 1 percent of its defense budget—complying with U.S. ITAR regulations.[88] Another assessment concluded, "When close U.S. allies—or their defense firms—wish to develop technology or acquire capability from the United States, they have to navigate a byzantine system of regulation. This costs time and money, undermines allies' sovereignty, stifles innovation, and blunts the United States' edge in the strategic competition with China."[89]

The chief of the U.K. Navy, Admiral Sir Ben Key, explained that "what we want to be able to do is move quicker" in today's competitive security environment. In periods of peace, regulators often predominate.[90] But in periods of war, in which countries must move quickly against cunning adversaries, "rat-catchers" need to dominate. Using language reminiscent of the British naval historian Andrew Gordon, Admiral Key asked, "Are we setting up the ITAR and all the rest of it to allow the regulators or the rat-catchers? And what is it we're trying to achieve?" He continued that "what we really want to do is in a contested environment, when the pressure is really on, we want the information to move between allies and partners and friends as fast as we possibly can with as few hurdles as we can."[91] But that has not been the case—at least not yet.

Despite these challenges, legions of skeptics have resisted change.

First, some see revitalization of the defense industry as giving money to greedy executives.[92] Concerns about corporate greed, waste, fraud, and abuse are not new. During World War II, Secretary of the Interior Harold Ickes and columnist Walter Lippmann accused—falsely—William Knudsen and others of lining the pockets of corporate executives.[93] The same was true during the Vietnam War, when some members of Congress and journalists bitterly complained about war profiteering. As journalist James Fallows wrote: "During the Vietnam era, the military-industrial complex was a shorthand reference to the interests that presumably kept profiting from the war. Brown and Root, building those bases in the jungle? Dow Chemical, with its napalm?"[94] Perhaps the quintessential Cold War example was Oliver Stone's movie *JFK*, which falsely portrayed the assassination of President Kennedy as a CIA plot to preserve the military-industrial complex in collusion with a right-wing cabal of generals and corporate profiteers. "The war is the biggest business in America, worth $80 billion a year," said district attorney Jim Garrison, who is played by Kevin Costner, to a packed courtroom in *JFK*.

Some have also warned about former defense officials working for venture capital, private equity, and defense firms. As one *New York Times* investigative piece concluded, "the close ties between venture capital firms and Defense Department decision makers have also put a new twist on long-running questions about industry access and influence at a time when the Pentagon is under pressure to rethink how it allocates its huge procurement budget."[95] Others have warned about waste, fraud, and abuse. For example, the CBS News investigative television show *60 Minutes* alleged that defense contractors had overcharged the Department of Defense for a wide array of equipment, boosting the profits of some companies by nearly 40 percent and sometimes as high as 4,000 percent.[96] In 2023, five U.S. senators, including Bernie Sanders and Elizabeth Warren, alleged in a letter to the secretary of defense that some companies had "abused the trust government has placed in them, exploiting their position as sole suppliers for certain items to increase prices far above inflation or any reasonable profit margin."[97]

All accusations of fraud, waste, and abuse need to be taken seriously, and any individuals and companies found guilty need to be appropriately punished. The Department of Justice, Department of Defense's Office of Inspector General, and other agencies are designed to conduct investigations and take necessary actions. But major waste, fraud, and abuse are the exceptions. The outlier cases should not be an excuse for failing to strengthen the defense industrial base.

Second, some don't want to provide additional funding to an industry involved in defense. Some Google employees protested when they discovered their company was involved in the Defense Department program Project Maven, telling CEO Sundar Pichai to "draft, publicize, and enforce a clear policy stating that neither Google nor its contractors will ever build warfare technology."[98] Others criticized Alex Karp and companies like Palantir for supporting the military-industrial complex. "While Palantir promises a more efficient and cost-effective way to conduct war, should our goal be to make it less expensive, onerous and painful?" asked journalist Kara Swisher, author of *Burn Book: A Tech Love Story*. "After all, war is not a video game, nor should it be."[99] In response to Palantir's work helping the Department of Homeland Security track down undocumented migrants, demonstrators protested at Palantir's office, shouting such slogans as "Immigrants are welcome here, time to cancel Palantir."[100]

Yet the primary goal of the defense industrial base is to strengthen defense to *deter* war. After all, a great power war between the United States and China would be devastating, particularly if it escalated to nuclear war.[101] How could the United States or other Western powers deter China, Russia, Iran, or North Korea with a weak defense industry? "I am actually a progressive. I want less war," explained Palantir's Karp, who grew up in a liberal family outside of Philadelphia. "You only stop war by having the best technology and by scaring the bejabbers—I'm trying to be nice here—out of our adversaries. If they are not scared, they don't wake up scared, they don't go to bed scared, they don't fear that the wrath of America will come down on them, they will attack us. They will attack us everywhere."[102]

Third, there are numerous bureaucratic obstacles to changes in the defense industry. Some government officials remain overly cautious about sharing sensitive technology with other countries, even with the closest U.S. allies with whom it shares its most sensitive intelligence. Of course the United States needs to prevent particularly sensitive technology—such as nuclear propulsion, stealth technology, and quantum navigation systems—from falling into the hands of its adversaries.[103] But these are a small subset of a vast supply chain.

Some policymakers oppose multiyear contracts because these types of contracts *commit* the government to fund the weapons systems or programs, reducing budget flexibility in out years. Government agencies lose liquidity, and it can be more difficult to move money over the course of a fiscal year if a military service or other entity wants to shift priorities. Munitions are sometimes a "bill payer," a part of the defense budget from which officials can trim to fund other programs.[104] Without multiyear contracts that guarantee funding, however, companies have little incentive to take financial risk and grow capacity. It's not worth investing if there is unreliable demand. And the costs and risks are high. Multiyear contracts keep supply lines warm, sustain supply chain subcontractors, increase production efficiencies that help industry better respond to surges, and encourage investment in facilities and equipment. In today's security environment, it increasingly makes sense for the government to take on more risk in buying defense systems because the risks associated with *underbuying* are so significant, especially for a protracted war.

The arguments opposed to revitalizing the defense industrial base are largely unpersuasive and ultimately counterproductive in today's competitive international landscape.

While the United States remains strong in some categories of national power, such as defense expenditures and GDP, its defense industrial base is in poor shape. The dire state of shipbuilding and the maritime industrial base are stark examples. The U.S. industrial base lacks the capacity, responsiveness, flexibility, and surge capability to meet the military's production, deterrence, and warfighting needs—especially with China's rise and growing cooperation between Beijing, Moscow, Tehran, and Pyongyang. Defense contracting and acquisitions policies and processes are slow and antiquated and stifle innovation. The United States does not have sufficient weapons systems—including munitions—to fight a protracted war. The problem is not just with the United States, but most of its allies. At the peak of the war in Ukraine, for example, Russia expended more ammunition in two days than the *entire U.K. military* had in stock.[105]

Unless there are urgent changes, the United States risks weakening deterrence and undermining its warfighting capabilities. As the previous chapter argued, China is heavily investing in munitions and acquiring high-end weapons systems and equipment faster than the United States and has a shipbuilding capacity much larger than that of the United States. And there are no quick fixes in the defense industrial base since there are long lead times.

What should be done? Thankfully, the United States has a rich tradition of innovators and entrepreneurs.

12

Rebuilding the Arsenal of Democracy

> Innovation distinguishes between a leader and a follower.
> —STEVE JOBS, founder of Apple

> Other countries may seek to compete with us; but in one vital area, as a beacon of freedom and opportunity that draws people of the world, no country on Earth comes close. This, I believe, is one of the most important sources of America's greatness.
> —PRESIDENT RONALD REAGAN

TWO CENTURIES AGO, THE FRENCH sociologist and philosopher Alexis de Tocqueville expressed deep admiration for the innovative spirit and boundless energy of Americans.[1] "When, near the end of a year filled with work," Tocqueville wrote in *Democracy in America*, "he takes his restless curiosity here and there across the vast limits of the United States."[2] For Tocqueville, a key to the American entrepreneurial spirit was the capacity to think freely, break with tradition, and develop new methods. These were important attributes of American national character. "The American taken randomly will therefore be a man ardent in his desires, enterprising, adventurous—above all, an innovator."[3]

Production and innovation have been important components of industry in the United States, and they have provided an advantage—the American edge—in times of peril. Take technology as an example.

"I'm constantly telling people 86 percent of the top 50 tech companies in the world just by market cap are American—and people fall out of their chair," said Palantir's Alex Karp. "It's hard for us to understand how dominant we are in certain industries."[4] Karp was correct: U.S. companies dominated the technology industry. Among the top 10 technology companies in 2025 by market capitalization—the total market value of a company traded on the stock market—eight were American: Apple, Microsoft, Nvidia, Alphabet (Google), Amazon, Meta Platforms (Facebook), Broadcom, and Tesla. As for the other two, one was from Taiwan (TSMC, the semiconductor firm) and the other was from China (Tencent, the technology and video game company).[5]

The American edge in production and innovation was apparent in how entrepreneurs from dramatically different sides of the political spectrum could come together in the spirit of creativity. Perhaps the quintessential examples were Alex Karp and Peter Thiel, who worked together at Palantir. Karp was a self-identified "progress warrior," and Thiel was a conservative libertarian.[6] While students at Stanford Law School, they debated the merits of socialism and capitalism. "We argued like feral animals," Karp recalled.[7] Their friendship and cerebral sparring continued after Stanford. "I think we bonded on this intellectual level where he was this crazy leftist and I was this crazy right-wing person," Thiel said, "but we somehow talked to each other."[8] They did more than talk, establishing Palantir as a unicorn with a market capitalization in 2025 of nearly $300 billion, larger than Lockheed Martin.[9]

As this book argues, countries in a wartime environment need to operate with urgency, spend money on defense to maximize production, minimize excessive red tape, and streamline their defense acquisition and contracting processes. The United States has a history of innovators and entrepreneurs capable of operating in wartime, such as George Schairer, Edward Wells, and Wellwood Beall with the B-29; Kelly Johnson and his team at Lockheed Skunk Works with the U-2; Weldon Word and his team at Texas Instruments with Paveway I, II, and III; Ben Rich, Denys Overholser, and others at Skunk Works with stealth; Abe Karem, Linden and Neal Blue, and Tom Cassidy at General Atomics with the Predator drone; Alex Karp, Akash "Aki" Jain, and Stephen Cohen at Palantir with defense software; Elon Musk, Mark Juncosa,

Gwynne Shotwell, and others at Space X, Starlink, and their government business unit Starshield with space capabilities; Brad Smith and engineers like John Lambert at Microsoft with cyber capabilities; and Anduril's Palmer Luckey, Brian Schimpf, and Trae Stephens with autonomous platforms, artificial intelligence, and sensor networks.

As the previous chapter argued, however, the U.S. defense industrial base is operating in a peacetime—not wartime—environment. The risks of failing to adequately revitalize the U.S. defense industrial base are significant and growing. The "peace dividend" that emerged at the end of the Cold War is over, especially with China putting significant resources into its defense industrial base, building advanced military capabilities, and partnering with Russia, Iran, and North Korea.[10] China's defense industrial base is increasingly operating on a wartime footing and is developing and producing weapons systems in all major domains: land, air, maritime, cyber, and space. As former U.S. Secretary of the Air Force Frank Kendall remarked, "China has been reoptimizing its forces for great power competition and to prevail against the U.S. and the Western Pacific for over 20 years. . . . China has been building a military capability specifically designed to achieve their national goals and to do so even if opposed by the United States."[11]

Without urgent changes, the United States will lose the ability to deter such adversaries as China and risk losing a great power war. The U.S. defense industrial base—led by a robust and strengthened commercial industry—needs to be a pillar of U.S. industrial policy strategy to compete with China economically, technologically, and militarily. There is good news, however. The U.S. private sector is innovative and has enormous production capacity. The United States also has a history of revitalizing its defense sector in the face of serious external threats. Revitalization occurred not just during World War II and the Korean War but also during times of increased strategic competition, such as during the first and second offsets.

The rest of this chapter outlines steps to dramatically revitalize the U.S. defense industrial base so that it can equip the U.S. military and intelligence community to deter China and—if deterrence fails—to fight and win a great power war on one or more fronts. The overall goal should be to *offset* Chinese advantages in size and scale by developing a mixture of weapons systems, technology, and concepts of operation to fight and win a major war. Doing this effectively will likely require a mix of high-end exquisite systems (such as submarines, bombers, and long-range precision missiles), cheap and attritable systems (such as unmanned underwater vehicles and drones), and cutting-edge technology (such as stealth, artificial intelligence, and quantum computing).

National Industrialization

One important component of a revitalized industrial base is a presidential-led initiative to urgently focus on the production of defense and dual-use hardware and software. National industrialization will not happen without leaders who recognize the current crisis, provide a vision for change, and demonstrate leadership to implement the vision. The Department of Defense cannot do it alone. The Department of State, Department of Commerce, Department of the Treasury, Congress, the private sector, and other elements also play important roles in the defense industrial base.[12] As noted in the previous chapter, there are numerous options: among them, variants of the War Industries Board during World War I, National Defense Advisory Commission and War Production Board during World War II, and Office of Defense Mobilization in the 1950s. An effective initiative—such as a modern-day Defense Production Board—should have several components.

First, it should be created by and report to the president of the United States. This ensures that the organization has the full weight of the president, which is necessary to break bureaucratic logjams and provide strategic guidance from the Oval Office. Second, it should conduct several types of activities: exercise general direction over U.S. defense procurement and production; help determine the policies, plans, and procedures of federal departments regarding procurement and production; and establish priorities in the distribution of materials and services. Third, members of the organization should include individuals with production experience from the private sector—the William Knudsens of the modern era who have the understanding and experience to manufacture and produce hardware and software. An alternative to a modern Defense Production Board would be for the president to direct the national security advisor and deputy national security advisor to revitalize the defense industrial base, in cooperation with the Office of Management and Budget and relevant departments and agencies. This option would have to be a national priority directed and overseen by the president.

Whatever the option, a national-level initiative should plan for long, protracted, and multi-theater wars—even though the goal is to deter war. As Johns Hopkins University professor Eliot Cohen wrote, "You will prefer to go short, but prepare to go long."[13] Wars between major powers can be long in duration. The mean duration for interstate wars is roughly 15 months. But wars involving one or more major powers can last longer, as happened in the Crimean War (28 months), Russo-Japanese War (16 months), World War I (52 months), World War II (over 60 months), Korean War (36 months), Vietnam War (121 months), and Sino-Vietnamese War (60 months).[14] In addition, wars involving major powers can use significant quantities of munitions, platforms, and systems. Weapons systems and platforms—such as main battle tanks, armored personnel carriers, artillery, and fighter aircraft—are destroyed or suffer wear and tear from constant use. The war in Ukraine highlighted that conventional wars involving one or more major powers require a robust defense industry (or access to the defense industry of allies) to produce sufficient quantities of munitions and weapons systems.

As President Roosevelt recognized before World War II and President Reagan acknowledged during heightened tension with the Soviet Union, presidential leadership is critical *before war* to strengthen deterrence and potentially avert war.

Bringing In the Commercial Sector

The U.S. government needs to better leverage the nation's innovative commercial sector and take advantage of technological advancements *outside* of defense.[15] Defense primes are still important to build such systems as submarines, long-range precision missiles, and strategic bombers. But the evolving character of warfare means that the defense industrial base needs to develop and produce such emerging technologies as artificial intelligence, quantum computing, unmanned and autonomous systems, biotechnology, directed energy, and electronic warfare capabilities. For example, advances in artificial intelligence could allow military units in the field to simulate thousands of operational and tactical options, decreasing the time between preparation and execution of a mission.[16] Developments in artificial intelligence could also help analysts and warfighters scan data from numerous sources, process the data, and manage a multilayered battlefield.[17] As already noted, China is developing through military-civil fusion a wide range of emerging technologies with defense applications, including artificial intelligence. Beijing has already deployed artificial intelligence–powered surveillance and electronic warfare systems.[18]

The tragedy is that some of the West's top technology companies are not significantly involved in the defense sector. One of the legacies of the 1993 Last Supper was a growing divide between defense and the private sector. "The most important consequence of the Last Supper wasn't a reduction in competition in the Defense Industrial Base, but the decoupling of commercial innovation from defense and the rise of the government Monopsony," one analysis concluded. "This was the Great Schism of the American industrial base."[19] Yet large technology companies, such as Apple, Nvidia, Google, and Microsoft, are producing some of the most innovative technologies and massively outspending defense companies in research and development. Between 2021 and 2023, the top six defense companies invested roughly $34 billion in internal research and development. During that same period, the top six commercial technology companies invested over $600 billion—nearly *20 times* the amount of the defense primes (Figure 12.1). Defense companies should not try to develop emerging technologies where they have little comparative advantage. It is a waste of taxpayer money.

Instead, the U.S. government needs to encourage strategic partnerships between technology companies and defense firms of all sizes to develop artificial intelligence, quantum computing, additive and

Company	Internal Research and Development (Thousands of Dollars)		
	2021	2022	2023
Big Tech			
Apple	$21,914	$26,251	$29,915
Nvidia	$5,268	$7,339	$8,675
Microsoft	$20,716	$24,512	$27,195
Google	$31,562	$39,500	$45,427
Amazon	$56,052	$73,213	$85,622
Meta	$24,655	$35,338	$38,483
Defense Primes			
Lockheed Martin	$1,500	$1,700	$1,500
Raytheon (RTX)	$2,730	$2,710	$2,810
Northrop Grumman	$1,100	$1,200	$1,200
General Dynamics	$415	$480	$510
Boeing	$184	$278	$315
L3Harris	$692	$603	$480

FIGURE 12.1 U.S. research and development investment by company, 2021-2023.[20]

digital manufacturing, autonomous and unmanned vehicles, sensors, and other technology that will give the United States and its allies and partners an advantage on the battlefield. It is amazing—and somewhat disheartening—that this type of cooperation has not yet occurred.

Mass Production

The United States needs to mass-produce critical defense systems by dramatically revising the acquisition and budgeting processes. Time is of the essence to deter China. Some of the most successful entrepreneurs over the past century—such as Kelly Johnson, Norm Augustine, and Elon Musk—were ruthless about speed and efficiency. As Johnson noted, "[T]he fundamental principle in our Skunk Works operation is that we operate with the minimum number of people and the least possible red tape."[21] In a Christmas speech to his staff, Johnson lauded his team for slashing bureaucracy even as they produced some of the country's most innovative defense systems. "You as American citizens and taxpayers can be proud of your contributions to our overall effort," Johnson said. "I hope that together we can reverse the trend toward more complex management, red tape and exorbitant costs by what we do here."[22] Johnson's 14 rules, Augustine's 52 laws, and Musk's algorithm and the five commandments focused, to a great extent, on slashing bureaucracy and maximizing production.

A defense industry operating on a wartime footing requires contracting and acquisitions processes that are faster, more flexible, and less risk-averse. A range of tools can be used to speed up acquisition and contracting. Examples include Rapid Acquisition Authority (which allows the secretary of defense to bypass the normal acquisition process, such as competitive bidding rules, to meet the immediate needs of the military), Other Transaction Authorities (which allow Pentagon leaders to bypass the Federal Acquisition Regulations), Defense Production Act authorities, and other emergency and experimental authorities.[23]

Defense production needs to increase so that industry can produce affordable systems at mass and scale. There are a significant number of small and midsize companies—including those backed by venture capital and private equity firms—that are highly innovative but struggle to operate in the Department of Defense's overly complicated contracting and acquisitions system. The Department of Defense—including the military services—need to cut the timelines for rewarding contracts and help innovative companies cross the Valley of Death from concept to prototype to production.[24] Innovation in the defense sector—especially in the United States—has generally occurred because of synergy between the government and the commercial sector, making it important to find ways for imaginative private sector firms to more easily sell to the government.

More broadly, the United States needs to significantly speed up the production of hardware and software. Some exquisite systems are important for deterrence and warfighting, but so are lower-cost, autonomous, and mass-producible systems and platforms. For its maritime industrial base, for example, the United States should build fewer exquisite manned surface ships and more large and small unmanned and autonomous surface and subsurface vessels.

Supply Chains and Strategic Stockpiles

Great powers in a wartime environment need to maintain stockpiles of key munitions, minerals, chemicals, technology, and medical supplies. In the United States, the Department of Defense and Congress should allocate additional funding for contracts and other incentives—such as tax incentives, regulatory relief, and long-term contracts—to build and maintain spare production capacity. Such funding should be used to modernize and expand facilities and develop flexible production.

In addition, the United States should increase funding to expand domestic production of components critical for deterrence and warfighting in such theaters as the Indo-Pacific. Examples include cruise missile motor capacity expansion, solid rocket motor capacity expansion, energetics, and batteries. The Department of Defense should also identify and establish stockpiles of the critical parts, finished goods, and commodities needed to meet production requirements for conducting sustained military campaigns against adversaries. Examples include iron and ferroalloy metals, such as vanadium and molybdenum; nonferrous metals, such as gallium, germanium, and, antimony; and industrial minerals, such as graphite and fluorite. A critical component of supply chains should be designing defense systems to maximize the use of easily available, low-cost components with robust *commercial* supply chains—not specialized defense components that are difficult to acquire.[25]

In addition, the Department of Defense should identify the stockpiling requirements of critical minerals and components necessary to reduce dependence on China and continue production in cases where international conflict or crisis may inhibit normal functioning of supply chains. The essential role of these stockpiles should be to mitigate supply chain vulnerabilities and ensure the military's operational freedom and effectiveness. One example is the field-programmable gate array chips that are manufactured in Taiwan and extensively used in U.S. weapons systems, such as F-35s, missiles, and command-and-control equipment. It will take years to set up the production capability in the United States, so the U.S. government needs to stockpile these chips in case of a Taiwan conflict.

Workforce

In a wartime environment, great powers need to strengthen their workforce, diversify their suppliers, and invest in new production methods. "Talent is a major discriminator among the major powers," remarked former deputy secretary of defense Robert Work.[26] The U.S. Department of Defense should look for opportunities to assist companies with upskilling and reskilling workers by offering financial incentives. One example is to increase investments in high schools, vocational schools, colleges, universities, and other institutions that train and educate individuals for defense industrial base jobs, such as welders, engineers, electricians, pipefitters, shipfitters, and metalworkers. Another example is to invest in institutions to address skill gaps in defense-related manufacturing and science, technology, engineering, and mathematics jobs.

The Department of Defense should consider increasing the use of defense industrial base programs, such as Defense Production Act Title III, to incentivize the expansion of existing sources within the supply chain and the establishment of new ones.[27] In addition, the United States needs to modernize and expand shipbuilding industrial capacity and develop a more capable and competitive shipbuilding workforce.[28]

Allies and Partners

Throughout the history of the U.S. defense industrial base, allies and partners have played an important role in developing and buying military capabilities. As the U.S. Defense Innovation Board concluded, "Since World War II, the United States' network of allies and partners has stood as the cornerstone of our global strength and the envy of our adversaries.... Yet, the Department of Defense (DoD) is failing to fully integrate allies and partners into a networked defense industrial base, and to modernize the concepts, systems, and processes that enable these relationships to flourish."[29]

Today cooperation with allies and partners is particularly important because of the advances in defense-related hardware and software. U.S. allies in Europe and Asia have significant capabilities: South Korea and Japan with shipbuilding; Japan, South Korea, and Taiwan with semiconductors; the United Kingdom with engines; Norway with anti-ship missiles and munitions; and Israel with air and missile defense—just to name a few examples. Allies and partners also possess critical raw materials for the defense sector, such as chromium (South Africa), lithium (Australia), rhodium and platinum (South Africa), and zirconium (Australia).[30] The reality is that modern weapons systems are products of a globalized market. Take the F-35 Lightning II combat aircraft program: production and sustainment relied on more than 1,900 companies around the globe, including suppliers in 48 U.S. states and over 10 countries.[31]

Foreign companies in allied nations can play a critical role in the U.S. defense industrial base in several ways. One is by building systems or subsystems from factories in the United States. Leonardo DRS (owned by Italy's Finmeccanica) and BAE Systems Inc. (owned by the United Kingdom's BAE Systems plc) are examples of U.S.-based defense contractors that can build sensitive defense capabilities at plants in the United States with U.S. workers, much like BMW, Toyota, Honda, and Mercedes-Benz can build cars in manufacturing plants in South Carolina, Indiana, Ohio, and Alabama, respectively. A second way is to help repair or maintain U.S. systems and platforms, such as ships, at locations overseas. A third way is for foreign companies in allied nations to export systems and materials in which they have a comparative advantage or that are part of the defense supply chain.[32]

Doing this effectively will require revising some U.S. laws, policies, and provisions that have weakened the defense industrial base, especially for allies that the United States will need to operate with and fight beside in future wars. For example, some Buy America provisions, which require companies to use goods made in the United States, have been inefficient, stifled innovation and competitiveness, and driven up costs.³³ U.S. laws prohibit ships that are home-ported in the United States or Guam from being overhauled, repaired, or maintained in a foreign shipyard, except to undergo mid-deployment voyage repairs or to fix battle damage.³⁴ The U.S. Navy cannot make significant use of high-quality shipyards in allied nations, such as Japan and South Korea, despite maintenance backlogs in U.S. shipyards.³⁵

Expanding reciprocal defense procurement agreements with allies could be helpful. The United States has such agreements with Australia and Japan, but not with South Korea. Such provisions as the Merchant Marine Act of 1920 (better known as the Jones Act) have made it difficult for the United States to effectively collaborate in such areas as shipbuilding with Japanese, South Korean, or other allies that have sufficient capacity.³⁶ The act is archaic and counterproductive in a world where defense collaboration is increasingly important with U.S. allies.

A Defense Budget for a Wartime Environment

Great powers need to spend significant amounts on defense to remain competitive, deter their adversaries, and win wars if they have to fight. As University of Chicago professor Hans Morgenthau wrote, "Since victory in modern war depends upon the number and quality of highways, railroads, trucks, ships, airplanes, tanks, and equipment and weapons of all kinds ... the competition among nations for power transforms itself largely into competition for the production of bigger, better, and more implements of war. The quality and productive capacity of the industrial plant, the know-how of the working man, the skills of the engineer, the inventive genius of the scientist, the managerial organization—all these are factors upon which the industrial capacity of a nation and, hence, its power depend."³⁷

The 2025 U.S. defense budget of approximately 3 percent of gross domestic product was historically low for a security environment in which authoritarian states, such as China, Russia, Iran, and North Korea, threatened the United States and its allies and partners. Even President Carter's defense budget was higher, at between 4.5 and 5.0 percent of gross domestic product (Figure 12.2).³⁸

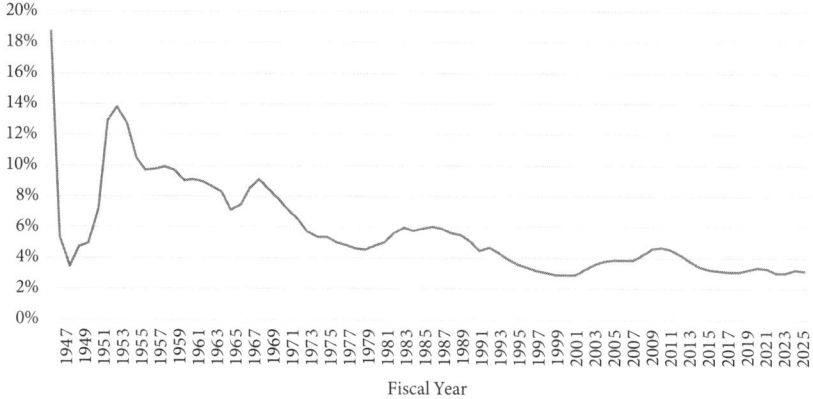

FIGURE 12.2 U.S. defense spending as a percentage of GDP, 1947–2025.[39]

Building a military force able to deter China and to fight and win wars will require a larger defense budget, closer to 1980s levels.[40] Any increase in defense spending will necessitate reforms to entitlement programs, an increase in taxes, or both.[41] As the history of the U.S. defense industrial base highlights, higher defense budgets are affordable. An important percentage of increased funding should go to the research, development, and production of defense systems that are essential for deterrence and warfighting—such as submarines, unmanned systems, and other hardware and software. The two most important parts of the defense budget to increase are research, development, test, and evaluation; and procurement.

An infusion of funds would be helpful for the supply chain, including such crucial components as rocket boosters, energetics, engines, and munitions. It would be useful for the government to increase investments in defense infrastructure, such as factories and shipyards, which can be difficult and risky for industry to invest in quickly.

———

These and other steps are important to offset Chinese capabilities and build a defense industrial base that can more effectively deter competitors and, if deterrence fails, provide the military with the weapons systems, material, and equipment to fight and win wars. "Production *is* deterrence," remarked Under Secretary of Defense for Acquisition and Sustainment William LaPlante.[42] Unless these types of urgent changes occur, the United States will lose deterrence and undermine its warfighting capabilities in the Indo-Pacific, Europe, and other regions against China and other adversaries. As Nobel Prize–winning economist Thomas Schelling explained, effective deterrence is a function of both the capabilities and the intentions of the deterrer.[43] Countries need to show that they possess the military capabilities (including the defense industrial capacity) and the willingness to use force if necessary.

A year before Pearl Harbor and the U.S. entry into World War II, President Roosevelt explained that the United States needed to "build now with all possible speed every machine, every arsenal, every factory that we need to manufacture our defense material."[44] The same is true today, and the failure to do so will have serious consequences. Winston Churchill warned his country in the 1930s about the importance of developing a robust industrial base as Germany rearmed, though most British politicians ignored him.

EPILOGUE

Want of foresight, unwillingness to act when action would be simple and effective, lack of clear thinking, confusion of counsel until the emergency comes, until self-preservation strikes its jarring gong—these are the features which constitute the endless repetition of history.

Look back upon the last five years—since, that is to say, Germany began to rearm in earnest and openly to seek revenge.... Now is the time at least to rouse the nation. Perhaps it is the last time it can be roused with a chance of preventing war, or with a chance of coming through to victory should our efforts to prevent war fail.

—Winston Churchill

When Germany began to rearm in the early 1930s, British leaders were at a decisive point.[1] Should they build up their defense industrial base and strengthen their naval, army, and air forces? Or not? Most of Britain's political establishment opposed rearmament. "I would close every recruiting station, disband the army and dismiss the air force," trumpeted George Lansbury, the Labour Party leader, in 1933. "I would abolish the whole dreadful equipment of war and say to the world 'Do your worst.'"[2] Germany had just announced its withdrawal from the Geneva Disarmament Conference and the League of Nations. Winston Churchill, who was then a member of Parliament for the constituency of Epping, was unimpressed. After Lansbury indicated that the Labour Party would never agree to Hitler's rearming, Churchill asked dryly, "Is the right honourable Gentleman quite sure that the Germans will come and ask him for his consent before they rearm? Does he not think that they might omit that formality and go ahead without even taking a card vote of the Trades Union Congress?"[3]

Opposition to strengthening the defense industrial base continued into the mid-1930s from the leadership of all Britain's major parties. When Churchill told the Oxford University Conservative Association in February 1935 that rearmament was necessary "for us to be safe in our Island home," he was derided with laughter.[4] During a House of Commons debate in 1935 on the merits of the U.K. Defence White Paper the government published on March 4, Clement Attlee, who had replaced Lansbury as Labour Party leader, said unequivocally, "We deny the proposition that an increased British air force will make for the peace of the world, and we reject altogether the plan of parity. We think that parity is an out-of-date, pre-war conception of the balance of power."[5] It proved to be a profoundly naïve statement. Neville Chamberlain, prime minister and leader of the Conservative Party, also refused to countenance additional spending necessary for rearmament and worried that it would undermine the country's precarious economic growth on the heels of the Great Depression.[6] Archie Sinclair, leader of the Liberal Party, denounced "the folly, danger and wastefulness of this steady accumulation of armaments."[7]

During the election campaign of 1935, Stanley Baldwin, the soon-to-be Conservative prime minister, told the British people in no uncertain terms, "I give you my word there will be no great armaments." Baldwin reaffirmed this statement a few months later—ironically several weeks after Mussolini invaded Abyssinia. "There has not been, there is not, and there will not be any question of huge armaments or materially increased forces," he said.[8] Following a speech by Churchill in the House of Commons in May 1935, Lieutenant-Colonel Thomas Moore, a Conservative member from Ayr, launched a personal attack against Churchill: "Although one hates to criticize anyone in the evening of his days, nothing can excuse the right honourable Member for Epping for having permeated his entire speech with the atmosphere that Germany is arming for war." Moore continued on a rant that would prove to be profoundly wrong: "[S]urely it is impossible to visualize a situation in which either the losers or the victors will ever again, at least in our lifetime, embark on such a disastrous conflict."9 Moore disparaged German rearmament, considered Germany a second-rate military power, and believed that a British move to revitalize its industrial base was wasteful, foolhardy, and ultimately unnecessary.

The reality, of course, was that Germany *was* rearming. German aircraft production jumped from 36 planes in 1932 to 1,938 in 1934 and 5,112 in 1936. The army expanded from a force of 7 divisions to 21, and in 1935 the German government announced conscription and raised the army's ceiling to 36 divisions. Germany also imported significant amounts of raw material for its defense industry, such as iron ore, copper, nickel, petroleum, bauxite, and rubber.[10] In 1936, Germany remilitarized the Rhineland by marching 19 infantry battalions into the region, violating the Treaty of Versailles and the Treaty of Locarno. But unwarranted pacifism and wishful thinking dominated British strategic thinking.

Churchill had been adamant from the early 1930s that Germany was rearming and that the United Kingdom needed to quickly rebuild its defense industrial base to strengthen deterrence and prepare for a much more dangerous adversary. On February 7, 1934, Churchill urged his fellow members of Parliament to confront their country's woeful defense unpreparedness. "What have we done?" he asked. "There is not an hour to lose. Those things cannot be done in a moment. The process should be started, and the very maximum of money that can be usefully spent should be spent from to-day on—if we act with wisdom."[11] On November 28, Churchill again warned of German rearmament and lamented that the U.K. defense industrial base was unprepared: "To urge the preparation of defence is not to assert the imminence of war. On the contrary, if war were imminent preparations for defence would be too late. I do not believe that war is imminent or that war is inevitable, but it seems very difficult to resist the conclusion that, if we do not begin forthwith to put ourselves in a position of security, it will soon be beyond our power to do so. What is the great new fact which has broken in upon us during the last 18 months? Germany is rearming."[12]

But Churchill was derided and scorned. "I felt a sensation of despair," he recalled. "To be so entirely convinced and vindicated in a matter of life and death to one's country, and not to be able to make Parliament and the nation heed the warning, or bow to the proof by taking action, was an experience most painful."[13] In anguish, Churchill recalled several lines from a poem he had learned as a teenager, which described a train accident at Eastleigh caused by an engine-driver and a stoker who were allegedly asleep:

> Who is in charge of the clattering train?
> The axles creak, and the couplings strain,
> And the pace is hot, and the points are near,
> And Sleep has deadened the driver's ear;
> And signals flash through the night in vain,
> For Death is in charge of the clattering train.[14]

For Churchill, the poem was a metaphor for what was occurring in the United Kingdom: policymakers were asleep in an hour of grave danger. While all periods of history are in some ways sui generis, the United States—and the West more broadly—face a China and a Russia that are increasing the pace and scope of military production. Both are on a wartime footing, with Moscow engaged in a bloody conflict in Ukraine and Beijing threatening military action in the Taiwan Strait, South China Sea, and East China Sea. There are a few lessons worth considering from Churchill's wilderness years, the period from 1929 to 1939, when Churchill remained a member of the House of Commons but did not serve in a senior government position.

One is the importance of building a strong military and defense industrial base in the face of authoritarian enemies that are arming. As Churchill repeatedly warned the U.K. population and its leaders, Nazi Germany was rapidly rebuilding its defense industrial base and a larger and more powerful military. Yet as Churchill presciently recognized, it would take his country years to strengthen its defense industrial base—to raise the money, build the factories, hire and train a workforce, acquire the supplies and raw materials, and ultimately produce ships, aircraft, tanks, artillery, and other defense items. Revitalizing the defense industrial base cannot be done quickly. As Churchill also appreciated, building a strong defense industrial base should, first and foremost, be about enhancing deterrence. This is why he argued that bolstering defense should not be confused with "the imminence of war."[15] Much like Reagan's defense buildup in the 1980s, during Churchill's time a robust defense was necessary to deter an aggressive great power and—if deterrence failed—to defeat it. Finally, a failure to prepare for adversaries that are arming can be catastrophic. Britain was woefully unprepared for the German threat in the late 1930s when it faced imminent invasion. The British people "should know the truth," Churchill said. "They should know that there has been gross neglect and deficiency in our defences."[16]

In a treacherous security environment with authoritarian regimes such as China and Russia arming, a strong defense industrial base is necessary. President George Washington was unambiguous in his 1793 State of the Union Address: "There is a rank due to the United States among nations which will be withheld, if not absolutely lost, by the reputation of weakness. If we desire to avoid insult, we must be able to repel it; if we desire to secure peace, one of the most powerful instruments of our rising prosperity, it must be known that we are at all times ready for war."[17] Nearly 200 years later, Reagan explained, "We know that peace is the condition under which mankind was meant to flourish. Yet peace does not exist of its own will. It depends on us, on our courage to build it and guard it and pass it on to future generations."[18]

As both Washington and Reagan believed, the goal of a strong defense industry is not war, but peace through strength.

APPENDIX 1

Kelly Johnson's 14 Rules

Kelly Johnson, the head of Lockheed Skunk Works from 1943 to 1975, had 14 basic operating rules:

1. The Skunk Works manager must be delegated practically complete control of his program in all aspects. He should report to a division president or higher.
2. Strong but small project offices must be provided both by the military and industry.
3. The number of people having any connection with the project must be restricted in an almost vicious manner. Use a small number of good people (10 percent to 25 percent compared to the so-called normal systems.)
4. A very simple drawing and drawing release system with great flexibility for making changes must be provided.
5. There must be a minimum number of reports required, but important work must be recorded thoroughly.
6. There must be a monthly cost review covering not only what has been spent and committed but also projected costs to the conclusion of the program. Don't have the books 90 days late, and don't surprise the customer with sudden overruns.
7. The contractor must be delegated and must assume more than normal responsibility to get good vendor bids for subcontract on the project. Commercial bid procedures are very often better than military ones.
8. The inspection system as currently used by the Skunk Works, which has been approved by both the Air Force and Navy, meets the

intent of existing military requirements and should be used on new projects. Push more basic inspection responsibility back to subcontractors and vendors. Don't duplicate so much inspection.

9. The contractor must be delegated the authority to test his final product in flight. He can and must test it in the initial stages. If he doesn't, he rapidly loses his competency to design other vehicles.
10. The specifications applying to the hardware must be agreed to well in advance of contracting. The Skunk Works practice of having a specification section stating clearly which important military specification items will not knowingly be complied with and reasons therefore is highly recommended.
11. Funding a program must be timely so that the contractor doesn't have to keep running to the bank to support government projects.
12. There must be mutual trust between the military project organization and the contractor with very close cooperation and liaison on a day-to-day basis. This cuts down misunderstanding and correspondence to an absolute minimum.
13. Access by outsiders to the project and its personnel must be strictly controlled by appropriate security measures.
14. Because only a few people will be used in engineering and most other areas, ways must be provided to reward good performance by pay not based on the number of personnel supervised.[1]

According to Johnson's successor at Skunk Works, there was a secretive 15th rule that was passed along by word of mouth: "Starve before doing business with the damned Navy. They don't know what the hell they want and will drive you up a wall before they break either your heart or a more exposed part of your anatomy."[2]

APPENDIX 2

Norman Augustine's 52 Laws

Norman R. Augustine, former chairman and CEO of Lockheed Martin Corporation, established 52 laws that covered every area of business:

1. The best way to make a silk purse from a sow's ear is to begin with a silk sow. The same is true of money.
2. If today were half as good as tomorrow is supposed to be, it would probably be twice as good as yesterday was.
3. There are no lazy veteran lion hunters.
4. If you can afford to advertise, you don't need to.
5. One-tenth of the participants produce over one-third of the output. Increasing the number of participants merely reduces the average output.
6. A hungry dog hunts best. A hungrier dog hunts even better.
7. Decreased business base increases overhead. So does increased business base.
8. The most unsuccessful four years in the education of a cost-estimator is fifth grade arithmetic.
9. Acronyms and abbreviations should be used to the maximum extent possible to make trivial ideas profound . . . Q.E.D.
10. Bulls do not win bullfights; people do. People do not win people fights; lawyers do.
11. If the Earth could be made to rotate twice as fast, managers would get twice as much done. If the Earth could be made to rotate twenty times as fast, everyone else would get twice as much done since all the managers would fly off.
12. It costs a lot to build bad products.

13. There are many highly successful businesses in the United States. There are also many highly paid executives. The policy is not to intermingle the two.
14. After the year 2015, there will be no airplane crashes. There will be no takeoffs either, because electronics will occupy 100 percent of every airplane's weight.
15. The last 10 percent of performance generates one-third of the cost and two-thirds of the problems.
16. In the year 2054, the entire defense budget will purchase just one aircraft. This aircraft will have to be shared by the Air Force and Navy 3-1/2 days each per week except for leap year, when it will be made available to the Marines for the extra day.
17. Software is like entropy. It is difficult to grasp, weighs nothing, and obeys the Second Law of Thermodynamics; i.e., it always increases.
18. It is very expensive to achieve high unreliability. It is not uncommon to increase the cost of an item by a factor of ten for each factor of ten degradation accomplished.
19. Although most products will soon be too costly to purchase, there will be a thriving market in the sale of books on how to fix them.
20. In any given year, Congress will appropriate the amount of funding approved the prior year plus three-fourths of whatever change the administration requests, minus 4-percent tax.
21. It's easy to get a loan unless you need it.
22. If stock market experts were so expert, they would be buying stock, not selling advice.
23. Any task can be completed in only one-third more time than is currently estimated.
24. The only thing more costly than stretching the schedule of an established project is accelerating it, which is itself the most costly action known to man.
25. A revised schedule is to business what a new season is to an athlete or a new canvas to an artist.
26. If a sufficient number of management layers are superimposed on each other, it can be assured that disaster is not left to chance.
27. Rank does not intimidate hardware. Neither does the lack of rank.
28. It is better to be the reorganizer than the reorganizee.
29. Executives who do not produce successful results hold on to their jobs only about five years. Those who produce effective results hang on about half a decade.
30. By the time the people asking the questions are ready for the answers, the people doing the work have lost track of the questions.

31. The optimum committee has no members.
32. Hiring consultants to conduct studies can be an excellent means of turning problems into gold, your problems into their gold.
33. Fools rush in where incumbents fear to tread.
34. The process of competitively selecting contractors to perform work is based on a system of rewards and penalties, all distributed randomly.
35. The weaker the data available upon which to base one's conclusion, the greater the precision which should be quoted in order to give the data authenticity.
36. The thickness of the proposal required to win a multimillion dollar contract is about one millimeter per million dollars. If all the proposals conforming to this standard were piled on top of each other at the bottom of the Grand Canyon it would probably be a good idea.
37. Ninety percent of the time things will turn out worse than you expect. The other 10 percent of the time you had no right to expect so much.
38. The early bird gets the worm. The early worm . . . gets eaten.
39. Never promise to complete any project within six months of the end of the year, in either direction.
40. Most projects start out slowly, and then sort of taper off.
41. The more one produces, the less one gets.
42. Simple systems are not feasible because they require infinite testing.
43. Hardware works best when it matters the least.
44. Aircraft flight in the 21st century will always be in a westerly direction, preferably supersonic, crossing time zones to provide the additional hours needed to fix the broken electronics.
45. One should expect that the expected can be prevented, but the unexpected should have been expected.
46. A billion saved is a billion earned.
47. Two-thirds of the Earth's surface is covered with water. The other third is covered with auditors from headquarters.
48. The more time you spend talking about what you have been doing, the less time you have to spend doing what you have been talking about. Eventually, you spend more and more time talking about less and less until finally you spend all your time talking about nothing.
49. Regulations grow at the same rate as weeds.
50. The average regulation has a life span one-fifth as long as a chimpanzee's and one-tenth as long as a human's, but four times as long as the official's who created it.

51. By the time of the United States Tricentennial, there will be more government workers than there are workers.
52. People working in the private sector should try to save money. There remains the possibility that it may someday be valuable again.[1]

APPENDIX 3

Elon Musk's Algorithm and the Five Commandments

Elon Musk developed what he called "the algorithm," which included five commandments:

1. Question every requirement. Each should come with the name of the person who made it. You should never accept that a requirement came from a department, such as from "the legal department" or "the safety department." You need to know the name of the real person who made that requirement. Then you should question it, no matter how smart that person is. Requirements from smart people are the most dangerous, because people are less likely to question them. Always do so, even if the requirement came from me. Then make the requirements less dumb.
2. Delete any part or process you can. You may have to add them back later. In fact, if you do not end up adding back at least 10 percent of them, then you didn't delete enough.
3. Simplify and optimize. This should come after step two. A common mistake is to simplify and optimize a part or a process that should not exist.
4. Accelerate cycle time. Every process can be speeded up. But only do this after you have followed the first three steps. In the Tesla factory, I mistakenly spent a lot of time accelerating processes that I later realized should have been deleted.

5. Automate. That comes last. The big mistake in Nevada and at Fremont was that I began by trying to automate every step. We should have waited until all the requirements had been questioned, parts and processes deleted, and the bugs were shaken out.[1]

NOTES

Introduction

1. The epigraphs are from Robert M. Gates, *Duty: Memoirs of Secretary at War* (New York: Alfred A. Knopf, 2014), 126; John Woodward, foreword to Andrew Gordon, *The Rules of the Game: Jutland and British Naval Command* (Annapolis, MD: Naval Institute Press, 1996), xi–xii.
2. Russell Buhite and David Levy, eds., *FDR's Fireside Chats*, (Norman: University of Oklahoma Press, 1992), 171–172.
3. Paul Kennedy, *The Rise and Fall of the Great Powers: Economic Change and Military Conflict from 1500 to 2000* (New York: Vintage Books, 1989), xxiv.
4. On overmatch, see the work of David Ochmanek, such as Octavian Manea, "Interview with David Ochmanek," Small Wars Journal, March 11, 2025, https://smallwarsjournal.com/2025/03/11/interview-with-david-ochmanek/; David A. Ochmanek, et al., *Inflection Point: How to Reverse the Erosion of U.S. and Allied Military Power and Influence* (Santa Monica, CA: RAND, 2023), 21, 32, 177.
5. Author interview with Robert Work, December 6, 2024.
6. See, for example, Ronald Reagan, Remarks at the Annual Convention of the National Association of Evangelicals in Orlando, Florida, March 8, 1983, https://www.reaganlibrary.gov/archives/speech/remarks-annual-convention-national-association-evangelicals-orlando-fl.
7. Andrew Gordon, *The Rules of the Game: Jutland and British Naval Command* (Annapolis, MD: U.S. Naval Institute Press, 1996).
8. Hansard, House of Commons Parliamentary Debates, vol. 301, col. 602, May 2, 1935.
9. Winston Churchill, "Sinews of Peace," speech at Westminster College, Fulton, MO, March 5, 1946 in Robert Rhodes James, ed., *Winston S. Churchill: His Complete Speeches*, Vol. VII (New York: Chelsea House Publishers, 1974), 7286.

10. Memo, Harold Brown for Jimmy Carter, December 23, 1980, folder Transition: Issues for President-Elect, Box 80, Brown Papers, Library of Congress (hereafter LC).
11. Robert M. Gates, *Duty: Memoirs of Secretary at War* (New York: Alfred A. Knopf, 2014), 126.
12. The role of the private sector has surprisingly been ignored in a large volume of work on defense innovation. See, for example, Stephen Peter Rosen, *Winning the Next War: Innovation and the Modern Military* (Ithaca, NY: Cornell University Press, 1991); Frank G. Hoffman, *Mars Adapting: Military Change during War* (Annapolis, MD: Naval Institute Press, 2021); Dima Adamsky, *The Culture of Military Innovation: The Impact of Cultural Factors on the Revolution in Military Affairs in Russia, the US, and Israel* (Stanford: Stanford University Press, 2010); Michael C. Horowitz and Shira Pindyck, "What Is a Military Innovation and Why It Matters," *Journal of Strategic Studies*, March 2022, 1–30; Adam Grissom, "The Future of Military Innovation Studies," *Journal of Strategic Studies* 29, no. 5 (2006): 905–934.
13. Margaret O'Mara, *The Code: Silicon Valley and the Remaking of America* (New York: Penguin Press, 2019), 7, emphasis in the original.
14. Buhite and Levy, *FDR's Fireside Chats*, 171–172.
15. Stanley McChrystal, *My Share of the Task: A Memoir* (New York: Portfolio, 2014), 153–155.
16. There is a voluminous literature on power. For historical examples, see Hans J. Morgenthau, *Politics among Nations: The Struggle for Power and Peace*, Fourth Edition (New York: Alfred A. Knopf, 1967); Inis L. Claude Jr., *Power and International Relations* (New York: Random House, 1962); David A. Baldwin, *Paradoxes of Power* (New York: Basil Blackwell, 1989); Klaus Knorr, *Military Power and Potential* (Lexington, MA: DC Heath, 1970); Kenneth N. Waltz, *Theory of International Politics* (New York: McGraw Hill, 1979).
17. See, for example, Joseph S. Nye Jr., *The Paradox of American Power: Why the World's Only Superpower Can't Go It Alone* (New York: Oxford University Press, 2002); Joseph S. Nye Jr., *The Future of Power* (New York: Public Affairs, 2011).
18. Bruce Russett and Harvey Starr, *World Politics: The Menu for Choice* (New York: Freeman, 1989); William Wohlforth, *The Elusive Balance: Power and Perceptions during the World War* (Ithaca, NY: Cornell University Press, 1993).
19. Robert Dahl, "The Concept of Power," *Behavioral Science* 2, no. 3 (July 1957): 202–203.
20. For good historical examples of economic power, see Richard N. Rosecrance, *The Rise of the Trading State* (New York: Basic Books, 1986); Robert Gilpin, *U.S. Power and the Multinational Corporation* (New York:

Basic Books, 1975); David A. Baldwin, *Economic Statecraft* (Princeton, NJ: Princeton University Press, 1985).
21. Joseph Nye first developed the concept of soft power in Joseph S. Nye Jr., *Bound to Lead: The Changing Nature of American Power* (New York: Basic Books, 1990).
22. Joseph S. Nye Jr., *Soft Power: The Means to Success in World Politics* (New York: PublicAffairs, 2004), 6.
23. See, for example, Eliot Cohen, *The Big Stick: The Limits of Soft Power and the Necessity of Military Force* (New York: Basic Books, 2016).
24. See, for example, Xi Jinping, "Working Together to Realize Rejuvenation of the Chinese Nation and Advance China's Peaceful Reunification," speech at the Meeting Marking the 40th Anniversary of the Issuance of the Message to Compatriots in Taiwan, January 2, 2019, http://www.gwytb.gov.cn/wyly/201904/t20190412_12155687.htm.
25. John J. Mearsheimer, *The Tragedy of Great Power Politics* (New York: W. W. Norton, 2001), 43, 56, 83.
26. See, for example, U.S. Department of Defense, *State of Competition within the Defense Industrial Base* (Washington, DC: U.S. Department of Defense, February 2022); U.S. Department of Defense, *Assessing and Strengthening the Manufacturing and Defense Industrial Base and Supply Chain Resiliency of the United States* (Washington, DC: U.S. Department of Defense, September 2018).
27. Jerry McGinn, *Building Resilience: Mobilizing the Defense Industrial Base in an Era of Great Power Competition* (Washington, DC: Heritage Foundation, November 17, 2020); C. Todd Lopez, "DoD Focuses on Sustaining Industrial Base through Pandemic," DOD News, May 5, 2020, https://www.defense.gov/News/News-Stories/Article/Article/2177093/dod-focuses-on-sustaining-industrial-base-through-pandemic/.
28. Stephen Biddle, *Military Power: Explaining Victory and Defeat in Modern Battle* (Princeton, NJ: Princeton University Press, 2004), 53.
29. Joseph S. Nye Jr., *The Future of Power* (New York: Public Affairs, 2011), 41.
30. Harvey M. Sapolsky, Eugene Gholz, and Caitlin Talmadge, *U.S. Defense Politics: The Origins of Security Policy*, 3rd edition (New York: Routledge, 2008), 134.
31. Sapolsky, Gholz, and Talmadge, *U.S. Defense Politics*, 129.
32. John C. Aquilino, U.S. Indo-Pacific Command Posture, Statement before the House Armed Services Committee, U.S. House of Representatives, March 20,"2024, 7.
33. U.S. Department of Defense, *Military and Security Developments Involving the People's Republic of China* (Washington, DC: Office of the Secretary of Defense, U.S. Department of Defense, 2024), vii.
34. Michael Evans, "China Leaves U.S. Trailing in Race to Build Warships," *Times* (London), July 12, 2023.

35. Brad Lendon and Haley Britzky, "U.S. Can't Keep Up with China's Warship Building, Navy Secretary Says," *CNN*, February 22, 2023.
36. U.S. Department of Defense, *Military and Security Developments Involving the People's Republic of China*, 2024, 59.
37. See the comments by Major General Cameron Holt at the Government Contracting Pricing Summit in July 2022: "Air Force Keynote Address (w/Q&A): Maj. Gen. Cameron Holt," YouTube, posted by Government Contract Pricing Summit, June 24, 2022. On Holt's comments, see Caleb Larson, "Catch Up: China Is Getting New Weapons Faster Than the U.S.," *National Interest*, July 7, 2022.
38. U.S. Department of Defense, *Military and Security Developments Involving the People's Republic of China*, 2024, 101; Statement of John C. Aquilino, 8.
39. U.S. Department of Defense, *Military and Security Developments Involving the People's Republic of China*, 2024, 45.
40. Clayton Swope et al., *Space Threat Assessment 2024* (Washington, DC: Center for Strategic and International Studies, 2024).
41. Christian Brose, *The Kill Chain: Defending America in the Future of High-Tech Warfare* (New York: Hachette Books, 2020), xxiii–xiv.
42. Tai Ming Cheung, *Innovate to Dominate: The Rise of the Chinese Techno-Security State* (Ithaca, NY: Cornell University Press, 2022) 171, 177.
43. John C. Demers, Statement before the Committee on the Judiciary, U.S. Senate, December 12, 2018, https://www.judiciary.senate.gov/imo/media/doc/12-12-18%20Demers%20Testimony.pdf.
44. Lawrence Freedman, *Command: The Politics of Military Operations from Korea to Ukraine* (New York: Oxford University Press, 2022), 505.
45. On In-Q-Tel, see, for example, Josh Krieger and Josh Lerner, "In-Q-Tel: Innovation on a Mission," Harvard Business School Teaching Note 823-042, Harvard Business School Case Collection, August 2022, 2.
46. Leon E. Panetta and Mike Gallagher, "The Pentagon Can't Wait to Innovate," *Wall Street Journal*, July 9, 2024.
47. See, for example, Rosen, *Winning the Next War*; Barry R. Posen, *The Sources of Military Doctrine: France, Britain, and Germany between the World Wars* (Ithaca, NY: Cornell University Press, 1984); Robert Gilpin, *War and Change in World Politics* (New York: Cambridge University Press, 1981); Michael C. Horowitz, *The Diffusion of Military Power: Causes and Consequences for International Politics* (Princeton, NJ: Princeton University Press, 2010); Cheung, *Innovate to Dominate*; Hoffman, *Mars Adapting*; Adamsky, *The Culture of Military Innovation*.
48. Horowitz and Pindyck, "What Is a Military Innovation and Why It Matters," 1–30. Also see, for example, Grissom, "The Future of Military Innovation Studies"; Rosen, *Winning the Next War*, 7.
49. Morgenthau, *Politics among Nations*, 115–116.
50. Horowitz, *The Diffusion of Military Power*, 2.

51. Rosen, *Winning the Next War*, 109–129.
52. Rosen, *Winning the Next War*.
53. Biddle, *Military Power*, 53.
54. Kendrick Kuo, "Dangerous Changes: When Military Innovation Harms Combat Effectiveness," *International Security* 47, no. 2 (Fall 2022): 48–87.
55. John Bartlett, *Familiar Quotations*, 10th edition (Boston: Little, Brown, 1919), no. 9707; Thucydides, *The Peloponnesian War*, trans. Martin Hammond (New York: Oxford University Press, 2009), 39.
56. See, for example, Biddle, *Military Power*; Basil Liddell Hart, *Strategy* (New York: Penguin, 1991); Michael Howard, *The Causes of War* (Cambridge, MA: Harvard University Press, 1983); Eliot A. Cohen, *Supreme Command: Soldiers, Statesmen, and Leadership in Wartime* (New York: Anchor, 2003); John J. Mearsheimer, *Conventional Deterrence* (Ithaca, NY: Cornell University Press, 1983); Mearsheimer, *Tragedy of Great Power Politics*; Ben Connable et al., *Will to Fight: Returning to the Human Fundamentals of War* (Santa Monica, CA: RAND, 2019); Horowitz, *The Diffusion of Military Power*; Dan Reiter and Alan C. Stam, *Democracies at War* (Princeton, NJ: Princeton University Press, 2002); Posen, *The Sources of Military Doctrine*.
57. Ali Javaheri and Matthew Nacionales, "Vertical Snapshot: Defense Tech Update," PitchBook, July 5, 2024, https://pitchbook.com/news/articles/global-vc-defense-tech-deals; Leah Hodgson, "Appetite Wanes for VC Defense-Tech Deals," Pitchbook, August 13, 2024; Marina Temkin, "Sizing Up the Boom in Defense Tech," PitchBook, November 2, 2023, https://pitchbook.com/news/articles/defense-tech-boom-ukraine-china-israel; Dale Swartz and Ryan Brukardt, "Creating a Modernized Defense Technology Frontier," McKinsey, February 12, 2025. https://www.mckinsey.com/industries/aerospace-and-defense/our-insights/creating-a-modernized-defense-technology-frontier

Chapter 1

1. The epigraphs are from Michael E. Haskew, *M4 Sherman Tanks: The Illustrated History of America's Most Iconic Fighting Vehicles* (New York: Voyageur Press, 2016), 70; Winston S. Churchill, *The Grand Alliance, The Second World War* (New York: Houghton Mifflin, 1986), 3:539–540.
2. The lead in a front-page *New York Times* article was full of foreboding: "Premier Reynaud of France announced in an early morning broadcast that the Belgian Army had collapsed and that King Leopold had given up the struggle." "The International Situation: On the Battle Fronts," *New York Times*, May 28, 1940.
3. Bernard M. Baruch, *Baruch: The Public Years* (New York: Holt, Rinehart and Winston, 1960), 283.
4. Norman Beasley, *Knudsen: A Biography* (New York: McGraw-Hill, 1947), 234.

5. Buhite and Levy, *FDR's Fireside Chats*, 158. Roosevelt gave the fireside chat on May 26, 1940.
6. David Farber, *Sloan Rules: Alfred P. Sloan and the Triumph of General Motors* (Chicago: University of Chicago Press, 2002), 205.
7. Beasley, *Knudsen*, 237.
8. Arthur Herman, *Freedom's Forge: How American Business Produced Victory in World War II* (New York: Random House, 2012), 70.
9. Beasley, *Knudsen*, 237–238.
10. Harold L. Ickes, *The Secret Diary of Harold L. Ickes* (New York: Simon and Schuster, 1954), 3, 194.
11. Herman, *Freedom's Forge*, ix.
12. Thomas Robertson and Christopher W. Wells, "A War of Mobility: Transportation, American Productive Power, and the Environment during World War II," in *Nature at War: American Environments and World War II*, ed. Thomas Robertson, Richard P. Tucker, Nicholas B. Breyfogle, and Peter Mansoor (New York: Cambridge University Press, 2020), 23–50.
13. On the role of the federal government in military mobilization, see Mark R. Wilson, *Destructive Creation: American Business and the Winning of World War II* (Philadelphia: University of Pennsylvania Press, 2016).
14. Richard Overy, *Why the Allies Won* (New York: W. W. Norton, 1995), 4.
15. Eugene Gholz and Harvey M. Sapolsky, "Restructuring the U.S. Defense Industry," *International Security* 24, no. 3 (Winter 1999–2000): 5–51; Merritt Roe Smith, "Military Arsenals and Industry before World War I," in *War Business and American Society: Historical Perspectives on the Military-Industrial Complex*, ed. Benjamin Franklin Cooling (Port Washington, NY: Kennikort Press, 1977), 36–37.
16. Samuel P. Huntington, *The Soldier and the State: The Theory and Politics of Civil-Military Relations* (Cambridge, MA: Harvard University Press, 1957), 364; Jacques Gansler, William C. Greenwalt, and William Lucyshyn, *Non-Traditional Commercial Defense Contractors* (College Park: Center for Public and Private Enterprise, School of Public Policy, University of Maryland, November 2013), 6.
17. Alfred E. Eckes, *The United States and the Global Struggle for Minerals* (Austin: University of Texas Press, 1979), 94–95.
18. Robertson and Wells, "A War of Mobility," 23–50; Eckes, *The United States and the Global Struggle for Minerals*, 94–95.
19. H. C. Hillman, "Comparative Strength of the Great Powers," in *The World in March 1939*, ed. Arnold Toynbee and Frank T. Ashton-Gwatkin (New York: Oxford University Press, 1952), 446; Kennedy, *The Rise and Fall of the Great Powers*, 331.
20. Herman, *Freedom's Forge*, 91–92.
21. William Langer and S. Everett Gleason, *The Undeclared War, 1940–1941* (New York: Harper and Brothers, 1953).

22. On the broader conclusions, see, for example, Reports of the Special Committee on Investigation of the Munitions Industry. U.S. Congress, Senate, 74th Congress, Second Session (Washington, DC: U.S. Government Printing Office, 1935-1936).
23. Kennedy, *The Rise and Fall of the Great Powers*, 328.
24. R. M. Hathaway, "Economic Diplomacy in a Time of Crisis," in *Economics and World Power: An Assessment of American Diplomacy Since 1789*, ed. Samuel F. Wells and William H. Becker (New York: Columbia University Press, 1984), 277–278.
25. Herman, *Freedom's Forge*, 7.
26. Herman, *Freedom's Forge*, 9–10.
27. Kennedy, *The Rise and Fall of the Great Powers*, 355.
28. Overy, *Why the Allies Won*, 331–332.
29. The National Archives of the UK, Kew, CAB 23/15.
30. See, for example, the discussion in Andrew Roberts, *Churchill: Walking with Destiny* (New York: Viking, 2018), 331.
31. U.S. Strategic Bombing Survey, Summary Reports, LC, September 30, 1945, 77.
32. See, for example, U.S. Strategic Bombing Survey, Kawamura Interview, LC, November 23, 1945, 7.
33. Kennedy, *The Rise and Fall of the Great Powers*, 355.
34. Quoted in Albert Seaton, *The German Army, 1933–45* (New York: St Martin's Press, 1982), 55.
35. Williamson Murray, *The Change in the European Balance of Power, 1938–1939: The Path to Ruin* (Princeton, NJ: Princeton University Press, 1984), 20–21; Hillman, "Comparative Strength of the Great Powers," 454.
36. Kennedy, *The Rise and Fall of the Great Powers*, 305.
37. Roger Munting, *Economic Development of the USSR* (London: Canberra, 1982), 118. On the Soviet defense industry before World War II, see, for example, John Barber and Mark Harrison, eds., *The Soviet Defence Industry Complex from Stalin to Khrushchev* (New York: Palgrave Macmillan, 2000).
38. Kennedy, *The Rise and Fall of the Great Powers*, 332.
39. Richard J. Overy, *The Air War: 1939–1945* (New York: Stein and Day, 1981), 26.
40. Rosen, *Winning the Next War*, 152.
41. Paul Kennedy, *Engineers of Victory: The Problem Solvers Who Turned the Tide in the Second World War* (New York: Random House, 2013), 78.
42. John A. Garraty and Mark C. Carnes, eds., *American National Biography* (New York: Oxford University Press, 1999), 12:843; Herman, *Freedom's Forge*, 16.
43. Christy Borth, "This Is Knudsen," *Forum and Century*, March 1939.
44. Kennedy, *The Rise and Fall of the Great Powers*, 330; Thomas H. Greer, *The Development of Air Doctrine in the Army Air Arm, 1917–1941* (Washington, DC: Office of Air Force History, U.S. Air Force, 1985), 95–100.

45. Detroit Public Library, Knudsen Collection, part 4, box 1: Keim Mills, May 1, 1940. See also Beasley, *Knudsen*, 10–14; Herman, *Freedom's Forge*, 16–17.
46. Christy Borth, *Master of Mass Production* (Indianapolis, IN: Bobbs-Merrill, 1945), 60.
47. Letter from Edsel Ford to William S. Knudsen, March 20, 1921, Detroit Public Library; Garraty and Carnes, *American National Biography*, 12:843.
48. Harry C. Thompson and Lida Mayo, *The Ordnance Department: Procurement and Supply* (Washington, DC: Center of Military History, 2003), 45–46, emphasis in original.
49. Herman, *Freedom's Forge*, 80.
50. Beasley, *Knudsen*, 254–255.
51. Biddle, *Military Power*.
52. Beasley, *Knudsen*, 250.
53. John Morton Blum, *V Was for Victory: Politics and American Culture during World War II* (New York: Harcourt Brace Jovanovich, 1976), 134–135.
54. Attorney General Francis Biddle, Secretary of War Henry L. Stimson, Secretary of the Navy Frank Knox, and Assistant Attorney General Thurman Arnold, Letter to the President Recommending Suspension of Anti-Trust Proceedings, March 20, 1942, Office Files 277, Box 3, Franklin D. Roosevelt Library.
55. Knudsen Papers: Speech to Army Ordnance Association, October 8, 1940. Detroit Public Library. Also *Time*, October 21, 1940, 23.
56. Overy, *Why the Allies Won*, 195.
57. Herman, *Freedom's Forge*, 110.
58. Jacob Vander Meulen, *Building the B-29* (Washington, DC: Smithsonian Museum Press), 28.
59. Francis Walton, The *Miracle of World War II: How American Industry Made Victory Possible* (New York: Macmillan, 1956), 237; Alan Clive, *State of War: Michigan in World War II* (Ann Arbor: University of Michigan Press, 1976), 22.
60. Henry Stimson, *Diary*, Henry Lewis Stimson Papers, Sterling Library, Yale University, New Haven, CT. December 20, 1940, 40. Also see, for example, Letter from William S. Knudsen to Franklin D. Roosevelt, January 10, 1941, Detroit Public Library; Letter from Franklin D. Roosevelt to William S. Knudsen, January 9, 1941, Detroit Public Library.
61. Stimson, *Diary*, December 21, 1940, 51.
62. Stimson, *Diary*, July 25, 1940, 36; August 14, 1940, 87.
63. Buhite and Levy, *FDR's Fireside Chats*, 172–173. Roosevelt gave this fireside chat on December 29, 1940.
64. Ickes, *The Secret Diary of Harold L. Ickes*, 212, 398.
65. Joseph Alsop and Robert D. Kinter, "Trust Buster: The Folklore of Thurman Arnold," *Saturday Evening Post*, August 12, 1939.

66. Quoted in Blum, *V Was for Victory*, 133.
67. A. H. Raskin, "C.I.O. Chief Says $1 Men Get 'Fat' Federal Contracts," *New York Times*, November 22, 1941.
68. Quoted in Craufurd D. Goodwin, *Walter Lippmann: Public Economist* (Cambridge, MA: Harvard University Press, 2014), 270.
69. H. H. Arnold, *Global Mission* (New York: Harper & Brother, 1940), 198.
70. Herman, *Freedom's Forge*, 129.
71. Donald Nelson, *Arsenal of Democracy: The Story of American War Production* (New York: Harcourt, 1946), 152.
72. The one no vote in the U.S. House of Representatives came from Jeannette Rankin, a Montana Republican and unreserved pacificist.
73. Franklin D. Roosevelt, Joint Address to Congress Leading to a Declaration of War against Japan, December 8, 1941, National Archives.
74. First War Powers Act, LC, 1941.
75. Second War Powers Act, LC, 1942.
76. Franklin D. Roosevelt, State of the Union Address, Franklin D. Roosevelt Library, January 6, 1942.
77. Franklin D. Roosevelt, State of the Union Address, January 6, 1942.
78. Quoted in "U.S. At War: Now, Mrs. Roosevelt!" *Time*, January 19, 1942.
79. Ickes, *The Secret Diary of Harold L. Ickes*, 509.
80. Executive Order 9024, "Establishing the War Production Board," LC.
81. Commissioning Knudsen into the army as a three-star general was controversial. See, for example, *Hearing before a Subcommittee of the Committee on Military Affairs, U.S. Senate, Seventy-seventh Congress, Second Session, on the Nomination of Hon. William Signius Knudsen for Temporary Appointment as a Lieutenant General in the Army of the United States, January 24, 1942* (Washington, DC: U.S. Government Printing Office, 1942).
82. Beasley, *Knudsen*, 260.
83. Herman, *Freedom's Forge*, 248–252.
84. Vander Meulen, *Building the B-29*, 28.
85. Mimi Sheller, *Aluminum Dreams: The Making of Light Modernity* (Cambridge, MA: MIT Press), 70.
86. H. Dewey Anderson, *Aluminum for Defense and Prosperity* (Washington, DC: Public Affairs Institute, 1951), 5.
87. Sheller, *Aluminum Dreams*, 70.
88. Phillips Payson O'Brien, *How the War Was Won* (New York: Cambridge University Press, 2015), 18.
89. Robertson and Wells, "A War of Mobility," 31.
90. Eckes, *The United States and the Global Struggle for Minerals*, 107.
91. Eckes, *The United States and the Global Struggle for Minerals*, 115.
92. Quoted in National Resources Planning Board, *Industrial Location and National Resources, December, 1942* (Washington, DC: Government Printing Office, 1943), 178.

93. Herman, *Freedom's Forge*, 247.
94. Hillman, "Comparative Strength of the Powers," 439, 446; Quincy Wright, *A Study of War* (Chicago: University of Chicago Press, 1942), 672; Raymond W. Goldsmith, "The Power of Victory: Munitions Output in World War II," *Military Affairs* 10 (Spring 1946): 69–80; Kennedy, *Rise and Fall of the Great Powers*, 355.
95. Rosen, *Winning the Next War*, 130.
96. Ronald Lewin, *The American Magic: Codes, Ciphers, and the Defeat of Japan* (New York: Farrar, Straus and Giroux), 224, 229.
97. Rosen, *Winning the Next War*, 131.
98. Rosen, *Winning the Next War*, 130.
99. Kennedy, *Engineers of Victory*, 306.
100. Thomas Collison, *The Superfortress Is Born: The Story of the Boeing B-29* (New York: Duell, Sloan and Pearce, 1945), 4.
101. Curtis Lemay and Bill Yenne, *Superfortress: The Boeing B-29 and American Air Power in World War II* (Yardley, PA: Westholme, 1988), 19–57.
102. Boeing, "Model Specifications and History, B-29 Superfortress," undated, Boeing Company Archives, Auburn, WA.
103. Herman, *Freedom's Forge*, 293.
104. Kenneth Werrell, *Blankets of Fire: US Bombers over Japan during World War II* (Washington, DC: Smithsonian, 1996), 82; Walter J. Boyne, "The B-29's Battle of Kansas," *Air Force Magazine* 95, no. 2 (February 2012): 95; O'Brien, *How the War Was Won*, 47–48.
105. Wellwood Beall File, Boeing Company Archives.
106. Edward Wells File, Boeing Company Archives.
107. George Schairer File, Boeing Company Archives.
108. Letter from W. E. Beall to P. G. Johnson, "Failure of Body under Pressure Test—XB-29," August 25, 1949, with Attachments, Boeing Company Archives.
109. Collison, *The Superfortress Is Born*, 60.
110. George Schairer File, Boeing Company Archives; Boeing, "Story of the Boeing B-29 Superfortress," undated, Boeing Company Archives.
111. Boeing, "Engineering Achievements in the B-29," undated, Boeing Company Archives.
112. Herman, *Freedom's Forge*, 315; Beasley, *Knudsen*, 368.
113. Kennedy, *Engineers of Victory*, 325.
114. Stephen Ambrose, *The Wild Blue: The Men and Boys Who Flew the B-24s over Germany* (New York: Simon and Schuster, 2001), 21–23, 79–80.
115. Collison, *The Superfortress Is Born*, 110–111.
116. Boeing, "B-29: Production and Construction Analysis," January 21, 1946, Boeing Company Archives.
117. Boeing, "The Battle of Kansas," undated, Boeing Company Archives.
118. Herman, *Freedom's Forge*, 299.

119. Boeing, "Boeing B-29 Superfortress," January 13, 1971, Boeing Company Archives.
120. Boeing, "B-29: Production and Construction Analysis," January 21, 1946, Boeing Company Archives.
121. Letter from W. E. Beall to P. G. Johnson, "Failure of Body under Pressure Test—XB-29," August 25, 1949, with Attachments, Boeing Company Archives; Boeing, "B-29: Production and Construction Analysis," January 21, 1946, Boeing Company Archives.
122. Kennedy, *Engineers of Victory*, 328.
123. Beasley, *Knudsen*, 371.
124. Herman, *Freedom's Forge*, 321.
125. Boeing, "Design Origin, Development, and Scope of Production of New B-29 Superfortress Revealed by Boeing," June 15, 1944, Boeing Company Archives.
126. Boeing, "Model Specifications and History, B-29 Superfortress," undated, Boeing Company Archives.
127. Boeing, "The Facts about the B-29," undated, Boeing Company Archives.
128. Jenns Robertson, "Theater History of Operations (THOR) Data: World War II," accessed June 10, 2024, https://www.af.mil/News/Article-Display/Article/466817/historic-airpower-database-now-online/.
129. Arnold, *Global Mission*, 371.
130. Arnold, *Global Mission*, 598.
131. There is some debate about the overall effectiveness of strategic bombing. Some argue that while strategic bombing was likely a *necessary* part of victory, it was not *sufficient* since Japanese leaders were also concerned about a potential U.S. and Soviet invasion of the island. See, for example, Robert A. Pape, *Bombing to Win: Air Power and Coercion in War* (Ithaca, NY: Cornell University Press, 1996), 87–136.
132. Kennedy, *Engineers of Victory*, 306.
133. Secretary of the Treasury (Morgenthau) to the President, Subject: Suggested Post-Surrender Program for Germany, Washington, September 5, 1944, Foreign Relations of the United States, Conference at Quebec 1944, eds. Richardson Dougall, Arthur G. Kogan, Richard S. Patterson, Irving L. Thomson (Washington, DC: Government Printing Office, 1972), Document 86.
134. David S. Landes, *The Unbound Prometheus: Technological Change and Industrial Development in Western Europe from 1750 to the Present* (New York: Cambridge University Press, 1969), 488.
135. U.S. Strategic Bombing Survey, Toyoda Interview, LC, October 5, 1945, 6.
136. O'Brien, *How the War Was Won*, 34–35.
137. See, for example, Paul M. Kennedy, *The Realities behind Diplomacy: Background Influences on British External Policy* (Boston: Allen and Unwin, 1981), 318.

138. Mark Harrison, "Wartime Mobilisation: A German Comparison," in Barber and Harrison, *The Soviet Defence Industry Complex from Stalin to Khrushchev*, 99–117.
139. Jonathan R. Adelman, *Prelude to the Cold War: The Tsarist, Soviet, and U.S. Armies in the Two World Wars* (Boulder, CO: Lynne Rienner, 1988), 219.
140. Adelman, *Prelude to the Cold War*, 219.
141. Mearsheimer, *The Tragedy of Great Power Politics*, 72.
142. Overy, *Why the Allies Won*, 331–332.
143. O'Brien, *How the War Was Won*, 52.
144. Overy, *Why the Allies Won*, 331.
145. Churchill, *The Grand Alliance*, 539–540.
146. Overy, *Why the Allies Won*, 331–332.
147. Knudsen Papers, June 1, 1945.
148. Arnold, *Global Mission*, 291–292.
149. Quoted in Bruce Catton, *The War Lords of Washington* (New York: Harcourt, Brace, 1948), 112–113.
150. U.S. Senate, *Economic Concentration and World War II*, report of the smaller war plants to the Special Committee to Study Problems of American Small Business U.S. Senate (Washington, DC: U.S. Government Printing Office, 1946), 30.
151. U.S. Department of State, *Lend-Lease and Military Aid to the Allies in the Early Years of World War II* (Washington, DC: Office of the Historian, U.S. Department of State, undated).
152. Goldsmith, "The Power of Victory," 70.
153. O'Brien, *How the War Was Won*.
154. Franklin D. Roosevelt, Annual Budget Message, Franklin D. Roosevelt Library, January 5, 1942, emphasis added.

Chapter 2

1. Both epigraphs are from Ben R. Rich, "Clarence Leonard (Kelly) Johnson, 1910–1990," in National Academy of Sciences, *Biographical Memoirs* (Washington, DC: National Academies Press, 1995), 231, 221.
2. City of Burbank, *Citywide Historic Context Report* (Redondo Beach, CA: Galvin Preservation Associates, September 2009).
3. Frank Whittle, *Jet: The Story of a Pioneer* (London: Muller, 1953); John D. Anderson Jr., *The Grand Designers: The Evolution of the Airplane in the 20th Century* (New York: Cambridge University Press, 2018).
4. See Pat Jefferson to Clarence L. Johnson, January 11, 1982, Box 2, Clarence L. Johnson Papers, Huntington Library, San Marino, CA.
5. Quoted in Mary Pat Kelly, *Irish above All* (New York: Forge, 2019), 268.
6. Clarence L. "Kelly" Johnson with Maggie Smith, *Kelly: More Than My Share of It All* (Washington, DC: Smithsonian Books, 1989), 7.

7. Michigan was proud of Kelly Johnson as an alumnus as soon as he went to Lockheed. See, for example, letter from H. C. Anderson, Dean, University of Michigan, to Clarence Leonard Johnson, July 19, 1938, Box 2, Clarence L. Johnson Papers, Huntington Library.
8. See Pat Jefferson to Clarence L. Johnson, January 11, 1982, Box 2, Clarence L. Johnson Papers, Huntington Library.
9. Johnson and Smith, *Kelly*, 96.
10. Jacques S. Gansler, *Democracy's Arsenal: Creating a Twenty-First Century Defense Industry* (Cambridge, MA: MIT Press, 2011), 10.
11. Executive Order 9638, "Creating the Civilian Production Administration and Terminating the War Production Board," October 4, 1945, https://www.trumanlibrary.gov/library/executive-orders/9638/executive-order-9638.
12. John M. Blair, *Economic Concentration: Structure, Behavior, and Public Policy* (New York: Harcourt Brace Jovanovich, 1972), 380.
13. Gansler, *Democracy's Arsenal*, 17.
14. Herman, *Freedom's Forge*, 337.
15. Herman, *Freedom's Forge*, 338.
16. James Dobbins et al., *America's Role in Nation-Building: From Germany to Iraq* (Santa Monica, CA: RAND, 2003), 9.
17. Office of the Under Secretary of Defense (Comptroller), *National Defense Budget Estimates for FY 2023* (Washington, DC: Department of Defense, July 2022).
18. Andrew Feickert, *Army Drawdown and Restructuring: Background and Issues for Congress* (Washington, DC: Congressional Research Service, February 28, 2014), 26.
19. Richard A. Bitzinger, *Assessing the Conventional Balance in Europe, 1945–1975* (Santa Monica, CA: RAND Corporation, May 1989), 6.
20. Alan S. Milward, *War, Economy, and Society, 1939–1945* (Berkeley: University of California Press, 1979), 63.
21. Benjamin M. Rowland, ed., *Balance of Power or Hegemony: The Interwar Monetary System* (New York: New York University Press, 1976), 220.
22. Kennedy, *The Rise and Fall of the Great Powers*, 369; S. H. Cohn, *Economic Development in the Soviet Union* (Lexington, MA: Heath, 1970), Appendix C, Table C-1.
23. Paul Bairoch, "International Industrialization Levels from 1750 to 1980," *Journal of European Economic History* 11, no. 2 (Fall 1982): 299, 302.
24. Phillip A. Karber and Jerald Combs, "The United States, NATO, and the Soviet Threat to Western Europe: Military Estimates and Policy Options, 1945–1963," *Diplomatic History* 22, no. 3 (Summer 1998): 403.
25. Kennedy, The Rise and Fall of the Great Powers, 369; Cohn, *Economic Development in the Soviet Union*.
26. Barber and Harrison, *The Soviet Defence Industry Complex from Stalin to Khrushchev*; Central Intelligence Agency, *A Comparison of the U.S. and*

Soviet Industrial Bases: A Reference Aid, SOV 89-10020 (Langley, VA: Directorate of Intelligence, Central Intelligence Agency, May 1989).

27. Central Intelligence Agency, *The Soviet Weapons Industry: An Overview*, DI 86-10016 (Langley, VA: Directorate of Intelligence, Central Intelligence Agency, September 1986).
28. Central Intelligence Agency, *The Soviet Defense Industry: Coping with the Military-Technological Challenge*, SOV 87-10035DX (Langley, VA: Directorate of Intelligence, Central Intelligence Agency, July 1987), iii.
29. See, for example, Andrei Antonovich Grechko, *The Armed Forces of the Soviet State: A Soviet View* (Washington, DC: U.S. Air Force, 1975). The U.S. Air Force translated the book from Russian.
30. See, for example, Barber and Harrison, *The Soviet Defence-Industry Complex from Stalin to Khrushchev*; Julian Cooper, *The Soviet Defence Industry: Conversion and Economic Reform* (New York: Council on Foreign Relations, 1991).
31. Halford J. Mackinder, "The Round World and the Winning of the Peace," *Foreign Affairs* 21, no. 4 (July 1943): 601.
32. Harold J. Mackinder, "The Geographical Pivot of History," *Geographical Journal* 23, no. 4 (April 1904): 298–321.
33. Truman to Acheson (unsent), March 15, 1957, in *Strictly Personal and Confidential: The Letters Harry Truman Never Mailed*, ed. Monte Poen (Boston: Little, Brown, 1982), 33.
34. See, for example, Marc Trachtenberg, *A Constructed Peace: The Making of the European Settlement 1945–1953* (Princeton, NJ: Princeton University Press, 1999), 35.
35. JCS 973/1, "Fundamental Military Factors in Relation to Discussions concerning Territorial Trusteeships and Settlements," July 28, 1944, CCS 092 (7-27-44), RG 218, U.S. National Archives, College Park, MD.
36. Report to the National Security Council, "United States Objectives and Programs for National Security" (NSC-68), April 14, 1950, Foreign Relations of the United States, 1950, National Security Affairs; Foreign Economic Policy, Volume I, eds. S. Everett Gleason and Frederick Aandahl (Washington, DC: Government Printing Office, 1977), Document 85.
37. Report to the National Security Council, "United States Objectives and Programs for National Security."
38. Johnson and Smith, *Kelly*, 95–106.
39. Huntington, *The Soldier and the State*, 364.
40. Lockheed, "The Air Superiority of Day Fighter or Defensive Fighter for USAF," January 5, 1957, Box 10, Clarence L. Johnson Papers, Huntington Library; Lockheed, Evolution of the F-104 Starfighter, Box 10, Clarence L. Johnson Papers, Huntington Library.
41. See, for example, Jack Broughton, "Pain and Gain in the Century Series," *Air Force Magazine*, September 2012, 80.
42. Gansler, *Democracy's Arsenal*, 11.

43. See, for example, Michael J. Hogan, *A Cross of Iron: Harry S. Truman and the Origins of the National Security State, 1945–1954* (New York: Cambridge University Press, 2000).
44. The Defense Production Act of 1950, September 8, 1950.
45. Alexander G. Neenan and Luke A. Nicastro, *The Defense Production Act of 1950: History, Authorities, and Considerations for Congress* (Washington, DC: Congressional Research Services, October 6, 2023), 3.
46. See, for example, Michael Brenes, *For Might and Right: Cold War Defense Spending and the Remaking of American Democracy* (Amherst: University of Massachusetts Press, 2020), 50–51.
47. Harry Truman, Radio and Television Address to the American People Following the Signing of the Defense Production Act, September 9, 1950, https://www.trumanlibrary.gov/soundrecording-records/sr62-81-president-trumans-radio-and-television-address-american-people.
48. Margaret O'Mara, *The Code: Silicon Valley and the Remaking of America* (New York: Penguin Press, 2019), 23.
49. O'Mara, *The Code*, 24.
50. Burbach et al., "Weighing the U.S. Navy," 261.
51. Tim Colton and LaVar Huntzinger, *A Brief History of Shipbuilding in Recent Times* (Alexandria, VA: Center for Naval Analysis, September 2002).
52. David T. Burbach et al., "Weighing the U.S. Navy," *Defense Analysis* 17, no. 3 (2001): 259–266.
53. Kennedy, *The Rise and Fall of the Great Powers*, 359.
54. Gansler, *Democracy's Arsenal*, 11.
55. Dwight D. Eisenhower, *The Eisenhower Diaries* (New York: Norton, 1981); Dwight D. Eisenhower, *Waging Peace, 1951–1961: The White House Years* (New York: Doubleday, 1965); Dwight D. Eisenhower meeting with Republican legislative leaders, April 30, 1953, Eisenhower Papers, Whitman File: DDE Diary, Box 2, "Staff Notes, Jan-Dec 53," Dwight D. Eisenhower Presidential Library, Abilene, KS.
56. Dwight D. Eisenhower, "The Chance for Peace," Addressed Delivered before the American Society of Newspaper Editors, April 16, 1953, Dwight D. Eisenhower Presidential Library.
57. Author interview with Robert Work, December 2, 2024.
58. Geoffrey Hosking, *A History of the Soviet Union: 1917–1991* (London: Fontana Press, 1985), Appendix C, 483; Munting, *The Economic Development of the USSR*, 133; Alec Nove, *An Economic History of the USSR* (New York: Penguin, 1982), 340, 387; J. P. Nettle, *The Soviet Achievement* (New York: Harcourt, Brace, 1967).
59. The strategy was laid out in National Security Council Paper 162/2. See, for example, Report to the National Security Council by the Executive Secretary, NSC 162/2, October 30, 1953, Foreign Relations of the United

States, 1952–1954, National Security Affairs, Volume II, Part 1, eds., Lisle A. Rose and Neal H. Petersen (Washington, DC: Government Printing Office, 1984), Document 101.

60. Report to the National Security Council by the Executive Secretary, NSC 162/2.
61. John Foster Dulles, "Policy for Security and Peace," *Foreign Affairs* 32, no. 3 (April 1954): 353–364.
62. Report to the National Security Council by the Executive Secretary, NSC 162/2.
63. Author interview with Robert Work, December 2, 2024.
64. Robert Work, "Remarks by Deputy Secretary Work on Third Offset Strategy," Brussels, Belgium, April 28, 2016, https://www.defense.gov/News/Speeches/Speech/Article/753482/remarks-by-deputy-secretary-work-on-third-offset-strategy/.
65. Quoted in Richard M. Leighton, *Strategy, Money, and the New Look, 1953-1956*, History of the Office of the Secretary of Defense, Vol. III (Washington, DC: Historical Office, Office of the Secretary of Defense, 2001), 373.
66. Leighton, *Strategy, Money, and the New Look*, 373, 395, 432-434.
67. In 1953, General Dynamics bought Convair, which developed and produced the B-58 and B-36, and operated it as the Convair Division.
68. Robert J. Watson, *Into the Missile Age, 1956-1960*, History of the Office of the Secretary of Defense, Vol. IV (Washington, DC: Historical Office, Office of the Secretary of Defense, 1997), 35.
69. Gansler, Greenwalt, and Lucyshyn, *Non-Traditional Commercial Defense Contractors*, 7.
70. William J. Perry, *My Journey at the Nuclear Brink* (Stanford: Stanford University Press, 2015), 35
71. Johnson and Smith, *Kelly*, 98.
72. Clarence L. Johnson, Christmas Speech, December 21, 1962, Box 7, Clarence L. Johnson Papers, Huntington Library.
73. See the official CIA history of the U-2 program, which was eventually declassified. Gregory W. Pedlow and Donald E. Welzenbach, *The Central Intelligence Agency and Overhead Reconnaissance: The U-2 and OXCART Programs, 1954–1974* (Washington, DC: History Staff, Central Intelligence Agency, 1992), 1–7.
74. James Killian, *Sputnik, Scientists, and Eisenhower: A Memoir of the First Special Assistant to the President for Science and Technology* (Cambridge, MA: MIT Press, 1977), 82.
75. Letter, Edwin Land to Allen Dulles, November 5, 1954, w/att: Memorandum for: Director of Central Intelligence, Subject: A Unique Opportunity for Comprehensive Intelligence, Dwight D. Eisenhower Library.

76. Johnson and Smith, *Kelly*, 120.
77. Pedlow and Welzenbach, *The Central Intelligence Agency and Overhead Reconnaissance*, 12.
78. Michael R. Beschloss, *Mayday: Eisenhower, Khrushchev, and the U-2 Affair* (New York: Harper & Row, 1986), 105–107.
79. Central Intelligence Agency, "Project Aquatone," CIA-RDP62B00844R000200030008-2, the CIA Records Search Tool (CREST), National Archives and Records Administration, College Park, Maryland, November 19, 1955; Memorandum from Lawrence R. Houston to Director of Central Intelligence, Subject: Project Aquatone, CIA-RDP62B00844R000200260063-6, the CIA Records Search Tool (CREST), National Archives and Records Administration, College Park, Maryland, January 26, 1956.
80. Johnson and Smith, *Kelly*, 123.
81. Ben R. Rich and Leon Janos, *Skunk Works: A Personal Memoir of My Years at Lockheed* (New York: Little, Brown, 1994), 120.
82. Rich and Janos, *Skunk Works*, 9, 107.
83. Rich and Janos, *Skunk Works*, 108.
84. Pedlow and Welzenbach, *The Central Intelligence Agency and Overhead Reconnaissance*, 47.
85. Pedlow and Welzenbach, *The Central Intelligence Agency and Overhead Reconnaissance*, 47.
86. Johnson and Smith, *Kelly*, 121.
87. Pedlow and Welzenbach, *The Central Intelligence Agency and Overhead Reconnaissance*, 45.
88. Pedlow and Welzenbach, *The Central Intelligence Agency and Overhead Reconnaissance*, 316.
89. See Kistiakowsky Diary, January 7 and July 8, 1960, in George B. Kistiakowsky, *A Scientist in the White House: The Private Diary of President Eisenhower's Special Assistant for Science and Technology* (Cambridge, MA: Harvard University Press, 1976), 219, 367.
90. Quoted in Pedlow and Welzenbach, *The Central Intelligence Agency and Overhead Reconnaissance*, 316.
91. Francis Gary Powers with Curt Gentry, *Operation Overflight: A Memoir of the U-2 Incident* (Washington, DC: Brassey's, 2004).
92. Adam R. Grissom, Caitlin Lee, and Karl P. Mueller, *Innovation in the United States Air Force: Evidence from Six Cases* (Santa Monica, CA: RAND, 2016).
93. "Eisenhower Describes Repercussions over Launching of 1st Soviet Sputnik," *Washington Post*, September 21, 1965.
94. Central Intelligence Agency, "Production of Semiconductor Devices in the USSR," CIA-RDP79R01141A001500150002-6, the CIA Records Search Tool (CREST), National Archives and Records Administration, College Park, Maryland, November 1959.

95. Rockefeller Brothers Fund, *Prospect for America: The Rockefeller Panel Reports* (Garden City, NY: Doubleday, 1961). The report's findings were covered on the front page of the *New York Times*. See Philip Benjamin, "Arms Rise Urged Lest Reds Seize Lead in 2 Years," *New York Times*, January 6, 1958.
96. William Greenwalt and Dan Patt, *Competing in Time: Ensuring Capability Advantage and Mission Success through Adaptable Resource Allocation* (Washington, DC: Hudson Institute, February 2021), 17.
97. Report to the President by the Security Resources Panel of the Science Advisory Committee [hereafter, Gaither Committee], *Deterrence and Survival in the Nuclear Age*, November 7, 1957, Foreign Relations of the United States, 1955-1957, National Security Policy, Volume XIX, eds. William Klingaman, David S. Patterson, and Ilana Stern (Washington, DC: Government Printing Office, 1990), Document 158.
98. Donald W. Mitchell, *History of Russian and Soviet Sea Power* (New York: Macmillan, 1974); Norman Polmar, *Soviet Naval Power: Challenge for the 1970s* (New York: Crane, Russak, 1974); Robert W. Herrick, *Soviet Naval Strategy: Fifty Years of Theory and Practice* (Annapolis, MD: U.S. Naval Institute, 1968); Michael MccGwire, ed., *Soviet Naval Developments* (New York: Praeger, 1973).
99. Central Intelligence Agency, *The Soviet Defense Industry*, 2.
100. Gaither Committee, *Deterrence and Survival in the Nuclear Age*, 7–8.
101. Eugene Gholz and Harvey M. Sapolsky, "The Defense Innovation Machine: Why the U.S. Will Remain on the Cutting Edge," *Journal of Strategic Studies* 44, no. 6 (2021): 854–872.
102. O'Mara, *The Code*, 44–47.
103. Edmund Beard, *Developing the ICBM: A Study in Bureaucratic Politics* (New York: Columbia University Press, 1976).
104. Walter S. Poole, *Adapting to Flexible Response, 1960–1968* (Washington, DC: Historical Office, Office of the Secretary of Defense, 2013), 182. On Schriever more broadly, see Neil Sheehan, *A Fiery Peace in a Cold War: Bernard Schriever and the Ultimate Weapon* (New York: Vintage Books, 2009).
105. Greenwalt and Patt, *Competing in Time*, 18.
106. Sharon Weinberger, *The Imagineers of War: The Untold Story of DARPA, the Pentagon Agency That Changed the World* (New York: Knopf, 2018), 9.
107. O'Mara, *The Code*, 39.
108. G. Pascal Zachary, *Endless Frontier: Vannevar Bush, Engineer of the American Century* (Cambridge, MA: MIT Press, 1999).
109. Gholz and Sapolsky, "The Defense Innovation Machine," 854–872; O'Mara, *The Code*, 20.
110. Chris Miller, *Chip War: The Fight for the World's Most Critical Technology* (New York: Scribner, 2022), 22, 29.

111. O'Mara, *The Code*, 47.
112. O'Mara, *The Code*, 51.
113. Brenes, *For Might and Right*, 72; Eugene Gholz and Harvey M. Sapolsky, "Restructuring the U.S. Defense Industry," *International Security* 24, no. 3 (Winter 1999–2000): 8.
114. Sapolsky, Gholz, and Talmadge, *U.S. Defense Politics*, 126.
115. Eugene Gholz, "The Curtiss-Wright Corporation and the Cold War–Era Defense Procurement," *Journal of Cold War Studies* 2, no. 1 (Winter 2000): 35–75; Sapolsky, Gholz, and Talmadge, *U.S. Defense Politics*, 127.
116. Brose, *The Kill Chain*, 46.
117. Gansler, Greenwalt, and Lucyshyn, *Non-Traditional Commercial Defense Contractors*, 7.
118. Quoted in Poole, *Adapting to Flexible Response*, 183.
119. Quoted in Michael Brenes, "How America Broke Its War Machine: Privatization and the Hollowing Out of the U.S. Defense Industry," *Foreign Affairs*, July 3, 2023.
120. Sapolsky, Gholz, and Talmadge, *U.S. Defense Politics*, 140.
121. Sapolsky, Gholz, and Talmadge, *U.S. Defense Politics*, 140.
122. Erik Lacitis, "Iconic 'Will the Last Person' Seattle Billboard Bubbles Up Again," *Seattle Times*, February 2, 2009.
123. O'Mara, *The Code*, 90.
124. O'Mara, *The Code*, 90–110.
125. Gholz and Sapolsky, "Restructuring the U.S. Defense Industry," 8.
126. Edward C. Keefer, *Harold Brown: Offsetting the Soviet Military Challenge, 1977–1981* (Washington, DC: Historical Office, Office of the Secretary of Defense, 2017), 594.
127. Report by President Nixon to the Congress, "U.S. Foreign Policy for the 1970s: A New Strategy for Peace," February 18, 1970, Foreign Relations of the United States, 1969-1976, Volume I, Foundations of Foreign Policy, 1969-1972, eds. Louis J. Smith and David H. Herschler (Washington, DC: Government Printing Office, 2003), Document 60. Also see, for example, Henry Kissinger, *White House Years* (Boston: Little, Brown, 1979), 195–198
128. Keefer, *Harold Brown*, 575–576.
129. Keefer, *Harold Brown*, 575.
130. U.S. Air Force, Strategic Air Command, SR-71, Brochure, undated, Box 11, Clarence L. Johnson Papers, Huntington Library. Also see C. L. "Kelly" Johnson, "White Paper on the SR-71 Aircraft," October 28, 1981, Box 11, Clarence L. Johnson Papers, Huntington Library.
131. Johnson and Smith, *Kelly*, 137.
132. Defense Science Board, *Report of the Acquisition Cycle Task Force, Defense Science Board 1977 Summer Study* (Washington, DC: Office of the Under Secretary of Defense for Research and Engineering, March 1978), vii.
133. Perry, *My Journey at the Nuclear Brink*, 35.

134. On the 3:1 rule, see, for example, John J. Mearsheimer, "Assessing the Conventional Balance: The 3:1 Rule and Its Critics," *International Security* 13, no. 4 (Spring 1989): 54–89.
135. See Pat Jefferson to Clarence L. Johnson, January 11, 1982, Box 2, Clarence L. Johnson Papers, Huntington Library.
136. Author interview with Robert Work, December 2, 2024.
137. Perry, *My Journey at the Nuclear Brink*, 33.
138. William Perry, Testimony before the U.S. Senate Armed Services Committee, Hearing on Department of Defense Appropriations for FY1979, Part 8: Research and Development, February 28, March 7, 9, 14, 16, 21, 1978, 95th Congress, Second Session, 5598. Also see Ashton B. Carter and William J. Perry, *Preventive Defense* (Washington, DC: Brookings Institution Press, 2000), 179-180.
139. Keefer, *Harold Brown*, 588.
140. Quoted in Keefer, *Harold Brown*, 588-589.
141. Perry, *My Journey at the Nuclear Brink*, 38–39.
142. Quoted in Keefer, Harold Brown, 589.
143. Keefer, *Harold Brown*, 582.
144. The exercise was Zapad-'81.
145. Quoted in Gordon S. Barrass, *The Great Cold War: A Journey through the Hall of Mirrors* (Stanford: Stanford University Press, 2009), 274.
146. Also see, for example, Michael J. Sterling, *Soviet Reactions to NATO's Emerging Technologies for Deep Attack* (Santa Monica, CA: RAND, August 1985).
147. House Armed Services Committee, *The Ailing Defense Industrial Base: Unready for Crisis* (Washington, DC: U.S. Government Printing Office, 1980), 1.
148. Ronald Reagan, *An American Life: The Autobiography* (New York: Simon and Schuster, 1990), 216.
149. In a controversial move, Walter Mondale agreed to meet with Soviet Foreign Minister Andrei Gromyko during the election campaign, a decision that even Jimmy Carter's national security advisor, Zbigniew Brzezinski, condemned: "It will contribute to the impression that [Mondale] is catering to the Soviets and that the Soviets are using the campaign. The prospect of American candidates rushing to the Soviets who bestow their favors is distasteful." Quoted in Charlotte Saikowski, "USSR Positions Itself in the Middle of the U.S. Election Campaign," *Christian Science Monitor*, September 18, 1984.
150. Central Intelligence Agency, *The Soviet Defense Industry*, iii.
151. Central Intelligence Agency, *The Soviet Defense Industry*, 1.
152. Central Intelligence Agency, *Soviet Acquisition of Militarily Significant Western Technology: An Update* (Langley, VA: Central Intelligence Agency, September 1985).
153. Central Intelligence Agency, *The Soviet Defense Industry*, 4.

154. U.S. Department of Defense, *Soviet Strategic Defense Programs* (Washington, DC: U.S. Department of Defense, October 1985); U.S. Department of Defense, *Soviet Military Power*, 5th edition (Washington, DC: U.S. Government Printing Office, 1986). Earlier editions of *Soviet Military Power* were released in September 1981, March 1983, April 1984, and April 1985.
155. Central Intelligence Agency, *The Soviet Defense Industry*, 4.
156. Edward C. Keefer, *Caspar Weinberger and the U.S. Military Build-up 1981–1985* (Washington, DC: Historical Office, Office of the Secretary of Defense, 2023), 623–624; Rich and Janos, *Skunk* Works, 73.
157. Gian Gentile et al., *A History of the Third Offset, 2014–2018* (Santa Monica, CA: RAND, 2021), 16.
158. Gansler, *Democracy's Arsenal*, 10.
159. Gansler, *Democracy's Arsenal*, 29.
160. Stockholm International Peace Research Institute, "SIPRI Military Expenditure Database," 2023, https://www.sipri.org/databases/milex.
161. See, for example, National Security Decision Directive Number 119, Strategic Defense Initiative, White House, January 6, 1984, https://www.reaganlibrary.gov/public/archives/reference/scanned-nsdds/nsdd119.pdf; National Security Decision Director Number 172, Presenting the Strategic Defense Initiative, White House, May 30, 1985, https://www.reaganlibrary.gov/public/archives/reference/scanned-nsdds/nsdd172.pdf.
162. Ronald Reagan, *Public Papers of the Presidents of the United States, 1983*, book 1: *January 1 to July 1, 1983* (Washington, DC: Government Printing Office, 1984), 440.
163. O'Mara, *The Code*, 246.
164. Keefer, *Caspar Weinberger and the U.S. Military Build-up 1981–1985*, 416–417.
165. Keefer, *Caspar Weinberger and the U.S. Military Build-up 1981–1985*, 578, 625.
166. The United Kingdom and France also had aircraft carriers. See, for example, *The Military Balance 1987* (London: International Institute for Strategic Studies, 1987), 46–91. Japan decommissioned its aircraft carriers after World War II. Its fearsome carrier strike force was known as the *Kido Butai*, or Mobile Force.
167. Edward C. O'Dowd, *Chinese Military Strategy in the Third Indochina War* (New York: Routledge, 2007), 28–30; King C. Chen, *China's War with Vietnam, 1979: Issues, Decision, and Implications* (Stanford: Hoover Institution Press, 1987), 88, 103.
168. *The Military Balance 1987* (London: International Institute for Strategic Studies, 1987).
169. See, for example, M. Taylor Fravel, *Active Defense: China's Military Strategy since 1949* (Princeton, NJ: Princeton University Press, 2019), 163–165; Gerald Segal, *Defending China* (New York: Oxford University

Press, 1985), 211–227; Nayan Chanda, *Brother Enemy: The War after the War* (New York: Harcourt Brace Jovanovich, 1986); Chen, *China's War with Vietnam*; Steven J. Hood, *Dragons Entangled: Indochina and the China Vietnam War* (Armonk, NY: M. E. Sharpe, 1992); Bruce Elleman, *Modern Chinese Warfare, 1785–1989* (London: Routledge, 2001), 284–297.

170. Segal, *Defending China*.
171. Kennedy, *Rise and Fall of the Great Powers*, 447.
172. Keefer, *Caspar Weinberger and the U.S. Military Build-up 1981–1985*, 166–173.
173. U.S. General Accounting Office, *DOD's Defense Acquisition Improvement Program: A Status Report* (Washington, DC: U.S. General Accounting Office, July 1986), 1.
174. On concerns about waste, fraud, and abuse—including Operation Ill Wind—see Andy Pasztor, *When the Pentagon Was for Sale: Inside America's Biggest Defense Scandal* (New York: Scribner, 1995); Robert F. Howe, "Navy Ex-Official Convicted in 'Ill Wind,'" *Washington Post*, March 8, 1992; Robert F. Howe, "United Technologies to Pay $6 Million in 'Ill Wind' Plea Pact," *Washington Post*, August 29, 1992; Andy Pasztor, "Lockheed Martin Settles Pentagon Contracts Case," *Wall Street Journal*, December 26, 1996.
175. President's Blue-Ribbon Commission on Defense Management [hereafter, Packard Commission], *A Quest for Excellence: Final Report to the President* (Washington, DC: The Commission, June 1986).
176. Packard Commission, *A Quest for Excellence*, 47.
177. Packard Commission, *A Quest for Excellence*, 52.
178. Gansler, Greenwalt, and Lucyshyn, *Non-Traditional Commercial Defense Contractors*, 8.
179. Gansler, *Democracy's Arsenal*, 29–30.
180. Steve Neal, *Happy Days Are Here Again: The 1932 Democratic Convention, the Emergence of FDR—and How America Was Changed Forever* (New York: Harper, 2005).
181. Robert Gottlieb and Robert Kimball, eds., *Reading Lyrics* (New York: Pantheon Books, 2000), 145.
182. Rich and Janos, *Skunk Works*, 73.
183. O'Mara, *The Code*, 224–225, 247.
184. Defense Science Board, *Report of the Defense Science Board Task Force on Defense Semiconductor Dependency* (Washington, DC: Office of the Under Secretary of Defense for Acquisition, February 1987), 1–2.
185. Gholz and Sapolsky, "Restructuring the U.S. Defense Industry," 9.
186. O'Mara, *The Code*, 112.
187. O'Mara, *The Code*, 249.

188. Vincent del Giudice, "Demonstrators Bomb Cars with Pumpkins to Protest President Reagan's 'Star Wars' Space Shield Program," United Press International, October 20, 1986.
189. Associated Press, "138 Protesters Arrested," April 17, 1986.
190. O'Mara, *The Code*, 260.
191. Memo, Harold Brown for Jimmy Carter, December 23, 1980, folder Transition: Issues for President-Elect, Box 80, Brown Papers, LC.
192. Office of Management and Budget, "Budget of the United States Government," https://www.govinfo.gov/app/collection/budget/2025/BUDGET-2025-TAB.
193. Stockholm International Peace Research Institute, "SIPRI Military Expenditure Database," 2024.
194. Gholz and Sapolsky, "Restructuring the U.S. Defense Industry," 5–51.
195. See, for example, Clarence L. Johnson, Memorandum to Col. Leo Geary, Rough Draft, Subject: Method of Contracting between the Government and ADP, August 26, 1964, Box 9, Clarence L. Johnson Papers, Huntington Library; Memorandum from Clarence L. Johnson to All Concerned, Subject: "Idiot" Charts and Related Subjects, January 29, 1963, Box 2, Clarence L. Johnson Papers, Huntington Library.
196. Johnson, Christmas Speech.
197. Letter from Barry Goldwater to Clarence Johnson, January 22, 1975, Box 2, Clarence L. Johnson Papers, Huntington Library. The quote was from Goldwater's remarks that were published in the *Congressional Record*.
198. Rich, "Clarence Leonard (Kelly) Johnson, 1910–1990," 232. Also see the Reagan administration decision to award him the National Security Medal. Memorandum for the President from William P. Clark, Subject: Award of the National Security Medal to Clarence L. (Kelly) Johnson, July 22, 1983, Box 2, Clarence L. Johnson Papers, Huntington Library.

Chapter 3

1. The epigraphs are from A. W. Marshall, "Some Thoughts on Military Revolutions—Second Version," Memorandum for the Record, Office of the Secretary of Defense, August 23, 1993, 4; Word quoted in Barrett Tillman and Stephen Coonts, "First Laser Bombs Bust the Dragon's Jaw," *American Heritage's Invention and Technology* 27, no. 1 (2021), https://www.inventionandtech.com/content/first-laser-bombs-bust-dragons-jaw.
2. H. Norman Schwarzkopf and Peter Petre, *It Doesn't Take a Hero* (New York: Bantam Books, 1992), 414.
3. U.S. Air Force, *Gulf War Air Power Survey*, vol. 2: *Operations and Effects and Effectiveness* (Washington, DC: Office of the Secretary of the Air Force, 1993), 120.

4. Schwarzkopf and Petre, *It Doesn't Take a Hero*, 415.
5. Schwarzkopf and Petre, *It Doesn't Take a Hero*, 415.
6. U.S. Air Force, *Gulf War Air Power Survey*, 2:96.
7. U.S. Air Force, *Gulf War Air Power Survey*, 2:308.
8. John T. Correll, "The Emergence of Smart Bombs," *Air and Space Forces Magazine*, March 1, 2010; Andrew F. Krepinevich Jr., *The Origins of Victory: How Disruptive Military Innovation Determines the Fates of Great Powers* (New Haven, CT: Yale University Press, 2023), 347.
9. Paul G. Gillespie, *Weapons of Choice: The Development of Precision Guided Munitions* (Tuscaloosa: University of Alabama Press, 2006), 75.
10. Tillman and Coonts, "First Laser Bombs Bust the Dragon's Jaw."
11. Gillespie, *Weapons of Choice*, 75.
12. Vernon Loeb, "Bursts of Brilliance," *Washington Post*, December 15, 2002.
13. Weldon Word interview with Paul Gillespie, March 19, 2001, Tyler, Texas, Tape 1, Side A.
14. Word interview with Gillespie, Tape 1, Side A.
15. Gillespie, *Weapons of Choice*, 81, 172.
16. Quoted in Correll, "The Emergence of Smart Bombs," 62.
17. Correll, "The Emergence of Smart Bombs"; Tillmann and Coonts, "First Laser Bombs Bust the Dragon's Jaw."
18. Texas Instruments, "Guidance Device for Sensing Direction of a Detectable Target," Patent application circa 1967, Texas Instruments Records, Southern Methodist University, Dallas, Texas, 10.
19. U.S. Air Force, *Development and Flight Test Evaluation of the M-117 Laser Guided Bomb*, DTIC AD Number 518403 (Baltimore, MD: U.S. Air Force Systems Command, December 1969), 48.
20. Tillmann and Coonts, "First Laser Bombs Bust the Dragon's Jaw."
21. Gillespie, *Weapons of Choice*, 130–131; Correll, "The Emergence of Smart Bombs."
22. Gillespie, *Weapons of Choice*, 130.
23. See, for example, U.S. Air Force, *Gulf War Air Power Survey*, 2:232.
24. Gillespie, *Weapons of Choice*, 163–165.
25. Nikolai Spassky, ed., *Russia's Arms*, vol. 7: *Precision Guided Weapons and Ammunition* (Moscow: Military Parade, 1997), 8.
26. Correll, "The Emergence of Smart Bombs"; Gillespie, *Weapons of Choice*, 137.
27. See, for example, U.S. Air Force, "AGM-65 Maverick," Fact Display Sheet, undated.
28. While an analyst at the RAND Corporation, I had the opportunity to work on several occasions with Andrew Marshall while he was running the Office of Net Assessment. Also see, for example, Andrew F. Krepinevich Jr., "Measures of Power: On the Lasting Value of Net Assessment," *Foreign Affairs*, April 19, 2019.

29. Andrew W. Marshall, Memorandum for the Record, Subject: Some Thoughts on Military Revolutions—Second Version, Office of the Secretary of Defense, August 23, 1993.
30. Marshall, Some Thoughts on Military Revolutions, 2.
31. President Dwight D. Eisenhower created the Advanced Research Projects Agency (ARPA) in 1958 to develop emerging technologies for use by the U.S. military. In 1972, the U.S. Department of Defense added "Defense" to the beginning of the name, so it became DARPA. Nevertheless, there was some pinball in the name of the organization over the next few decades. The name switched back to ARPA in 1993 and then to DARPA in 1996.
32. See, for example, Robert Work, "The Third Offset Strategy," Comments at the Reagan Defense Forum, Simi Valley, CA, November 7, 2015, https://www.defense.gov/News/Speeches/Speech/Article/628246/reagan-defense-forum-the-third-offset-strategy/.
33. William J. Perry, *Written Statement before the Committee on Armed Services, U.S. House of Representatives, Hearings on Military Posture and H.R. 10929* (Washington, D.C., U.S. Government Printing Office, 1978), 1049.
34. See the overview of Soviet thinking in Andrew F. Krepinevich Jr., *The Military-Technical Revolution: A Preliminary Assessment* (Washington, DC: Center for Strategic and Budgetary Assessments, 2002), 1.
35. Marshall, "Some Thoughts on Military Revolutions."
36. Николай Васильевич Огарков [Nikolai Vasilyevich Ogarkov], "Надежная защита мира" [A Reliable Defense to Peace], Красная звезда [*Red Star*], September 23, 1983, 2.
37. Николай Васильевич Огарков [Nikolai Vasilyevich Ogarkov], "Защита социализма: опыт истории и современность" [Defense of Socialism: The Experience of History and the Present], Красная звезда [*Red Star*], May 9, 1984, 2–3. Also see Николай Васильевич Огарков [Nikolai Vasilyevich Ogarkov], История учит бдительность [*History Teaches Vigilance*] (Moscow: Voyenizdat, 1985), 51.
38. Валерий Герасимов [Valery Gerasimov], "Влияние современного характера вооруженной борьбы на направленность строительства и развития Вооруженных Сил Российской Федерации. Приоритетные задачи военной науки в обеспечении обороны страны" [The Influence of the Contemporary Nature of Armed Struggle on the Focus of the Construction and Development of the Armed Forces of the Russian Federation. Priority Tasks of Military Science in Safeguarding the Country's Defense], Вестник Академии Военных Наук [*Journal of the Academy of Military Sciences*], Vol. 62, No. 2, 2018; Valery Gerasimov, "Remarks by Chief of General Staff of the

Russian Federation General of the Army Valery Gerasimov at the Russian Defence Ministry's Board Session," Ministry of Defence of the Russian Federation, November 7, 2017; Виктор Худолеев [Viktor Khudoleev], "Военная наука смотрит в будущее" [Military Science Looks to the Future], Красная звезда [*Red Star*], March 26, 2018.

39. П. Я. Уфимцев [P. Ya. Ufimtsev], "Метод краевых Волн в Физической Теорли Дифрактсли" [Method of Edge Waves in the Physical Theory of Diffraction] (Moscow: Izd-Vn Svptskoe Radio, 1962). The U.S. Force's Foreign Technology Division, at Air Force Systems Command, translated the document.
40. See the interview with Denys Overholser in Capi Lynn, "Secret Weapon for Stealth Tech Is from Dallas," *Statesman Journal*, April 16, 2016.
41. Rich and Janos, *Skunk Works*, 21.
42. Rich and Janos, *Skunk Works*, 20.
43. Rich and Janos, *Skunk Works*, 21.
44. Rich and Janos, *Skunk Works*, 21.
45. Rich and Janos, *Skunk Works*, 26–27.
46. Rich and Janos, *Skunk Works*, 51–52.
47. Keefer, *Harold Brown*, 575.
48. Rich and Janos, *Skunk Works*, 34–35.
49. Center for Strategic and International Studies, "S-200 (SA-5 Gammon)," July 6, 2021, https://missilethreat.csis.org/defsys/s-200-sa-5-gammon/.
50. Clarence L. Johnson Speech to Air Force Academy, September 6, 1979, Box 8, Clarence L. Johnson Papers, Huntington Library, San Marino, CA.
51. Rich and Janos, *Skunk Works*, 28–86.
52. Rich and Janos, *Skunk Works*, 28–105.
53. U.S. Air Force, *Gulf War Air Power Survey*, 2:97.
54. U.S. Air Force, *Gulf War Air Power Survey*, 2:45.
55. U.S. Air Force, *Gulf War Air Power Survey*, 2:115.
56. Krepinevich, *The Origins of Victory*, 388.
57. U.S. Air Force, *Gulf War Air Power Survey*, 2:144, emphasis in original.
58. U.S. Air Force, *Gulf War Air Power Survey*, 2:123.
59. U.S. Air Force, *Gulf War Air Power Survey*, 2:115–146.
60. James A. Winnefeld, Preston Niblack, and Dana J. Johnson, *A League of Airmen: U.S. Air Power in the Gulf War* (Santa Monica, CA: RAND, 1994), 120.
61. U.S. Air Force, *Gulf War Air Power Survey*, 2:236.
62. U.S. Air Force, *Gulf War Air Power Survey*, 2:318.
63. U.S. Air Force, *Gulf War Air Power Survey*, 2:204, 206.
64. U.S. Air Force, *Gulf War Air Power Survey*, 2:271.
65. Gillespie, *Precision Guided Munitions*, 182.
66. Quoted in Richard P. Hallion, *Precision Guided Munitions and the New Era of Warfare* (Fairbairn, Australia: Air Power Studies Centre, 1997), 16.

67. Gillespie, *Precision Guided Munitions*, 182.
68. Krepinevich, *The Origins of Victory*, 390–392.
69. See, for example, U.S. Air Force, *Gulf War Air Power Survey*, 2:96.
70. U.S. Air Force, *Gulf War Air Power Survey*, 2:294.
71. U.S. Air Force, *Gulf War Air Power Survey*, 2:95.
72. Krepinevich, *The Origins of Victory*, 394.
73. Office of the Under Secretary of Defense for Acquisition and Technology, *Report of the Defense Science Board on Tactical Air Warfare* (Washington, DC: Department of Defense, November 1993), 17.
74. U.S. Air Force, *Gulf War Air Power Survey*, 2:95.
75. Krepinevich, *The Origins of Victory*, 393.
76. Quoted in Krepinevich, *The Origins of Victory*, 38–39.
77. William J. Perry, "Desert Storm and Deterrence," *Foreign Affairs*, September 1, 1991.
78. Krepinevich, *The Military-Technical Revolution*, 51.
79. Eliot Cohen, "A Revolution in Warfare," *Foreign Affairs* 75, no. 2 (March–April 1996): 40.
80. Cohen, "A Revolution in Warfare," 40.
81. See, for example, James A. Kitfield, "Another Look at the Air War That Was," *Air Force Magazine*, October 1999; Craig R. Whitney, "Air Wars Won't Stay Risk Free, General Says," *New York Times*, June 18, 1999; Rebecca Grant, "Airpower Made It Work," *Air and Space Forces*, November 1, 1999.
82. Daniel L. Byman and Matthew C. Waxman, "Kosovo and the Great Air Power Debate," *International Security* 24, no. 4 (Spring 2000): 5–38.
83. Cyril Falls, *A Hundred Years of War*, 2nd edition (London: Duckworth, 1961), 13.
84. David A. Deptula, "Air Force Transformation: Past, Present, and Future," *Aerospace Power Journal* 15 (Fall 2001): 86.
85. Marshall, "Some Thoughts on Military Revolutions," 4.
86. Keefer, *Harold Brown*, 577.
87. Keefer, *Caspar Weinberger and the U.S. Military Build-up 1981–1985*, 426–429.

Chapter 4

1. James Clarity, "On Moscow's Streets, Worry and Regret," *New York Times*, December 26, 1991. The epigraphs are from Norman R. Augustine, *Augustine's Laws*, 6th edition (Reston, VA: American Institute of Aeronautics and Astronautics, 1997), 331; Perry quoted in John A. Tirpak, "The Distillation of the Defense Industry," *Air Force Magazine* 81 (July 1998): 56.
2. Serge Schmemann, "The Soviet State, Born of a Dream Dies," *New York Times*, December 26, 1991.
3. Author interview with Norm Augustine, October 11, 2024.

4. Nathaniel C. Nash, "Teaching Marietta the Law of Diversity," *New York Times*, April 27, 1986.
5. Augustine, *Augustine's Laws*, 107.
6. See, for example, Clarence L. Johnson Speech to Air Force Academy, September 6, 1979, Box 8, Clarence L. Johnson Papers, Huntington Library, San Marino, CA.
7. Augustine, *Augustine's Laws*, p. 331.
8. Charles Krauthammer, "The Unipolar Moment," *Foreign Affairs* 70, no. 1 (1990–1991): 23–33.
9. The U.S. defense budget was $325.03 billion in 1992 and $287.96 billion in 1996. See World Bank, Military Expenditures, DataBank, World Development Indicators, 2023, https://databank.worldbank.org/home.
10. Brose, *The Kill Chain*, 47.
11. William Easterly and Stanley Fischer, *The Soviet Economic Decline: Historical and Republican Data*, Policy Research Working Paper 1284 (Washington, DC: World Bank, Policy Research Department, April 1994), Summary Findings.
12. There is a rich historical debate about Soviet economic growth. See, for example, Abram Bergson, "Comparative Productivity: The USSR, Eastern Europe, and the West," *American Economic Review* 77, no. 3 (1987): 342–357; Padma Desai, *The Soviet Economy: Problems and Prospects* (Oxford: Blackwell, 1987); Gur Ofer, "Soviet Economic Growth: 1982–1985," *Journal of Economic Literature* 24, no. 4 (December 1987): 1767–1833; Martin L. Weitzman, "Soviet Postwar Economic Growth and Capital-Labor Substitution," *American Economic Review* 60, no. 5 (December 1970): 676–692.
13. Easterly and Fischer, *The Soviet Economic Decline*, Table 3: Soviet Defense Burden as Share of GDP.
14. Daniel Landau, "The Impact of Military Expenditures on Economic Growth in the Less Developed Countries," *Defence and Peace Economics* 5 (1994): 205–220; Daniel Landau, *The Economic Impact of Military Expenditures*, Policy Research Working Paper 1138 (Washington, DC: World Bank, 1993); Easterly and Fischer, *The Soviet Economic Decline*.
15. Central Intelligence Agency, *Soviet Defense Industry: Confronting Ruin*, SOV 91-10042 (Washington, DC: Directorate of Intelligence, Central Intelligence Agency, October 1991), iii.
16. International Institute for Strategic Studies, *The Military Balance 1993*, 98.
17. Central Intelligence Agency, *Soviet Defense Industry*, 3.
18. Siemon T. Wezeman, "China, Russia, and the Shifting Landscape of Arms Sales," SIPRI, July 5, 2017, https://www.sipri.org/commentary/topical-backgrounder/2017/china-russia-and-shifting-landscape-arms-sales.
19. International Institute for Strategic Studies, *The Military Balance 1993* (London: International Institute for Strategic Studies, 1993), 98.
20. International Institute for Strategic Studies, *The Military Balance 1993*.

21. International Institute for Strategic Studies, *The Military Balance 1993*, 20, 41, 45, 62, 98, 152, 157.
22. International Institute for Strategic Studies, *The Military Balance 1993*.
23. Andrew Scobell, David Lai, and Roy Kamphausen, eds., *Chinese Lessons from Other Peoples' Wars* (Carlisle, PA: Strategic Studies Institute, U.S. Army War College, November 2011).
24. 江泽民 [Jiang Zemin], 江泽民国防和军队建设思想 [*On National Defense and Army Building*] (Beijing: Jiefangjun chubanshe, 2002), 32. On Mao's inspiration from Stalin, see Yi Wang, "'The Backward Will Be Beaten': Historical Lesson, Security, and Nationalism in China," *Journal of Contemporary China* 29, no. 126 (2020): 887–900.
25. 江泽民 [Jiang Zemin], 江泽民文选 [*Jiang Zemin's Selected Works*] (Beijing: Renmin chubanshe, 2006), 1:285.
26. William J. Clinton, "A New Covenant for American Security: Remarks to Students at Georgetown University," Washington, DC, December 12, 1991. Secured from William J. Clinton Presidential Library, Little Rock, Arkansas.
27. Clinton, "A New Covenant for American Security."
28. "Transcript of Speech by Clinton Accepting Democratic Nomination," *New York Times*, July 17, 1992.
29. U.S. Department of Defense, *Report on the Bottom-Up Review* (Washington, DC: U.S. Department of Defense, October 1993).
30. Author interview with John Deutch, September 25, 2024.
31. John Deutch, "Consolidation of the U.S. Defense Industrial Base," *Acquisition Review* 8, no. 3 (Fall 2001): 138–139.
32. See, for example, Gholz and Sapolsky, "Restructuring the U.S. Defense Industry."
33. Thanks to several people, especially Rudy deLeon, for helping identify the date and location of the dinner.
34. Author interview with Norm Augustine, October 11, 2024.
35. Author interview with Norm Augustine, October 11, 2024.
36. On a peace dividend, see Gansler, *Democracy's Arsenal*, xiii, 10.
37. Interview with William Perry, February 21, 2006, William J. Clinton Presidential History Project, Miller Center, University of Virginia, Charlottesville.
38. Jonathan Chang and Meghna Chakrabarti, "'The Last Supper': How a 1993 Pentagon Dinner Reshaped the Defense Industry," interview with Norman Augustine, National Public Radio, March 1, 2023.
39. Author interview with Norm Augustine, October 11, 2024.
40. Interview with William J. Perry, December 2, 2015, Defense Writers Group, Washington, DC, https://www.wbur.org/onpoint/2023/03/01/the-last-supper-how-a-1993-pentagon-dinner-reshaped-the-defense-industry.

41. U.S. Department of Defense, chart briefed at the Pentagon dinner with chief executive officers, May 18, 1993.
42. Author interview with Norm Augustine, October 11, 2024.
43. "'The Last Supper.'"
44. Sandra I. Erwin, "Former SecDef Perry: Defense Industry Consolidation Has Turned Out Badly," *National Defense*, December 2, 2015.
45. Author interview with Norm Augustine, October 11, 2024.
46. Author interview with John Deutch, September 25, 2024.
47. Gansler, *Democracy's Arsenal*, 31–34.
48. Author interview with Norm Augustine, October 11, 2024.
49. John Mintz, "How a Dinner Led to a Feeding Frenzy," *Washington Post*, July 4, 1997.
50. Norman R. Augustine, "Reshaping an Industry: Lockheed Martin's Survival Story," *Harvard Business Review*, May–June 1997, 83–94.
51. Stockholm International Peace Research Institute, *SIPRI Yearbook 1992: World Armaments and Disarmament* (Stockholm: Stockholm International Peace Research Institute, 1992), 392. Stockholm International Peace Research Institute, *SIPRI Yearbook 2000: World Armaments and Disarmament* (Stockholm: Stockholm International Peace Research Institute, 2000), 328.
52. Gholz and Sapolsky, "Restructuring the U.S. Defense Industry," 23.
53. Augustine, "Reshaping an Industry," 83–94.
54. Brose, *The Kill Chain*, 14.
55. Gansler, *Democracy's Arsenal*, 36.
56. Gansler, *Democracy's Arsenal*, 31–34.
57. Gansler, *Democracy's Arsenal*, 36.
58. Gholz and Sapolsky, "Restructuring the U.S. Defense Industry," 11.
59. Gholz and Sapolsky, "Restructuring the U.S. Defense Industry," 11.
60. Gansler, *Democracy's Arsenal*, 31.
61. Peter J. Dombrowski, Eugene Gholz, and Andrew Ross, *Military Transformation and the Defense Industry after Next: The Defense Industrial Implications of Network-Centric Warfare* (Newport, RI: Naval War College), 22.
62. Dombrowski, Gholz, and Ross, *Military Transformation and the Defense Industry after Next*, 22.
63. Author interview with multiple defense and industry officials present at the meeting, 2024.
64. U.S. v. Lockheed Martin Corp. and Northrop Grumman Corp., Verified Complaint, the United States District Court for the District of Columbia, March 23, 1998, U.S. Department of Justice, "Justice Department Goes to Court to Block Lockheed Martin's Purchase of Northrop Grumman," March 23, 1998, https://www.justice.gov/archive/opa/pr/1998/March/131.htm.html.
65. U.S. Department of Justice, "Justice Department Goes to Court to Block Lockheed Martin's Purchase of Northrop Grumman."

NOTES 343

66. See, for example, U.S. v. General Dynamics Corporation and Newport News Shipbuilding Inc., Civil No. 1:01CV02200, U.S. District Court for the District of Columbia, October 23, 2001.
67. Gansler, *Democracy's Arsenal*, 37–38.
68. Jeff Cole and Anne Mari Squeo, "Defense Industry Questions Move by Pentagon to Spur Competition," *Wall Street Journal*, December 3, 1999.
69. Author interview with senior Clinton administration defense official, August 2024.
70. Erwin, "Former SecDef Perry."
71. Deutch, "Consolidation of the U.S. Defense Industrial Base," 138.
72. Author interview with John Hamre, October 21, 2024, and April 17, 2025.
73. Deutch, "Consolidation of the U.S. Defense Industrial Base," 141, 144.
74. Department of Defense, Office of the Inspector General, Audit of Major Defense Acquisition Programs Cycle Time, Report Number D-2002-032, December 28, 2001, 2, https://media.defense.gov/2001/Dec/28/2001714031/-1/-1/1/02-032.pdf. Also see, for example, Donald H. Rumsfeld, *Annual Report to the President and Congress* (Washington, DC: U.S. Department of Defense, 2004), 61. Initial operational capability, or IOC, refers to the time when a product works as designed and is fielded to operational units.
75. Author interview with John Hamre, April 17, 2025.
76. Author interview with John Hamre, April 14, 2025.
77. Author interview with Norm Augustine, October 11, 2024.
78. Author interview with Norm Augustine, October 11, 2024.

Chapter 5

1. Epigraphs are from R. James Woolsey, *Hearing before the Select Committee on Intelligence of the United States Senate, February 2–3, 1993* (Washington, DC: U.S. Government Printing Office, 1993), 76; author interview with Neal Blue, Poway, CA, January 24, 2024.
2. Chris Woods, "The Story of America's First Drone Strike," *Atlantic*, May 30, 2015.
3. Tommy Franks with Malcolm McConnell, *American Soldier* (New York: Regan Books, 2004), 290–291.
4. On the legal debates, for using Predators to conduct strikes see, for example, U.S. Department of the Air Force, e-mails, "Predator Weaponization and INF Treaty," September 2000, National Security Archive, George Washington University, Washington, DC.
5. Franks and McConnell, *American Soldier*, 290.
6. Scott Swanson, "War Is No Video Game—Not Even Remotely," *Breaking Defense*, November 18, 2014.
7. Franks and McConnell, *American Soldier*, 292.
8. Richard Whittle, *Predator: The Secret Origins of the Drone Revolution* (New York: Henry Holt, 2014), 255.
9. Whittle, *Predator*, 256.

10. Franks and McConnell, *American Soldier*, 293.
11. Swanson, "War Is No Video Game."
12. Whittle, *Predator*, 258.
13. Swanson, "War Is No Video Game."
14. Swanson, "War Is No Video Game."
15. There was significant tension involving U.S. military and intelligence officials about the drone strike. For example, some senior officials involved in the air campaign, such as Lieutenant General Chuck Wald, located in U.S. Central Command's Combined Air Operations Center in Saudi Arabia, were surprised and furious about the strike since no one had told them it would happen. Wald was apparently so irate that he threatened to call off bombings on the first night of the war.
16. There are a range of other terms for a drone, such as unmanned aircraft system (UAS), remotely piloted aircraft, and unmanned aerial vehicle. There are also other specific weapons, such as loitering munitions, which have built-in warheads and are designed to wait passively and then strike a target. There are some differences in the terms. For example, the word "system" in "unmanned aircraft system" refers to various components (not just the aircraft), such as the remote pilot station, command-and-control link, payload, and the aircraft itself. I have opted to use the term "drone" in this book, which is more familiar to a wide audience.
17. Diana G. Cornelisse, *Splendid Vision, Unswerving Purpose: Developing Air Power for the United States Air Force during the First Century of Powered Flight* (Wright-Patterson Air Force Base, OH: History Office, Aeronautical Systems Center, Air Force Materiel Command, 2002).
18. The quote comes from Rebecca Grant in the preface to Thomas P. Ehrhard, *Air Force UAVs: The Secret History* (Washington, DC: Mitchell Institute, July 2010), 2.
19. Ehrhard, *Air Force UAVs*, 9.
20. Kelly Johnson to John Parangosky, Wendell Mangis, Col. Leo Geary, October 9, 1962, Box 11, Clarence L. Johnson Papers, Huntington Library, San Marino, CA.
21. Rich and Janos, *Skunk Works*, 22.
22. Tony Landis and Dennis R. Jenkins, *Lockheed Blackbirds* (Plantation, FL: Specialty Press, 1997).
23. Ehrhard, *Air Force UAVs*, 9–10.
24. Rich and Janos, *Skunk Works*, 270.
25. Ehrhard, *Air Force UAVs*, 25.
26. Ehrhard, *Air Force UAVs*, 9.
27. Quoted in "News and Comments," *Army, Navy, Air Force Register*, November 3, 1956, 6.
28. Richard Whittle, "The Man Who Invented the Predator," *Air and Space Magazine*, April 13, 2013.
29. Ehrhard, *Air Force UAVs*, 44.

30. Whittle, "The Man Who Invented the Predator."
31. Whittle, "The Man Who Invented the Predator."
32. Whittle, *Predator*, 9, emphasis in original.
33. Whittle, *Predator*, 14.
34. Quoted in Whittle, *Predator*, 18.
35. Whittle, "The Man Who Invented the Predator."
36. Justin Rowlatt, "The Business and Morality of Drone War," interview with Abraham Karem, BBC, May 7, 2013.
37. Whittle, "The Man Who Invented the Predator."
38. Rowlatt, "The Business and Morality of Drone War."
39. Frank Strickland, "The Early Evolution of the Predator Drone," *Studies in Intelligence* 57, no. 1 (March 2013): 2.
40. Ehrhard, *Air Force UAVs*, 21.
41. Ehrhard, *Air Force UAVs*, 21.
42. Whittle, *Predator*, 59.
43. Whittle, *Predator*, 62.
44. Whittle, *Predator*, 63.
45. Author interview with Neal and Linden Blue, Poway, CA, January 24, 2024.
46. Whittle, "The Man Who Invented the Predator."
47. Author interview with Neal and Linden Blue.
48. John M. Deutch, Memorandum for Assistant Secretary of the Navy for Research, Development, and Acquisition, Subject: Endurance Unmanned Aerial Vehicle (UAV) Program, U.S. Department of Defense, July 12, 1993, National Security Archive, George Washington University.
49. James Neal Blue, George Morgan Browne Jr., Charles White Trippe, and Henry G. Von Maur, "U.S. Students Find Contrasts on Balkan Tour," *New York Times*, July 4, 1955.
50. James Neal Blue, George Morgan Browne Jr., Charles White Trippe, and Henry G. Von Maur, "4 Yale Men Greeted by Afghans with Free Tea and Free Shave," *New York Times*, September 28, 1955.
51. The cover of the April 8, 1957, *Life* magazine (which cost 20 cents) had the title "The Flying Blue Brothers" next to a photo of Neal and Linden in a bright blue aircraft.
52. Author interview with Linden Blue, Poway, CA, January 24, 2024.
53. Strickland, "The Early Evolution of the Predator Drone."
54. Author interview with Neal Blue.
55. Author interview with John Deutch, September 25, 2024.
56. Author interview with Neal Blue.
57. Author interview with John Deutch.
58. Deutch, Memorandum for Assistant Secretary of the Navy for Research, Development, and Acquisition, Subject: Endurance Unmanned Aerial Vehicle (UAV) Program.
59. Author interview with Neal Blue.

60. Whittle, *Predator*, 86.
61. Author interview with Neal Blue.
62. Vanderbilt Television News Archive, "NBC Evening News," October 19, 1994.
63. Strickland, "The Early Evolution of the Predator Drone."
64. Whittle, *Predator*, 108.
65. Headquarters Air Combat Command Langley AFB VA, Cable, Subject: RQ-1, Predator, Program Direction, May 1, 2000, National Security Archive, George Washington University.
66. Author interview with Neal Blue.
67. Headquarters Air Combat Command Langley AFB VA, Cable, Subject: RQ-1.
68. See, for example, Stephen B. Plummer to Henry Obering, email, Subject: RE: Predator Weaponization, September 23, 2000, National Security Archive, George Washington University.
69. John P. Jumper to Michael E. Ryan, email, Subject: FW: Predator Weaponization, September 24, 2000, National Security Archive, George Washington University.
70. Jacques Gansler, Memorandum for Secretary of the Air Force Director, Defense Advanced Research Projects Agency, Subject: Compliance Certification of Predator Tests and the DARPA/USAF X-45A, December 21, 2000, National Security Archive, George Washington University.
71. Michael G. Vickers, *By All Means Available: Memoirs of a Life in Intelligence, Special Operations, and Strategy* (New York: Alfred A. Knopf, 2023), 209.
72. Stephen Hadley to John McLaughlin, Paul Wolfowitz, and Richard Mayers, NSC Memo, Re: Predator, July 11, 2001, National Security Archive, George Washington University, Washington, DC.
73. Michael Mosely to several Members of Congress, Letter, July 11, 2000, National Security Archive, George Washington University; Stephen B. Plummer, Memorandum for HQ US Army Deputy Chief of Staff Operations and Plans, Subject: Request for HELLFIRE II Missiles and Launchers in Support of Expanded Predator UAV Weaponization Demo, July 12, 2001, National Security Archive, George Washington University.
74. Memorandum from John E. Campbell, Department of the Air Force, Headquarters Air Combat Command, Special Order GB-52, September 18, 2001, National Security Archive, George Washington University; Memorandum from John E. Campbell, Department of the Air Force, Headquarters Air Combat Command, Special Order GB-73, May 29, 2002, National Security Archive, George Washington University.
75. Vickers, *By All Means Available*, x.
76. National Intelligence Council, "The Terrorist Threat to the U.S. Homeland," National Intelligence Estimate, July 2007.

77. That data is in current US$. Stockholm International Peace Research Institute, SIPRI Military Expenditures Database, https://www.sipri.org/databases/milex.
78. That data is in current US$. Stockholm International Peace Research Institute, SIPRI Military Expenditures Database, https://www.sipri.org/databases/milex.
79. Gansler, *Democracy's Arsenal*, 46.
80. General Atomics, "GA-ASI's Predator A UAS Series Achieves 300,000 Flight Hours," Press Release, August 30, 2007, https://www.ga.com/ga-asis-predator-a-uas-series-achieves-300000-flight-hours.
81. Tom Vanden Brook, "New Vehicles Protect Marines in 300 Attacks in Iraq Province," *USA Today*, April 19, 2007.
82. Robert M. Gates, *Duty: Memoirs of Secretary at War* (New York: Alfred A. Knopf, 2014), 122.
83. Gates, *Duty*, 124.
84. Gates, *Duty*, 126.
85. Government Accountability Office, *Warfighter Support: DOD Needs Strategic Outcome-Related Goals and Visibility over Its Counter-IED Efforts* (Washington, DC: U.S. Government Accountability Office, February 2012).
86. Gates, *Duty*, 447.
87. Gates, *Duty*, 447.
88. Gates, *Duty*, 448.
89. Defense Science Board, *Transformation: A Progress Assessment*, vol. 2: *Supporting Reports* (Washington, DC: U.S. Department of Defense, April 2006).
90. Defense Science Board, *Transformation: A Progress Assessment*, vol. 1 (Washington, DC: U.S. Department of Defense, February 2006), 33.
91. Gates, *Duty*, 320; Gansler, *Democracy's Arsenal*, 206, 210.
92. Gansler, *Democracy's Arsenal*, 40.
93. Gansler, *Democracy's Arsenal*, 48.
94. Vickers, *By All Means Available*, 228.
95. Vickers, *By All Means Available*, 231.
96. Vickers, *By All Means Available*, 232.
97. Admiral Michael Mullen, Statement before the Senate Armed Services Committee, "The U.S. Strategy in Afghanistan and Iraq," Hearing Before the Committee on Armed Services, United States Senate, 112th Congress, First Session, September 22, 2011 (Washington, DC: U.S. Government Printing Office, 2012) 17.
98. Amnesty International, *"Will I Be Next?" U.S. Drone Strikes in Pakistan* (London: Amnesty International, October 2013), 24.
99. Rowlatt, "The Business and Morality of Drone War."
100. Vickers, *By All Means Available*, 232–233.
101. Vickers, *By All Means Available*, 238.

102. Author interview with Stanley McChrystal, October 3, 2024.
103. "Generation Kill: A Conversation with Stanley McChrystal," *Foreign Affairs* 92, no 2 (March–April 2013): 2.
104. McChrystal, *My Share of the Task*, 153–155.
105. Author interview with Stanley McChrystal.
106. Author interview with Stanley McChrystal.
107. Author interview with Stanley McChrystal.
108. National Security Agency, "National Cryptologic Museum Debuts Service & Sacrifice, Real Time Regional Gateway Exhibits," July 12, 2017, https://www.nsa.gov/Press-Room/News-Highlights/Article/Article/1670296/national-cryptologic-museum-debuts-service-sacrifice-real-time-regional-gateway/.
109. Author interview with Michael Hayden, November 19, 2024.
110. Vickers, *By All Means Available*, 235, 249.
111. On U.S. concerns about Awlaki, see, for example, U.S. Department of Justice, Office of Legal Counsel, "Memorandum for the Attorney General, Re: Applicability of Federal Criminal Laws and the Constitution to Contemplated Lethal Operations Against Shaykh Anwar al-Aulaqi," July 16, 2010.
112. Vickers, *By All Means Available*, 250–251.
113. Vickers, *By All Means Available*, 253.
114. James Clapper, "Worldwide Threat Assessment of the U.S. Intelligence Community for the Senate Select Committee on Intelligence," Office of the Director of National Intelligence, January 31, 2012.
115. Rowlatt, "The Business and Morality of Drone War."
116. McChrystal, *My Share of the Task*, 153–155.
117. Gates, *Duty*, 126.
118. Donald H. Rumsfeld, Secretary's Foreword in *Transformation Planning Guidance* (Washington, DC: U.S. Department of Defense, April 2003), 1, emphasis added. Also see, for example, U.S. Department of Defense, *Quadrennial Defense Review Report* (Washington, DC: U.S. Department of Defense, September 30, 2001).
119. Gansler, *Democracy's Arsenal*, 40.
120. Ashton B. Carter and William J. Perry, "China on the March," *National Interest*, March–April 2007, 21.
121. Gansler, *Democracy's Arsenal*, 45.

Chapter 6

1. The epigraphs are from 习近平 [Xi Jinping], "在《复兴之路》展览的讲话" [Speech at "The Road to Rejuvenation" Exhibition], Beijing, November 29, 2012; Karp quoted in Eve Driver, "9 Candid Insights on the Future of Technology from Palantir CEO Alex Karp," *Better Magazine*, April 5, 2021.

2. 习近平 [Xi Jinping], "在《复兴之路》展览的讲话" [Speech at "The Road to Rejuvenation" Exhibition].
3. Author interview with Robert Work, December 2, 2024.
4. Christopher Darby, "The Unseen Conflict: Strategic Technology Competition," Testimony before the Strategic Technology and Advanced Research Subcommittee, House Permanent Select Committee on Intelligence, February 12, 2020, https://www.congress.gov/116/meeting/house/110489/witnesses/HHRG-116-IG10-Bio-DarbyC-20200212.pdf.
5. Quoted in Anne Laurent, "Raising the Ante," *Government Executive*, June 1, 2002.
6. 习近平 [Xi Jinping], 在第十二届全国人民代表大会第一次会议上的讲话 [Address to the First Session of the 12th National People's Congress], National People's Congress, March 17, 2023.
7. Cai Xia, "The Party That Failed," *Foreign Affairs* 100, no. 1 (January–February 2020): 78–96.
8. Susan L. Shirk, *Overreach: How China Derailed Its Peaceful Rise* (New York: Oxford University Press, 2023), 89–80.
9. "The Decision on Major Issues concerning Comprehensively Deepening Reforms," Third Plenary Session, 18th CPC Central Committee, November 16, 2013.
10. See, for example, Mearsheimer, *The Tragedy of Great Power Politics*, 61; Gilpin, *War and Change in World Politics*; Kennedy, *The Rise and Fall of the Great Powers*.
11. 习近平 [Xi Jinping], 在第十二届全国人民代表大会第一次会议上的讲话 [Address to the First Session of the 12th National People's Congress].
12. Chris Miller, *Chip War: The Fight for the World's Most Critical Technology* (New York: Scribner, 2022), 173.
13. Quoted in Miller, *Chip War*, 173. The quote was from an article in *Survey of the Chinese Mainland Press*, no. 4520 (October 21, 1969): 11–13.
14. Bates Gill, "Chinese Military-Technical Development: The Record for Western Assessments, 1979–1999," in *Seeking Truth from Facts: A Retrospective on Chinese Military Studies in the Post-Mao Era*, ed. James C. Mulvenon and Andrew N. D. Yang, 141–172 (Santa Monica, CA: RAND, 2001).
15. See, for example, "习近平在印度尼西亚国会的演讲" ["Xi Jinping's Speech at the Indonesian Parliament"], 新华 [*Xinhua*], October 3, 2013.
16. See, for example, Jonathan E. Hillman, *The Emperor's New Road: China and the Project of the Century* (New Haven, CT: Yale University Press, 2020).
17. On China's desire to create a world-class military, see, for example, 习近平 [Xi Jinping], 习近平同志在中共中央政治局第八次集体学习时的讲话 [Comrade Xi Jinping's Remarks to the Eighth Collective Study Session of the CCP Politburo], *Pacific Journal*, July 30, 2013, CSIS

Interpret: China Database, https://interpret.csis.org/translations/comrade-xi-jinpings-remarks-to-the-eighth-collective-study-session-of-the-ccp-politburo/.

18. 习近平 [Xi Jinping], 习近平同志在中共中央政治局第八次集体学习时的讲话 [Comrade Xi Jinping's Remarks to the Eighth Collective Study Session of the CCP Politburo].

19. 习近平 [Xi Jinping], 决胜全面建成小康社会夺取新时代中国特色社会主义伟大胜利 [Secure a Decisive Victory in Building a Moderately Prosperous Society in All Respects and Strive for the Great Success of Socialism with Chinese Characteristics for a New Era], Speech at the 19th National Congress of the Communist Party of China, October 18, 2017, CSIS Interpret: China Database, https://interpret.csis.org/translations/secure-a-decisive-victory-in-building-a-moderately-prosperous-society-in-all-respects-and-strive-for-the-great-success-of-socialism-with-chinese-characteristics-for-a-new-era-delivered-at-the/.

20. Office of Naval Intelligence, *The PLA Navy: New Capabilities and Missions for the 21st Century* (Washington, DC: U.S. Navy, December 2014), 13.

21. Tai Ming Cheung, *Fortifying China* (Ithaca, NY: Cornell University Press, 2013); Tai Ming Cheung, *Innovate to Dominate: The Rise of the Chinese Techno-Security State* (Ithaca, NY: Cornell University Press, 2022).

22. Office of the Secretary of Defense, *Military and Security Developments Involving the People's Republic of China 2023: A Report to Congress* (Washington, DC: U.S. Department of Defense, October 2023), 33.

23. Wendy Leutert, "The Political Mobility of China's Central State-Owned Enterprise Leaders," *China Quarterly* 233 (March 2018): 1–2.

24. Mark Ashby et al., *Defense Acquisition in Russia and China* (Santa Monica, CA: RAND, 2021), 22–23; Cheung, *Innovate to Dominate*, 96, 176.

25. Tai Ming Cheung and Thomas G. Mahnken, *The Decisive Decade: United States–China Competition in Defense Innovation and Defense Industrial Policy in and beyond the 2020s* (Washington, DC: Center for Strategic and Budgetary Assessments, 2023), 11; Office of Naval Intelligence, *The PLA Navy*, 33–40.

26. *The Science of Military Strategy* is an important document that conveys the view of key strategists at China's Academy of Military Science, an organization that includes some of the PLA's most influential military thinkers. But it does not contain China's official military strategy. For a good summary of *The Science of Military Strategy*, see, for example, M. Taylor Fravel, "China's Changing Approach to Military Strategy: The Science of Military Strategy from 2001 to 2013," in *China's Evolving Military Strategy*, ed. Joe McReynolds (Washington, DC: Jamestown Foundation, 2016), 40–73.

27. 寿晓松 [Shou Xiaosong, ed.], 战略学 [*The Science of Military Strategy*] (Beijing: Junshi kexue chubanshe, 2013), 105.

28. The PLA did not publicly release the 2014 strategic guideline, but new language in China's 2015 defense white paper suggests that the guideline had evolved. See 中国的军事战略 [*China's Military Strategy*] (Beijing: Guowuyuan xinwen bangongshi, 2015).

29. See, for example, "牢牢把握国防和军队建设的重要指导方针" [Firmly Grasp the Important Guidelines for National Defense and the Army Building], 解放军报 [*PLA Daily*], January 1, 2006. On discussions of "informatization," see Taylor Fravel, *Active Defense: China's Military Strategy since 1949* (Princeton, NJ: Princeton University Press, 2019), 218–219; Joe McReynolds and James Mulvenon, "The Role of Informatization in the People's Liberation Army under Hu Jintao," in *Assessing the People's Liberation Army in the Hu Jintao Era*, ed. Roy Kamphausen, David Lai, and Travis Tanner (Carlisle, PA: Strategic Studies Institute, Army War College, 2014).

30. 中国的军事战略 [*China's Military Strategy*].

31. See, for example, 苗圩 [Miao Wei], 制造强国和网络强国建设迈出坚实步伐: 党的十八大以来我国工业和信息化发展新成就 [Taking Solid Steps in the Construction of a Manufacturing Power and a Cyberpower: New Achievements in China's Industry and Information Technology Development since the 18th Party Congress], Ministry of Industry and Information Technology, October 17, 2017.

32. Alex Stone and Peter Wood, *China's Military-Civil Fusion Strategy* (Montgomery, AL: China Aerospace Studies Institute, U.S. Air Force, June 15, 2020).

33. Xi Jinping, "Uphold and Develop Socialism with Chinese Characteristics," speech to the CCP Central Committee, January 5, 2013.

34. 习近平 [Xi Jinping], "习近平: 积极树立亚洲安全观 共创安全合作新局面" [New Asian Security Concept for New Progress in Security Cooperation], Speech at the Conference on Interaction and Confidence Building Measures in Asia (CICA), May 21, 2014.

35. 寿晓松 [Shou Xiaosong, ed.], 战略学 [*The Science of Military Strategy*], 79.

36. 寿晓松 [Shou Xiaosong, ed.], 战略学 [*The Science of Military Strategy*], 79.

37. Stephen G. Brooks and William C. Wohlforth, "The Once and Future Superpower: Why China Won't Overtake the United States," *Foreign Affairs* 95, no. 3 (May–June 2016): 95.

38. Barry R. Posen, "Command of the Commons: The Military Foundation of U.S. Hegemony," *International Security* 28, no. 1 (Summer 2003): 5–46.

39. Stephen G. Brooks and William C. Wohlforth, "The Rise and Fall of the Great Powers in the Twenty-First Century: China's Rise and the Fate of America's Global Position," *International Security* 40, no. 3 (Winter 2015–2016): 22.

40. Stockholm International Peace Research Institute, SIPRI Military Expenditure Database, accessed March 1, 2024, https://www.sipri.org/databases/milex.
41. See, for example, David Ochmanek, *Restoring the Power Projection Capabilities of the U.S. Armed Forces* (Santa Monica, CA: RAND, 2017); David A. Shlapak and Michael W. Johnson, *Reinforcing Deterrence on NATO's Eastern Flank* (Santa Monica, CA: RAND, 2016).
42. Data from Stockholm International Peace Research Institute, "SIPRI Military Expenditure Database," accessed June 11, 2024; Sam Perlo-Freeman, "Military Expenditure: Overview," in *SIPRI Yearbook 2015* (Stockholm: Stockholm International Peace Research Institute, 2015), https://www.sipri.org/databases/milex; and Organisation for Economic Co-operation and Development, "Main Science and Technology Indicators (MSTI Database)," accessed June 11, 2024, https://www.oecd.org/en/data/datasets/main-science-and-technology-indicators.html.
43. Brooks and Wohlforth, "The Rise and Fall of the Great Powers in the Twenty-First Century," 26. Note that the author updated the numbers for 2014.
44. International Monetary Fund, "World Economic Outlook Database, April 2024," accessed May 23, 2024, https://www.imf.org/en/Publications/SPROLLs/world-economic-outlook-databases#sort=%40imfdate%20descending; World Bank, "GDP (Current US$)," accessed May 23, 2024; Organisation for Economic Co-operation and Development, "OECD Data Explorer," accessed May 23, 2024, https://www.oecd.org/en/data/datasets/oecd-DE.html. Also see Brooks and Wohlforth, "The Rise and Fall of the Great Powers in the Twenty-First Century," 27.
45. Brooks and Wohlforth, "The Rise and Fall of the Great Powers in the Twenty-First Century," 26.
46. World Bank, "High-Technology Exports (Current US$)," accessed June 7, 2024, https://databank.worldbank.org/home.aspx; Organisation for Economic Co-operation and Development, "Main Science and Technology Indicators (MSTI Database)," accessed June 7, 2024, https://www.oecd.org/en/data/datasets/oecd-DE.html; Organisation for Economic Co-operation and Development, "Patents by Technology," accessed June 7, 2024; Science and Engineering Indicators 2020 (Alexandria, VA: National Science Board and National Science Foundation, 2019); UNESCO Institute for Statistics, "9.5.2 Researchers (in Full-Time Equivalent) per Million Inhabitants," accessed June 7, 2024, https://uis.unesco.org/; Science and Engineering Indicators 2024 (Alexandria, VA: National Science Board and National Science Foundation, 2023).
47. World Bank, "High-Technology Exports (Current US$)," accessed June 7, 2024, https://databank.worldbank.org/home.aspx; Organisation for

Economic Co-operation and Development, "Main Science and Technology Indicators (MSTI Database)," accessed June 7, 2024, https://www.oecd.org/en/data/datasets/main-science-and-technology-indicators.html; Organisation for Economic Co-operation and Development, "Patents by Technology," accessed June 7, 2024; *Science and Engineering Indicators 2020* (Alexandria, VA: National Science Board and National Science Foundation, 2019); UNESCO Institute for Statistics, "9.5.2 Researchers (in Full-Time Equivalent) per Million Inhabitants," accessed June 7, 2024, https://uis.unesco.org/; *Science and Engineering Indicators 2024* (Alexandria, VA: National Science Board and National Science Foundation, 2023).
48. Josh Krieger and Josh Lerner, "In-Q-Tel: Innovation on a Mission," Harvard Business School, 822-093, July 20, 2022, 4.
49. Krieger and Lerner, "In-Q-Tel," 4.
50. Gansler, *Democracy's Arsenal*, 157.
51. Gansler, *Democracy's Arsenal*, 199.
52. George Tenet with Bill Harlow, *At the Center of the Storm: My Years at the CIA* (New York: HarperCollins, 2007), 26.
53. "Taking Stock: An Interview with Dr. Ruth David, CIA's Deputy Director for Science and Technology," *Studies in Intelligence* 40, no. 3 (Fall 1996): 63–64.
54. In-Q-Tel Charter Agreement, July 1999. The CIA set up In-Q-Tel as a nonprofit, nonstock corporation exempt from federal income taxation under section 501(c)(3) of the Internal Revenue Code.
55. In-Q-Tel, "In-Q-Tel Announces Christopher Darby as New CEO," August 29, 2006, https://www.iqt.org/library/in-q-tel-announces-christopher-darby-as-new-ceo.
56. John T. Reinert, "In-Q-Tel: The Central Intelligence Agency as Venture Capitalist," *Northwestern Journal of International Law and Business* 33, no. 3 (Spring 2013): 677–709.
57. Author interview with Norm Augustine, October 11, 2024.
58. Michael Morell, "Intelligence Matters," interview with Chris Darby, CBS News, April 19, 2019.
59. Keith W. Crane et al., *Assessment of the Utility of a Government Strategic Investment Fund* (Alexandria, VA: Institute for Defense Analyses, 2019), B-1.
60. Morell, "Intelligence Matters."
61. Author interview with Norm Augustine; author interview with Chris Darby, December 1, 2024.
62. Author interview with Chris Darby.
63. Morell, "Intelligence Matters."
64. Morell, "Intelligence Matters."
65. Quoted in Louisa Thomas, "The Echoes of Loss and Legacy as the NHL Returns," *New Yorker*, October 6, 2024.

66. Author interview with Chris Darby.
67. Terence O'Hara, "In-Q-Tel, CIA's Venture Arm, Invests in Secrets," *Washington Post*, August 14, 2005.
68. Author interview with In-Q-Tel personnel, November 2024; Damian Paletta, "The CIA's Venture-Capital Firm, Like Its Sponsor, Operates in the Shadows," *Wall Street Journal*, August 30, 2016.
69. SAIC, "SAIC Purchases Simulation and Collaboration Product Line from Forterra Systems Inc.," Press Release, February 1, 2010, https://www.prnewswire.com/news-releases/saic-purchases-simulation--collaboration-product-line-from-forterra-systems-inc-83237277.html.
70. Paletta, "The CIA's Venture-Capital Firm, Like Its Sponsor, Operates in the Shadows."
71. O'Hara, "In-Q-Tel, CIA's Venture Arm, Invests in Secrets."
72. O'Hara, "In-Q-Tel, CIA's Venture Arm, Invests in Secrets."
73. Michael Steinberger, "Does Palantir See Too Much?," *New York Times Magazine*, October 21, 2020.
74. Andy Greenberg, "How a 'Deviant' Philosopher Built Palantir, a CIA-Funded Data-Mining Juggernaut," *Forbes*, August 14, 2013.
75. Josh Tyrangiel, "Let AI Remake the Whole U.S. Government (Oh, and Save the Country)," *Washington Post*, March 6, 2024; Greenberg, "How a 'Deviant' Philosopher Built Palantir."
76. Rob Copeland and Maureen Farrell, "Palantir Finally Raking in Cash," *Wall Street Journal*, February 7, 2019.
77. Steinberger, "Does Palantir See Too Much?"
78. Eric Schmidt, remarks during a panel discussion with Debby Hopkins, Kevin Kelly, and Lisa Randall, Techonomy Conference, Lake Tahoe, CA, August 4, 2010.
79. Peter Lyman and Hal R. Varian, *How Much Information 2003?* (Berkeley: School of Information Management and Systems, University of California at Berkeley, 2003).
80. Greenberg, "How a 'Deviant' Philosopher Built Palantir."
81. Quentin Hardy, "Unlocking Secrets, If Not Its Own Value," *New York Times*, May 31, 2014.
82. Greenberg, "How a 'Deviant' Philosopher Built Palantir."
83. See, for example, Palantir, *Palantir Cyber* (Palo Alto, CA: Palantir Technologies, 2013).
84. Greenberg, "How a 'Deviant' Philosopher Built Palantir."
85. See, for example, Palantir, *Palantir Cyber*; Palantir, "The Palantir Platform," undated PowerPoint slides. National Security Archive, George Washington University, Washington, DC.
86. Steinberger, "Does Palantir See Too Much?"
87. Akash Jain, "Forget the AI Race: Let's Invest in a Data Grid for AI," *Cipher Brief*, November 16, 2020.
88. Greenberg, "How a 'Deviant' Philosopher Built Palantir."

89. Greenberg, "How a 'Deviant' Philosopher Built Palantir."
90. See, for example, Palantir USG, Inc. v. United States, Opinion, 2017-1465, September 7, 2018, U.S. Court of Appeals for the Federal Circuit, 904 F.3d 980 (Fed. Cir. 2018).
91. Palantir USG, Inc. vs. United States.
92. Matt Burns, "Leaked Palantir Doc Reveals Uses, Specific Functions and Key Clients," *TechCrunch*, January 11, 2015.
93. Ashlee Vance and Brad Stone, "Palantir, the War on Terror's Secret Weapon," *Bloomberg*, November 22, 2011.
94. Memorandum from Secretary of Defense Chuck Hagel, Subject: The Defense Innovation Initiative, November 14, 2014.
95. Robert Work, "Remarks by Deputy Secretary Work on Third Offset Strategy," Brussels, April 28, 2016, https://www.defense.gov/News/Speeches/Speech/Article/753482/remarks-by-deputy-secretary-work-on-third-offset-strategy/.
96. "An Interview with Robert O. Work," *Joint Forces Quarterly* 84, no. 1 (2017): 6.
97. See, for example, Ochmanek, *Restoring the Power Projection Capabilities of the U.S. Armed Forces*; Shlapak and Johnson, *Reinforcing Deterrence on NATO's Eastern Flank*.
98. Author interview with Robert Work, December 3, 2024.
99. Robert Work, "Video: The Third U.S. Offset Strategy and Its Implications for Partners and Allies," *War on the Rocks*, January 30, 2015.
100. Stockholm International Peace Research Institute, *SIPRI Yearbook 2014: Armaments, Disarmament and International Security* (Stockholm: SIPRI, 2014), 258
101. See Work's concerns about Russia in "Remarks by Deputy Secretary Work on Third Offset Strategy."
102. Robert Work, Remarks at the CNAS Inaugural National Security Forum, Washington, DC, December 14, 2015, https://www.cnas.org/publications/transcript/remarks-by-defense-deputy-secretary-robert-work-at-the-cnas-inaugural-national-security-forum.
103. Gian Gentile et al., *A History of the Third Offset, 2014–1018* (Santa Monica, CA: RAND, 2021).
104. Author interview with Robert Work, December 2, 2024.
105. "An Interview with Robert O. Work," 7.
106. Memorandum from Secretary of Defense Chuck Hagel, Subject: The Defense Innovation Initiative.
107. Defense Science Board, *Summer Study on Autonomy* (Washington, DC: U.S. Department of Defense, June 2016), 1.
108. "An Interview with Robert O. Work," 7.
109. Gentile et al., *A History of the Third Offset*.
110. Work, "Video: The Third U.S. Offset Strategy and Its Implications for Partners and Allies."

111. "An Interview with Robert O. Work," 9.
112. Cheung and Mahnken, *The Decisive Decade*, 8–9. On the Defense Department and innovation see Silicon Valley Defense Working Group, "Department of Defense Emerging Technology Strategy: A Venture Capital Perspective," April 2019, https://www.siliconvalleydefense.org/initiatives/dod-emerging-technology-strategy-venture-capital-perspective.
113. Distributed Maritime Operations included dispersing naval units and weapons systems across a large area to deceive and confuse adversaries, particularly China. Agile Combat Employment involved the U.S. Air Force's use of small, dispersed air bases abroad—rather than relying on large overseas bases—to reduce vulnerability to attack by China and other adversaries.
114. Author interview with Robert Work, December 6, 2024.
115. Author interview with Robert Work, December 2, 2024.
116. Author interview with Robert Work, December 2, 2024.
117. Author interview with Robert Work, December 2, 2024, and April 17, 2025.
118. Author interview with Robert Work, December 2, 2024.
119. Author interview with Robert Work, December 6, 2024, and April 17, 2025.
120. See, for example, Raj M. Shah and Christopher Kirchhoff, *Unit X: How the Pentagon and Silicon Valley Are Transforming the Future of War* (New York: Scribner, 2024); Defense Innovation Unit Experimental, *Annual Report 2017* (Mountain View, CA: DIUx, 2018).
121. Ash Carter, *Inside the Five-Sided Box: Lessons from a Lifetime of Leadership in the Pentagon* (New York: Dutton, 2019).
122. Author interview with Robert Work, December 2, 2024. Also see, for example, Cheryl Pellerin, "DoD Strategic Capabilities Office Gives Deployed Military Systems New Tricks," *DoD News*, April 4, 2016.
123. David E. Sanger and Rick Gladstone, "Piling Sand in a Disputed Sea, China Literally Gains Ground," *New York Times*, April 8, 2015.
124. Asia Maritime Transparency Initiative, *An Accounting of China's Deployments to the Spratly Islands* (Washington, DC: Center for Strategic and International Studies, May 9, 2018); Amanda Macias, "China Quietly Installed Missile Systems on Strategic Spratly Islands in Hotly Contested South China Sea," CNBC, May 2, 2018.
125. "China Tests 'Magic Island Maker,'" *Maritime Executive*, November 4, 2017.
126. Office of the Secretary of Defense, *Military and Security Developments Involving the People's Republic of China 2019: Annual Report to Congress* (Washington, DC: U.S. Department of Defense, 2019), ii.
127. 国务院 [State Council], 中国制造2025 [Made in China 2025], May 19, 2015, https://www.gov.cn/zhengce/content/2015-05/19/content_9784.htm.

128. 国务院 [State Council], 中国制造2025 [Made in China 2025].
129. Christian Curriden, *The Chinese Acquisition Process* (Santa Monica, CA: RAND, 2023), 6.
130. Tai Ming Cheung, *Strengths and Weaknesses of China's Defense Industry and Acquisition System and Implications for the United States* (Monterey, CA: Naval Postgraduate School, June 2018).
131. Cheung, *Strengths and Weaknesses of China's Defense Industry and Acquisition System and Implications for the United States*.
132. Keith Crane et al., *The Effectiveness of China's Industrial Policies in Commercial Aviation Manufacturing*, RR-245 (Santa Monica, CA: RAND, 2014).
133. Cheung, Strengths and Weaknesses of China's Defense Industry and Acquisition System and Implications for the United States.
134. Ashby, *Defense Acquisition in Russia and China*, 24.
135. 国家统计局 [National Bureau of Statistics], 中国统计年鉴*2017* [*China Statistical Yearbook 2017*] (Beijing: China Statistics Press, 2017).
136. Ashby, *Defense Acquisition in Russia and China*, 19.
137. Tai Ming Cheung, "An Uncertain Transition: Regulatory Reform and Industrial Innovation in China's Defense Research, Development, and Acquisition System," in *Forging China's Military Might*, ed. Tai Ming Cheung (Baltimore: Johns Hopkins University Press, 2014).
138. Ashby, *Defense Acquisition in Russia and China*, 21.
139. Ashby, *Defense Acquisition in Russia and China*, 22.
140. Cheung, "An Uncertain Transition."
141. Christina Larson, "With a Stealth Fighter, China Points to Advances in Its Arms Industry," *New York Times*, November 11, 2014.
142. See, for example, Deborah Kidwell, *Cyber Espionage for the Chinese Government* (Quantico, VA: U.S. Air Force, Office of Special Investigations, September 17, 2020). Also see the plea agreement between the U.S. government and Su Bin at United States of America v. Su Bin, SA CR No. 14-131, March 23, 2016 U.S. District Court for the Central District of California,; U.S. Department of Justice, "Chinese National Pleads Guilty to Conspiring to Hack into U.S. Defense Contractors' Systems to Steal Sensitive Military Information," March 23, 2016, https://www.justice.gov/archives/opa/pr/chinese-national-pleads-guilty-conspiring-hack-us-defense-contractors-systems-steal-sensitive#:~:text=Su%20Bin%2C%20also%20known%20as,for%20National%20Sec urity%20John%20P.
143. Office of the Secretary of Defense, *Military and Security Developments Involving the People's Republic of China 2019*, 48.
144. Government Accountability Office, *Military Airlift: Cost and Complexity of the C-17 Aircraft Research and Development Program* (Washington, DC: Government Accountability Office, March 1991); Congressional Research Service, *Air Force F-22 Fighter Program* (Washington, DC: U.S.

Government Printing Office, July 2013); John R. Hoehn, *F-35 Joint Strike Fighter (JSF) Program* (Washington, DC: Congressional Research Service, May 2022).

145. Xi Jinping, Speech at the World Economic Forum, Davos, January 17, 2017.
146. Xi Jinping, Speech at the Work Conference for Cyber Security and Informatization, April 19, 2016.

Chapter 7

1. Epigraphs are from Elon Musk (@elonmusk), Twitter, October 22, 2019; U.S. Space Force, *U.S. Space Force Commercial Space Strategy: Accelerating the Purposeful Pursuit of Hybrid Space Architectures* (Washington, DC: U.S. Space Force, April 8, 2024), 2.
2. Matthew Weinzierl, "Space, the Final Economic Frontier," *Journal of Economic Perspectives* 32, no. 2 (Spring 2018): 173.
3. Quoted in Eric M. Johnson and Joey Roulette, "Musk Shakes Up SpaceX in Race to Make Satellite Launch Window: Sources," Reuters, November 1, 2018.
4. Walter Isaacson, *Elon Musk* (New York: Simon and Schuster, 2023), 322.
5. Isaacson, *Elon Musk*, 355.
6. See, for example, Valerie Insinna, "SpaceX Beating Russian Jamming Attack Was 'Eyewatering': DoD Official," Breaking Defense, April 20, 2022.
7. Andy Pasztor, "Third Failed SpaceX Launch Raises Concerns about Rocket," *Wall Street Journal*, August 4, 2008.
8. Matthew Weinzierl and Mehak Sarang, "The Commercial Space Age Is Here," *Harvard Business Review*, February 12, 2021.
9. Isaacson, *Elon Musk*, 284–285.
10. Marina Temkin, "Sizing Up the Boom in Defense Tech," PitchBook, November 2, 2023, https://pitchbook.com/news/articles/defense-tech-boom-ukraine-china-israel.
11. John F. Sargent Jr., *Department of Defense Research, Development, Test, and Evaluation (RDT&E): Appropriations Structure* (Washington, DC: Congressional Research Service, September 7, 2022), 18.
12. The data is from PitchBook.
13. See, for example, U.S. Space Force, U.S. *Space Force Commercial Space Strategy*.
14. Bruce Berkowitz, *The National Reconnaissance Office at 50 Years: A Brief History*, Second Edition (Chantilly, VA: Center for the Study of National Reconnaissance, National Reconnaissance Office, July 2018), 11–12.
15. On the history of U.S. space, see, for example, Henry R. Hertzfeld, "Globalization, Commercial Space, and Spacepower in the USA," *Space Policy* 23 (2007): 210–220.

16. President's Commission on Implementation of United States Space Exploration Policy, *A Journey to Inspire, Innovate, and Discover*, (Washington, DC: U.S. Government Printing Office, June 2004), 7.
17. Matthew Weinzierl, "Blue Origin, NASA, and New Space," Harvard Business School Case 716-037, May 2016.
18. Elon Musk, "Blastar," *PC and Office Technology*, December 1984, 6.
19. Elon Musk (@elonmusk), "Just dropping some friends off at the pool," Twitter, November 29, 2021.
20. Elon Musk (@elonmusk), "At least 50% of my tweets were made on a porcelain throne," Twitter, November 22, 2021; Elon Musk (@elonmusk), "It gives me solace," Twitter, November 22, 2021.
21. Eric Berger, *Liftoff: Elon Musk and the Desperate Early Days That Launched SpaceX* (New York: HarperCollins, 2021).
22. Isaacson, *Elon Musk*, 77.
23. Isaacson, *Elon Musk*, 183.
24. Isaacson, *Elon Musk*, 183.
25. Pasztor, "Third Failed SpaceX Launch Raises Concerns about Rocket."
26. *Orbital Transportation Service: A New Era in Spaceflight*, NASA/SP-2014-617 (Washington, DC: National Aeronautics and Space Administration, February 2014).
27. Matthew Weinzierl et al., "Your Company Needs a Space Strategy. Now," *Harvard Business Review*, 100(6): 80–91, November–December 2022; Bryce Tech, *Start-up Space: Update on Investment in Commercial Space Ventures* (Alexandria, VA: Bryce Tech, 2023).
28. Weinzierl, "Space, the Final Economic Frontier," 173–192.
29. Quoted in Christian Davenport and Brian Fung, "Elon Musk's SpaceX to Sue Government over Space Launch Contract," *Washington Post*, April 25, 2014.
30. Quoted in Doug Cameron, "SpaceX to Drop Pentagon Suit Over Rocket Deals," *Wall Street Journal*, January 23, 2015.
31. Isaacson, *Elon Musk*, 321.
32. SpaceX, "Improving Starlink's Latency," undated, https://www.starlink.com/public-files/StarlinkLatency.pdf.
33. A chunk of the leadership team fired by Musk went on to start Project Kuiper, a subsidiary of Amazon to establish a satellite internet constellation in low Earth orbit.
34. Isaacson, *Elon Musk*, 389.
35. Reed Albergotti, "Who's the Boss? At Musk's Companies He Is, but Also Young Loyalists," *Washington Post*, April 28, 2022; SAE International, *Formula SAE Student Handbook: Formula SAE Michigan, Brooklyn, Michigan, May 13–16, 2015*, 80, https://www.sae.org/images/cds/selfservice/430417418_2015_FSAE_Student_Handbook.pdf.
36. Isaacson, *Elon Musk*, 232.
37. "Polar Explorer Erling Kagge on the Value of Silence," *Financial Times*, January 19, 2018.

38. Isaacson, *Elon Musk*, 323–324.
39. Isaacson, *Elon Musk*, 284–286.
40. Kenneth Chang, "SpaceX Launches 60 Starlink Internet Satellites into Orbit," *New York Times*, May 23, 2019.
41. Defense Intelligence Agency, *Russia Military Power: Building a Military to Support Great Power Aspirations* (Washington, DC: Defense Intelligence Agency, 2017), 42.
42. U.S. Space Force, *U.S. Space Force Commercial Space Strategy*.
43. Isaacson, *Elon Musk*, 612.
44. Space Foundation, *The Space Report 2022* Q2 (Colorado Springs, CO: Space Foundation, July 2022).
45. Bryce Tech, *Start-up Space: Update on Investment in Commercial Space Ventures* (Alexandria, VA: Bryce Tech, 2022).
46. Bryce Tech, *Start-up Space*, 2022, 2.
47. Bryce Tech, *Start-up Space*, 2023.
48. Bryce Tech, *Smallsats by the Numbers* (Alexandria, VA: Bryce Tech, 2021); Christian Davenport, "The Revolution in Satellite Technology Means There Are Swarms of Spacecraft No Bigger Than a Loaf of Bread in Orbit," *Washington Post*, April 6, 2021.
49. Brukardt, "How Will the Space Economy Change the World?"
50. Ryan D'Agostino, "Elon Musk: Why I'm Building the Starship Out of Stainless Steel," *Popular Mechanics*, January 22, 2019; Thomas G. Roberts, "Space Launch to Low Earth Orbit: How Much Does It Cost?" Center for Strategic and International Studies, September 1, 2022, https://aerospace.csis.org/data/space-launch-to-low-earth-orbit-how-much-does-it-cost/.
51. U.S. Department of Defense, *Commercial Space Integration Strategy* (Washington, DC: U.S. Department of Defense, 2024), 1.
52. U.S. Department of Defense, *Commercial Space Integration Strategy*; U.S. Space Force, *U.S. Space Force Commercial Space Strategy*.
53. The data comes from the Union of Concerned Scientists, UCS Satellite Database, accessed July 9, 2024, https://www.ucs.org/resources/satellite-database.
54. Bryce Tech, *Smallsats by the Numbers*.
55. Kari A. Bingen, "2024: The Year that Launched China's Commercial Space Sector?" in Craig Cohen and Alexander Kisling, eds., *The China Challenge* (Washington, DC: Center for Strategic and International Studies, 2024), 19-22.
56. State Council Information Office of the People's Republic of China, *China's Space Program: A 2021 Perspective* (Beijing: State Council Information Office of the People's Republic of China, January 2022).
57. Katharina Buchholz, "The Countries with the Most Satellites in Space," *Forbes*, September 29, 2023.
58. Todd Harrison et al., *Space Threat Assessment 2022* (Washington, DC: Center for Strategic and International Studies, April 2022).

59. Harrison et al., *Space Threat Assessment 2022*.
60. Florian Vidal and Roman Privalov, "Russia in Outer Space: A Shrinking Space Power in the Era of Global Change," *Space Policy*, August 2023.
61. Office of the Director of National Intelligence, *Annual Threat Assessment of the U.S. Intelligence Community* (Washington, DC: Office of the Director of National Intelligence, February 2022).
62. Harrison et al., *Space Threat Assessment 2022*.
63. Harrison et al., *Space Threat Assessment 2022*.
64. Peter Garretson, ed., *State of the Space Industrial Base 2022: Winning the New Space Race for Sustainability, Prosperity and the Planet* (Mountain View, CA: Defense Innovation Unit, U.S. Space Force, and Air Force Research Laboratory, August 2022), 7.
65. Ali Javaheri, "Vertical Snapshot: Defense Tech," PitchBook, May 22, 2023, 4, https://pitchbook.com/news/reports/2023-vertical-snapshot-defense-tech.
66. See the interview with Gordon Moore in Rodes Fishburne and Michael Malone, "Laying Down the Laws," *Forbes*, February 21, 2000.
67. Tad Friend, "Tomorrow's Advance Man," *New Yorker*, May 11, 2015.
68. See, for example, Peter Thiel with Blake Masters, *Zero to One: Notes on Startups, or How to Build the Future* (New York: Crown Business, 2014), 83.
69. See, for example, Aileen Lee, "Welcome to the Unicorn Club: Learning from Billion-Dollar Startups," *Tech Crunch*, November 2, 2023. Aileen Lee was the founder of Cowboy Ventures, a Palo Alto–based venture capital fund.
70. Friend, "Tomorrow's Advance Man."
71. The data is from PitchBook.
72. Quoted in Steven Overly, "Peter Thiel Explains Why His Company's Defense Contracts Could Lead to Less War," *Washington Post*, November 8, 2016.
73. Temkin, "Sizing Up the Boom in Defense Tech."
74. Katherine Boyle (@KTmBoyle), "To those at Reagan National Defense Forum #RNDF, if there's one BLUF you take away from the weekend, you should know: Time is running out with Silicon Valley," Twitter, December 3, 2021.
75. Roberto J. González, *How Big Tech and Silicon Valley Are Transforming the Military-Industrial Complex* (Providence, RI: Watson Institute of International and Public Affairs, Brown University, April 17, 2024).
76. Charles W. Mahoney, Benjamin K. Tkach, and Craig J. Rethmeyer, "Defense Contractors, Private Equity Firms, and US National Security," *Journal of Global Security Studies* 7, no. 4 (December 2022): 1–20. Also see, for example, Bryan Burrough and John Helyar, *Barbarians at the Gate: The Fall of RJR Nabisco* (New York: Harper & Row, 1990).

77. In contrast to private equity firms, which generally invest in established companies, venture capital firms typically invest in start-up companies. Charles W. Mahoney, Benjamin K. Tkach, and Craig J. Rethmeyer, "Leveraging National Security: Private Equity and Bankruptcy in the United States Defense Industry," *Business and Politics* 26, no. 3 (September 2024): 362-381; Mahoney, Tkach, and Rethmeyer, "Defense Contractors, Private Equity Firms, and US National Security," 1–20.
78. Felix Barber and Michael Goold, "The Strategic Secret of Private Equity," *Harvard Business Review*, 85(9): 53–61 September 2007.
79. Lorenzo Scarazzato and Madison Lipson, "Going Private (Equity): A New Challenge to Transparency in the Arms Industry," Stockholm International Peace Research Institute, March 1, 2023, https://www.securityincontext.com/posts/going-private-equity-a-new-challenge-to-transparency-in-the-arms-industry.
80. KPMG, *The Private Equity Opportunity in Aerospace and Defense* (Amstelveen: KPMG, 2021).
81. KPMG, *Future of M&A in Aerospace and Defense* (Amstelveen: KPMG, 2021); KPMG, *The Private Equity Opportunity in Aerospace and Defense*.
82. The data is from PitchBook. Also see Mahoney, Tkach, and Rethmeyer, "Leveraging National Security," 362–381.
83. KPMG, *Future of M&A in Aerospace and Defense*.
84. The data is from PitchBook. Also see Scarazzato and Lipson, "Going Private (Equity)"; Mahoney, Tkach, and Rethmeyer, "Leveraging National Security," 362–381.
85. Fairmont Consulting Group, *Mergers and Acquisitions: 2021's Most Interesting Transactions in Aerospace, Defense, & Government Services* (Boston: Fairmont Consulting Group, January 2022).
86. Colin Kellaher, "KPS Capital to Buy Humvee Maker AM General from MacAndrews & Forbes," *Wall Street Journal*, July 22, 2020.
87. Mahoney, Tkach, and Rethmeyer, "Defense Contractors, Private Equity Firms, and US National Security," 1–20.
88. Cheryl Pellerin, "Project Maven to Deploy Computer Algorithms to War Zone by Year's End," *U.S. Department of Defense News*, July 21, 2017.
89. Letter from Google employees to Sundar Pichai, 2018. Several news sources published the text of the letter; see, for example, Scott Shane and Daisuke Wakabayashi, "'The Business of War': Google Employees Protest Work for the Pentagon," *New York Times*, April 4, 2018.
90. Letter from Google employees to Sundar Pichai, 2018.
91. Google, "AI Principles: Objectives for Building Beneficial AI," 2018.
92. KPMG, The *Private Equity Opportunity in Aerospace and Defense*.
93. González, *How Big Tech and Silicon Valley Are Transforming the Military-Industrial Complex*.
94. Mahoney, Tkach, and Rethmeyer, "Defense Contractors, Private Equity Firms, and US National Security," 1–20.

95. KPMG, *The Private Equity Opportunity in Aerospace and Defense.*
96. U.S. Department of Defense, *Summary of the 2018 National Defense Strategy of the United States of America: Sharpening the American Military's Competitive Edge* (Washington, DC: U.S. Department of Defense, 2018), 1.
97. Eric Lipton, "New Spin on a Revolving Door: Pentagon Officials Turned Venture Capitalists," *New York Times*, December 30, 2023.
98. See, for example, Ickes, *The Secret Diary of Harold L. Ickes*, 3:212, 398; Goodwin, *Walter Lippmann*, 270. Henry Lewis Stimson Papers, Sterling Library, Yale University, New Haven, CT; Henry Stimson, *Diary*, May 29, 1941.
99. Dwight D. Eisenhower, "Scientific and Technological Resources as Military Assets," Memorandum for Directors and Chiefs of War Department General and Special Staff Divisions and Bureaus and the Commanding Generals of the Major Commands, Office of the Chief of Staff, War Department, Washington, DC, April 30, 1946; Louis Galambos ed., *The Papers of Dwight D. Eisenhower*, Vol. VII, The Chief of Staff (Baltimore: Johns Hopkins University Press, 1978), 1046–1049.
100. Dwight D. Eisenhower, Farewell Address, January 17, 1961. Speech Series, Box 38, Final TV Talk, Dwight D. Eisenhower Presidential Library, Abilene, KS.
101. Charles J. Dunlap Jr., "The Military-Industrial Complex," *Daedalus* 140, no. 3 (Summer 2011): 135–147.
102. Eisenhower, Farewell Address.
103. Lipton, "New Spin on a Revolving Door."
104. Lipton, "New Spin on a Revolving Door."
105. Letter from Senator Elizabeth Warren to Heidi Shyu, Under Secretary of Defense for Research and Engineering, Department of Defense, July 9, 2023, https://www.warren.senate.gov/imo/media/doc/2023.07.09%20Letter%20to%20DoD%20on%20Strategic%20Capital%20Office%20Conflict%20of%20Interest %20Concerns.pdf.
106. James Fallows, "The Military-Industrial Complex," *Foreign Policy*, no. 133 (November–December 2022): 47–48.
107. Mahoney, Tkach, and Rethmeyer, "Leveraging National Security," 362-381.
108. Steven N. Kaplan and Per Strömberg, "Leveraged Buyouts and Private Equity," *Journal of Economic Perspectives* 23, no. 1 (2009): 121–146.
109. Mahoney, Tkach, and Rethmeyer, "Defense Contractors, Private Equity Firms, and US National Security," 1–20.
110. See, for example, William D. Hartung, *Prophets of War: Lockheed Martin and the Making of the Military-Industrial Complex* (New York: Nations Books, 2011); James Ledbetter, *Unwarranted Influence: Dwight D. Eisenhower and the Military-Industrial Complex* (New Haven, CT: Yale University Press, 2011).

111. James Ledbetter, "What Ike Got Right," *New York Times*, December 13, 2010.
112. Ron Paul, "More Blank Checks to the Military-Industrial Complex," Antiwar.com, May 25, 2010.
113. "Elon Musk's U.S. Department of Defense Contracts," Reuters, February 11, 2025; Joey Roulette and Marisa Taylor, "Musk's SpaceX Is Building Spy Satellite Network for U.S. Intelligence Agency, Sources Say," Reuters, March 16, 2024.
114. The data comes from the Union of Concerned Scientists, UCS Satellite Database, accessed July 9, 2024, https://www.ucs.org/resources/satellite-database.
115. Molly Ball, Jeffrey Kluger, and Alejandro de la Garza, "Time 2021 Person of the Year: Elon Musk," *Time*, December 13, 2021.

Chapter 8

1. Epigraphs are from "A Front Row View of the NSA: Reflections from General Paul M. Nakasone," CSIS, August 10, 2023, https://www.csis.org/analysis/front-row-view-nsa-reflections-general-paul-m-nakasone; Brad Smith, "Countering Foreign Information Operations: Developing a Whole Society Approach to Build Resilience," Reagan Institute, June 22, 2022, https://www.reaganfoundation.org/events/countering-foreign-information-operations?srsltid=AfmBOoqmoh6XcqbfSfDIVa2HGkoafzWHnWhDncZKtCW8WC3nY5VqYxjF.
2. Microsoft, *Defending Ukraine: Early Lessons from the Cyber War* (Redmond, WA: Microsoft, June 22, 2022), 7.
3. See, for example, Andy Greenberg, *Sandworm: A New Era of Cyberwar and the Hunt for the Kremlin's Most Dangerous Hackers* (New York: Doubleday, 2019).
4. Office of the Director of National Intelligence, *Annual Threat Assessment of the U.S. Intelligence Community 2022* (Washington, DC: Office of the Director of National Intelligence, February 2022), 12.
5. Microsoft, *Special Report: Ukraine* (Redmond, WA: Digital Security Unit, Microsoft, April 27, 2022).
6. Brad Smith, "Digital Technology and the War in Ukraine," Microsoft, February 28, 2022, https://blogs.microsoft.com/on-the-issues/2022/02/28/ukraine-russia-digital-war-cyberattacks/.
7. David E. Sanger, Julian E. Barnes, and Kate Conger, "As Tanks Rolled into Ukraine, So Did Malware. Then Microsoft Entered the War," *New York Times*, February 28, 2022.
8. Microsoft, *Special Report: Ukraine*, 3.
9. Tom Burt, "The Hybrid War in Ukraine," Microsoft, April 27, 2022, https://blogs.microsoft.com/on-the-issues/2022/04/27/hybrid-war-ukraine-russia-cyberattacks/.

10. Mykhailo Federov (@FederovMykhailo), Twitter, 4:51 a.m. Eastern, July 4, 2002.
11. Microsoft, *Defending Ukraine*, 14.
12. Office of the Director of National Intelligence, *Annual Threat Assessment of the U.S. Intelligence Community 2022*, 8.
13. John Lambert, LinkedIn post, September 2, 2022.
14. Lambert, LinkedIn post.
15. Lambert, LinkedIn post.
16. Peter Loftus and Frank ByrtDow, "Nimda Virus Continues to Spread, Is Called One of Worst Bugs Ever," *Wall Street Journal*, September 20, 2001.
17. Robert A Guth, "Keeping Your PC Safe from the Blaster Worm," *Wall Street Journal*, August 14, 2003.
18. Lambert, LinkedIn post.
19. Author interview with John Lambert, October 1, 2024.
20. U.S. Department of Justice, "Six Russian GRU Officers Charged in Connection with Worldwide Deployment of Destructive Malware and Other Disruptive Actions in Cyberspace," Office of Public Affairs, October 19, 2020, https://www.justice.gov/archives/opa/pr/six-russian-gru-officers-charged-connection-worldwide-deployment-destructive-malware-and.
21. Anton Cherepanov, *GreyEnergy: A Successor to BlackEngergy*, GreyEnergy White Paper (Bratislava: ESET, October 2018).
22. Jack Stubbs and Pavel Polityuk, "Family Firm in Ukraine Says It Was Not Responsible for Cyber Attack," Reuters, July 3, 2017.
23. MalwareHunterTeam (@malwarehunterteam), "Here is an IDR based heatmap for past 24 hours of XData ransomware. 91% of victims from Ukraine, 3% from RU. @BleepinComputer @demonslay335," Twitter, May 19, 2017.
24. David Maynor et al., "The MeDoc Connection," *Talos* blog, Cisco, July 5, 2017, https://blog.talosintelligence.com/the-medoc-connection/; Anton Ivanov and Orkhan Mamedov, "ExPetr/Petya/NotPetya Is a Wiper, Not Ransomware," *Securelist* blog, AO Kaspersky Lab, June 28, 2017, https://securelist.com/expctrpctyanotpctya-is-a-wiper-not-ransomware/78902/.
25. Author interview with John Lambert.
26. Lennart Maschmeyer, "The Subversive Trilemma: Why Cyber Operations Fall Short of Expectations," *International Security* 46, no. 2 (Fall 2021): 51–90.
27. On the damages caused by NotPetya, see Matteo Crosignani, Marco Macchiavelli, and André F. Silva, *Pirates without Borders: The Propagation of Cyberattacks through Firms' Supply Chains* (New York: Federal Reserve Bank of New York, July 2021).
28. Bharath Aiyer et al., "New Survey Reveals $2 Trillion Market Opportunity for Cybersecurity Technology and Service Providers," McKinsey & Company, October 27, 2022, https://www.mckinsey.com/capabilities/

29. "A New Global Ranking of Cyber-Power Throws Up Some Surprises," *Economist*, September 17, 2020.
30. Julia Voo, Irfan Hemani, and Daniel Cassidy, *National Cyber Index 2022* (Cambridge, MA: Belfer Center for Science and International Affairs, Harvard University, September 2022).
31. Office of the Director of National Intelligence, *Annual Threat Assessment of the U.S. Intelligence Community 2022*, 8.
32. Daniel R. Coats, *Worldwide Threat Assessment of the U.S. Intelligence Community* (Washington, DC: Office of the Director of National Intelligence, January 29, 2019), 6.
33. U.S. Department of Homeland Security, *Ransomware Attacks on Critical Infrastructure Fund DPRK Malicious Cyber Activity* (Washington, DC: Cybersecurity and Infrastructure Security Agency, U.S. Department of Homeland Security, February 9, 2023).
34. Microsoft, "Decoding Nobelium," *Security Unlocked: The Microsoft Security Podcast*, December 8, 2021.
35. Microsoft, "Decoding Nobelium."
36. Alexandra Roland, "How Internet Telemetry Data Becomes Threat Intelligence," Microsoft Defender Threat Intelligence Blog, October 25, 2022, https://techcommunity.microsoft.com/blog/defenderthreatintelligence/how-internet-telemetry-data-becomes-threat-intelligence/3657881.
37. John Lambert, "Microsoft Digital Defense Report Shares New Insights on Nation-State Attacks," Microsoft, October 25, 2021, https://www.microsoft.com/en-us/security/blog/2021/10/25/microsoft-digital-defense-report-shares-new-insights-on-nation-state-attacks/.
38. Roland, "How Internet Telemetry Data Becomes Threat Intelligence."
39. Microsoft, "Decoding Nobelium."
40. Microsoft, "Decoding Nobelium."
41. White House, "Fact Sheet: Imposing Costs for Harmful Foreign Activities by the Russian Government," April 15, 2021, https://bidenwhitehouse.archives.gov/briefing-room/statements-releases/2021/04/15/fact-sheet-imposing-costs-for-harmful-foreign-activities-by-the-russian-government/; John Lambert, "The Hunt for Nobelium, the Most Sophisticated Nation-State Attack in History," Microsoft, 10, 2021, https://www.microsoft.com/en-us/security/blog/2021/11/10/the-hunt-for-nobelium-the-most-sophisticated-nation-state-attack-in-history/.
42. National Counterintelligence and Security Center, Office of the Cyber Executive, "SolarWinds Orion Software Supply Chain Attack," August 19, 2021, https://www.dni.gov/files/NCSC/documents/SafeguardingOurFuture/SolarWinds%20Orion%20Software%20Supply%20Chain%20Attack.pdf.

43. Lambert, "The Hunt for Nobelium."
44. White House, "Fact Sheet: Imposing Costs for Harmful Foreign Activities by the Russian Government"; Joint Statement by the Federal Bureau of Investigation, the Cybersecurity and Infrastructure Security Agency, the Office of the Director of National Intelligence, and the National Security Agency, January 5, 2021.
45. Microsoft, *Special Report: Ukraine*.
46. Author interview with John Lambert.
47. Microsoft, *Special Report: Ukraine*.
48. Microsoft, *Special Report: Ukraine*.
49. On Aqua Blizzard and the FSB, see Microsoft Threat Intelligence, "ACTINIUM Targets Ukrainian Organizations," February 4, 2022, https://www.microsoft.com/en-us/security/blog/2022/02/04/actinium-targets-ukrainian-organizations/; Microsoft Threat Intelligence, "Russian Threat Actors Dig In, Prepare to Seize on War Fatigue," December 7, 2023, https://www.microsoft.com/en-us/security/security-insider/intelligence-reports/russian-threat-actors-dig-in-prepare-to-seize-on-war-fatigue.
50. On Forest Blizzard and the GRU, see U.S. Department of Justice, "Justice Department Conducts Court-Authorized Disruption of Botnet Controlled by the Russian Federation's Main Intelligence Directorate of the General Staff (GRU)," February 15, 2024, https://www.justice.gov/archives/opa/pr/justice-department-conducts-court-authorized-disruption-botnet-controlled-russian.
51. Microsoft, *Special Report: Ukraine*.
52. Ofir Dor, "How Threat Intelligence Became Key to Microsoft's Computer Security," *Globes: Israeli Business News*, September 1, 2022.
53. Microsoft, *Special Report: Ukraine*.
54. Microsoft, "How Technology Helped Ukraine Resist during Wartime," January 20, 2023, https://news.microsoft.com/en-cee/2023/01/20/how-technology-helped-ukraine-resist-during-wartime/.
55. Jack Watling and Nick Reynolds, *Operation Z: The Death Throes of an Imperial Delusion* (London: Royal United Services Institute for Defence and Security Studies, April 22, 2022), 2.
56. For an overview of the initial stages of the war, see, for example, Owen Matthews, Overreach: The Inside Story of Putin's War against Ukraine (London: Mudlark, 2023); Hal Brands, ed., *War in Ukraine: Conflict, Strategy, and the Return of a Fractured World* (Baltimore: Johns Hopkins University Press, 2024); Yaroslav Trofimov, *Our Enemies Will Vanish: The Russian Invasion and Ukraine's War of Independence* (New York: Penguin Press, 2024).
57. Sam Jones, John Paul Rathbone, and Demetri Sevastopulo, "'A Serious Failure': Scale of Russia's Military Blunders Becomes Clear," *Financial Times*, March 12, 2022.
58. Watling and Reynolds, *Operation Z*, 3.

59. U.K. Ministry of Defense, Defence Intelligence, Twitter post, March 1, 2022; Center for Strategic and International Studies.
60. Author interviews with senior Ukrainian military and defense officials in Ukraine, April 2024.
61. Mason Clark, George Barros, and Kateryna Stepanenko, *Russian Offensive Campaign Assessment, February 25* (Washington, DC: Institute for the Study of War, February 25, 2022), 4.
62. Watling and Reynolds, *Operation Z*, 4–5.
63. While Moscow's specific strategic objectives are unclear, captured FSB documents strongly suggest that the goal of Russian military operations in February 2022 was decapitation of the Ukrainian government and installation of a pro-Russian regime. See, for example, FSB documents highlighted in Greg Miller and Catherine Belton, "Russia's Spies Misread Ukraine and Misled Kremlin as War Loomed," *Washington Post*, August 19, 2022.
64. Karoun Demirjian and Dan Lamothe, "Pentagon: Russia Has Fully Withdrawn from Kyiv, Chernihiv," *Washington Post*, April 6, 2022.
65. Mary Ilyushina et al., "Russia Vows New Push for Eastern Ukraine," *Washington Post*, April 19, 2022.
66. Thomas Gibbons-Neff, Michael Schwirtz, and Eric Schmitt, "More Cautious, Russia Embarks on New Phase of Ukraine War," *New York Times*, April 19, 2022.
67. Karolina Hird, Mason Clark, and George Barros, *Russian Offensive Campaign Assessment, April 29* (Washington, DC: Institute for the Study of War, April 29, 2022).
68. "Senior Defense Official Holds a Background Briefing, April 28, 2022," U.S. Department of Defense, April 28, 2022, https://www.defense.gov/News/Transcripts/Transcript/Article/3014131/senior-defense-official-holds-a-background-briefing-april-28-2022/.
69. "Britain Says Russia Has Lost a Third of Its Forces in Ukraine," Reuters, May 15, 2022.
70. For data on the number of military personnel, defense budget, economy, and military capabilities, see International Institute for Strategic Studies, *The Military Balance* (London: International Institute for Strategic Studies, 2022), 164–217. https://www.sipri.org/databases/milex; "SIPRI Military Expenditure Database," Stockholm International Peace Research Institute; "The World Factbook," Central Intelligence Agency. https://www.cia.gov/the-world-factbook/.
71. Microsoft, *Special Report: Ukraine*.
72. Microsoft, *Special Report: Ukraine*.
73. Author interview with John Lambert.
74. Microsoft, *Defending Ukraine*, 9.
75. Matt Grossman, "Microsoft to Buy Cybersecurity Firm RiskIQ," *Wall Street Journal*, July 12, 2021.

76. RiskIQ, *RiskIQ for Government Overview* (San Francisco: RiskIQ, 2019).
77. Dor, "How Threat Intelligence Became Key to Microsoft's Computer Security."
78. Author interview with John Lambert.
79. Microsoft, *Defending Ukraine*, 9.
80. Microsoft, *Special Report: Ukraine*.
81. David Vergun, "Partnering with Ukraine on Cybersecurity Paid Off, Leaders Say," *DOD News*, U.S. Department of Defense, December 3, 2022; Patty Nieberg, "'Hunt Forward' Cyber Teams Have Deployed to 24 Countries, Including Ukraine," *Task and Purpose*, September 28, 2023; Gordon Corera, "Inside a U.S. Military Cyber Team's Defence of Ukraine," BBC, October 29, 2022.
82. Сергей Чекинов и Сергей Богданов [Sergey Chekinov and Sergey Bogdanov], "Эволюция сущности и содержания понятия 'война' в XXI столетии" [The Evolution of the Nature and the Content of the Concept of "War" in the Twenty-First Century"], Военная мысль [*Military Thought*], no. 1 (2017), 30–43.
83. Author interview with John Lambert.
84. Dor, "How Threat Intelligence Became Key to Microsoft's Computer Security."
85. See, for example, John Arquilla and David Ronfeldt, "Cyberwar Is Coming," *Comparative Strategy* 12, no. 2 (1993): 141–165; Richard A. Clarke and Robert K. Knake, *Cyber War: The Next Threat to National Security and What to Do about It* (New York: HarperCollins, 2010); James J. Wirtz, "The Cyber Pearl Harbor," in *Cyber Analogies*, ed. Emily O. Goldman and John Arquilla, 7–14 (Monterey, CA: U.S. Naval Postgraduate School, 2014).
86. For an overview of these issues, see Maschmeyer, "The Subversive Trilemma."
87. Dor, "How Threat Intelligence Became Key to Microsoft's Computer Security."
88. Author interview with John Lambert.

Chapter 9

1. Epigraphs are from Palmer Luckey (@PalmerLuckey), "Anduril has won billions of dollars in contracts," Twitter, November 18, 2024; author interview with William LaPlante, September 26, 2023.
2. Michael Kofman, "The Russia-Ukraine War: Military Operations and Battlefield Dynamics," in *War in Ukraine: Conflict, Strategy, and the Return of a Fractured World*, ed. Hal Brands (Baltimore: Johns Hopkins University Press, 2024), 113; Mari Saito, Maria Tsvektova, and Anton Zverev, "Abandoned Russian Base Holds Secret of Retreat in Ukraine," Reuters, October 26, 2022.

3. "Ukraine Liberated Hundreds of Settlements in Past Month, Kyiv Says, as Russian Strikes Continue," Radio Free Europe/Radio Liberty Ukrainian Service, October 14, 2022; "Ukraine Must Demine 12,000 km² of Liberated Areas in Kharkiv Region: Official," Reuters, September 21, 2022; Amy Woodyatt et al., "November 11, 2022, Russia-Ukraine News," CNN, November 11, 2022.
4. See, for example, U.S. Department of Defense, "Fact Sheet on U.S. Security Assistance to Ukraine," November 20, 2024, https://media.defense.gov/2024/Nov/20/2003590818/-1/-1/0/UKRAINE-FACT-SHEET-PDA-70.PDF.
5. Valerie Insinna, "Northrop Grumman Finalizes Deal to Coproduce Ammo in Ukraine," *Breaking Defense*, July 11, 2024.
6. Palmer Luckey (@PalmerLuckey), "Never judge people for their body or what they wear!," Twitter, April 6, 2022.
7. Steven Levy, "Palmer Luckey Says Working with Weapons Isn't as Fun as VR," *Wired*, March 14, 2022.
8. Erica Sweeney and Poll Thompson, "Who Is Palmer Luckey? The Founder of Oculus and Anduril," *Business Insider*, June 23, 2024; Kirsten Grind and Keach Hagey, "Why Did Facebook Fire a Top Executive? Hint: It Had Something to Do with Trump," *Wall Street Journal*, November 11, 2018.
9. Facebook, "Facebook to Acquire Oculus," March 25, 2014; Gideon Resnick and Ben Collins, "Palmer Luckey: The Facebook Near-Billionaire Secretly Funding Trump's Meme Machine," *Daily Beast*, April 13, 2017; Grind and Hagey, "Why Did Facebook Fire a Top Executive?"
10. Sharon Weinberger and Heather Somerville, "Tech Bros Are Betting They Can Help Win a War with China," *Wall Street Journal*, August 9, 2024.
11. Quoted in Weinberger and Somerville, "Tech Bros Are Betting They Can Help Win a War with China."
12. Vago Muridian, *Defense and Aerospace Report Podcast*, interview with Trae Stephens, June 28, 2022.
13. Emily Chang, "Can Anduril Reboot the U.S. Defense Industry?," *Bloomberg*, interview with Palmer Luckey, May 15, 2024.
14. Schumpeter, "Palmer Luckey and Anduril Want to Shake Up Armsmaking," *Economist*, June 20, 2024.
15. See, for example, Aaron Mehta, "Anduril Nabs DIU 'Service' Contract for Counter-Drone AI," *Breaking Defense*, July 27, 2021.
16. Schumpeter, "Palmer Luckey and Anduril Want to Shake Up Armsmaking."
17. González, *How Big Tech and Silicon Valley Are Transforming the Military-Industrial Complex*.
18. Chris Brose, "Rebuilding the Arsenal of Democracy: The Imperative to Strengthen America's Defense Industrial Base and Workforce," Testimony before the Select Committee on the CCP, U.S. House of Representatives, December 5, 2024, https://www.youtube.com/watch?v

=KXoji1sAXl8https://selectcommitteeontheccp.house.gov/sites/evo-subsites/selectcommitteeontheccp.house.gov/files/evo-media-document/Brose%20Testimony%20--%20CCP%20Select%20Committee%20Hearing%20-%20Rebuilding%20the%20Arsenal%20of%20Democracy.pdf; Anduril Industries, "Anduril Lattice Counter Drone System," demo video, January 23, 2022.
19. Sweeney and Thompson, "Who Is Palmer Luckey?"; Contrary Research, Anduril Industries, April 11, 2023, https://research.contrary.com/company/anduril.
20. Levy, "Palmer Luckey Says Working with Weapons Isn't as Fun as VR"; Berber Jin, "Defense Startup Founder Predicts Russia Will Use 'Tactical Nuclear Weapon,'" *Wall Street Journal*, October 26, 2022.
21. Weinberger and Somerville, "Tech Bros Are Betting They Can Help Win a War with China."
22. Weinberger and Somerville, "Tech Bros Are Betting They Can Help Win a War with China."
23. National Cyber Security Centre, "Russia behind Cyber Attack with Europe-Wide Impact an Hour before Ukraine Invasion," May 10, 2022, https://www.ncsc.gov.uk/news/russia-behind-cyber-attack-with-europe-wide-impact-hour-before-ukraine-invasion.
24. Juan Andrés Guerrero-Saade, "AcidRain: A Modern Wiper Rains Down on Europe," *SentinelOne*, March 31, 2022.
25. Isaacson, *Elon Musk* 428.
26. Isaacson, *Elon Musk*, 428–429.
27. Kevin Collier, "Starlink Internet Becomes a Lifeline for Ukrainians," *NBC News*, April 29, 2022.
28. Elon Musk (@elonmusk), "Bad reporting by FT," Twitter, October 7, 2022.
29. Adela Suliman, "SpaceX Questions Ukraine's Use of Starlink for War," *Washington Post*, February 9, 2023.
30. Matthew Fitzgerald and Cort Thompson, "What Does Starlink's Participation in Ukrainian Defense Reveal about U.S. Space Policy?," *Lawfare*, April 26, 2022; Collier, "Starlink Internet Becomes a Lifeline for Ukrainians."
31. "UkraineX: How Elon Musk's Space Satellites Changes the War on the Ground," *Politico*, June 8, 2022.
32. On the use of Starlink for offensive operations—and SpaceX concerns—see Matthew Luxmoore and Ievgeniia Sivorka, "Soldiers in Ukraine Say Some Drones Affected after SpaceX Limits Starlink," *Wall Street Journal*, February 10, 2023.
33. See Juana Summers, "This U.S. Company Is Helping Arm Ukraine against Russia—with AI Drones," interview with Palmer Luckey, National Public Radio, July 11, 2024.
34. Vera Bergengruen, "How Tech Giants Turned Ukraine into an AI War Lab," *Time*, February 8, 2024.

35. Vera Bergengruen, "The First AI War," *Time*, February 26, 2024.
36. Bergengruen, "How Tech Giants Turned Ukraine into an AI War Lab."
37. "Baykar Bayraktar Tactical UAS," Janes, July 29, 2022, https://www.janes.com/.
38. Michael C. Horowitz, "Battles of Precise Mass: Technology Is Remaking War—and America Must Adapt," *Foreign Affairs*, 103, no. 6 (November–December 2024): 34–40; "Switchblade," Janes, July 15, 2022, https://www.janes.com/.
39. See, for example, Gerald Gilbert, *The Evolution of Tactics* (London: Hugh Rees, 1907); Jonathan M. House, *Toward Combined Arms Warfare: A Survey of 20th-Century Tactics, Doctrine, and Organization* (Leavenworth, KS: Combat Studies Institute, U.S. Army Command and General Staff College, August 1984).
40. See the Nagorno-Karabakh case study in Seth G. Jones et al., *Combined Arms Warfare and Unmanned Aircraft Systems* (Lanham, MD: Rowman & Littlefield, November 2022).
41. Jeffrey Edmonds and Samuel Bendett, *Russian Military Autonomy in a Ukraine Conflict* (Arlington, VA: Center for Naval Analyses, February 2022).
42. Miko Vranic, "Ukraine Conflict: Russia Weaponizes Orlan-10 UAV," *Janes Defence Weekly*, May 20, 2022; Zachary Kallenborn, "Seven (Initial) Drone Warfare Lessons from Ukraine," Modern War Institute, May 12, 2022, https://mwi.westpoint.edu/seven-initial-drone-warfare-lessons-from-ukraine/; Alexander Freund, "Ukraine Using Starlink for Drone Strikes," DW, March 27, 2022, https://www.dw.com/en/ukraine-is-using-elon-musks-starlink-for-drone-strikes/a-61270528.
43. Yaroslav Trofimov, "As Ukraine Holds the Line in Donbas, Russian Fire Shatters Cities in Moscow's Path," *Wall Street Journal*, August 10, 2022.
44. Laura Kahn, "How Ukraine Is Using Drones against Russia," Council on Foreign Relations, March 2, 2022, https://www.cfr.org/in-brief/how-ukraine-using-drones-against-russia; Sebastien Roblin, "Russia's War in Ukraine," Inside Unmanned Systems, June 30, 2022, https://insideunmannedsystems.com/russias-war-in-ukrainer/; Kallenborn, "Seven (Initial) Drone Warfare Lessons from Ukraine."
45. Roblin, "Russia's War in Ukraine."
46. On Kropyva—including its use on Ukrainian computers and tablets—see Trofimov, "Ukraine's Drone Spotters on Front Lines Wage New Kind of War."
47. Author interviews with members of Aerorozvidka, Kyiv, Ukraine, April 2024.
48. U.S. Department of Defense, "Fact Sheet on U.S. Security Assistance to Ukraine," December 21, 2022, https://media.defense.gov/2022/Dec/21/2003136422/-1/-1/0/20221216-UKRAINE-FACT-SHEET-PDA28-USAI1.PDF.

49. The data comes from Seth G. Jones, Riley McCabe, and Alexander Palmer, *Ukrainian Innovation in a War of Attrition* (Washington, DC: Center for Strategic and International Studies, February 2023).
50. Lloyd J. Austin III, "The Common Defence," Remarks at the Reagan National Defense Forum, December 7, 2024; author interviews with senior U.S. and U.K. officials, November and December 2024, https://www.defense.gov/News/Speeches/Speech/Article/3989588/the-common-defence-remarks-by-secretary-of-defense-lloyd-j-austin-iii-at-the-re/.
51. In the Molotov-Ribbentrop Pact, named after the two main individuals who negotiated the agreement (German Foreign Minister Joachim von Ribbentrop and Soviet Foreign Minister Vyacheslav Molotov), Germany and the Soviet Union agreed not to attack each other. In a secret protocol, they also divided Eastern Europe into spheres of influence, with the two countries sharing Poland and the Soviet Union getting Finland, Lithuania, Latvia, Estonia, and Bessarabia.
52. "Research Starters: Worldwide Deaths in World War II," National WWII Museum, New Orleans, LA. https://www.nationalww2museum.org/students-teachers/student-resources/research-starters/research-starters-worldwide-deaths-world-war; "Estimated Number of Military and Civilian Fatalities Due to the Second World War per Country or Region between 1939 and 1945," Statista, accessed December 2, 2024, https://www.statista.com/statistics/1293510/second-world-war-fatalities-per-country/.
53. G. F. Krivosheev, ed., *Soviet Casualties and Combat Losses in the Twentieth Century* (Mechanicsburg, PA: Stackpole Books, 1997), 281–290; Lester W. Grau and Michael A. Gress, eds., *The Soviet-Afghan War: How a Superpower Fought and Lost* (Lawrence: University of Kansas Press, 2002); Lester W. Grau, *The Bear Went over the Mountain: Soviet Combat Tactics in Afghanistan* (New York: Frank Cass, 1998), xiv; John B. Dunlop, "How Many Soldiers and Civilians Died during the Russo-Chechen War of 1994–1996?," *Central Asia Survey* 19, nos. 3–4 (2000): 329–339; Simon Saradzhyan, "Army Learned Few Lessons from Chechnya," *Moscow Times*, March 9, 2005; Robert M. Kennedy, *Russia in Afghanistan and Chechnya: Military Strategic Culture and the Paradoxes of Asymmetric Conflict* (Carlisle, PA: Strategic Studies Institute, U.S. Army War College, February 2003); Robyn Dixon et al., "Russia's War Dead Belie Its Slogan That No One Is Left Behind," *Washington Post*, April 8, 2022; Mark Galeotti, *The Modern Russian Army 1992–2016* (New York: Osprey, 2017); "Chechen Official Puts Death Toll for 2 Wars at Up to 160,000," *New York Times*, August 16, 2005; Nabi Abdullaev, "Death Toll Put at 160,000 in Chechnya," *Moscow Times*, August 16, 2005; "Russia Lost 64 Troops in Georgia War, 283 Wounded," Reuters, February 21, 2009; "Nearly 585,000 People Have Been Killed since the Beginning of the Syrian Revolution," Syrian Observatory for Human Rights, January 4, 2020; United Nations, Office of the High Commissioner for Human Rights, "Conflict-Related

Civilian Casualties in Ukraine," January 27, 2022; Ukraine Ministry of Defence, Twitter post, February 17, 2023, 1:45 a.m.; "The Total Combat Losses of the Enemy from 24.02.22 to 18.02.23," Ukraine Ministry of Defence; Helene Cooper, Eric Schmitt, and Thomas Gibbons-Neff, "Soaring Death Toll Gives Grim Insight into Russian Tactics," *New York Times*, February 2, 2023; Ольга Ившина [Olga Ivshina], "В пять раз больше, чем обычно: что известно о потерях России в Украине к середине февраля" [Five Times More Than Usual: What Is Known about the Losses of Russia in Ukraine by Mid-February], BBC, February 17, 2023; Anatoly Kurmanaev and Constant Méheut, "Ukraine is Losing Fewer Soldiers Than Russia—But It's Still Losing the War," *New York Times*, January 23, 2025, https://www.nytimes.com/2025/01/23/world/europe/ukraine-russia-soldiers-loss.html; Ольга Ившина [Olga Ivshina], "90 тысяч погибших: что известно о потерях России в Украине к концу января" [90,000 Dead: What Is Known About Russia's Losses in Ukraine by the End of January], BBC, January 24, 2025, https://www.bbc.com/russian/articles/c93lklg89e80; Anatoly Kurmanaev, "Russia Has Suffered Colossal Losses in Ukraine. Is Its Army Depleted?" *New York Times*, November 19, 2024, https://www.nytimes.com/2024/11/19/world/europe/russia-troops-losses-ukraine.html; analysis of data collected by Russian news outlet Mediazona and the BBC Russian Service; "UK Ministry of Defence, X post, May 8, 2025," https://x.com/DefenceHQ/status/1920532827344400527; author estimates based on interviews with U.S. and European government officials, 2022–2025.

54. Author interviews with officials in the U.S. Department of Defense and defense industry, November and December 2022.

55. Author interviews with officials in the U.S. Department of Defense and defense industry.

56. U.S. Department of Defense, "Fact Sheet on U.S. Security Assistance to Ukraine," December 21, 2022.

57. U.S. Department of Defense, "Fact Sheet on U.S. Security Assistance to Ukraine," December 21, 2022.

58. See, for example, U.S. Department of Defense, "Under Secretary of Defense (Acquisition and Sustainment) LaPlante and Deputy Under Secretary of Defense (Policy) Baker Hold a Media Roundtable on the Recent Meeting of the National Armaments Directors under the Auspices of the Ukraine Defense Contract Group," September 30, 2022, https://www.defense.gov/News/Transcripts/Transcript/Article/3176537/under-secretary-of-defense-acquisition-and-sustainment-laplante-and-deputy-unde/; "Pentagon's Top Buyer Is 'Worried' about Small Suppliers," *Defense News*, September 7, 2022; U.S. Department of Defense, "Secretary of Defense Lloyd J. Austin III and Chairman of the Joint Chiefs of Staff General Mark A. Milley, Press Conference Following the Ukraine Defense

59. Contact Group Meeting, October 12, 2022, Brussels, Belgium," October 12, 2022, https://www.defense.gov/News/Transcripts/Transcript/article/3186611/secretary-of-defense-lloyd-j-austin-iii-and-chairman-of-the-joint-chiefs-of-sta/.

59. The data on systems committed to Ukraine is from U.S. Department of Defense, "Fact Sheet on U.S. Security Assistance to Ukraine," December 21, 2022, https://media.defense.gov/2022/Dec/21/2003136422/-1/-1/0/20221216-UKRAINE-FACT-SHEET-PDA28-USAI1.PDF. For the status of U.S. inventories, the author interviewed officials in the U.S. Department of Defense and the defense industry.

60. See, for example, Joe Gould, "Army Plans 'Dramatic' Ammo Production Boost as Ukraine Drains Stocks," *Defense News*, December 5, 2022. Companies that won contracts to produce and deliver 155mm artillery shells included General Dynamics Ordnance and Tactical Systems, American Ordnance, and IMT Defense.

61. U.S. Army, "Army Awards $431 Million Contract for HIMARS," U.S. Army Public Affairs, December 2, 2022, https://www.army.mil/article/262457/army_awards_431_million_contract_for_himars.

62. Office of the Under Secretary of Defense for Acquisition and Sustainment, *State of Competition within the Defense Industrial Base* (Washington, DC: U.S. Department of Defense, February 2022), 18.

63. Gates, *Duty*, 126.

64. Author interview with individuals from multiple U.S. defense companies; Linda J. Bilmes, William D. Hartung, and Stephen Semler, *United States Spending on Israel's Military Operations and Related U.S. Operations in the Region, October 7, 2023–September 30, 2024* (Providence, RI: Watson Institute for International and Public Affairs, Brown University, October 7, 2024).

65. "Top 100 Defense Companies," *Defense News*, 2024, https://people.defensenews.com/top-100/.

66. Quoted in Anders Fogh Rasmussen, "The West Needs a War Footing," *Wall Street Journal*, March 28, 2024.

67. Alex Vershinin, "The Return of Industrial Warfare," RUSI, June 17, 2022, https://www.rusi.org/explore-our-research/publications/commentary/return-industrial-warfare.

Chapter 10

1. See, for example, Ministry of National Defense the People's Republic of China, "东部战区圆满完成 '联合利剑-2024B' 演习" [The PLA Eastern Theater Command Successfully Completed "Joint Sword-2024B" Drills], October 14, 2024. Epigraphs are from Statement of John C. Aquilino, U.S. Indo-Pacific Command Posture, March 20, 2024, https://www.armed-services.senate.gov/imo/media/doc/aquilino_statement.pdf; Frank Kendall III, "Accelerating Readiness for Great Power Competition," Air,

Space & Cyber Conference, National Harbor, MD, September 11, 2023, https://www.airandspaceforces.com/watch-read-secretary-kendall-great-power-competition/.
2. Rupert Wingfield-Hayes and Nick Marsh, "Taiwan's President Vows to Resist 'Annexation,'" BBC News, October 10, 2024.
3. Dzirhan Mahadzir, "China Targets Taiwan in Major Military Exercise, Pentagon Condemns 'Irresponsible' Action," *USNI News*, October 14, 2024.
4. Center for Strategic and International Studies.
5. "东部战区已展开环台岛战备警巡和'联合利剑' 演习" [The Eastern Theater Command Has Launched Combat Readiness Patrols and "Joint Sword" Exercises around the Island of Taiwan], 新华网 [Xinhuanet], April 8, 2023.
6. Bonny Lin et al., *Analyzing China's Escalation after Taiwan President Tsai's Transit through the United States* (Washington, DC: Center for Strategic and International Studies, June 2023).
7. Statement of John C. Aquilino.
8. "PLA Eastern Theater Command Conducts Joint Exercises around Taiwan Island," *Xinhua*, August 4, 2022.
9. "东部战区将在台岛周边开展一系列联合军事行动" [The Eastern Theater Command Will Launch a Series of Joint Military Operations around Taiwan Island], 新华网 [Xinhuanet], August 2, 2022.
10. "Japan Protests after Chinese Missiles Land in Its Exclusive Economic Zone," Associated Press, August 4, 2022.
11. Statement of Admiral Samuel J. Paparo, commander of U.S. Indo-Pacific Command, before the House Armed Services Committee, April 9, 2025, https://armedservices.house.gov/uploadedfiles/indopacom_posture_statement_2025.pdf.
12. Michael Evans, "China Leaves U.S. Trailing in Race to Build Warships," *The Times* (London), July 12, 2023.
13. Testimony of Admiral Samuel J. Paparo, commander of U.S. Indo-Pacific Command, before the Senate Armed Services Committee, April 10, 2025, https://www.armed-services.senate.gov/imo/media/doc/4102025fulltranscript.pdf; Statement of John C. Aquilino.
14. Cameron Holt, Keynote Address, Government Contract Pricing Summit, June 24, 2022, https://www.youtube.com/watch?v=uyxJ36I2dLo.
15. Juro Osawa, "Huawei Ad Debate Offers Look Inside Company," *Wall Street Journal*, July 19, 2015.
16. Amir Mizrach and Sam Schechner, "Huawei's Elusive Ren Zhengfei Steps Out in London," *Wall Street Journal*, May 2, 2014; Raymond Zhong, "Huawei's Reclusive Founder Rejects Spying and Praises Trump," *New York Times*, January 15, 2019.
17. Chris Miller, *Chip War: The Fight for the World's Most Critical Technology* (New York: Scribner, 2022), 269.

18. 任正非 [Ren Zhengfei], "我的父亲母亲" [My Father and My Mother], 华为人 [*Huawei People*], February 8, 2001.
19. 任正非 [Ren Zhengfei], "我的父亲母亲" [My Father and My Mother].
20. Miller, *Chip War*, 270–271.
21. Tim Bowler, "Ren Zhengfei: Huawei's Reclusive Founder," BBC, February 18, 2019; Carter Center, *Who Is Ren Zhengfei?* (Atlanta, GA: Carter Center, August 2021).
22. Karishma Vaswani, "Huawei: The Story of a Controversial Company," BBC, March 6, 2019.
23. Carter Center, *Who Is Ren Zhengfei?*
24. 任正非 [Ren Zhengfei], "赴美考察散记" [Notes from a Trip to America], 华为人 [*Huawei People*], January 28, 1994. *Huawei People* is an internal Huawei newspaper.
25. Miller, *Chip War*, 272.
26. "A Transcript of Ren Zhengfei's Interview," *Economist*, September 12, 2019.
27. Miller, *Chip War*, 270.
28. Carter Center, *Who Is Ren Zhengfei?*
29. Quoted in Raymond Zhong, "Huawei's 'Wolf Culture' Helped It Grow, and Got It into Trouble," *New York Times*, December 18, 2018.
30. Tian Tao and Wu Chunbo, *The Huawei Story* (Thousand Oaks, CA: Sage, 2015).
31. Zhong, "Huawei's 'Wolf Culture' Helped It Grow, and Got It into Trouble."
32. Liza Lin, Stu Woo, and Raffaele Huang, "The U.S. Wanted to Knock Down Huawei. It's Only Getting Stronger," *Wall Street Journal*, July 29, 2024; Chuin-Wei Yap, "State Support Helped Fuel Huawei's Global Rise," *Wall Street Journal*, December 25, 2019.
33. George Gilder, "Huawei Is an Asset, Not a Threat," *Wall Street Journal*, May 20, 2019; Dan Strumpf, "How Huawei Took Over the World," *Wall Street Journal*, December 25, 2018; Zhong, "Huawei's 'Wolf Culture' Helped It Grow, and Got It into Trouble."
34. Rachel Lerman, "Jury Awards T-Mobile $4.8M in Trade-Secrets Case against Huawei," *Seattle Times*, May 18, 2017.
35. U.S. Department of Justice, "Chinese Telecommunications Device Manufacturer and Its U.S. Affiliate Indicted for Theft of Trade Secrets, Wire Fraud, and Obstruction of Justice," January 28, 2019, https://www.justice.gov/archives/opa/pr/chinese-telecommunications-device-manufacturer-and-its-us-affiliate-indicted-theft-trade; U.S. Department of Justice, "Chinese Telecommunications Conglomerate Huawei and Huawei CFO Wanzhou Meng Charged with Financial Fraud," January 28, 2019, https://www.justice.gov/archives/opa/pr/chinese-telecommunications-conglomerate-huawei-and-huawei-cfo-wanzhou-meng-charged-financial.
36. Miller, *Chip War*, 272.

37. Christopher Marquis and Kunyuan Qiao, *Mao and Markets: The Communist Roots of Chinese Enterprise* (New Haven, CT: Yale University Press), 9, 11.
38. "A Transcript of Ren Zhengfei's Interview," *Economist*, September 12, 2019.
39. Liza Lin and Raffaele Huang, "Huawei Bounces Back from U.S. Sanctions as Profit Doubles," *Wall Street Journal*, March 29, 2024; Michelle Toh, "Huawei Wants to Go All In on AI for the Next Decade," CNN, September 21, 2023.
40. Author interviews with multiple U.S. Department of Defense officials, May 2024. Around 2022, the CCP began to use the term "integrated national strategic systems and capabilities" rather than military-civil fusion.
41. See, for example, Katie Bo Lillis, "FBI Investigation Determined Chinese-Made Huawei Equipment Could Disrupt U.S. Nuclear Arsenal Communications," CNN, July 25, 2022.
42. U.S. Department of Defense, "DOD Releases List of People's Republic of China (PRC) Military Companies in Accordance with Section 1260H of the National Defense Authorization Act for Fiscal Year 2021," January 31, 2024, https://www.defense.gov/News/Releases/Release/article/3661985/dod-releases-list-of-peoples-republic-of-china-prc-military-companies-in-accord/; U.S. Department of Defense, "Entities Identified as Chinese Military Companies Operating in the United States in Accordance with Section 1260H of the William M. ('Mac') Thornberry National Defense Authorization Act for Fiscal Year 2021 (Public Law 116–283)," 2024, https://media.defense.gov/2025/Jan/07/2003625471/-1/-1/1/ENTITIES-IDENTIFIED-AS-CHINESE-MILITARY-COMPANIES-OPERATING-IN-THE-UNITED-STATES.PDF.
43. Thanks to Alexander Palmer for the research and analysis in this and several other sections of this chapter.
44. See, for example, Lingling Wei, "Xi Digs In with Top-Down Economic Plan Even as China Drowns in Debt," *Wall Street Journal*, December 23, 2024; Jason Douglas, "What's Wrong with China's Economy, in Eight Charts," *Wall Street Journal*, March 1, 2024.
45. Cortney Weinbaum et al., *Assessing Systemic Strengths and Vulnerabilities of China's Defense Industrial Base: With a Repeatable Methodology for Other Countries* (Santa Monica, CA: RAND, 2022), v.
46. Weinbaum, *Assessing Systemic Strengths and Vulnerabilities of China's Defense Industrial Base*.
47. Tai Ming Cheung and Thomas G. Mahnken, *The Decisive Decade: United States-China Competition in Defense Innovation and Defense Industrial Policy in and Beyond the 2020s* (Washington, DC: Center for Strategic and Budgetary Assessments, 2023), 20.
48. "Top 100 Defense Companies, 2024," *Defense News*;, "Top 100 Defense Companies, 2013," *Defense News*.
49. "Top 100 Defense Companies, 2024," *Defense News*;, "Top 100 Defense Companies, 2013," *Defense News*.

50. Weinbaum, *Assessing Systemic Strengths and Vulnerabilities of China's Defense Industrial Base*, iv.
51. "Top 100 Defense Companies, 2024," *Defense News*.
52. J. J. Long, Thomas Corbett, and Dan Shats, *Organization and Structure of the Aviation Industry Corporation of China (AVIC)* (Montgomery, AL: China Aerospace Studies Institute, January 2024), 13.
53. Aviation Industry Corporation of China, *Social Responsibility Report* (Beijing: AVIC, 2017), 7.
54. See, for example, Tai Ming Cheung, *Strengths and Weaknesses of China's Defense Industry and Acquisition System and Implications for the United States* (Monterey, CA: U.S. Naval Postgraduate School, June 25, 2018), 7.
55. China Power Team, "How Developed Is China's Arms Industry?," CSIS, February 25, 2021.
56. See, for example, Cheung, *Strengths and Weaknesses of China's Defense Industry and Acquisition System and Implications for the United States*, 10–11.
57. Christian Curriden, *The Chinese Acquisition Process* (Santa Monica, CA: RAND, 2023).
58. Mark Ashby et al., *Defense Acquisition in Russia and China* (Santa Monica, CA: RAND, 2023), 17–18.
59. William Greenwalt and Dan Patt, *Competing in Time: Ensuring Capability Advantage and Mission Success through Adaptable Resource Allocation* (Washington, DC: Hudson Institute, February 2021), 35.
60. Author interview with William LaPlante, CSIS, Washington, DC, September 26, 2023.
61. Office of the Secretary of Defense, *Military and Security Developments Involving the People's Republic of China 2023* (Washington, DC: U.S. Department of Defense, 2023), 34, 41; Joel Wuthnow, *System Destruction Warfare and the PLA* (Washington, DC: Institute for National Strategic Studies, National Defense University, March 2023).
62. International Institute for Strategic Studies, *The Military Balance 2025*; Hans M. Kristensen et al., "Chinese Nuclear Weapons, 2024," *Bulletin of the Atomic Scientists* 80, no. 1 (January 2, 2024): 49–72; Hans M. Kristensen and Matt Korda, "United States Nuclear Weapons, 2023," *Bulletin of the Atomic Scientists* 79, no. 1 (January 2, 2023): 28–52; Stockholm International Peace Research Institute, "SIPRI Military Expenditure Database," 2023, https://www.sipri.org/databases/milex; Stockholm International Peace Research Institute, "World Military Expenditure Reaches New Record High as European Spending Surges," Press Release, April 24, 2023, https://www.sipri.org/media/press-release/2023/world-military-expenditure-reaches-new-record-high-european-spending-surges#:~:text=World%20military%20expenditure%20reaches%20new%20record%20high%20as%20European%20spending%20surges,-24%20April%202023&text=(Stockholm%2C%2024%20April%2020 23),in%20at%20least%2030%20years; Office of the Secretary of Defense,

Military and Security Developments Involving the People's Republic of China 2023.
63. Evans, "China Leaves U.S. Trailing in Race to Build Warships."
64. Brad Lendon and Haley Britzky, "U.S. Can't Keep Up with China's Warship Building, Navy Secretary Says," CNN, February 22, 2023.
65. Office of the Secretary of Defense, *Military and Security Developments Involving the People's Republic of China 2023*, 166–167.
66. China Power Team, "How Advanced Is China's Third Aircraft Carrier?," CSIS, May 17, 2023; Office of the Secretary of Defense, *Military and Security Developments Involving the People's Republic of China 2023*, 54.
67. International Institute for Strategic Studies, *The Military Balance 2024* (London: Routledge, 2024), 218.
68. Office of the Secretary of Defense, *Military and Security Developments Involving the People's Republic of China 2023*, xii.
69. International Institute for Strategic Studies, *The Military Balance 2025* (London: Routledge, 2025), 221.
70. David Axe, "Yes, China Has More Warships Than the USA. That's Because Chinese Ships Are Small," *Forbes*, November 5, 2021.
71. David Axe, "Yes, the Chinese Navy Has More Ships Than the U.S. Navy. But It's Got Far Fewer Missiles," *Forbes*, November 10, 2021.
72. Sarah Kirchberger, *China's Submarine Industrial Base: State-Led Innovation with Chinese Characteristics* (Newport, RI: U.S. Naval War College, September 2023), 5.
73. Long, Corbett, and Shats, *Organization and Structure of the Aviation Industry Corporation of China (AVIC)*, 7.
74. U.S. Department of Defense, *Military and Security Developments Involving the People's Republic of China 2024*, 59; International Institute for Strategic Studies, *The Military Balance 2017* (London: Routledge, 2017); International Institute for Strategic Studies, *The Military Balance 2024*, 237.
75. International Institute for Strategic Studies, *The Military Balance 2025*, 224. Office of the Secretary of Defense, *Military and Security Developments Involving the People's Republic of China 2024*, vii, 46, 62.
76. Stephen Chen, "Mainland China's Norinco Unveils Drone That Can Reach Taiwan and May Outperform U.S. Rival," *South China Morning Post*, September 23, 2024.
77. "China To Make about 100 Space Launches in 2024," *Xinhua*, February 26, 2024.
78. Clayton Swope et al., *Space Threat Assessment 2024* (Washington, DC: Center for Strategic and International Studies, April 2024), 9
79. Office of the Secretary of Defense, *Military and Security Developments Involving the People's Republic of China 2023*, 94.
80. Office of the Secretary of Defense, *Military and Security Developments Involving the People's Republic of China 2024* (Washington, DC: U.S.

Department of Defense, 2024), 101; International Institute for Strategic Studies, *The Military Balance 2024*, 218.

81. Peter Wood and Alex Stone, *China's Ballistic Missile Industry* (Montgomery, AL: China Aerospace Studies Institute, 2021), ii.
82. The U.S. Navy and Army finally completed a flight test of a hypersonic missile in June 2024. See, for example, U.S. Department of Defense, "DoD Completes Flight Test of Hypersonic Missile," June 28, 2024, https://www.defense.gov/News/Releases/Release/Article/3821376/dod-completes-flight-test-of-hypersonic-missile/.
83. Wood and Stone, *China's Ballistic Missile Industry*, 18–20.
84. "Top 100 Defense Companies, 2024," *Defense News*; Weinbaum, *Assessing Systemic Strengths and Vulnerabilities of China's Defense Industrial Base*, 48.
85. International Institute for Strategic Studies, *The Military Balance 2025*, 220-221; Office of the Secretary of Defense, *Military and Security Developments Involving the People's Republic of China 2024*, 45-47.
86. "强化政治自觉，下决心根治'和平病'" [Strengthen Political Awareness and Resolve to Eradicate "Peace Disease"], 中国军网 [*China Military Network*], July 2, 2018; 倪文鑫 [Ni Wenxin], "实战化训练必须聚焦明天的战场—军区空军实战化训练对联合训练的启示" [Training Made Realistic to Actual War Must Focus on Tomorrow's Battlefield: What Military Region Air Force's Training Made Realistic to Actual War Can Tell Us about Joint Training], 人民前线 [*People's Front*], October 25, 2013; 陈永义 [Chen Yongyi] and 刘媛媛 [Liu Yuanyuan], "'和平病'亦须心药医" [Peace Disease Also Requires Careful Medicine], 解放军报 [*People's Liberation Army Daily*], July 16, 2019.
87. See, for example, Taylor Fravel, *Active Defense: China's Military Strategy since 1949* (Princeton, NJ: Princeton University Press, 2019), 163–165; Gerald Segal, *Defending China* (New York: Oxford University Press, 1985), 211–227; Nayan Chanda, *Brother Enemy: The War after the War* (New York: Harcourt Brace Jovanovich, 1986); King C. Chen, *China's War with Vietnam, 1979: Issues, Decision, and Implications* (Stanford, CA: Hoover Institution Press, 1987); Steven J. Hood, *Dragons Entangled: Indochina and the China Vietnam War* (Armonk, NY: M. E. Sharpe, 1992); Bruce Elleman, *Modern Chinese Warfare, 1785–1989* (London: Routledge, 2001), 284–297.
88. Office of the Secretary of Defense, *Military and Security Developments Involving the People's Republic of China 2023*, viii.
89. See, for example, Mark F. Cancian, Matthew Cancian, and Eric Heginbotham, *The First Battle of the Next War: Wargaming a Chinese Invasion of Taiwan* (Washington, DC: Center for Strategic and International Studies, January 2023); Stacie Pettyjohn, Becca Wasser, and Chris Dougherty, *Dangerous Straits: Wargaming a Future Conflict over Taiwan* (Washington, DC: Center for New American Security, June

2022); Chris Dougherty, Jennie Mutuschak, and Ripley Hunter, *The Poison Frog Strategy* (Washington, DC: Center for New American Security, October 2021). Also see David Ochmanek et al., *U.S. Military Capabilities and Forces for a Dangerous World: Rethinking the U.S. Approach to Force Planning* (Santa Monica, CA: RAND, 2017), 14–19.

90. Cancian, Cancian, and Heginbotham, *The First Battle of the Next War*, 1.
91. Long, Corbett, and Shats, *Organization and Structure of the Aviation Industry Corporation of China (AVIC)*, 25.
92. See, for example, Cheung, *Strengths and Weaknesses of China's Defense Industry and Acquisition System and Implications for the United States*, 21–22.
93. Weinbaum, *Assessing Systemic Strengths and Vulnerabilities of China's Defense Industrial Base*, 28; Curriden, *The Chinese Acquisition Process*, 6.
94. Ashby et al., *Defense Acquisition in Russia and China*, 23.
95. Cheung and Mahnken, *The Decisive Decade*, 24.
96. Weinbaum, *Assessing Systemic Strengths and Vulnerabilities of China's Defense Industrial Base*, 26.
97. See, for example, Cheung, *Strengths and Weaknesses of China's Defense Industry and Acquisition System and Implications for the United States*, 22.
98. World Intellectual Property Organization, "Huawei, Samsung and Qualcomm Are Top Users of WIPO's International Patent System," PR/2024/914, March 7, 2024, https://www.wipo.int/pressroom/en/articles/2024/article_0002.html; Eva Dou and Ellen Nakashima, "Commerce Department Revokes More Export Licenses to China's Huawei," *Washington Post*, May 7, 2024.
99. Brian Buntz, "Top 30 R&D Spending Leaders of 2023: Big Tech Firms Spending Hit New Heights," *R&D World*, June 17, 2024.
100. U.S. Department of Defense, *Military and Security Developments Involving the People's Republic of China* (Washington, DC: Office of the Secretary of Defense, U.S. Department of Defense, 2024); Cheung and Mahnken, *The Decisive Decade*, 25.
101. Colin Clark, "In China's Military 'Urge,' Final Outcomes Remain to Be Seen," *Breaking Defense*, October 16, 2023; Christian Shepherd, "Chinese Defense Minister Removed after Just Seven Months in Latest Purge," *Washington Post*, October 24, 2023; Greg Torode and Laurie Chen, "The Public Face of China's Military under Corruption Probe," Reuters, September 17, 2023; "China Watchdog Says Is Probing the Head of Chip-Focused Big Fund," Reuters, August 1, 2022.
102. See, for example, Chun Han Wong, "Xi Is Trying to Secure the Devotion of China's Military," *Wall Street Journal*, February 20, 2025; Trevor Hunnicutt, Idrees Ali, and Laurie Chen, "China Defence Minister Dong Jun's Fate Unclear as Corruption Probe Sparks Differing Account," Reuters, November 28, 2024.

103. U.S. Department of Defense, *Military and Security Developments Involving the People's Republic of China 2024*, xii, 159.
104. "Former CSIC Chairman Sentenced to 13 Years in Jail for Bribery, Abuse of Power," *Xinhua*, December 26, 2023; Minnie Chan, "12 Years Behind Bars for Corrupt Former Boss of Chinese Warship Builder CSIS," *South China Morning Post*, July 4, 2019.
105. See, for example, Transparency International, *Corruption Perceptions Index 2023* (Berlin: Transparency International, January 2024); World Bank, Worldwide Governance Indicators, 2022, https://www.worldbank.org/en/publication/worldwide-governance-indicators.
106. Michael Peck, "Pay-for-Promotion: Some Chinese Generals Paid for Their Positions," *National Interest*, July 19, 2021.
107. Weinbaum, *Assessing Systemic Strengths and Vulnerabilities of China's Defense Industrial Base*.
108. U.S. Office of Naval Intelligence, "Naval Construction Trends vis-à-vis Navy Shipbuilding Plans, 2020–2030," February 6, 2020; Amanda Rivkin, "German Technology Found in China's Warships: Report," *DW*, June 11, 2021; Kirchberger, *China's Submarine Industrial Base*.
109. International Institute for Strategic Studies, *The Military Balance 2024*, 242; Peter Wood and Robert Stewart, *China's Aviation Industry: Lumbering Forward* (Montgomery, AL: China Aerospace Studies Institute, 2019), 31–32.
110. China Power Team, "How Developed Is China's Arms Industry?"
111. Weinbaum, *Assessing Systemic Strengths and Vulnerabilities of China's Defense Industrial Base*, vi; Ashby et al., *Defense Acquisition in Russia and China*, vii; Gregory C. Allen, "China's New Strategy for Waging the Microchip Tech War," CSIS, May 3, 2023.
112. Daxue Consulting, *China's Machine Tools Industry: Can Local Companies Catch Up with Foreign Manufacturers?* (Beijing: Daxue Consulting, November 9, 2022).
113. Daxue Consulting, *China's Machine Tools Industry*.
114. Weinbaum, *Assessing Systemic Strengths and Vulnerabilities of China's Defense Industrial Base*, 56.
115. Wood and Stewart, *China's Aviation Industry*, 27.
116. Wood and Stewart, *China's Aviation Industry*, 32–33.
117. Office of the Secretary of Defense, *Military and Security Developments Involving the People's Republic of China 2023*, 166.
118. Weinbaum, *Assessing Systemic Strengths and Vulnerabilities of China's Defense Industrial Base*, 44, 59.
119. Fudan University, Tsinghua University, and J. P. Morgan, *Skills Shortages in the Chinese Labor Market: Executive Summary*, October 2016, 13, https://china.usc.edu/sites/default/files/skillsgap-in-chineselabor-market-exec-summary.pdf.
120. Curriden, *The Chinese Acquisition Process*, 9.

121. Kirchberger, *China's Submarine Industrial Base*, 12–13.
122. Curriden, *The Chinese Acquisition Process*, 8.
123. Office of the Secretary of Defense, *Military and Security Developments Involving the People's Republic of China 2022*, 53.
124. See, for example, Mike Sweeney, "Submarines Will Reign in a War with China," U.S. Naval Institute, *Proceedings* 149, no. 3 (March 2023). https://www.usni.org/magazines/proceedings/2023/march/submarines-will-reign-war-china.
125. Quoted in "Failed Eradication," *Economist* 451, no. 9401, p.14 (June 15, 2024).
126. Quoted in Sijia Jiang, "Huawei Founder Details 'Battle Mode' Reform Plan to Beat U.S. Crisis," Reuters, August 20, 2019.
127. Statement of John C. Aquilino.

Chapter 11

1. Epigraphs are from *Commission on the National Defense Strategy* (Santa Monica, CA: RAND, July 2024), vii; Statement of Admiral Samuel J. Paparo, commander of U.S. Indo-Pacific Command, before the House Armed Services Committee, April 9, 2025, https://armedservices.house.gov/uploadedfiles/indopacom_posture_statement_2025.pdf.
2. Cancian, Cancian, and Heginbotham, *The First Battle of the Next War*.
3. Carmelia Scott-Skillern and Peter Singer, "The Forgotten Part of the Contest: Army Logistics in the Pacific," *War on the Rocks*, April 29, 2024.
4. Quoted in Michael Bayer, "Marine Corps Rebalances for New Realities," *National Defense*, May 30, 2023.
5. See, for example, Cancian, Cancian, and Heginbotham, *The First Battle of the Next War*, 88; Seth G. Jones, "The U.S. Is Losing the Ability to Deter War with China," *Wall Street Journal*, November 26, 2024; Mark A. Gunzinger, *Affordable Mass: The Need for a Cost-Effective PGM Mix for Great Power Conflict* (Washington, DC: Mitchell Institute for Aerospace Studies, November 2021).
6. On the timeline for production of LRASMs, see Seth G. Jones, *Empty Bins in a Wartime Environment: The Challenge to the U.S. Defense Industrial Base* (Washington, DC: CSIS, January 2023).
7. See, for example, David A. Ochmanek et al., *Inflection Point: How to Reverse the Erosion of U.S. and Allied Military Power and Influence* (Santa Monica, CA: RAND, 2023); Stacie Pettyjohn, "The Pentagon Isn't Buying Enough Ammo," *Foreign Policy*, May 21, 2024; Joslyn Fleming et al., *Naval Logistics in Contested Environments: Examination of Stockpiles and Industrial Base Issues* (Santa Monica, CA: RAND, 2024).
8. *Commission on the National Defense Strategy*, 17.
9. Kennedy, *The Rise and Fall of the Great Powers*, 355.
10. Kennedy, *The Rise and Fall of the Great Powers*, 304–305.
11. Kennedy, *The Rise and Fall of the Great Powers*, 384.

12. International Monetary Fund, "World Economic Outlook Database, April 2024," accessed May 23, 2024, https://www.imf.org/en/Publications/SPROLLs/world-economic-outlook-databases#sort=%40imfdate%20descending; Organisation for Economic Co-operation and Development, Main Science and Technology Indicators, MSTI database. https://www.oecd.org/en/data/datasets/main-science-and-technology-indicators.html.
13. World Bank, "High-Technology Exports (Current US$)," accessed June 7, 2024, https://databank.worldbank.org/home.aspx; Organisation for Economic Co-operation and Development, Main Science and Technology Indicators, MSTI database. https://www.oecd.org/en/data/datasets/main-science-and-technology-indicators.html; *Science and Engineering Indicators 2020* (Alexandria, VA: National Science Board and National Science Foundation, 2019); *Science and Engineering Indicators 2024* (Alexandria, VA: National Science Board and National Science Foundation, 2023).
14. In 2000, U.S. defense expenditures were $543,989 billion in constant 2022 dollars. The same year, China's defense expenditures were $44,578 billion in constant 2022 U.S. dollars. The data is from Stockholm International Peace Research Institute, SIPRI Military Expenditure Database. https://www.sipri.org/databases/milex
15. The range of Chinese defense spending was reached following author interviews with senior U.S. government officials and a review of such analyses as *Commission on the National Defense Strategy*; Fravel, Gilboy, and Heginbotham, "Estimating China's Defense Spending"; Eaglen, *Keeping Up with the Pacing Threat*; Rogin, "The U.S. Military Plans a 'Hellscape' to Deter China from Attacking Taiwan." Rogin used estimates from U.S. Indo-Pacific Command.
16. Peter Robertson and Wilson Beaver, "China's Defense Budget Is Much Bigger Than It Looks," *Foreign Policy*, September 19, 2023.
17. Helen Warrell and John Paul Rathbone, "UK Military Unprepared for 'Conflict of Any Scale,' Warns Ex-Defence Official," *Financial Times*, July 1, 2024.
18. Defense budget numbers and percentage of GDP are from Stockholm International Peace Research Institute, SIPRI Military Expenditure Database. https://www.sipri.org/databases/milex; U.S. Department of Defense, *Military and Security Developments Involving the People's Republic of China* (Washington, DC: Office of the Secretary of Defense, U.S. Department of Defense, 2024), xi. Military force sizes are from International Institute for Strategic Studies, *Military Balance 2024* (London: International Institute for Strategic Studies, 2024), 542–547.
19. Daniel Byman and Seth G. Jones, "Legion of Doom? China, Russia, Iran and North Korea," *Survival* 66, no. 4 (August–September 2024): 29–50; Andrea Kendall-Taylor and Richard Fontaine, "The Axis of Upheaval:

How America's Adversaries Are Uniting to Overturn the Global Order," *Foreign Affairs* 103, no. 3 (May–June 2024): 50–63.
20. Mark Green, *China and Russia: Quietly Going Steady?* (Washington, DC: Wilson Center, October 29, 2024).
21. Antoni Slodkowski and Laurie Chen, "China's Xi Affirms 'No Limits' Partnership with Putin in Call on Ukraine War Anniversary," Reuters, February 24, 2025.
22. Hyonhee Shin, "Key Points of North Korea, Russia Landmark Strategic Partnership Treaty," Reuters, June 20, 2024.
23. "Treaty on the Comprehensive Strategic Partnership between the Islamic Republic of Iran and the Russian Federation," January 17, 2025, https://president.ir/en/156874.
24. See, for example, Mackenzie Eaglen, "China's Real Military Budget Is Far Bigger Than It Looks," American Enterprise Institute, June 16, 2023, https://www.aei.org/op-eds/chinas-real-military-budget-is-far-bigger-than-it-looks/; Todd Harrison and Seamus P. Daniels, *Analysis of the FY 2019 Defense Budget* (Washington, DC: Center for Strategic and International Studies, September 2018), 7–9.
25. The data on U.S. defense spending as percentage of GDP comes from Stockholm International Peace Research Institute, SIPRI Military Expenditure Database. https://www.sipri.org/databases/milex.
26. Eugene Gholz and Harvey M. Sapolsky, "Restructuring the U.S. Defense Industry," *International Security* 24, no. 3 (Winter 1999–2000): 5–51.
27. Stephen G. Brooks and William C. Wohlforth, "The Myth of Multipolarity," *Foreign Affairs* 102, no. 3 (May–June 2023): 78.
28. See, for example, Randall B. Kester, "The War Industries Board, 1917–1918: A Study in Industrial Mobilization," *American Political Science Review* 34, no. 4 (August 1940): 655–685.
29. Morton H. Halperin and Priscilla A. Clapp, *Bureaucratic Politics and Foreign Policy*, 2nd ed. (Washington, DC: Brookings Institution, 2006), 362.
30. Halperin and Clapp, *Bureaucratic Politics and Foreign Policy*, 16.
31. Herman, *Freedom's Forge*, 70.
32. Beasley, *Knudsen*, 237–238.
33. "Executive Order 9024—Establishing the War Production Board," Federal Register 7, no. 12 (January 16, 1942): 329-330.
34. Truman abolished the War Production Board in "Executive Order 9638: Creating the Civilian Production Administration and Terminating the War Production Board," Federal Register 10, no. 197 (October 4, 1945): 12591.
35. Gansler, *Democracy's Arsenal*, 11.
36. See, for example, Michael J. Hogan, *A Cross of Iron: Harry S. Truman and the Origins of the National Security State, 1945–1954* (New York: Cambridge University Press, 2000).

37. Defense Production Act of 1950, Pub. L. No. 81-774, 64 Stat. 798 (1950).
38. In 1981, President Reagan created the Emergency Mobilization Preparedness Board to improve mobilization and interagency cooperation within the federal government to respond to major peacetime or war-related emergencies. It was not a war production board and did not focus on the revitalization of the defense industrial base. Instead, it was led by the Federal Emergency Management Agency and focused on developing plans and procedures for a national emergency. The board consisted of the representatives of 22 key federal agencies at the deputy secretary or under secretary level and was chaired by the assistant to the president for national security affairs. A full-time secretariat was established to support the board and monitor the implementation of its recommendations by federal agencies. It included senior representatives from several departments and agencies, such as the Departments of Defense, Commerce, Agriculture, Treasury, Justice, Health and Human Services, and Labor. See, for example, "Announcement of Establishment of the Emergency Mobilization Preparedness Board," December 29, 1981, Ronald Reagan Presidential Library, Simi Valley, CA. https://www.reaganlibrary.gov/archives/speech/announcement-establishment-emergency-mobilization-preparedness-board.
39. President Ronald Reagan, Address to the National on Defense and National Security, March 23, 1983, https://www.reaganlibrary.gov/archives/speech/address-nation-defense-and-national-security.
40. Michael C. Horowitz, "Battles of Precise Mass: Technology is Remaking War—and America Must Adapt," *Foreign Affairs* 103, no. 6 (November-December 2024): 34-40.
41. Brose, "Rebuilding the Arsenal of Democracy."
42. J. Ronald Fox, *Defense Acquisition Reform 1960–2009: An Elusive Goal* (Washington, DC: Center of Military History, U.S. Army, 2009), 189.
43. Gansler, *Democracy's Arsenal*, 200.
44. U.S. Government Accountability Office, *Weapons Systems Annual Assessment: DOD Is Not Yet Well-Positioned to Field Systems with Speed* (Washington, DC: U.S. Government Accountability Office, June 2024), 1.
45. Thomas Ritter and Carsten Lund Pedersen, "An Entrepreneur's Guide to Surviving the 'Death Valley Curve,'" *Harvard Business Review*, April 13, 2022, https://hbr.org/2022/04/an-entrepreneurs-guide-to-surviving-the-death-valley-curve.
46. Quoted in Aaron Mehta, "'The Math Doesn't Make Sense': Why Venture Capital Firms Are Wary of Defense-Focused Investments," *Defense News*, January 30, 2020.
47. Greg Allen and Doug Berenson, *Why Is the U.S. Defense Industrial Base So Isolated from the U.S. Economy?* (Washington, DC: Center for Strategic and International Studies, August 20, 2024).

48. Clarence L. "Kelly" Johnson with Maggie Smith, *Kelly: More Than My Share of It All* (Washington, DC: Smithsonian Books, 1989), 160.
49. Author interview with William LaPlante, September 26, 2023.
50. D. Scott Bennett and Allan C. Stam III, "The Duration of Interstate Wars, 1816–1985," *American Political Science Review* 90, no. 2 (June 1996): 239–257.
51. See, for example, Mark F. Cancian et al., *Industrial Mobilization: Assessing Surge Capabilities, Wartime Risk, and System Brittleness* (Washington, DC: Center for Strategic and International Studies, January 8, 2021).
52. Author interviews with multiple individuals in the U.S. government and defense industry.
53. U.S. Department of Defense data from Under Secretary of Defense (Comptroller), "DoD Budget Request"; author interviews with multiple individuals in the U.S. defense industry.
54. See, for example, U.S. Army Corps of Engineers, "Environmental Assessment for Establishing Mine Resistant Ambush Protected (MRAP) Vehicle Storage and Repair Facilities at Joint Base Charleston/Army Strategic Logistics Activity Charleston, South Carolina," U.S. Army Corps of Engineers, Charleston District, November 21, 2014, https://www.sac.usace.army.mil/Portals/43/docs/civilworks/nepadocuments/ASLACMRAPEADraft.pdf.
55. Author interview with William LaPlante.
56. Luke A. Nicastro, *The U.S. Defense Industrial Base: Background and Issues for Congress*, CRS Report no. R47751 (Washington, DC: Congressional Research Service, October 12, 2023), 34.
57. U.S. Department of Defense, *Securing Defense-Critical Supply Chains*, 19.
58. Weinbaum et al., *Assessing Strengths and Vulnerabilities of China's Defense Industrial Base*, 56.
59. U.S. Department of Defense, *Securing Defense-Critical Supply Chains*, 27.
60. Liza Lin and Jiahui Huang, "China Hits Back at U.S. Chip Controls with Limits on Key Raw Materials," *Wall Street Journal*, December 3, 2024.
61. Brian Daigle and Samantha DeCarlo, "Antimony: A Critical Mineral You've Probably Never Heard Of," U.S. International Trade Commission, Executive Briefing on Trade, October 2021, https://www.usitc.gov/publications/332/executive_briefings/ebot_a_critical_material_probably_never_heard_of.pdf.
62. Gracelin Baskaran and Meredith Schwartz, "The Consequences of China's New Rare Earths Export Restrictions," Center for Strategic and International Studies, April 14, 2025, https://www.csis.org/analysis/consequences-chinas-new-rare-earths-export-restrictions.
63. Weinbaum et al., *Assessing Strengths and Vulnerabilities of China's Defense Industrial Base*, 56.

64. Office of the Assistant Secretary of Defense for Sustainment, *Supply Chain Risk Management Framework, Project Report—Phase I* (Washington, DC: U.S. Department of Defense, February 2023), iv.
65. Jennifer Stewart et al., *Vital Signs 2023: Posturing the U.S. Defense Industrial Base for Great Power Competition* (Arlington, VA: National Defense Industrial Association, February 2023).
66. Author interview with William LaPlante.
67. Author interviews with executives at multiple factories and shipyards, 2023 and 2024.
68. Mallory Shelbourne and Sam Lagrone, "First Constellation Frigate Delayed at Least a Year, Schedule Assessment 'Ongoing,'" *USNI News*, January 11, 2024; Megan Eckstein, "Frigate Program Delayed as Shipyard Is a 'Few Hundred' Workers Short," *Defense News*, January 11, 2024.
69. Megan Eckstein, "Workforce Woes Are Top 'Strategic Challenge' for Navy, Admiral Says," *Defense News*, January 31, 2023.
70. U.S. Government Accountability Office, *Weapons System Annual Assessment: Programs Are Not Consistently Implementing Practices That Can Help Accelerate Acquisitions* (Washington, DC: U.S. Government Accountability Office, June 2023), 205.
71. Author interview with senior industry and navy officials, 2024.
72. Lord Alanbrooke, *War Diaries, 1939–1945* (Berkeley: University of California Press, 2001), 680.
73. Another major option for the sale and export of defense articles is through direct commercial sales.
74. Christina L. Arabia, Nathan J. Lucas, and Michael J. Vassalotti, *Transfer of Defense Articles: U.S. Sale and Export of U.S.-Made Arms to Foreign Entities*, CRS Report No. R46337 (Washington, DC: Congressional Research Service, March 23, 2023).
75. U.S. Department of State officials report that they approve 95 percent of cases within 48 hours for their portion of foreign military sales. Testimony of Jessica Lewis, assistant secretary of state for political-military affairs, before the House Foreign Affairs Committee, May 24, 2023, https://www.dcfcnsc.gov/News/Transcripts/Transcript/Article/3408956/assistant-secretary-of-defense-for-strategy-plans-and-capabilities-dr-mara-karl/.
76. Jerry McGinn and Michael T. Roche, *A "Build Allied" Approach to Increase Industrial Base Capacity* (Fairfax, VA: George Mason University, Center for Government Contracting, School of Business, June 2023), 5–6.
77. Sam Skove, "Meet the Tiny State Department Offices Clearing Billions of Dollars' Worth of Weapons for Ukraine," *Defense One*, August 24, 2023.
78. A direct commercial sale involves the sale of a U.S.-licensed defense article or service directly from a U.S. firm to an eligible foreign entity or international organization. Direct commercial sales are generally more flexible than foreign military sales since the purchaser can consult directly with industry about the systems and services it needs.

79. On ITAR, see, for example, "International Traffic in Arms Regulations: Consolidation and Restructuring of Purposes and Definitions," Federal Register 87, no. 56 (March 23, 2022): 16396-16401. ITAR was established under 22 U.S. Code § 2778, Arms Export Control Act.
80. Christopher A. Casey, *Export Controls—International Coordination: Issues for Congress*, CRS Report No. R47684 (Washington, DC: Congressional Research Service, September 2023).
81. 22 Code of Federal Regulations §126.5, Canadian Exemptions; Government of Canada, *A Guide to Canada's Export Control List* (Ottawa: Government of Canada, January 2024).
82. U.S. Department of State, Office of the Spokesperson, "AUKUS Defense Trade Integration Determination," August 15, 2024, https://2021-2025.state.gov/aukus-defense-trade-integration-determination/; U.S. Department of State, Bureau of Political-Military Affairs, "Key Elements of the International Traffic in Arms Regulations Exemption for Defense Trade and Cooperation among Australia, the United Kingdom, and the United States," January 20, 2025, https://www.state.gov/key-elements-of-the-international-traffic-in-arms-regulations-exemption-for-defense-trade-and-cooperation-among-australia-the-united-kingdom-and-the-united-states/.
83. See, for example, "Polaris Sales Agreement," U.S. Department of the Navy, n.d., https://www.ssp.navy.mil/About-Us/SSP-Mission/Safeguard/Polaris-Sales-Agreement/.
84. See, for example, "Address by Secretary of Defense McNamara at the Ministerial Meeting of the North Atlantic Council," May 5, 1962, Foreign Relations of the United States, 1961–1963, Volume VIII, National Security Policy, ed. David W. Mabon (Washington, DC: Government Printing Office, 1996), Document 82; "Address by Secretary of Defense McNamara at the Ministerial Meeting of the North Atlantic Council," December 14, 1962, Foreign Relations of the United States, 1961–1963, Volume VIII, National Security Policy, ed. David W. Mabon (Washington, DC: Government Printing Office, 1996), Document 120.
85. William Greenwalt, *Leveraging the National Technology Industrial Base to Address Great-Power Competition: The Imperative to Integrate Industrial Capabilities of Close Allies* (Washington, DC: Atlantic Council, April 2019).
86. See, for example, Sean Monaghan and Deborah Cheverton, "What Allies Want: Delivering the U.S. National Defense Strategy's Ambition on Allies and Partners," *War on the Rocks*, July 24, 2023.
87. Greenwalt, *Leveraging the National Technology Industrial Base to Address Great-Power Competition*, 13.
88. John Christianson, Sean Monaghan, and Di Cooke, *AUKUS Pillar Two: Advancing the Capabilities of the United States, United Kingdom, and*

Australia (Washington, DC: Center for Strategic and International Studies, July 10, 2023), 8.
89. Christianson, Monaghan, and Cooke, *AUKUS Pillar Two*, 8.
90. Andrew Gordon, *The Rules of the Game: Jutland and British Naval Command* (Annapolis, MD: Naval Institute Press, 1996).
91. Author interview with Admiral Sir Ben Key, First Sea Lord, October 27, 2023.
92. See War Horse News, "Jon Stewart Full Interview of DepSec of Defense: War Horse Symposium," YouTube, April 8, 2023; Leo Shane III, "Jon Stewart Blasts 'Corruption' in Pentagon Spending Priorities," *Military Times*, April 7, 2023.
93. See, for example, Harold L. Ickes, *The Secret Diary of Harold L. Ickes*, vol. 3 (New York: Simon and Schuster, 1954), 212, 398; Goodwin, *Walter Lippmann*, 270.
94. James Fallows, "The Military-Industrial Complex," *Foreign Policy*, no. 133, p. 46 (November–December 2002).
95. Eric Lipton, "New Spin on a Revolving Door: Pentagon Officials Turned Venture Capitalists," *New York Times*, December 30, 2023.
96. Bill Whitaker, "Weapons Contractors Hitting Defense Department with Inflated Prices," CBS News, May 21, 2023; Senators Bernard Sanders (VT), Charles Grassley (IA), Elizabeth Warren (MA), Mike Braun (IN), and Ron Wyden (OR), "Letter to Secretary Austin," U.S. Senate, May 24, 2023.
97. Sanders et al., "Letter to Secretary Austin."
98. Letter from Google employees to Sundar Pichai, 2018.
99. Maureen Dowd, "Alex Karp Has Money and Power. So What Does He Want?," *New York Times*, August 17, 2024. See also Kara Swisher, *Burn Book: A Tech Love Story* (New York: Simon and Schuster, 2024).
100. Rosalie Chan, "Protesters Blocked Palantir's Cafeteria to Pressure the $20 Billion Big Data Company to Drop Its Contracts with ICE," *Business Insider*, August 16, 2019; Dowd, "Alex Karp Has Money and Power."
101. Jennifer Welch et al., "Xi, Biden and the $10 Trillion Cost of War over Taiwan," *Bloomberg*, January 8, 2024; *Commission on the National Defense Strategy*; David C. Gompert, Astrid Stuth Cevallos, and Cristina L. Garafola, *War with China: Thinking through the Unthinkable* (Santa Monica, CA: RAND, 2016).
102. Dowd, "Alex Karp Has Money and Power."
103. See, for example, Damien Cave, "American Can't Produce the Weapons It Needs for the Future. This Could Help," *New York Times*, August 15, 2024.
104. See, for example, Army Science Board, *Surge Capacity in the Defense Munitions Industrial Base* (Washington, DC: U.S. Department of the Army, September 2023), 15, 19.

105. Mykhaylo Zabrodskyi et al., *Preliminary Lessons in Conventional Warfighting from Russia's Invasion of Ukraine: February–July 2022* (London: Royal United Services Institute, November 30, 2022), 55.

Chapter 12

1. Epigraphs are from Steve Jobs, quoted in Ben Woo, "Innovation Distinguishes between a Leader and a Follower," *Forbes*, February 14, 2013; Ronald Reagan, Remarks at the Presentation Ceremony for the Presidential Medal of Freedom, Washington, DC, January 19, 1989, https://www.reaganlibrary.gov/archives/speech/remarks-presentation-ceremony-presidential-medal-freedom-5.
2. Alexis de Tocqueville, *Democracy in America*, trans. Harvey C. Mansfield and Delba Winthrop (Chicago: University of Chicago Press, 2000), 944.
3. Tocqueville, *Democracy in America*, 388.
4. Dowd, "Alex Karp Has Money and Power."
5. "Top 10 Largest Tech Companies in the World by Market Cap in 2025," Forbes India, February 17, 2025.
6. Quoted in Michael Steinberger, "Does Palantir See Too Much?," *New York Times Magazine*, October 21, 2020.
7. Steinberger, "Does Palantir See Too Much?"
8. Dowd, "Alex Karp Has Money and Power."
9. Samantha Subin, "Palantir Now Among 10 Most Valuable U.S. Tech Companies–Its Earnings Multiple is Astronomical," CNBC, May 8, 2025.
10. On peace dividends, see Gansler, *Democracy's Arsenal*, xiii, 10.
11. Frank Kendall, speech, National Harbor, MD, September 11, 2023, https://www.airandspaceforces.com/watch-read-secretary-kendall-great-power-competition/.
12. On the role of the government in the defense industrial base, see, for example, Michael Brenes, "How America Broke Its War Machine: Privatization and the Hollowing Out of the U.S. Defense Industry," *Foreign Affairs*, July 3, 2023.
13. Eliot Cohen, *The Big Stick: The Limits of Soft Power and the Necessity of Military Force* (New York: Basic Books, 2016), 219.
14. Bennett and Stam, "The Duration of Interstate Wars, 1816–1985."
15. See, for example, Defense Science Board, *21st Century Industrial Base for National Defense: Final Report* (Washington, DC: U.S. Department of Defense, February 2024).
16. Mark A. Milley and Eric Schmidt, "America Isn't Ready for the Wars of the Future," *Foreign Affairs* 103, no. 5 (September–October 2024): 26–37.
17. Emily Harding and Harshana Ghoorhoo, *Seven Critical Technologies for Winning the Next War* (Washington, DC: Center for Strategic and International Studies, April 2023).
18. Eric Schmidt et al., *Mid-Decade Challenges to National Competitiveness* (Washington, DC: Special Competitive Studies Project, September 2022).

19. Shyam Sankar, *The Defense Reformation* (Denver, CO: Palantir, October 31, 2024), 5.
20. The data are from the company public filings (10-K reports) of Apple, Nvidia, Microsoft, Google, Amazon, Meta, Lockheed Martin, Raytheon (RTX), Northrop Grumman, General Dynamics, Boeing, and L3 Harris. Note that the numbers for the defense primes represent company-funded research and development only, not customer-funded research and development. In addition, Nvidia's numbers represent research and development expenses for the following fiscal year, since Nvidia's fiscal year runs from February to January. For example, the data for 2023 correspond to Nvidia's Fiscal Year 2024, which ran from February 2023 to January 2024.
21. Clarence L. Johnson, Memorandum to Col. Leo Geary, Rough Draft, Subject: Method of Contracting between the Government and ADP, August 26, 2964, Box 9, Clarence L. Johnson Papers, Huntington Library, San Marino, CA. Also see, for example, Clarence L. Johnson, Christmas Speech, December 21, 1962, Box 7, Clarence L. Johnson Papers, Huntington Library. The RAND Corporation drafted a study on Kelly Johnson's principles. See *"The Kelly Johnson" Approach to Development: An Exposition* (Santa Monica, CA: RAND, February 18, 1963), Draft Document, Box 11, Clarence L. Johnson Papers, Huntington Library.
22. Johnson, Christmas Speech.
23. See, for example, John G. McGinn, *Before the Balloon Goes Up: Mobilizing the Defense Industrial Base Now to Prepare for Future Conflict*, Report No. 10 (Fairfax, VA: Greg and Camille Baroni Center for Government Contracting, October 3, 2024).
24. Remarks by Secretary of Defense Lloyd J. Austin III at the Reagan National Defense Forum, December 4, 2021, https://www.defense.gov/News/Speeches/Speech/Article/2861931/remarks-by-secretary-of-defense-lloyd-j-austin-iii-at-the-reagan-national-defen/.
25. Brose, "Rebuilding the Arsenal of Democracy."
26. Author interview with Robert Work, December 6, 2024.
27. Luke A. Nicastro, *The U.S. Defense Industrial Base: Background and Issues for Congress*, CRS Report no. R47751 (Washington, DC: Congressional Research Service, October 12, 2023), 34.
28. Carlos del Toro, Speech at Harvard University, Cambridge, MA, September 26, 2023, https://www.navy.mil/Press-Office/Speeches/display-speeches/Article/3538420/secnav-delivers-remarks-at-harvard-kennedy-school/.
29. Defense Innovation Board, *Optimizing Innovation Cooperation with Allies and Partners* (Washington, DC: Defense Innovation Board, 2024), 2.
30. Cortney Weinbaum et al., *Assessing Systemic Strengths and Vulnerabilities of China's Defense Industrial Base: With a Repeatable Methodology for Other Countries* (Santa Monica, CA: RAND, 2022), 56.

31. Lockheed Martin, "F-35 Lightning II," 2022, https://www.lockheedmartin.com/content/dam/lockheed-martin/aero/documents/F-35/f35-brochure.pdf.
32. Defense Innovation Board, *Optimizing Innovation Cooperation with Allies and Partners*, 6–7.
33. Jerry McGinn, "More 'Buy America' Provisions Threaten Our Industrial Base and National Security," *The Hill*, October 27, 2023.
34. Douglas Robb, "Repair Deployed Ships in Theater to Optimize Combat Power," *Defense News*, January 17, 2024.
35. See, for example, Brian T. DiMascio, "Foreign Shipyards Can Help the U.S. Navy Build Its Fleet," *Proceedings* 150, no. 10 (October 2024). https://www.usni.org/magazines/proceedings/2024/october/foreign-shipyards-can-help-us-navy-build-its-fleet; Alistair MacDonald and Gordon Lubold, "The Warship that Shows Why the U.S. Navy Is Falling Behind China," *Wall Street Journal*, March 20, 2025.
36. Merchant Marine Act, 1920, 46 U.S.C. §§ 861–889.
37. Hans J. Morgenthau, *Politics among Nations: The Struggle for Peace and Power*, 4th ed. (New York: Alfred A. Knopf, 1967), 113.
38. Gansler, *Democracy's Arsenal*, 21.
39. Office of Management and Budget, "Budget of the United States Government," https://www.govinfo.gov/app/collection/budget/2025/BUDGET-2025-TAB.
40. See, for example, Roger Zakheim, "U.S. Defense Spending Will Have to Go Up," *Washington Post*, February 16, 2023. A rise in the U.S. defense budget would require an analysis of additional options, such as trimming other programs or generating more revenue through taxation.
41. *Commission on the National Defense Strategy* (Santa Monica, CA: RAND, July 2024), xii.
42. Author interview with William LaPlante, September 26, 2023.
43. Thomas Schelling, *Arms and Influence* (New Haven, CT: Yale University Press, 1966), 35.
44. Russell Buhite and David Levy, eds., *FDR's Fireside Chats* (Norman: University of Oklahoma Press, 1992), 171–173.

Epilogue

1. Epigraphs are from Hansard, House of Commons Parliamentary Debates, vol. 301, col. 602, May 2, 1935; Winston Churchill, *Arms and the Covenant* (London: G. G. Harrap, 1938), 465–466.
2. Robert Rhodes James, *Memoirs of a Conservative: J. C. C. Davidson's Memoirs and Papers, 1910–37* (London: Macmillan, 1970), 398.
3. James, "Winston S. Churchill," in *Memoirs of a Conservative*, 5:5297.
4. Martin Gilbert, *Winston Churchill: The Wilderness Years* (London: Macmillan, 1981), 106.

5. Hansard, House of Commons Parliamentary Debates, vol. 292, col. 2348, July 30, 1934.
6. Andrew Roberts, *Churchill: Walking with Destiny* (New York: Viking, 2018), 376.
7. James, *Memoirs of a Conservative*, 403.
8. The quote is from Churchill in the parliamentary debate. Hansard, House of Commons Parliamentary Debates, vol. 317, col. 1104, November 12, 1936.
9. Hansard, House of Commons Parliamentary Debates, vol. 301, col. 666, May 2, 1935.
10. Kennedy, *The Rise and Fall of the Great Powers*, 305–307.
11. James, "Winston S. Churchill," 5:5324.
12. James, "Winston S. Churchill," 5:5449.
13. Winston Churchill, *The Gathering Storm: The Second World War*, vol. 1 (Boston: Houghton Mifflin, 1948), 96.
14. Churchill, *The Gathering Storm*, 1:96. The poem was "Death and His Brother Sleep," *Punch, or the London Charivari* vol. 99 (October 4, 1890).
15. James, "Winston S. Churchill," 5:5449.
16. James, "Winston S. Churchill," 6:6013.
17. George Washington, State of the Union Address, Philadelphia, PA, December 3, 1793, https://millercenter.org/the-presidency/presidential-speeches/december-3-1793-fifth-annual-message-congress.
18. Ronald Reagan, Address to the Nation on National Security, Washington, DC, February 26, 1986, https://www.reaganlibrary.gov/archives/speech/address-nation-national-security.

Appendix 1

1. Rich and Janos, *Skunk Works*, 51–52.
2. Rich and Janos, *Skunk Works*, 272.

Appendix 2

1. Norman R. Augustine, *Augustine's Laws* (New York: Viking, 1986).

Appendix 3

1. Isaacson, *Elon Musk*, 284–285.

ACKNOWLEDGMENTS

The research, writing, and editing process of a book is a deeply rewarding, though frustratingly arduous, journey. "Writing a book is an adventure," wrote British prime minister Winston Churchill after receiving the Times Literary Prize in November 1949. "To begin with it is a toy, an amusement; then it becomes a mistress, and then a master, and then a tyrant, and then the last phase is that, just as one is about to be reconciled to one's servitude, one kills the monster."

David McBride at Oxford and Eric Lupfer, my agent, were particularly helpful in conceptualizing the book and its focus on a history of the defense industrial base. Along the way, it was extremely helpful to hold discussions on the defense industrial base with a wide range of government officials, including Chairman of the Joint Chiefs of Staff General C. Q. Brown; Mike Waltz; Senator Mark Kelly; Vice Chairman of the Joint Chiefs of Staff Admiral Christopher Grady; Chief of Naval Operations Admiral Linda Franchetti; Under Secretary of Defense for Acquisition and Sustainment William LaPlante; Assistant Secretary of the Army for Acquisition, Logistics, and Technology Doug Bush; Assistant Secretary of Defense for Industrial Base Policy Laura Taylor-Kale; National Security Advisor Jake Sullivan; and many others. Thanks also to several allies, including discussions with U.K. First Sea Lord and Chief of the Naval Staff Admiral Sir Ben Key and Commander of the Royal Canadian Navy Vice-Admiral Angus Topshee.

I owe an enormous debt of gratitude to Riley McCabe at the Center for Strategic and International Studies for help with the research, analysis, and figures. Riley was hardworking, assiduous, and a true pleasure to work with. Iselin Brady was helpful in reviewing the entire draft manuscript for errors. I also owe a special thanks to Eliot Cohen for hosting a dinner at CSIS on the manuscript, in which Eliot and the participants appropriately skewered the draft and sent me back to the drawing board. Richard "Otter" Bew, Dan Byman, Mark Cancian, Cynthia Cook, Andrew Hunter, John Koehn, Louis Lauter, Andrew May, and Katie Wheelbarger provided frank and helpful comments. Chris Park and Christina Nordby were valuable in organizing the dinner and providing a summary of the main comments.

Krista Auchenbach, Kari Bingen, Emily Harding, Ben Jensen, Tom Karako, Wes Rumbaugh, Clayton Swope, and Heather Williams were also helpful along the way. In addition, thanks to Victor Cha, Bonny Lin, Jude Blanchette, Charlie Edel, Eric Heginbotham, and Tai Ming Cheung for conversations on China. Several others were helpful on the industrial base, especially Jeremy Bayer, Laura Brent, Jacob Cohn, Eric Edelman, Paul Gillespie, Matt Green, Bill Greenwalt, Jake Harrington, Arthur Herman, Michael Horowitz, Niki Johnson, Jerry McGinn, Tim Morrison, CJ Oates, Greg Sanders, Goodloe Sutton, Mark Webber, and Roger Zakheim. At Oxford, thanks to Kennedy Anderson, Angela Chnapko, Morgan Jones, Sindhu Padmanaban, and Bailey Vehslage for their superb help with the manuscript.

This book could not have been written without the willingness of several individuals to be interviewed, including Norman Augustine, Chris Darby, Rudy De Leon, John Deutch, John Hamre, John Lambert, William Lynn, Stan McChrystal, Michael Vickers, and Robert Work. A big thanks to Boeing for allowing me access to the Boeing archives in Seattle; the Huntington Library in San Marino, California, for access to the Kelly Johnson papers; and the Ronald Reagan Presidential Library in Simi Valley, California, especially Ray Wilson, for access to Reagan administration debates about the industrial base and the defense buildup. The Smith Richardson Foundation, particularly Marin Strmecki and Chris Griffin, and the Diana Davis Spencer Foundation, especially Diana Davis, Abby Spencer Moffat, and Chris Burn, provided critical support to write and research the manuscript. This book would not have been possible without the extensive assistance and expertise of numerous individuals from the U.S. government (especially the Departments of Defense and State), members of Congress and their staff, allies and partners, industry executives, and other subject-matter experts. Many of them did not want to be identified by name, but this book could not have been written without their insights.

Finally, a big thanks to my wife, Suzanne, and daughters, Elizabeth and Alexandra, for their support and patience over the course of the manuscript. I dedicate this book to them.

INDEX

For the benefit of digital users, indexed terms that span two pages (e.g., 52–53) may, on occasion, appear on only one of those pages.

Abdulmutallab, Umar Farouk, 147
Accel Partners, 196
Achen, Christian, 25–26
AcidRain malware, 228
acquisition process, 3, 20–21, 52, 71–73, 82–83, 86, 99–100, 118–119, 124–125, 148–149, 162, 164–165, 200–201, 271–274, 283, 286–287, 291–292
    in China, 248–249, 255
    See also bureaucracy; regulations
Advanced Research Projects Agency Network (ARPANET), 69–70
Aerorozvidka, 232
AeroVironment, 224, 230–231
Aevex Aerospace, 224, 230–231
Afghanistan, 5, 13–14, 128, 129, 139–142, 144–147, 168, 195–196, 198–199, 234–236, 264, 267–268, 277
    Soviet Union in, 78, 232–233
air power, air defense, 64, 68–69, 74, 90, 93, 94–95, 99–107, 152–153, 158, 214–215, 223–224
Airbus, 247

Albania, 138
Alexander, Bretton, 184
Allen, Edmund "Eddie," 37–40
Alphabet. *See* Google
AM General, 198–199
Amalgamated Clothing Workers of America, 19, 29
Amazon, Amazon Web Services, 8, 171–172, 214, 224, 285–286
Amber drones, 133–135
Amnesty International, 145
Andreesen, Marc, 8
Andreessen Horowitz, 183, 195, 196–197, 226–227
Anduril, 7–8, 197, 224–230, 255–256, 272–273, 286–287
Apple, 84–85, 171–172, 255–256, 285–286, 290
Aquilino, John, 258–259
Area-I, 226–227
Argentina, 163
Arlington Capital Partners, 183, 198–199
Arnold, Henry "Hap," 31, 36, 45–46, 130

399

Arnold, Thurman, 30–31, 46, 201–202
artificial intelligence, 7–8, 171, 173, 230, 286–287, 289–290
Aspin, Les, 111, 114–118, 267–268
Assad, Bashar al-, 170
Atlas ICBM, 62, 69
Attlee, Clement, 300
Augustine, Norman, 109–111, 116, 118–120, 125, 162–163, 291–292
Australia, 254, 262, 278–279, 296
  space capabilities of, 193
autonomous platforms, 7–8, 171, 173, 226–227, 292–293
Aviation Industry Corporation of China, 10–11, 246–247, 251–252
Awlaki, Anwar al-, 147

B-17 Flying Fortress, 24–25, 35–37
B-29 Superfortress, 6–7, 20, 35–41, 98
B-52 Stratofortress, 62–63, 98
BAE Systems Inc., 295
Baker, David, 131–132
Baldwin, Ed "Baldy," 100
Baldwin, Stanley, 300–301
Balkans, 106, 135
Baruch, Bernard, 17–18
Baykar, 230–231
Bayraktar, Selcuk, 230–231
Beall, Wellwood, 6–7, 20, 37–39, 46–47, 188–189, 286–287
BeiDou, 192–193
Bell Aircraft Corporation, 37, 39
Bell Labs, 243–244
Bezos, Jeff, 184, 186, 190–191
Biddle, Francis, 28
bin Laden, Osama, 139–140
Bissell, Richard, 6–7, 65, 66–67
Blaster worm, 208
blitzkrieg, 12–13, 20, 216–217
Blue, James E., 135–136

Blue, Neal and Linden, 7, 129–130, 135–139, 147, 148, 188–189, 286–287
Blue, Virginia Neal, 135–136
Blue Origin, 184, 186
BMW, 295
Boeing, 6–8, 20, 22, 33–40, 59, 62–63, 76–77, 98, 120–121, 123, 131, 171–172, 186, 188–189, 223–224, 236–237, 247, 273–274
bombing, strategic, 6–7, 12–13, 20, 35–36, 39–40, 42, 47, 98
Bosnia, 136, 138, 277
Boyle, Katherine, 196–197
Bradley, Omar, 262
Branson, Richard, 186
Brazil, 265–266
Broadcom, 285–286
Brokaw, Tom, 138
Brook, Tom Vanden, 141
Brooks, Stephen, 158, 268
Brose, Chris, 11
Brown, Alan, 100
Brown, Harold, 5, 75–78, 86, 91, 96, 107
Browne, George Morgan, Jr., 135–136
Budd, Ralph, 19
bureaucracy, 2–3, 14, 20–21, 27–29, 72, 75, 86–87, 92, 110, 141–143, 196, 268–269, 282, 288–289, 291–292. *See also* acquisition process; regulations
Burt, Tom, 206
Bush, Doug, 234–235
Bush, George H. W., 91, 107
Bush, George W., 144, 184
Bush, Vannevar, 70
Byrnes, James Francis, 56–57

CaddyWiper malware, 218
Caedmon Group, 165
California Microwave, 118–119
Canada, 278–279
  space capabilities of, 193

Carlucci, Frank, 82
Carlyle Group, 183, 198–199
Carmakal, Charles, 211
Carroll, Frank, 50–51, 57
Carter, Ashton, 61–62, 142–143, 148–149, 152–153, 173–174, 178
Carter, Jimmy, 5, 76–78, 85–86, 107
Cassidy, Tom, 7, 129–130, 137–139, 147, 148, 188–189, 286–287
Center for a New American Security, 152, 169
Center for Strategic and International Studies, 262
Challenger, 184
Chamberlain, Neville, 300
Chengdu Aerospace Corporation, 175–176
Cheung, Tai Ming, 175–176, 255
China, 1, 4, 7–8, 14–15, 53–54, 277, 296–298
   Belt and Road Initiative, 155
   corruption and, 11, 176, 247–248, 256
   cyber capabilities of, 207, 210, 220, 252–253
   defense industrial base, 2–4, 10–11, 15, 80–81, 113, 152–160, 169–171, 175–178, 204, 241–242, 246–259, 263, 264–268, 275–276, 283, 287, 289–290, 302, 303
   electronic warfare, 189–190
   espionage and, 11, 176–177
   General Armaments Department (Equipment Development Department), 175
   Great Leap Forward, 242–243
   "Made in China 2025" strategic plan, 175
   multi-domain precision warfare, 249
   "One China" policy, 155
   Russia and, 4, 266–267
   Science of Military Strategy, 156–157
   in South China Sea, 4, 155, 174–175, 201, 220
   space capabilities of, 192–194, 204, 252
   Taiwan and, 8–9, 155, 239–241, 251–252, 254, 258–259, 261–263, 302
   Uyghurs in, 155
   Volt Typhoon hacking group, 220
China Aerospace Science and Industry Corporation Limited, 252–253
China Aerospace Science and Technology Corporation, 252–253
China Electronics Technology Group, 247
China North Industries Group Corporation Limited, 11, 247, 251–254
China South Industries Group Corporation, 11, 247, 253–254
China State Shipbuilding Corporation Limited, 10, 246–247, 249–251
Chinese Communist Party (CCP), 151–156, 175–176, 245, 248, 255–256
Chrysler, 28–29, 46–47, 53, 59, 62, 118–119
Churchill, Winston, 4–5, 15, 23, 44, 277, 298, 299–303
CIA (Central Intelligence Agency), 64, 66–67, 127–128, 131–132, 136–140, 161–164

CIA (Central Intelligence Agency) (*Continued*)
  In-Q-Tel, 7, 12, 153, 162–168, 173, 178–179, 190–191
Cisco, 244–245
Clapp, Priscilla, 268–269
Clarium Capital Management, 167–168
Clinton, Bill, 14–15, 114, 135
Clinton, Hillary, 225
Code Red, 208
Cohen, Bill, 121–123
Cohen, Eliot, 105–106, 289
Cohen, Stephen, 7, 153, 165–168, 178–179, 286–287
Cold War, 1, 5, 6–8, 14, 51–52, 63, 67, 81, 85–87, 95, 111–112, 114–117, 183, 184, 267–271, 287
Colt Arms, 22
Columbia, 184
Commander Nazir Group, 145
Commercial Aircraft Corporation, 10–11
Congress of Industrial Organizations, 30–31, 46
Continental Aerospace Technologies, 257
Convair, 60, 62
Corning, 118–119
Crimean War, 289
Cubic Corporation, 198–199
Curtiss-Wright Corporation, 22, 46–47, 71–72
cyber domain, 7–8, 15, 164–165, 173, 182, 193–194, 205–214, 218–221, 286–287
Czechoslovakia, 54

D-21 drone, 130–131
Dahl, Robert, 8
Darby, Chris, 153, 162–164
Data Collective, 190–191
David, Ruth, 7, 153, 161–162, 178–179
Davies, Joe, 56–57
Davis, Chester C., 19
Davis, Joseph, 7, 92–93
Davis, Tommy, 194–195
Dayton-Wright Airplane Company, 130
Defense Advanced Research Projects Agency (DARPA), 8, 69–70, 84, 99–100, 133–134, 160–161, 183
  Long Range Research and Development Planning Program, 96
Defense budget, 1–2, 5, 53–54, 79–80, 107, 111, 113, 140–141, 265, 296–298
defense industrial base, 1–3, 9–10, 12–14
  consolidation of, 1–4, 14–15, 111, 114–125
  cooperation and, 266–267, 277–280, 294–296
  cyber domain and, 206–207, 210, 220–221
  first offset, 60–62, 169, 178
  innovation and, 36–40, 47, 55–56, 72, 74–75, 97, 100–101, 110, 143, 160–163, 188–189, 255–256, 273–274
  interaction between private sector and government in, 1, 6–8, 12–13, 18, 19–21, 27–31, 36–38, 46–47, 58–59, 71–73, 91, 100–101, 107, 129–130, 148, 153, 161–162, 166–167, 171–172, 183, 206–207, 236–237, 288–289
  mass production and, 291–293
  national industrialization of, 288–289
  regulations and, 82–83, 92, 110, 118–119, 124–125, 160–163,

182–183, 274–276, 282,
  291–292
 second offset, 14–15, 51–52,
  61–62, 75–77, 79–80, 86, 169,
  178, 264, 269–271, 287
 supply chain and, 294
 third offset, 14–15, 152–153,
  168–173, 178
 venture capital and private equity
  investment in, 15, 182–186,
  194–204, 226–228, 281
 wartime *versus* peacetime, 2–6,
  10, 13–14, 31–32, 46, 51–52,
  54, 57–58, 68, 77–78, 85–
  86, 91, 109–111, 113–114,
  116, 117–118, 125, 129, 148,
  152–153, 178–179, 182–183,
  196–197, 200–201, 210, 224–
  225, 234–238, 254, 258–259,
  262, 267–268, 271, 274, 280,
  283, 286–289, 292, 296–298,
  302–303
 workforce and, 276–277, 294
Demers, John, 11
demobilization, 21, 51–52, 85–86
Deng Xiaoping, 81, 154–155
Department of Defense, 8, 71, 77–78,
  99–100, 140, 171, 191, 200–203,
  275–276, 293–294
 acquisition process, 12, 71–73,
  82–83, 124–125, 136, 141–143,
  148, 160–161, 187–188, 196–
  197, 200–201, 226, 234–235,
  271–273, 281, 292
 *Commercial Space Integration
  Strategy*, 191
 Compliance Review Groups, 139
 consolidation and, 1–2, 111,
  115–118, 120–121, 123–124,
  143
 corruption and waste in, 73,
  202–203, 281
 Counter-IED Task Force, 142–143
 Defense Innovation Unit, 12, 173

 Detachment 1, Air Combat
  Command, Pentagon, 140
 Directive 3200.9, 72–73
 Joint Improvised Explosive Device
  Defeat Organization, 142–143
 military sales process, 278
 National Reconnaissance
  Office, 184
 Office of Net Assessment, 95, 105
 Office of Strategic Capital, 12
 Persistent Hobgoblin, 172–173
 Project Maven, 173, 199–200,
  281–282
Deptula, David, 106–107
DesertBlade malware, 218
deterrence, 3–5, 52, 61–62, 68–69,
  71, 74–75, 78, 86, 91, 178, 236,
  263–264, 269–271, 274, 283,
  287–288, 292–293, 296–298,
  301, 302–303
Deutch, John, 114–116, 118,
  123–124, 129–130, 136–137,
  148
Developmental Sciences, 133
Diamond Aircraft Industries, 257
Dive Technologies, 226–227
Douglas Aircraft Company, 46–47,
  59, 60, 62, 109–110
Dragon Lady. *See* U-2 reconnaissance
  aircraft
drones, drone warfare, 1–2, 7, 14–15,
  127–141, 144–148, 230–232. *See
  also* Predator drones
Dulles, Allen, 65–67
Dulles, John Foster, 61
DuPont, 38–39

E-systems, 120
East China Sea, 4, 302
Egtvedt, Claire, 37
Egypt, 74
Eisenhower, Dwight D., 60–64,
  66–69, 184, 201–202, 267,
  269–271

Electric Boat, 22
Elliott, Harriet, 19
England, Gordon, 141–142
Epirus, 197
Esper, Mark, 202–203
espionage, 11, 54–55, 78, 176–177, 205–206, 210–211, 244–245, 248
Estonia, 54
Evergreen Coast Capital, 198–199

F-117 Nighthawk, 7, 12–13, 51, 77, 90, 98–102, 104–105, 107, 153
Facebook (Meta), 225, 285–286
Fairchild Semiconductor, 84
Fallows, James, 203, 280–281
Falls, Cyril, 106
Federov, Mykhailo, 206, 228
FiberLake malware, 218
Finland, 54, 232
Finmeccanica, Leonardo DRS, 295
FireEye (Mandiant), 164–165, 211, 212, 224
First offset, 61–62, 153
Ford, Henry, 26, 28–29
Ford Motor Company, 26, 28–29, 31, 39, 46–47, 53, 72, 118–119, 273
Forterra Systems, 164
Founders Fund, 182–183, 185–186, 190–191, 194, 196, 225–227
FoxBlade malware, 205–206, 218
France, 1–2, 53–54
  defense industrial base, 24–25, 42–43, 113, 158, 263–266
  in Iraq, 102–103
  space capabilities of, 193
Franks, Tommy, 127–128
French, John, 13
Frigidaire, 33–34
Fritsch, Werner von, 23–24

Gaither Report, 68–69
Gallagher, Mike, 12

Gansler, Jacques "Jack," 139, 143–144, 160–161, 271–272
Gates, Robert, 5, 141–144, 148, 234–235
General Atomics, 7, 127, 129–130, 135, 136–139, 141, 147, 188–189, 286–287
General Catalyst, 183, 196–197
General Dynamics, 8, 62–63, 119, 120–123, 223–224, 236–237, 247, 249–251
General Electric, 22, 33–34, 38–39, 46–47, 118–119, 247
General Motors, 6–7, 17, 18–19, 22, 26, 28–29, 31, 46–47, 53, 118–120, 269
  Fisher Body Division, 37
Germany, 53–54, 228
  defense industrial base, 23–25, 34–35, 42, 113, 158, 263–266, 299–303
  in World War II, 1–2, 4–5, 13, 14–15, 17, 20–25, 29–32, 34–36, 42, 43–44, 49–50, 233
Gettings, Nathan, 165–166
Glenn L. Martin Company, 39
Global Navigation Satellite System, 193
Global Positioning System (GPS), 76–77
GNAT-750 drone. *See* Predator drones
Golden, Neal, 208
Goldstein, Ken, 92
Goldwater, Barry, 86–87
Google (Alphabet), 8, 171–172, 199–200, 224, 229–230, 255–256, 281–282, 285–286, 290
Gorbachev, Mikhail, 112
Gordon, Andrew, 3, 280
Gotham, 167–169
government:
  defense industry base and, 1, 6, 9–14, 18, 19–22, 27–28, 32–33,

52, 58–59, 71–73, 91, 107, 129–130, 160–161, 164–165, 190, 206–207, 246, 282–283, 289–292, 297
  private sector and, 1, 6, 12–13, 91, 100–101, 129–130, 148, 153, 160–163, 166–168, 178–179, 183–184, 203, 204, 206–207, 218–219, 272–273, 289–292
  regulations and, 2–3, 9–12, 72, 82–83, 110, 118–119, 160–161, 166–167, 178–179, 271–273
  space domain and, 184–186, 190, 191
  See also private sector
Gramm, Phil, 115
Grumman Aerospace, 60, 120. *See also* Northrop Grumman
GTE, 118–119
Guay, Jeff, 128
Guderian, Heinz, 13
Gulf War, 101–105, 264. *See also* Operation Desert Storm

Habermas, Jürgen, 165
Hadley, Stephen, 139–140
Hagel, Chuck, 168–171
Haggerty, Pat, 70
Haig, Douglas, 13
Halperin, Morton, 268–269
Hamas, 8–9, 13–14, 224–225, 236–237
Hamre, John, 124
Haqqani Network, 144–145
Hasan, Nidal, 147
Have Blue. *See* F-117 Nighthawk
HawkEye 360, 197
Hayden, Mike, 144, 147
Henderson, Leon, 19
Herman, Arthur, 22–23
Hewlett Packard, 118–119, 243–244
Hezbollah, 13–14, 224–225, 236–237
Hillman, Sidney, 19, 29

Hitler, Adolf, 23–24, 31, 43–44, 233, 299–300
Hollings, Fritz, 115
Honda, 295
Honeywell, 85, 118–119
Hoover, Herbert, 22
Hopkins, Harry, 18–19
Horner, Chuck, 90
Houthis, 224–225
Huawei, 242–246, 254–256, 258
Hughes Aircraft Company, 91–92, 94–95, 120
Hu Jintao, 154–155
Human Capital, 226
Huntington, Samuel, 57–58
Huntington Ingalls Industries, 236–237, 249–251
Hussein, Saddam, 89–90, 101–102
Hu Yaobang, 154–155

IBM, 33–34, 118–119, 208, 243–244
Ickes, Harold, 29–33, 46, 201–202, 280–281
improvised explosive devices (IEDs), 141–143, 148, 168
In-Q-Tel. *See under* CIA
India, 158–159
  defense industrial base, 265–266
  space capabilities of, 193
Industroyer2 malware, 218
information technology, 143–144, 148–149, 156–157, 161–163, 166, 167–168, 172–173, 199–200, 220–221, 227
informatization, 156–157
innovation, 11–14, 35–36, 38–39, 47, 82, 143, 159–160, 172, 243–244, 254–256, 285–287

innovation (*Continued*)
    private sector and, 6, 12–13, 20, 45–46, 51, 64, 66, 67, 72, 74–75, 97, 99–101, 148, 161–163, 178–179, 182–183, 188–189, 191, 204, 273–274, 287, 290, 292
    regulations and, 110, 160–163, 283
Intel, 84–85, 194–195, 255–256
Intellect Services, 209
intelligence, 65, 67, 97, 130, 135, 146–147, 153, 161–164, 167, 172–173, 184, 189–190, 230, 231–232. *See also* reconnaissance
Intermediate-Range Nuclear Forces Treaty, 139
International Space Station, 186
Iran, 4, 8–9, 13–14, 56–57, 224–225, 236–237, 277, 296
    China and, 266–268, 287
    cyber capabilities of, 210–211, 220
    Elfin hacking group, 210–211
    Russia and, 266–267
    space capabilities of, 193
Iraq, 4–5, 7, 13–14, 89–91, 100–107, 113, 114–115, 129, 138, 140–142, 145–146, 168, 195–196, 198–199, 234–236, 264, 267–268, 277
Isaacson, Walter, 190
Isham, Joanne, 153, 161–162, 178–179
Israel, 4, 8–9, 13–14, 74, 131–133, 224–225, 236–237, 295
    space capabilities of, 193
Israel Aircraft Industries (Israel Aerospace Industries), 132–133
Italy, 28–29, 34–35, 53–54
    defense industrial base, 42–43, 263–264

Jain, Akash "Aki," 7, 153, 167–168, 178–179, 286–287
Japan, 53–54, 191–192, 295–296
    China and, 239–241, 254, 256–257, 261–262
    defense industrial base, 21–23, 34–35, 42, 113, 158, 263–266
    space capabilities of, 193
    in World War II, 1–2, 6–7, 14, 20–25, 31–32, 34–36, 40–42, 44–45, 47, 263–264
Jaza'iri, Sulayman al-, 147
Jeremiah, David, 136–137
Jiang Zemin, 113, 154–155
Johnson, Clarence "Kelly," 6–7, 49, 50–51, 57, 63–67, 72, 74–75, 83–84, 86–87, 97–100, 110, 130–131, 183, 188–189, 243–244, 255–256, 273–274, 286–287, 291–292
Johnson, Dick, 92
Johnson, Jesse, 89–90
Johnson, Lyndon B., 5, 52, 71, 86–87, 267
Johnson, Rob, 265–266
Joint Surveillance Target Attack Radar System, 76–77
Jumper, John, 128, 138–139
Juncosa, Mark, 7–8, 181–184, 187–190, 252, 255–256, 286–287
Junkers, 49–51

Kaiser, Henry, 20, 32, 34–35, 46, 52–53
Karem, Abraham "Abe," 7, 129–130, 132–135, 137–138, 145, 147–148, 183, 188–189, 286–287
Karp, Alex, 7, 153, 164–168, 177, 178–179, 230, 243–244, 255–256, 281–282, 285–287
Kendall, Frank, 287
Kennan, George, 56–57
Kennedy, John F., 5, 52, 71, 81, 86, 267, 280–281
Kennedy, Paul, 2, 22, 23–24, 40, 175, 263–264

Kettering, Charles, 130
Kettering Bug, 130
Key, Ben, 280
Keynes, John Maynard, 42–43
Khrushchev, Nikita, 67–68
Kilby, Jack, 70, 84
Kimmons, Jeff, 127
Kishi Nobuo, 241
Kissinger, Henry, 68, 95
Kleiner Perkins, 166–167
Knox, Frank, 28
Knudsen, William, 6–7, 17–20, 25–35, 38, 39–40, 44–46, 52–53, 237–238, 269, 280–281
Kodak, 273
Kohlberg Kravis Roberts & Company, 197–198
Korean War, 3–5, 13–14, 51–52, 57–61, 63, 79–80, 85–86, 264, 267, 269–271, 289
Kosovo, 106, 277
KPS Capital Partners, 198–199
Krauthammer, Charles, 110–111
Krepinevich, Andrew, 105
Kresa, Kent, 121–122
Kropyva, 232
Kuwait, 89–91, 101, 102–104, 106

Lai Ching-te, 239–241
Lambert, John, 7–8, 206–209, 211, 212–214, 218–221, 255–256, 286–287
Lansbury, George, 299–300
LaPlante, William "Bill," 234–235, 248–249, 276–277, 297–298
Lattice open software platform, 227
Latvia, 54
Lavrov, Sergey, 217
Lawrence Livermore Laboratories, 80
Leading Systems, 133–135, 183
Lebanon, 224–225
Leide, Jack, 90
LeMay, Curtis, 40, 64–65
Libi, Abu Layth al-, 147

Libya, 264
Lightning Bug, 130
Lippmann, Walter, 30–31, 46, 201–202, 280–281
Li Shangfu, 256
Lithuania, 54
Litton, 120–121
Lockheed Aircraft Company, Lockheed Martin, 8, 46–47, 49, 50–51, 60, 62, 70–71, 73, 84–85, 119–125, 131–132, 171–172, 186, 196, 223–224, 236–237, 247, 251–252, 255–256, 286
  Skunk Works (Advanced Development Projects), 6–7, 51, 57–58, 63–67, 72, 74–75, 83–84, 86–87, 91, 97–101, 107, 110, 130–131, 183, 188–189, 273–274, 286–287
Lonsdale, Joe, 165–166
Loral Corporation, 119
Lucent, 118–119
Luckey, Palmer, 7–8, 224–230, 243–244, 255–256, 273, 286–287
Lux Capital, 183, 196
Lynn, Bill, 114–115

MacArthur, Douglas, 63
Mackinder, John, 56
Magnavox, 118–119
Mandiant. *See* FireEye
Manhattan Project, 37
manufacturing, 18, 21–22, 25, 27–28, 34–35, 39, 46–47, 59, 73–74, 248, 256–257
Mao Zedong, 154–155, 157, 242–243
Marietta, Martin, 62
Marshall, Andrew, 95–96, 106–107
Marshall, George C., 27, 44–45
Martin Marietta, 109–110, 119
Masri, Abu Khabab al-, 147
Matos, 133
Maverick missiles, 76–77, 94–95

Maxar, 224
McCarthy, Kevin, 240–241
McCarthy, Ryan, 202–203
McChrystal, Stanley, 7, 145–146
McDonald, Bob, 73–74
McDonnell Douglas, 60, 99–100, 120
McLaughlin, John E., 139–140
McNamara, Robert, 71–73
Mearsheimer, John, 43–44
M.E.Doc, 209
Mercedes-Benz, 295
Meta Platforms. *See* Facebook
MetaConstellation, 230
Microsoft, 7–8, 15, 255–256, 273–274, 285–287, 290
    Threat Intelligence Center, 206–209, 211–214, 218–221
    Windows Security Group, 208
Milošević, Slobodan, 106
mine-resistant ambush-protected (MRAP) vehicles, 129, 141–142, 148
Minuteman missiles, 69–70
Mitsubishi Electric, 23, 42, 255–256
Moldova, 54
MongoDB, 164–165
Moonraker worm, 209
Moore, Thomas, 300–301
Morgenthau, Hans, 296
Morgenthau, Henry, Jr., 22–23, 42
Moritz, Michael, 166–167
Mullen, Mike, 144–145
Murray, Philip, 30–31, 46
Musk, Elon, 7–8, 181–190, 204, 228–229, 243–244, 252, 255–256, 286–287, 291–292
Myers, Richard, 139–140

National Aeronautics and Space Administration (NASA), 183–185, 191
    Commercial Orbital Transportation Services, 186

National Geospatial-Intelligence Agency, 146–147, 174
National Postal Meter, 33–34
National Security Agency, 210, 213
    Real Time Regional Gateway (RT-RG), 146–147
NATO (North Atlantic Treaty Organization), 4, 53, 77, 106, 135, 213, 232, 279
Nazir, Maulvi, 145
Nelson, Donald, 20, 33, 34–35, 46
Neuberger, Anne, 206
Newport News Shipbuilding, 122–123
Nimble America, 225
Nimda virus, 208
Nixon, Richard, 5, 74, 95
North American Aviation, 37, 59
North Korea, 4, 57–58, 60–61, 114–115, 296
    China and, 266–268, 287
    cyber capabilities of, 210–211, 220
    Russia and, 266–267
    space capabilities of, 193
Northrop, Northrop Grumman, 8, 99–100, 107, 120–123, 223–224, 236–237, 251–252
Norway, 295
Nosek, Luke, 185–186
Noyce, Bob, 84
nuclear weapons, 10–13, 52, 60–64, 67, 68–69, 74, 75–77, 85, 96, 99–100, 130, 139, 169, 173, 178, 241–242, 279, 282. *See also* deterrence
Nvidia, 285–286, 290

Nye, Gerald, 22
Nye, Joseph, 8

Obama, Barack, 170
Oculus VR, 225
Offset, 61–62, 75–76, 91, 96, 169, 171, 178
Ogarkov, Nikolai, 77
Okonite, 33–34
Omar, Muhammad, 127–129
O'Mara, Margaret, 6, 85
OneWeb, 181–182, 186
Operation Allied Force, 138
Operation Barbarossa, 233
Operation Deny Flight, 135
Operation Desert Storm, 7, 13–15, 87, 89–91, 100–107, 113, 264
  Instant Thunder, 102
Operation Dynamo, 20
Operation Meetinghouse, 40
Operation Rolling Thunder, 93
Operation Sky Monitor, 135
Operation Southern Watch, 138
Ogarkov, Nikolai, 96–97
O'Sullivan, Stephanie, 171–172
Overholser, Denys, 7, 91, 97–100, 106–107, 286–287
Overy, Richard, 20–21

Pace, Frank, 134–135
Pace, Peter, 141–142
Packard, David, 82–83
Packard Commission, 82–83
Pakistan, 129, 135–136, 144–147, 264
  Directorate for Inter-Services Intelligence (ISI), 144–145
Palantir, 7, 153, 164–169, 171–172, 178–179, 182, 197, 224, 225–226, 230, 255–256, 272–274, 281–282, 285–287
Palmer, Don, 51
Panama, 100–101
Panetta, Leon, 12

Paparo, Samuel, 241
Patel, Harsh, 167
Paul, Ron, 203–204
Paveway bombs, 93–94, 104–105, 286–287
Paxton, Jay, 142–143
PayPal, 166, 185
Perry, William, 7, 63, 75–78, 91, 96, 105, 107, 111, 114–117, 121–122, 148–149, 267–268
Philippines, 262
Phillips, 118–119
Pichai, Sundar, 200, 281–282
PitchBook, 194
Planet Labs, 224
Poland, 54
Polaris missiles, 62, 279
Pontiac, 28–29
Powers, Francis Gary, 67
precision-guided weapons, 7, 12–15, 79–80, 90, 91–97, 100–105, 107. *See also* Paveway bombs
Predator drones, 127–130, 135–141, 144, 145–147, 286–287. *See also* drones, drone warfare
private equity, 8, 15, 182–184, 197–204, 281. *See also* venture capital
private sector:
  cyber domain and, 220
  defense industrial base and, 1, 3–4, 6, 7–8, 10, 12–13, 15, 18–21, 27–31, 33–34, 36–38, 46–47, 58–60, 64, 67, 71–73, 86–87, 91, 148, 166–167, 183–184, 199–204, 206–207, 272–273, 281, 289–292
  government and, 1, 6, 12–13, 46, 91, 100–101, 107, 115–116, 129–130, 148, 153, 160–163, 166–168, 178–179, 183–184, 186,

private sector (*Continued*)
  202–204, 206–207, 218–219,
  272–273, 289–292
 innovation and, 64, 86–87,
  153, 157, 160–162, 178–179,
  182–183, 191, 287, 290
 space domain and, 179, 182–184,
  186, 190–191, 204
 See also government
Promus Ventures, 190–191
Proxmire, William, 73
Puritano, Vincent, 82
Putin, Vladimir, 170, 232

al-Qa'ida, 1–2, 127, 128, 138–140,
  144–148
Qualcomm, 255–256
Quality Hardware, 33–34
Quso, Fahd al-, 147

Rabia, Hamza, 140
Ralston, W. P., 51
RAND Corporation, 95
Raytheon (RTX), 8, 70, 91–92,
  94–95, 120–121, 123, 171–172,
  223–224, 236–237, 247
 Raytheon Ventures, 196
Reagan, Ronald, 3, 51–52, 77–80,
  82–86, 91, 107, 267, 269–271,
  289, 302–303
Rebellion Defense, 227–228
reconnaissance, 64–67, 74–75, 131,
  135. *See also* U-2 reconnaissance
  aircraft
reconnaissance strike complex, 97
Red Star, 96–97
regulations, 3–4, 9–12, 22, 27–28,
  31, 46, 58, 71–73, 75, 77, 82–83,
  92, 99, 110, 118–119, 124–125,
  160–161, 272–273, 278, 279–
  280. *See also* acquisition process;
  bureaucracy
Ren Zhengfei, 242–246, 248,
  255–256, 258

Reno, Janet, 122–123
Rich, Ben, 7, 83–84, 91, 97–101,
  106–107, 130–131, 286–287
RiskIQ, 218–219
Rock, Arthur, 194–195
Rockefeller Brothers Fund, 68
Rock Island Arsenal, 59
Rock-Ola, 33–34
Rockwell, 120
Romania, 54
Roosevelt, Eleanor, 32–33
Roosevelt, Franklin D., 1–2, 6, 14,
  18–22, 26, 28–33, 42, 46–47, 70,
  201–202, 269, 289, 298
 "The Victory Program," 29–30
Roper, Will, 173
Roscosmos, 193
Rosen, Stephen, 35
Route 128 (Massachusetts), 8, 70, 183
Rudman, Warren, 115
Rumsfeld, Donald, 128, 148–149
Russia, 262, 277, 296
 annexation of Crimea, 170, 201
 Aqua Blizzard cyber unit, 213–214
 Cadet Blizzard cyber unit, 213–214
 China and, 266–268, 287
 cyber capabilities of, 205–210,
  212–214, 218–221, 228–229
 defense industrial base, 158,
  169–171, 178, 223, 302, 303
 electronic warfare, 189–190
 Federal Security Service
  (FSB), 213–214
 Forest Blizzard cyber unit, 213–214
 Intelligence Service
  (SVR), 212–213
 invasion of Ukraine, 4, 8–9,
  13–15, 170, 201, 205–207, 213,
  214–221, 223–225, 228–236,
  266–268, 279, 283, 289
 Iran and, 267
 Main Intelligence Directorate
  (GRU), 205–206, 208–209,
  213–214

Nobelium group, 212–213
North Korea and, 267
NotPetya cyber attack, 208–209
Sandworm (Military Unit 74455), 205–206, 208–209, 218–219
space capabilities of, 193–194
See also Soviet Union; Ukraine
Russo-Japanese War, 289
Rutan, Burt, 186
Ryan, Mike, 139
Ryan Aeronautical, 130

Samsung, 255–256
Sanders, Bernie, 281
Sarang, Mehak, 182
Sasser worm, 208
Saudi Arabia, 89–91, 102–103
Schairer, George, 6–7, 20, 37–38, 46–47, 286–287
Schelling, Thomas, 297–298
Scherrer, Dick, 100
Schimpf, Brian, 7–8, 225–226, 273, 286–287
Schmemann, Serge, 109
Schmidt, Eric, 166
Schriever, Bernard, 69, 72–73, 119
Schwarzkopf, Norman, 89–90
Sears Roebuck, 20, 33
Second offset, 14–15, 61–62, 75–77, 79–80, 169, 264, 287
Selva, Paul, 171–172
Sequoia Capital, 166–167, 183, 196
Seraphim Capital, 190–191
Serbia, 106, 135, 138
Shah, Raj, 202–203
Shamoon malware, 210–211
Shield AI, 197, 227–228
Shield Capital, 183, 196
Shirk, Susan, 154
Shotwell, Gwynne, 7–8, 183–184, 188–189, 228, 243–244, 252, 255–256, 286–287
Sickle, Jack, 92

Silicon Valley, 6, 8, 12, 59, 69–71, 73, 84–85, 153, 160, 163, 166–167, 173, 183
Sinclair, Archie, 300
Sino-Vietnamese War, 11, 254, 289
Skydio, 197
Sloan, Alfred P., 18–19, 26
Smith, Brad, 7–8, 206–207, 286–287
Smith, Leighton "Snuffy," 138
SolarWind, 212–213
Somalia, 236
SonicVote malware, 218
South Africa, 295
South Korea, 4, 60–61, 254, 262, 295–296
space capabilities of, 193
Soviet Union, 1, 3–4, 14, 21–22, 31, 47, 53–54, 233
collapse of, 14–15, 109–113, 154, 264, 267–268
defense industrial base, 1–2, 23–25, 34–35, 43–44, 51–52, 54–57, 60–62, 64, 66–69, 74, 75–80, 85, 86, 95, 96–97, 99–100, 110–113, 178, 263–264, 279
enlargement of, 5, 54
First Five-Year Plan, 43–44
Military Industrial Commission, 54–55, 112
nuclear capabilities of, 74–75, 99–100
Sputnik launch, 67–68, 72–73, 85–86, 202
See also Russia
Space Capital, 190–191
space domain, 7–8, 11, 15, 171, 173, 181, 182–186, 190, 191–194, 286–287

space domain (*Continued*)
   private investment in, 179, 182–184, 186, 190–191, 204
Space X, 7–8, 15, 181–189, 191, 194, 197, 204, 224, 225–226, 229, 255–256, 273–274, 286–287
Spalding, George, 24–25
Sparx Space Frontier Fund, 190–191
Speer, Albert, 23–24
Sperry Gyroscope, 38–39
Sputnik, 51–52, 67–69, 85–86, 202
Stalin, Joseph, 23–24, 52, 54, 56–57, 86, 113
Star Wars. *See* Strategic Defense Initiative
Starlink, 7–8, 181–184, 186–191, 204, 224, 228–229, 286–287
Starshield, 204
stealth technology, 77, 91, 97–102, 104–105, 107, 286–287
Stellex Capital Management, 198–199
Stephens, Trae, 7–8, 225–226, 273, 286–287
Stettinius, Edward, Jr., 19
Stimson, Henry, 28–29, 201–202
Stone, Oliver, 280–281
Strategic Arms Reduction Treaty, 139
Strategic Computing Initiative, 84
Strategic Defense Initiative (SDI), 80, 85
Stratemeyer, Edward, 50
Streisand, Barbra, 83–84
Su Bin, 176–177
Superior Air Parts, 257
SV Angel, 226
Swanson, Scott, 128–129
Sweden, 232
Swisher, Kara, 281–282
Syria, 4, 74, 170

Taiwan, Taiwan Strait, 4, 8–9, 155, 239–241, 251–252, 254, 258–259, 261–263, 268, 293–295, 302
Taliban, 128, 140, 144–145
Tan Ruisong, 248
TechStars, 190–191
Tehreek-e-Taliban Pakistan, 145
Telesat, 181–182
Teller, Edward, 80
Tencent, 285–286
Tenet, George, 128, 139, 153, 161–162, 178–179
terrorism, counterterrorism, 1–2, 7, 12–15, 127, 129, 141, 142, 144–149, 166, 170, 172–173, 201, 236, 264
Tesla, 285–286
Texas Instruments, 7, 70, 84, 91–94, 118–120, 286–287. *See also* Paveway bombs
Textron, 273
Thiel, Peter, 8, 165–168, 182, 185–186, 195–196
Thielert Aircraft, 257, 286
Third offset, 14–15, 152–153, 168–172, 178
Thomas, Joseph, 134
3-M, 118–119
Tibet, 155
T-Mobile, 244–245
Tocqueville, Alexis de, 285
Toyoda, Teijiro, 42
Toyota, 295
Transnational and Technology Mission Center, 12
Transparency International, 256
Treaty on Conventional Armed Forces in Europe, 139
Trippe, Charles White, 135–136
Truman, Harry, 5, 52–53, 56–59, 63, 86, 269–271
Trump, Donald, 201, 225
Tsai Ing-wen, 240–241

TSMC, 285–286
Turkey, 56–57
Twining, Nathan, 62

U-2 aircraft (Dragon Lady), 6–7, 64, 65–67, 72, 86–87, 286–287. *See also* reconnaissance
Ufimtsev, Pyotr, 97–98
Ukraine, 112–113
   Crimea and, 201
   cyber attacks on, 208–209, 213–214, 218–221, 228–229
   invasion by Russia, 4, 8–9, 13–15, 170, 201, 205–207, 213, 214–221, 223–225, 228–236, 266–268, 279, 283, 289
Underwood, 33–34
United Kingdom, 1–2, 53–54, 278–280, 295
   defense industrial base, 4–5, 15, 23–25, 34–35, 42–43, 113, 158, 263–266, 298, 299–303
   in Iraq, 102–103
   Office of Net Assessment, 265–266
   Polaris Sales Agreement, 279
   space capabilities of, 193
   Ten Year Rule, 23
United Launch Alliance, 186
United States:
   Advanced Capabilities and Deterrence Panel, 171–172
   in Afghanistan, 5, 13–14, 128, 129, 139–142, 144–147, 168, 195–196, 198–199, 234–236, 264, 267–268, 277
   Agile Combat Employment, 172
   Assault Breaker program, 75–77
   Base Reduction and Consolidation, 115–116
   Big Safari Air Force program, 7, 136, 148
   Bottom-Up Review, 114–115
   Commission on the National Defense Strategy, 263
   Commission on Implementation of United States Space Exploration Policy, 184
   Council of National Defense, 19
   cyber capabilities of, 206–207, 210
   Defense Federal Acquisition Regulation Supplement, 272
   defense industrial base of, 1–15, 18, 19–38, 40, 44, 46–47, 51–54, 56–63, 67–69, 71–87, 91–97, 99–101, 107, 110–111, 113–125, 129–130, 140–144, 148–149, 152–153, 158–161, 170–173, 177–179, 183–184, 188–189, 202, 204, 224–225, 233–236, 249, 251–252, 261–265, 267–283, 286–298, 302, 303
   Defense Priorities and Allocation System, 58
   Defense Production Act, 58–59, 269–271, 288–289, 292, 294
   Defense Science Board, 75, 143, 171
   Department of Defense Reorganization Act (1986), 83
   Distributed Maritime Operations, 172
   Federal Acquisition Regulation, 160–163, 272
   Flexible Response, 267
   Fort Hood attack (November 2009), 147
   Government Accountability Office, 272
   Gulf War Air Power Survey, 102–104

414   INDEX

in Iraq, 4–5, 7, 13–14, 89–91,
    100–107, 113, 114–115, 129,
    138, 140–142, 145–146, 168,
    195–196, 198–199, 234–236,
    264, 267–268, 277
Indo-Pacific Command, 10
International Traffic in Arms
    Regulations (ITAR), 278–280
Joint Interagency Combined Space
    Operations Center (National
    Space Defense Center), 173
Korean War and, 57–61, 63, 85–86
Last Supper, 1–2, 111, 116–118,
    120–121, 129, 267–268, 273, 290
Merchant Marine Act (Jones
    Act), 296
National Defense Advisory Commission, 19, 26, 27, 29, 269,
    288
National Reconnaissance
    Office, 204
National Security Resources
    Board, 58, 269–271
Neutrality Acts, 22
New Covenant, 114–116
New Deal, 29–30
New Look strategy, 61–63, 86, 202,
    267
Northwest Airlines attack
    (December 2009), 147
nuclear capabilities of, 76–77
Nye Commission, 22
Office of Defense and Civil
    Mobilization, 269–271
Office of Defense Mobilization, 58,
    60–61, 269–271, 288
Office of Net Assessment, 95
Office of Production
    Management, 29, 32–33
Office of Scientific Research and
    Development, 70
Other Transaction Authorities, 292
Pearl Harbor attack, 31–32, 44

Planning, Programming, Budgeting
    System, 72
Polaris Sales Agreement, 279
Project AQUATONE, 65
Project Forecast, 72–73
Rapid Acquisition Authority, 292
Russo-Ukraine War and, 4,
    223–225, 228–236
Securities and Exchange
    Commission, 19, 198
September 11, 2001, terrorist
    attacks, 1–2, 14–15, 127, 140,
    148–149, 152, 264
Smoot-Hawley Tariff Act, 22
space capabilities of, 191–192, 194,
    204
Special Program Missile
    Defeat, 173
State of the Space Industrial
    Base, 194
Strategic Capabilities Office, 173
Truth in Negotiations Contract, 72
Vietnam War and, 91–94
War Industries Board, 17–18, 268,
    288
War Powers Act (1941), 32
War Production Board, 14, 20–21,
    33, 34, 46, 52–53, 58, 269–271,
    288
Wargaming Incentive
    Fund, 172–173
Washington Naval Treaty, 22–23
unmanned aerial vehicles (UAVs). *See*
    drones, drone warfare
USS *Cole*, 147
U.S. Steel, 19
Ustinov, Dmitri, 77–78

venture capital, 8, 15, 166–167, 182–
    186, 194–197, 199, 200–204,
    225–228, 281
    space domain and, 190–191
    See also private equity
Veritas Capital, 183, 198–199

INDEX   415

Vickers, Mike, 144
Viereck, Art, 51
Vietnam, Vietnam War, 5, 13–14, 73–74, 80–81, 86, 91–94, 119, 131, 280–281, 289
Virgin Galactic, 186
Von Maur, Henry G., 135–136

Wagner, Herbert, 49–50
Wagner, Robert, 92
Warren, Elizabeth, 201–203, 281
Warsaw Pact, 77, 80
Washington, George, 303
Wazir, Nek Mohammad, 140
Weinberger, Casper "Cap," 79–80, 82, 107
Weinberger, Sharon, 69–70
Weinzierl, Matthew, 182
Wells, Edward "Ed," 6–7, 20, 37, 46–47, 286–287
Westinghouse Electric Corporation, 33–34, 118–120
WhisperGate malware, 214, 218
Whittle, Frank, 49–51
William Foster & Company, 13
Wilson, Charles E., 62–63
Wilson, Woodrow, 268
Wohlforth, William, 158, 268
Wolfowitz, Paul, 139–140
Woolsey, Jim, 7, 129–130, 135, 148
Word, Weldon, 7, 91–92, 106–107, 286–287

Work, Bob, 3, 61–62, 152–153, 168–174, 178, 199–200, 294
World Bank, 256
World War I, 1–2, 19, 21, 119, 130, 268, 288–289
World War II, 1–7, 13–15, 17, 18–25, 29–36, 40, 42–47, 49, 51–52, 70, 85–86, 119, 129–130, 201–202, 233, 263–264, 269, 280–281, 288, 289, 298
Wormuth, Christine, 234–235
Wright Aeronautics, 37
Wyler, Greg, 186

XData, 209
Xi'an Aircraft Industrial Corporation, 175–176
Xi Jinping, 2, 7–8, 14–15, 151–157, 177–178, 192–193, 254–256, 264–265
"The China Dream," 152

Yemen, 4, 129, 147, 224–225, 236, 264
Young, Shelly, 128
Youngren, Jim, 73–74
Yugoslavia, 135

Zarqawi, Abu Musab al-, 145–146
Zelensky, Volodymyr, 206, 230
Zhao Ziyang, 154–155
Zoom, 224, 229–230